Ozzy Osbourne was born in Aston, Birmingham in 1948. He has sold over a hundred million records both with Black Sabbath and as an award-winning solo artist. He has five children and lives with his wife Sharon in California and Buckinghamshire.

I AM OZZY

Ozzy Osbourne

with

CHRIS AYRES

sphere

SPHERE

First published in Great Britain in 2009 by Sphere
This paperback edition published in 2010 by Sphere
Reprinted 2010 (twice)

Chris Ayres and Sphere would like to thank *The Times* for its support of this book.
For information about Chris Ayres, go to www.chrisayres.net

The author acknowledges permission to quote from the following: 'Evil Woman, Don't Play Your Games With Me': L. Weigand, R. Weigand, Waggoner. EMI Music Pub Ltd. 'Spiral Architect': Ward, Butler, Osbourne, Iommi. Westminster Music. 'Suicide Solution': Osbourne, Daisley, Rhoads. Blizzard Music/Westminster Music.

A CIP catalogue record for this book is available from the British Library.

ISBN 978-0-7515-4340-7

Typeset in Bembo by M Rules
Printed and bound in Great Britain by
Clays Ltd, St Ives plc

Papers used by Sphere are natural, renewable and recyclable products sourced from well-managed forests and certified in accordance with the rules of the Forest Stewardship Council.

Sphere
An imprint of
Little, Brown Book Group
100 Victoria Embankment
London EC4Y 0DY

An Hachette UK Company
www.hachette.co.uk

www.littlebrown.co.uk

I would like to dedicate this book to all my fans. Because of you I've had such an amazing life. I thank you from the bottom of my heart.

God bless you all.

Ozzy

And not forgetting the one special guy who meant so much to me, Mr Randy Rhoads, R.I.P. I will never forget you and I hope we meet again somewhere, somehow.

Contents

They said I would never write this book.

Well, fuck 'em – 'cos here it is.

All I have to do now is remember something . . .

Bollocks. I can't remember *anything*.

Oh, apart from this . . .*

*'Other people's memories of the stuff in this book might not be the same as mine. I ain't gonna argue with 'em. Over the past forty years I've been loaded on booze, coke, acid, Quaaludes, glue, cough mixture, heroin, Rohypnol, Klonopin, Vicodin, and too many other heavy-duty substances to list in this footnote. On more than a few occasions I was on all of those at the same time. I'm not the fucking *Encyclopaedia Britannica*, put it that way. What you read here is what dribbled out of the jelly I call my brain when I asked it for my life story. Nothing more, nothing less . . .

Part One

In the Beginning . . .

1

John the Burglar

My father always said I would do something big one day.

'I've got a feeling about you, John Osbourne,' he'd tell me, after he'd had a few beers. 'You're either going to do something very special, or you're going to go to prison.'

And he was right, my old man.

I was in prison before my eighteenth birthday.

Burglary – that's what they sent me down for in the end. Or, as the charge sheet said, 'Breaking and entering and stealing goods to the value of £25.' That's about three hundred quid in today's dough. It wasn't exactly the Great Train Robbery, put it that way. I was a fucking crap burglar. I kept going back and doing the same job, over and over. I'd scoped out this clothes shop called Sarah Clarke's, on the street behind my house in Aston. During the first break-in I grabbed a load of hangers and thought, Magic, I'll be able to flog this stuff down the pub. But I'd forgotten to take a torch with me, and it turned out that the clothes I'd nicked were a bunch of babies' bibs and toddlers' underpants.

I might as well have tried to flog a turd.

So I went back. This time I nicked a 24-inch telly. But the fucking thing was too heavy for me to carry, and when I was climbing over the back wall it fell on my chest and I couldn't move for about an hour. I was just lying there in this ditch full of nettles, feeling like a twat. I was like Mr Magoo on drugs, I was. Eventually I got the telly off me but I had to leave it behind.

On my third attempt I managed to nick some shirts. I even had the bright idea to wear a pair of gloves, like a true professional. The only problem was that one of the gloves was missing a thumb, so I left perfect prints all over the place. The cops came to my house a few days later and found the gloves and my pile of swag. 'A thumbless glove, eh?' the copper goes to me, as he slaps on the cuffs. 'Not exactly Einstein, are we?'

About a week later I went to court and was fined forty quid by the judge. That was more dough than I'd ever had in my life. There was no way I could pay it, unless I robbed a bank . . . or borrowed it from my dad. But my old man wouldn't help me out. 'I earn an honest wage,' he said. 'Why should I give any of it to you? You need to be taught a fucking lesson.'

'But Dad—'

'For your own good, son.'

End of discussion.

The judge sentenced me to three months in Winson Green for 'non-payment of fines'.

I almost shit my pants when they told me I was going to prison, to be honest with you. Winson Green was an old Victorian slammer that had been built in 1849. The screws in there were notorious bastards. In fact, the chief inspector of prisons for the entire country later said that Winson Green was the most violent, piss-reeking, lawless fucking hole he'd ever set eyes on. I pleaded with my dad to pay the fine, but he just kept saying that it might finally knock some sense into me, being inside.

Like most kids who get into crime, I'd only ever wanted to be accepted by my mates. I thought it would be cool to be a bad guy, so I tried to be a bad guy. But I soon changed my mind when I got to Winson Green. In the admissions room my heart was pounding so loud and fast I thought it was gonna fly out of my chest and land on the concrete floor. The screws emptied my pockets and put all my stuff in this little plastic bag – wallet, keys, fags – and they had a good old laugh about my long, flowing brown hair.

'The boys in Block H are gonna love you,' one of 'em whispered to me. 'Enjoy the showers, sweetie pie.'

I had no idea what he meant.

But I found out soon enough.

Unless your life's ambition was to work in a factory, killing yourself with all-night shifts on an assembly line, there wasn't much to look forward to, growing up in Aston. The only jobs to be had were in the factories. And the houses people lived in had no indoor shitters and were falling down. Because a lot of tanks and trucks and planes had been made in the Midlands during the war, Aston had taken a pounding during the Blitz. On every other street corner when I was a kid there were 'bomb building sites' – houses that had been flattened by the Germans when they were trying to hit the Castle Bromwich Spitfire factory. For years I thought that's what playgrounds were called.

I was born in 1948 and grew up at number 14 in the middle of a row of terraced houses on Lodge Road. My father, John Thomas, was a toolmaker and worked nights at the GEC plant on Witton Lane. Everyone called him Jack, which for some reason was a common nickname for John back then. He'd often tell me about the war – like the time he was working in King's Stanley, Gloucestershire, in the early 1940s. Every night, the Germans were bombing the fuck out of Coventry, which was about fifty miles away. They'd drop high-explosives and parachute mines, and the light from the fires was so bright my dad could read the newspaper during the blackout. When I was a kid I never really understood how heavy-duty that must have been. Imagine it: people went to bed at night not knowing if their houses would still be standing the next morning.

Life after the war wasn't that much easier, mind you. When my dad got home in the morning after a night's work at GEC, my mum, Lillian, would start her shift at the Lucas factory. It was a grinding fucking routine, day in, day out. But you didn't hear them complaining about it.

She was a Catholic, my mum, but she wasn't religious. None of the Osbournes went to church – although for a while I went to a Church of England Sunday school, 'cos there was fuck-all else to do, and they gave you free tea and biscuits. Didn't do me much good, all those mornings spent learning Bible stories and drawing pictures of the baby Jesus. I don't think the vicar would be proud of his ex-pupil, put it that way.

Sunday was the worst day of the week for me. I was the kind of kid who always wanted to have fun, and there wasn't much of that to be had in Aston. There were just grey skies and corner pubs and sickly looking people who worked like animals on assembly lines. There was a lot of working-class pride, though. People even put those fake stone bricks on the outside of their council houses, to make it look like they were living in fucking Windsor Castle. All they were missing were the moats and the drawbridges. Most of the houses were terraced, like ours, so the stone cladding on one would end where the pebbledash on the next began. It looked so bad.

I was the fourth kid in my family and the first boy. My three older sisters were Jean, Iris and Gillian. I don't know when my parents found time to go at it with each other, but before long I also got two younger brothers, Paul and Tony. So there were six kids at 14 Lodge Road. It was pandemonium. Like I said, there was no indoor plumbing in the early days, just a bucket to piss in at the end of the bed. Jean, the eldest, eventually got her own bedroom, in an annexe at the back. The rest of us had to share until Jean grew up and got married, when the next in line took her place.

I tried to stay out of my sisters' way most of the time. They were always fighting with each other, like girls do, and I didn't want to get caught in the crossfire. But Jean always made a special effort to look out for me. She was almost like another mum, my big sis. Even to this day, we talk on the phone every Sunday, no matter what.

I don't know what I would have done without Jean, to be honest with you, because I was a very nervous kid. Fear of impending doom ruled my life. I convinced myself that if I stepped on the cracks in the pavement while I was running home, my mother would die. And when my dad was sleeping through the day, I'd start freaking out that he was dead, and I'd have to poke him in the ribs to make sure he was still breathing. He wasn't too fucking pleased about that, I can tell you. But all of these spooky things kept swirling through my head.

I was terrified most of the time.

Even my first memory is of being scared. It was 2 June 1953: Queen Elizabeth's Coronation Day. At that time my father was crazy about Al Jolson, the American vaudeville star. My old man would sing Jolson's songs around the house, he'd recite Jolson's comedy routines, he'd even dress up like Al Jolson whenever he got the chance.

Now, Al Jolson was most famous for these blackface numbers – the kind of politically incorrect stuff they'd flog you for today. So my father asked my aunty Violet to make a couple of Black and White Minstrel-type suits for me and him to wear during the Coronation celebrations. They were amazing, these suits. Aunty Violet even got us matching white top hats and matching white bow ties and a couple of red-and-white-striped walking canes. But when my dad came downstairs in blackface, I went fucking nuts. I was screaming and crying and wailing, 'What have you done to him? *Give me back my dad!*' I wouldn't shut up until someone explained that he was just wearing boot polish. Then they tried to put some of it on me, and I went fucking nuts all over again. I would not have any of that stuff on me. I thought it would stick for ever.

'No! No! No! *Noooooooo!*' I screamed.

'Don't be such a scaredy-cat, John,' snapped my dad.

'No! No! No! *Noooooooo!*'

I've since learned that craziness runs in the family. My grandmother on my father's side was borderline certifiable. Really fucking nuts. She'd knock me around all the time for no reason. I have this memory of her slapping my thighs over and over again. Then there was my mum's younger sister, Aunty Edna, who committed suicide by jumping in a canal. She just walked out of the funny farm one day and decided to throw herself in a canal. My grandmother on my mother's side was a bit Radio Rental, too. She had my granddad's initials – A. U. for Arthur Unitt – tattooed on her arm. I think about her every time I see one of those gorgeous chicks on the telly with ink all over her body. It looks all right when you're footloose and fancy free, but, believe me, it doesn't look too fucking hot when you're a grandma, and you've got a floppy dagger and two wrinkly snakes on your biceps when you're rocking your grandkids to sleep. But she didn't give a fuck, my nan. I liked her a lot. She lived until she was ninety-nine. When I started to drink too much she'd hit me on the arse with a rolled-up copy of the *Mirror* and go, 'You're getting too fat! Stop drinking! You smell like a bloody beer mat!'

My folks were relatively normal in comparison. My dad was strict but he never beat me up or locked me in the coal house or anything. The worst I'd get was a smack if I did anything bad, like when I tried to kneecap my grandfather with a hot poker while he was asleep. But my dad did have big rows with my mother, and I later learned that he slapped her around. She even took him to court once, apparently, although I knew nothing of that at the time. I'd hear them shouting, but I never knew what any of it was about – money, I suppose. Mind you, no one who lives in the real world spends the whole time going around saying, 'Oh yes, darling, I understand, let's talk about our "feelings", lah-dee-fucking-dah.' People who say they've never had a cross word are living on another fucking planet. And being married was different in those days. I can't even imagine what it must have been like, working every night while your missus works every day, and still not having any dough to show for it.

He was a good guy, my old man: simple, old-fashioned. Physically, he was built like a featherweight, and he wore these thick, black Ronnie Barker glasses. He would say to me, 'You might not have a good education, but good manners don't cost you anything.' And he practised what he preached: he'd always give up his seat on the bus for a woman or help an old lady across the road.

A good man. I really miss him.

But I can now see that he was a bit of a hypochondriac. Maybe that's where I got it from. He always had some kind of trouble with his leg. He'd have bandages wrapped around it all the time but he'd never go and see a doctor. He'd rather have dropped dead than go to a doctor. He was terrified of them, like a lot of people his age were. And he'd never take a day off work. If he ever stayed at home feeling ill, it was time to call the undertaker.

One thing I didn't inherit from the old man was my addictive personality. My dad would have a few beers when he went out, but he wasn't an excessive drinker. He used to like Mackeson Stout, of all things. He'd go to the working men's club, have a laugh with the boys from the factory, and come home singing 'Show Me the Way to Go Home'. And that was it. I'd never see him rolling around on the floor or pissing his pants or throwing up in the house. He'd just get merry. Sometimes I'd go with him to the pub on a Sunday then play in the street outside and listen to him singing his head off through the door. And I'd think, Fucking hell, that lemonade my dad drinks must be *amazing* . . . I had an incredible imagination. I spent years wondering what beer must be like, until I finally drank some and thought, What the fuck is this shit? My dad would never drink this! But I soon found out how it could make you feel, and I loved anything that could change the way I felt. By the time I was eighteen I could down a pint in five seconds.

My dad wasn't the only one in our family who liked to sing when he'd had a few. My mum and my sisters did, too. Jean would come home with these Chuck Berry and Elvis Presley records, and they'd all learn them and organise these little family shows on a Saturday night. My sisters even had some of those Everly Brothers harmonies down pat. The first time I ever performed was at one of those Osbourne get-togethers. I sang Cliff Richard's 'Living Doll', which I'd heard on the radio. Never in a million years did I think I'd end up making a career out of singing. I didn't think it was possible. As far as I knew, the only way I could make any dough was to go and work in a factory, like everyone else in Aston. Or rob a fucking bank.

And that wasn't completely out of the question.

Crime came naturally to me. I even had an accomplice – a kid on my street called Patrick Murphy. The Murphys and the Osbournes were tight, even though the Murphy kids were proper Catholics and went to a different school. We started out scrumping apples, me and Pat. We didn't sell them or anything – we just used to eat the fuckers because we were hungry.

Every so often you'd get a rotten one and you'd shit your guts out for days. Not far from where we lived was a place called Trinity Road, which backed on to a lower street, so you could just lean over a wall, turn your shirt into a kind of sling and fill it with apples from the trees on the other side. Once I was standing on the wall like a pregnant fucking apple smuggler and the owner of the land set these two German shepherds on me. They rushed up at me from behind and I fell head first over the wall, into the orchard. Within seconds, my eye swelled up like a big black balloon. My old man went fucking nuts when I went home. Then I went to hospital, and the doctor gave me another bollocking.

It didn't stop me and Pat, though.

After the apples we moved on to robbing parking meters. Then we got into some petty shoplifting. My folks had six kids and not much dough, and if you're in that kind of desperate situation, you'll do whatever you can for your next meal. I'm not proud of it, but I'm not one of those guys who'll go, 'Oh, I'm fine now, I've got plenty of dough, I'll just forget about my past.'

It's what made me who I am.

Another scam we came up with was standing outside Aston Villa's ground on match days and charging the fans a half-shilling each to 'mind' their cars. Everyone would leave their car unlocked in those days, so during the game we'd get inside them and just fuck around. Sometimes we'd try to make extra dough by washing them. That was a brilliant plan until we decided to wash one poor fucker's car with a wire brush. Half the paint was gone by the time we'd finished. The guy went fucking *insane*.

I wasn't really a bad guy, even though I wanted to be. I was just a kid trying to be accepted by the local gangs. We used to have great games, I remember. One street would fight the other by throwing stones down the road and using dustbin lids as shields, like it was the Greeks versus the Romans or something. It was fun until someone got hit in the face with a rock and had to go to the emergency room with blood gushing out of his eye socket. We played war games, too, and made our own bombs: you'd get a load of penny bangers, empty the gunpowder out, flatten one end of a copper tube, drill a hole in the middle, pack it with the gunpowder, fold the other end over, then take the fuse out of one of the bangers and put it in the hole. Then all you had to do was put a match to the fuse and fuck off out of the way, quick.

Bang!

Heh-heh-heh.

Not everything we did was as dodgy as bomb-making, but most of it was just as dangerous.

Me and Pat built this underground den one time, carved out of a hard clay embankment. We put an old bed frame in there and bits of wood, and there was this hole in the roof for a chimney. Next to it were these rusty oil drums, and we'd jump off the drums onto this piece of old corrugated metal that served as a perfect springboard – *Boing!* – then we'd land on the roof of the den. We did that for weeks until one day I crashed through the fucking chimney hole and almost broke my neck.

Pat thought I was a goner for a few seconds.

The bomb building sites were the best, though. We'd fuck around on them for hours, building stuff out of the rubble, smashing things, lighting fires. And we were always looking for treasure . . . our imaginations went crazy. There were also a lot of derelict Victorian houses to play in, because they were doing up Aston at the time. They were magnificent, those old houses – three or four storeys – and you could do all kinds of shit in them. We'd buy a couple of tuppenny cigarettes and lounge around in bombed-out drawing rooms or whatever, having a smoke. Woodbine or Park Drive, they were our fags of choice. You'd be sitting there in all this dirt and dust, smoking a cigarette and breathing in all this thick, yellow Birmingham smog at the same time.

Ah, them were the days.

I hated school. *Hated* it.

I can still remember my first day at Prince Albert Juniors in Aston: they had to drag me in there by the scruff of my neck, because I was kicking and screaming so much.

The only thing I ever looked forward to at school was the bell ringing at four o'clock. I couldn't read properly so I couldn't get good marks. Nothing would stick in my head, and I couldn't understand why my brain was such a useless piece of fucking jelly. I'd look at a page in a book and it might as well have been written in Chinese. I felt like I was no good, like I was a born loser. It wasn't until I was in my thirties that I found out about my dyslexia and attention deficit hyperactivity disorder. No one knew anything about any of that shit back then. I was in a class of forty kids, and if you didn't understand, the teachers didn't try to help – they just let you fuck around. So that's what I did. And when I got the piss taken out of me – like when I had to read out loud – I'd try to entertain the class. I'd think up all sorts of insane things to do to make the other kids laugh.

The only good thing about having dyslexia is that dyslexics are usually very creative people, or so I've been told. We think in unusual ways. But it's a very bad stigma to have, not being able to read like normal people can. To this day I wish I'd had a proper education. I think books are great, I do. To be able to lose yourself in a book is fucking phenomenal. Everyone should be able to do it. But I've been able to get through an entire book only a few times in my life. Every blue moon this thing in my head will release, and I'll try to read as many books as I can, because when it closes up it goes straight back to the way it was, and I end up just sitting there, staring at Chinese.

For as long as I can remember people called me 'Ozzy' at school. I haven't got a clue who first came up with it, or when, or why. It was just a nickname for Osbourne, I suppose, but it fitted my clownish personality. As soon as it stuck, only my immediate family kept calling me John. I don't even recognise my birth name now. If someone says, 'Oi, John! Over 'ere!' I don't even look up.

After Prince Albert Juniors, I went to Birchfield Road Secondary Modern in Perry Barr. They had a uniform there. It wasn't mandatory, but most of the kids wore it, including my goody two-shoes little brother Paul. He'd turn up every day in the blazer and the grey flannels and the tie and shirt. Me, I'd walk around in fucking wellies and jeans and smelly old jumpers. The headmaster, Mr Oldham, would give me a bollocking every time he set eyes on me. 'John Osbourne, tidy yourself up, you're a disgrace!' he'd shout down the hallway. 'Why can't you be more like your brother?'

The only time Mr Oldham ever said a good word about me was when I told him that one of the older kids had tried to kill the school fish by putting Fairy Liquid in the aquarium. He even praised me in assembly. 'Because of John Osbourne,' he said, 'we were able to apprehend the villain responsible for this dastardly deed.' What Mr Oldham didn't know was that it was me who'd tried to kill the school fish by putting Fairy Liquid in the aquarium – but I'd bottled out halfway through. I knew everyone would blame me for all the bubbles in the tank, 'cos they blamed me for *everything*, so I thought if I blamed someone else first, I could get away with it. And it worked.

There was one teacher I liked: Mr Cherrington. He was a local-history buff and he once took us to this place called Pimple Hill, the site of an old castle in Birmingham. It was fucking great. He talked about forts and burial grounds and medieval torture devices. It was the best lesson I ever had, but I still didn't get good marks because I couldn't write any of it down. Funnily enough, the only thing I got gold stars for at Birchfield Road was 'heavy metalwork'. I suppose that was 'cos my dad was a toolmaker and it came naturally to me. I even won first prize in a class competition for a metal window catch. It didn't stop me fucking around, though. The teacher, Mr Lane, would end up slapping me on the arse with this big piece of wood. He would hit me so hard I thought my arse was going to fall off. He was actually a nice guy, Mr Lane. Terrible racist, though. Fucking hell, the things he'd say . . . you'd get put in jail for it today.

My favourite prank in heavy metalwork was to get a penny and spend three or four minutes making it really hot with a blowtorch, and then leave it on Mr Lane's desk, so that he'd see it and pick it up out of curiosity.

First you'd hear: 'Waaaaahhhhhh!'

Then: 'Osbourne, you little bastard!'

Heh-heh-heh.

The old hot-penny trick. Priceless, man.

I got bullied for a while when I was younger. Some older kids used to wait for me on the way home from school and pull my trousers down and fuck around with me. I was maybe eleven or twelve at the time. It was a bad scene. They didn't fuck me or wank me off or any of that stuff – it was just boys playing boys' games – but it made me feel ashamed, and it freaked me out because I couldn't tell my parents. There was a lot of teasing in my family – which is normal when you've got six kids in one little terraced house – but it meant I didn't feel I could ask anyone for help. I felt like it was all my fault.

At least it made me determined that when I grew up and had my own kids, I'd tell them, 'Don't ever be afraid to come to your mum and dad with any problems. You know what's right and you know what's wrong, and if somebody ever messes with parts of your body that you don't think are cool, just tell us.' And believe me, if I ever found out that anything dodgy was happening to one of my own, there'd be fucking *blood*.

Eventually I worked out a way to get around the bullies. I found the biggest kid in the playground and clowned around until I made him laugh. By doing that he became my friend. He was built like a cross between a brick shithouse and Mount fucking Snowdon. If you fucked around with him you'd be drinking your school dinners through a straw for the next month and a half. But deep down he was a gentle giant. The bullies left me well alone once we became pals, which was a relief because I was as crap at fighting as I was at reading.

One kid at school who *never* beat me up was Tony Iommi. He was in the year above me, and everyone knew him 'cos he could play the guitar. He might not have beaten me up, but I still felt intimidated by him: he was a big guy, and good-looking, and all the girls fancied him. And no one could beat Tony Iommi in a fight. You could not put the guy down. As he was older than me he might have kicked me in the bollocks a few times and given me some stick, but nothing more than that. What I remember most about him from school is the day when we were allowed to bring our Christmas presents to class. Tony showed up with this bright red electric guitar. I remember thinking it was the coolest thing I'd ever seen in my life. I'd always wanted to play an instrument myself, but my folks didn't have the dough to buy me one, and I didn't have the patience to learn anyway. My attention span was five seconds. But Tony could really play. He was incredible, just one of those naturally talented guys: you could have given him some Mongolian bagpipes and he'd have learned how to do a blues riff on them in a couple of hours. At school I always wondered what would happen to Tony Iommi.

But it would be a few more years before our paths would cross again.

As I got older, I started to spend less time in class and more in the boys' toilets, smoking. I smoked so much I was always turning up late for morning registration, which was taken by the school rugby teacher, Mr Jones. He hated me. He was always putting me in detention and picking on me in front of the other kids. His favourite thing in the whole world was to beat me with a shoe. He'd tell me to go to the tennis-shoe rack at the back of the classroom and pick out the biggest one and bring it to him. Then he'd go and inspect the rack, and if he found a bigger shoe I'd get whacked on the arse twice as many times. He was the worst bully in the whole place.

Another thing Mr Jones would do is, he'd get all the kids to stand in a row every morning in the classroom, and then he'd walk up and down behind us, looking at our necks to make sure we were washing ourselves in the morning. If he thought you had a dirty neck, he'd rub a white towel over it – and if it came up soiled, he'd drag you by the collar over to the sink in the corner and scrub you down like an animal.

He was the worst bully in the whole school, Mr Jones was.

It didn't take me long to realise that my folks had less dough than most other families. We certainly weren't having holidays in Majorca every summer – not with six little Osbournes to clothe and feed. I never even saw the sea until I was fourteen. That was thanks to my aunty Ada, who lived in Sunderland. And I didn't see an ocean – with the kind of water that doesn't have Geordie turds floating in it and won't give you hypothermia in three fucking seconds – until I was well into my twenties.

There were other ways I could tell we were skint. Like the squares of newspaper we had to use instead of toilet roll. And the wellies I had to wear in the summer 'cos I had no shoes. And the fact that my mum never bought me underwear. There was also this dodgy bloke who'd come round to the house all the time, asking for money. We called him the 'knock-knock' man. He was a door-to-door salesman, basically, and he'd flog my mum all this stuff out of his catalogue on the never-never, then come around every week to collect the payments. But my mum never had the cash, so she'd send me to the door to tell him she wasn't at home. I got sick of it eventually. 'Mum says she ain't in,' I'd say.

Years later, I made up for it by opening the door to the knock-knock man and settling my mum's bill in full. Then I told him to fuck off and never come back again. But it didn't do any good. Two weeks later I came home to find my mum getting a brand new three-piece suite delivered. It didn't take much imagination to work out where she'd got it from.

Money was so tight when I was a kid; one of the worst days of my entire childhood was when my mum gave me ten shillings on my birthday to go and buy myself a torch – it was the kind that could light up in different colours – and on the way home I lost the change. I must have spent at least four or five hours searching every last ditch and drain hole in Aston for those few coppers. The funny thing is, I can't even remember now what my mum said when I got home. All I can remember is being fucking terrified.

It's not that life at 14 Lodge Road was bad. But it was hardly fucking domestic bliss, either.

My mother was no Delia Smith, for a start.

Every Sunday she'd be sweating in the kitchen, making lunch, and we'd all be dreading the final result. But you couldn't complain. One time, I'm eating this cabbage and it tastes like soap. Jean sees the look on my face, so she jabs me in the ribs and goes, 'Don't say a word.' But I'm sick to my guts and I don't want to die from fucking cabbage poisoning. I'm just about to say something when my dad gets back from the pub, hangs up his coat, and sits down in front of his dinner. He picks up his fork, stabs it down into the cabbage, and when he lifts it up to his mouth there's this lump of tangled wire on the end of it! God bless my old mum, she'd boiled a Brillo pad!

We all ran to the bog to make ourselves throw up.

Another time my mum made me some boiled-egg sandwiches for a packed lunch. I opened up the bread and there was cigarette ash and bits of shell in it.

Cheers, Mum.

All I can say is, school dinners saved my life. That was one small part of my shitty fucking education that I liked. They were magic, school dinners were. You got a main course *and* a pudding. It was incredible. Nowadays, you pick up something and you automatically go, 'Oh, that's got two hundred calories,' or, 'Oh, that's got eight grams of saturated fat.' But there was no such thing as a fucking calorie back then. There was only food on yer plate. And there was never enough of it, as far as I was concerned.

Every morning I'd try to think of an excuse to skive off school. So no one believed me when my excuses were real.

Like the time I heard a ghost.

I'm in the kitchen, about to leave the house. It's winter and freezing cold, and we don't have hot water on tap, so I'm boiling the kettle and getting ready to fill the sink to do the dishes. Then I hear this voice going, 'Osbourne, Osbourne, *Osbourne*.'

Because my father worked nights in those days, he would get us ready for school in the morning, before he went to bed. So I turned to my old man and said, 'Dad! Dad! I can hear someone shouting our name! I think it's a ghost! I think our house is haunted!'

He looked up from his paper.

'Nice try, son,' he said. 'You're going to school, ghost or no ghost. Hurry up with the dishes.'

But the voice wouldn't go away.

'Osbourne, Osbourne, *Osbourne*.'

'But, Dad!' I shouted. 'There's a voice! There is, there *is*. Listen!'

Finally my dad heard it, too.

'Osbourne, Osbourne, *Osbourne*.'

It seemed to be coming from the garden. So we both legged it outside – me without any shoes – but the garden was empty. Then we heard the voice again, louder this time. 'Osbourne, Osbourne, *Osbourne*.' It was coming from the other side of the fence. So we peer over into the garden next door and there's our neighbour, an old lady who lived alone, lying on the ground on a patch of ice. She must have slipped and fallen, and didn't have any way of getting help. If it hadn't been for us, she would have frozen to death. So me and my dad climb over the fence and lift her into her living room, which we'd never been in before, even though we'd lived next door to this woman for as long as anyone could remember. It was just the saddest thing. The old lady had been married with kids during the war but her husband had been sent off to France and had been shot by the Nazis. On top of that, her kids had died in a bomb shelter. But she lived as though they were all still alive. There were photographs everywhere and clothes laid out and children's toys and everything. The entire house was frozen in time. It was the most heartbreaking thing I'd ever seen. I remember my mum bawling her eyes out after she came out of that place later in the day.

It's amazing, isn't it? You can live a few inches away from your next-door neighbour and never know a thing about them.

I was late for school that day, but Mr Jones didn't care why, because I was late for school every day. It was just another excuse for him to make my life hell. One morning – it might have been the day we found the old lady on the ice, but I can't be sure – I was so late for registration that it had ended, and there was already a new class filing in.

It was a special day for me at school, because my dad had

given me a bunch of metal rods from the GEC factory so I could make some screwdrivers in Mr Lane's heavy metalwork class. The rods were in my satchel, and I couldn't wait to get them out and show them to my mates.

But the day was ruined almost before it had begun. I remember standing there in front of Mr Jones's desk as he went fucking insane at me as the kids from the other class were taking their seats. I was so embarrassed, I wanted to crawl into a hole and never come out.

'OSBOURNE!' he shouted. 'YOU'RE A DISGRACE TO YOURSELF AND TO THIS SCHOOL. BRING ME A SHOE.'

The room went so quiet you could have heard a mouse fart.

'But, sir!'

'BRING ME A SHOE, OSBOURNE. AND MAKE SURE IT'S THE BIGGEST, OR I'M GOING TO HIT YOUR BACKSIDE SO BLOODY HARD YOU WON'T BE ABLE TO SIT DOWN AGAIN FOR A MONTH.'

I looked around at all these strange faces staring at me. I wanted to fucking die, man. The kids were in the next year up from me and were just staring at me like I was a fucking freak. I put my head down and did the walk of shame to the back of the class. Someone tried to trip me up. Then another kid pushed his bag in front of me so I had to walk around it. My whole body was shaking and numb, and my fucking face was on fire. I didn't want to cry in front of all these older kids, but I could already feel myself beginning to blubber. I went to the rack and found a shoe – I was so nervous with everyone looking at me that I couldn't even tell which one was the biggest – and I carried it back to where Mr Jones was standing. I gave it to him without looking up.

'YOU CALL THIS THE BIGGEST?' goes Mr Jones. Then he strides to the back of the class, looks at the rack, comes back with another, bigger shoe, and orders me to bend over.

Everyone's still staring. At this point I'm trying incredibly hard to stop myself bawling and there's fucking snot running out of my nose, so I wipe my face with the back of my hand.

'I SAID BEND OVER, OSBOURNE.'

So I do as he says. Then he lifts up his arm as far as it'll go and brings down this fucking size-ten shoe as hard as he can.

'ARRRGGGHHHHHH!!'

It hurts like a motherfucker. Then the bastard does it again. And again. But by the third or fourth time I've fucking had enough. I suddenly get angry. Just blind fucking rage. So, as he brings the shoe down for another wallop, I reach into my satchel and take out my dad's metal rods and throw them as hard as I can at Mr Jones's fat, sweaty face. I was never any good at sport, but for those two seconds I could have bowled for the English cricket team. Mr Jones staggers backwards with blood spurting out of his nose and I realise what I've done. The class gasps. Oh, *fuuuuuck*. And I'm off, legging it as fast as I can, out of the classroom, down the corridor, out of the school, up the fucking driveway, through the gates, and all the way back to 14 Lodge Road. I run straight upstairs to where my father's sleeping and shake him awake. Then I burst into tears.

He went mental.

Not with me, thank God, but with Mr Jones. He marched straight back to school and demanded to see Mr Oldham. You could hear the shouting from the other end of the school. Mr Oldham said he had no idea about Mr Jones and the tennis shoes, but promised to look into the situation. My father said fucking right he should look into the situation.

I never got another beating again after that.

I wasn't exactly a Romeo at school – most chicks thought I was insane – but for a while I had a girlfriend called Jane. She went to the all-girls school up the road. I was nuts about her. Big time. Whenever we were due to meet, I'd first go to the boys' toilets at school and rub soap into my hair to slick it back, so she'd think I was cool. But one day it started to rain, and by the time I arrived my head looked like a bubble bath, with all this soap dripping down my forehead and into my eyes. She took one look at me and went, 'What the *fuck* are you doing?' Dumped. On the spot. I was fucking heartbroken. Then, a few years later, I saw her coming out of a club in Aston when she was off her face, and I wondered what I'd been so upset about.

There were other girls, but most of the time it never came to anything. I soon found out how painful it is when you see a girl you fancy walking around with another guy. Getting stood up wasn't much fun, either. One time, I planned to meet this chick outside the Crown and Cushion in Perry Barr. It was pissing down with rain when I got there at seven-thirty, and she was nowhere to be seen. I told myself, 'Oh, she'll be here in half an hour.' So I waited until eight. No sign. I'll gave it another half an hour. Still no sign. I was there until ten o'clock in the end. Then I just walked home, soaking wet and feeling so sad and rejected. Now that I'm a parent, of course, I just think, What the fuck was wrong with me? I wouldn't let my daughter go out in the lashing rain to meet some kid from school.

It was all only puppy love in those days. You felt like you were being a grown-up, but you weren't. Another time, when I was about fourteen, I took this girl to the movies. I thought I was Jack the Lad, so I decided to smoke to impress her. I'd been smoking for a while by then, but not like heavy-duty. This night I've got five fags and a penny book of matches in my pocket. So I'm sitting in this movie theatre, trying to be a big shot, and suddenly I break out in a fucking cold sweat. I'm thinking, What the fuck's up with me? Then I burp and taste vomit. I run to the bathroom and lock myself in a stall and cough my fucking guts up. I was so fucking sick, man. I dragged myself out of the exit and went straight home, throwing up the whole way. I don't know what happened to the chick, but at least she got a box of Maltesers out of it.

That wasn't my only bad experience with cigarettes, growing up. Another night around that time, I remember smoking a fag in my bedroom at Lodge Road, then pinching the end of it so I could have the rest in the morning. I woke up a few hours later choking. Smoke everywhere. *Fucking hell*, I thought, *I've set the house on fire!* But then I looked down at the ashtray by my bed and saw that my cigarette wasn't even lit. What I didn't know is that my dad had come home a bit merry that night and had also been smoking inside the house. But instead of putting out his cigarette he'd dropped it down the back of the settee, and now all the foam in the cushions was smouldering and giving off this horrendous black smoke.

Next thing I knew I was legging it downstairs to the living room to find my dad looking hungover and guilty, and my mum with tears streaming down her face, doubled over, coughing.

'Jack Osbourne,' she was saying, between splutters. 'What the bloody hell did you d—'

Then she coughed so hard, her false teeth literally flew out of her mouth and smashed through the window, letting in this freezing cold wind from outside, which fanned the flames – making the settee go up like a fucking bonfire. I didn't know whether to laugh or shit myself. Anyway, somehow me and my dad managed to put the fire out while my mum went out into the garden to look for her choppers.

But the house didn't smell right for weeks.

It didn't put me off smoking, mind you. I was convinced it made me look cool. And maybe I was right, 'cos a few weeks after the fire, I got my merry end away for the first time. I'd only just discovered that my penis wasn't just for pissing through and I was banging it all over the fucking place. Jacking off, tossing everywhere. I couldn't sleep for milking the old maggot. Anyhow, I was at a dance in a pub in Aston. This was before I was drinking, so maybe it was a birthday party or something in a back room. There was an older girl there – I can't for the life of me remember her name, I swear to God – and she danced with me for a bit. Then she took me back to her parents' house and shagged the shit out of me all night. I had no fucking idea why she decided to pick me. Maybe she felt a bit horny and I was the only spare dick in the room. Who knows? But I wasn't complaining. Of course, I wanted more after that. I wanted seconds. So, the next day, I went running back to her house like a dog sniffing around the old pole again.

But she just blurted out, 'What the fuck do *you* want?'

'How about another shag?'

'Fuck off.'

That was the end of our beautiful romance.

I was fifteen when I left school. And what did I get to show for my ten years in the British education system? A piece of paper which said,

> John Osbourne attended Birchfield Road Secondary Modern.
>
> Signed,
> Mr Oldham (Headmaster)

That was fucking it. Not a single qualification. Nothing. I had two career choices: manual labour or manual labour. The first thing I did was look for jobs in the back of the *Birmingham Evening Mail*. That week they happened to be running a special feature on occupations for people who'd just left school. I looked at them all – milkman, bin man, assembly-line worker, brickie, street cleaner, bus driver, that kind of thing – and decided on plumbing, because at least it was a trade. And I'd been told that I wouldn't get anywhere in life without a trade.

By the time I got the job I wanted it was late in the year and starting to get cold. I didn't realise that plumbers work their arses off in the middle of winter, when all the pipes burst. So you spend most of your time bending over a manhole when it's minus five degrees, freezing your fucking nut sack off. I didn't last a week. It wasn't the cold that did me in, though. I got fired for scrumping apples during my lunch break.

Old habits die hard.

My next job was less ambitious. It was at an industrial plant outside Aston. This place made car parts, and I was in charge of a big fucking degreasing machine. You'd get baskets full of bits – rods, springs, levers, whatever – and you dropped them into this vat of bubbling chemicals which cleaned them. The chemicals were toxic and there was a sign on top of the machine which said, 'EXTREME HAZARD! PROTECTIVE MASKS MUST BE WORN AT ALL TIMES. NEVER LEAN OVER THE TANK.'

I remember asking what was in the vat and someone told me it was methylene chloride. I thought to myself, Hmm, I wonder if you can get a buzz off that stuff? So one day I pull down my mask and lean over the tank, just for a second. And I go, '*Whooooooaaaah!*' It was like sniffing glue . . . times a fucking hundred. So every morning I started taking a whiff of the old degreasing machine. It was a lot cheaper than going down the pub. Then I started doing it twice a day. Then three times a day. Then every five fucking minutes. Trouble was, every time I leant over the vat I got a big black greasy face. So it didn't take long for the other guys in the plant to work out what was going on. I'd be taking a tea break and they'd see my face covered in all this black stuff and they'd go, 'You've been at that fucking degreasing machine again, haven't you? You'll fucking kill yourself, man.'

'What do you mean?' I'd say, all innocent.

'It's fucking toxic, Ozzy.'

'That's why I wear a protective mask at all times and *never* lean over the tank, just like the sign says.'

'Bollocks. Stop doing it, Ozzy. You'll kill yourself.'

After a few weeks it got to the point where I was just out of my brains all the time, wobbling around the place, singing songs. I even started to have hallucinations. But I kept doing it – I couldn't stop myself. Then, one day I went missing for a while. They found me slumped over the tank, passed out. 'Get 'im an ambulance,' said the supervisor. 'And don't ever let that idiot back in this place again.'

My parents went nuts when they found out I'd been fired again. I was still living at 14 Lodge Road, and they expected me to chip in for the rent, even though I tried to spend as little time at home as possible. So my mum talked to her bosses and sorted me out with a job at the Lucas factory, where she could keep an eye on me. 'It's an apprenticeship, John,' she said. 'Most people your age would give their right arm for this kind of opportunity. You'll have a skill. You're going to be a trained car horn tuner.'

My heart sank.

A car horn tuner?

In those days, the working person's mentality went like this: you got what little education you could, you found an apprenticeship, they gave you a shit job, and then you took pride in it, even though it was a shit job. And then you did that same shit job for the rest of your life. Your shit job was *everything*. A lot of people in Birmingham never even made it to retirement. They just dropped down dead on the factory floor.

I needed to get the fuck out before I got stuck in the same trap. But I had no idea how to leave Aston. I tried to do this 'emigrate to Australia' thing, but I couldn't afford the ten-quid fare. I even tried to join the army, but they wouldn't have me. The bloke in the uniform took one look at my ugly mug and said, 'Sorry, we want subjects, not *objects*.'

So I took the job in the factory. I told my friend Pat that I'd got a gig in the music business.

'What do you mean, the music business?' he said.

'Tuning stuff,' I told him, vaguely.

'What kind of stuff?'

'Mind your own fucking business.'

On my first day at the Lucas plant the supervisor showed me into this sound-proofed room, where I'd do my shift. My job was to pick up the car horns as they came along a conveyor belt and put them into this helmet-shaped machine. Then you'd hook them up to an electrical current and adjust them with a screwdriver, so they went, 'BAGH, BOOO, WEEE, URRH, BEEOOP.' Nine hundred a day – that's how many car horns they wanted tuned. They kept count, because every time you did one you clicked a button. There were five of us in the room, so that's five car horns burping and beeping and booping all at the same time, from eight in the morning until five in the afternoon.

You came out of that fucking place with your ears ringing so loud you couldn't hear yourself think.

This was my day:

Pick up horn.

Attach connectors.

Adjust with screwdriver.

BAGH, BOOO, WEEE, URRH, BEEOOP.

Put horn back on belt.

Click the button.

Pick up horn.

Attach connectors.

Adjust with screwdriver.

BAGH, BOOO, WEEE, URRH, BEEOOP.

Put horn back on belt.

Click the button.

Pick up horn.

Attach connectors.

Adjust with screwdriver.

BAGH, BOOO, WEEE, URRH, BEEOOP.

Put horn back on belt.

Click the button.

While I was doing this, my mum would be watching me proudly through this glass screen. But after a couple of hours of listening to that fucking din I was starting to go insane. I was ready to murder someone. So I started to click the button twice for every horn I did, thinking I could knock off early. Anything to get out of that fucking booth. When I realised I was getting away with it, I started to click three times. Then four. Then five.

This went on for a few hours until I heard a tap-tap and a squeal of feedback from somewhere above me. The conveyor belt juddered to a halt. Then this angry voice comes over the Tannoy:

'OSBOURNE. SUPERVISOR'S OFFICE. *NOW*.'

They wanted to know how come I'd done five hundred car horns in twenty minutes. I told them there was obviously something wrong with the clicker. They told me they weren't born fucking yesterday and that the only thing wrong with the clicker was the fucking idiot operating it, and that if I did it again, I'd be thrown out on my fucking arse, end of story. Did I understand? I said, 'Yeah, I understand,' and sloped back to my little booth.

Pick up horn.

Attach connectors.

Adjust with screwdriver.

BAGH, BOOO, WEEE, URRH, BEEOOP.

Put horn back on belt.

Click the button.

After a few more weeks of this bullshit I decided to strike up a conversation with the old guy next to me, Harry.

'How long have you be working 'ere?' I asked him.

'Eh?'

'How long you been 'ere?'

'Stop whispering, son.'

'HOW LONG HAVE YOU WORKED HERE?' I shouted. Harry had obviously gone completely deaf from listening to car horns all day.

'Twenty-nine years and seven months,' he said with a grin.

'You're kidding me.'

'Eh?'

'Nothing.'

'Stop whispering, son.'

'THAT'S A LONG FUCKING TIME, HARRY.'

'You know what the best thing is?'

I raised my hands and shook my head.

'In five months' time, I'll get my gold watch. I'll have been here thirty years!'

The thought of thirty years in that room made me want the Russians to drop the bomb and get it over with.

'If you wanted a gold watch that badly,' I said. 'You should have nicked one from the fucking jeweller's. Even if you got caught, you'd only do a tenth of the time that you've done in this shithole.'

'Say again, son?'

'Nothing.'

'Eh?'

'NOTHING.'

I'd had enough. I threw down my screwdriver, walked out of the door, past my mum, out of the factory gate, and straight to the nearest pub. That was the end of my first job in the music business.

The idea of getting a real job in the music business was a fucking joke. It was just one of those impossible things, like becoming an astronaut or a stuntman, or shagging Elizabeth Taylor. Still, ever since the time I'd sung 'Living Doll' at our family knees-up, I'd been thinking about starting a band. I even went around for a while boasting that I was a member of a group called the Black Panthers. Bollocks, I was. My 'band' was an empty guitar case with 'The Black Panthers' written on the side (I'd used some emulsion paint which I'd found in the garden shed). It was all in my imagination. I used to tell people I had a dog, too: it was a Hush Puppy that I'd found in a skip, which I put on the end of a lead. I'd walk around the streets of Aston with my empty guitar case, pulling this old fucking shoe behind me, thinking I was some kind of Mississippi bluesman. Everyone else thought I was fucking insane.

When I wasn't spending time with my imaginary band and my Hush-Puppy dog, I used to hang around with the Teddy Boys. It was a bit before my time, the Teddy Boy scene, so I never got into the long coats and the brothel creepers and all that shit. But I liked the music they played on the jukebox. I went around singing 'Hey Paula' by Paul & Paula for weeks. Those old tunes were great. Then I got into the mod stuff – I used to like the slim-fit mohair suits. Then I was a rocker, with the leather jackets and the studded belts. I'd switch back and forth all the fucking time. I was just looking for adventure, me. Anything that didn't involve working in a factory.

Then the Beatles happened.

All of a sudden, these four moptop Scousers were all over the radio and the telly. Using my last pay cheque from the job at the Lucas plant, I bought their second LP, *With the Beatles*.

The moment I got it home, everything changed.

A light went on in my head when I heard that record. It just sucked me in. Lennon and McCartney's harmonies were like magic. They took me away from Aston and into this fantasy Beatleworld. I couldn't stop listening to those fourteen songs (eight were originals, six were covers, including a version of Chuck Berry's 'Roll Over Beethoven'). It might sound over-the-top to say it now, but for the first time I felt as though my life had meaning. I played that record over and over again on my dad's big, polished radiogram, which was a combination of a valve radio and an old-fashioned phonograph, made to look like a piece of furniture, which took pride of place in our living room. Then I'd go to the Silver Blades ice rink and they'd be playing it on the Tannoy system there. Sometimes I would just walk around with the album under my arm, I was so fucking chuffed with it. Soon I began to collect anything with 'The Beatles' written on it. Photographs. Posters. Cards. *Anything*. It would all go up on the bedroom wall. My brothers didn't mind – they were mad about the Beatles, too.

But not half as mad as me.

Obviously, I had to save up some dough to buy the Beatles' first album, *Please Please Me*. Then, when *A Hard Day's Night* came out, I was one of the first in the queue at the record shop to buy that. Thanks to Beatlemania, it seemed all right that I didn't want to work in a factory. John Lennon and Paul McCartney hadn't wanted to work in a factory either! And they were just like me – working-class kids from the back streets of a run-down, far-from-London industrial town. The only difference was that their town was Liverpool, not Aston. I reckoned if they could be in a band, then maybe I could, too. I was eight years younger than Lennon and six years younger than McCartney, so I still had plenty of time to get my first big break. Trouble was, I had no idea how to get a big break. Apart from Tony Iommi – who I'd never seen again since leaving school – I didn't even know anyone who could play a musical instrument. So, instead, I decided to grow my hair long and get some tattoos. At least I'd *look* the part.

The hair was easy. The tattoos stung like a fucking bastard.

First it was a dagger on my arm. Then I learned how to do them myself with a needle and some Indian ink. All you needed was a big enough blob of ink on the end of the needle and then you'd poke it far enough through the skin to make it permanent. When I was seventeen, I spent a whole afternoon in Sutton Park – a posh area of Birmingham – spelling out 'O-Z-Z-Y' across my knuckles. I went home that night feeling really fucking pleased with myself.

My dad wasn't so happy. He went white when he saw me.

'Son, you look like a fucking idiot,' he said.

In 1964 something totally unexpected happened.

I got a job I enjoyed.

It turned out that although I was no good at plumbing or tuning car horns or working on building sites or doing any of the other half a dozen shit jobs I'd been fired from, I was a natural at killing animals. They say that when the average person sees the inside of a slaughterhouse, they become a vegetarian. Not me. Having said that, though, it was an education. I quickly learned that there aren't any little nugget-shaped chickens, or little hamburger-shaped cows. Animals are big fucking smelly things. I think that anyone who eats meat should visit a slaughterhouse at least once in their life, just to see what goes on. It's a bloody, filthy, putrid fucking business.

The slaughterhouse that hired me was in Digbeth, one of the older parts of Birmingham. My first job was puke remover. They showed me to this big pile of sheep's stomachs in the corner, and I had to cut them open, one by one, and remove all the puke from inside. I was throwing up like a son of a bitch the entire first day. And it didn't get any better for a long time. I threw up every hour or so for a solid four weeks. My stomach muscles were on fire, man. Sometimes the other guys would have a laugh by giving me the stomach of a condemned animal – like a crippled old sheep that was unfit for human consumption or something. One time I picked up this dodgy stomach and it just burst in my hands – all this fucking pus and blood squirted into my face. They all thought that was extremely fucking funny.

But I grew to like the slaughterhouse. I got used to the smell, and once I'd proved myself as puke remover they promoted me to cow killer.

What a fucking job that was. I'll tell you something: if you ever get kicked by a cow, you'll know about it. When one of them got me in the marbles I thought I was going to cough up my left ball.

The process starts with a gang of five or six guys roping the animal into the kill room. It walks up this ramp and I'm standing at the other end with a pressurised bolt gun. The gun is loaded with a blank cartridge, which creates enough pressure to fire out a big spike, like a round chisel, straight into the cow's brain. It's designed to make sure the animal doesn't feel any pain – apart from at the moment when it gets this big fucking bolt through its head – but doesn't actually kill it. Trouble is, you have to be up close and personal with the cow to use the bolt gun, and if you get an animal that's pissed off, you won't be able to knock it out the first time. But there's no escape for either of you. I can't tell you how many man-on-cow death matches I had in the Digbeth slaughterhouse. I had to shoot one bull five or six times before it went down. Fuck me, he was pissed off. At one point I thought I'd be the one who'd end up in a bun, covered in ketchup.

Once you've knocked out the cow you shackle its legs and attach them to a kind of moving rail, which pulls the animal upside down and carries it down the processing line. Then someone cuts its throat and the blood drains out into a chute underneath. So, eventually, the animal dies through loss of blood. One time, this cow was still conscious when I shackled it to the rail, but I didn't know it. Just as it was swinging upside down it fucking hoofed me in the arse and I went flying head first down the blood chute. When they got me out, I looked like fucking afterbirth. My clothes were soaked in blood, my shoes were full of blood, and my hair was matted with blood.

I even got a mouthful of the stuff. And it's not just blood in the chute. There are all kinds of other unmentionable substances in that fucking thing. No one would sit next to me on the bus for weeks, I reeked so bad.

I had lots of different jobs at Digbeth. I specialised in tripe for a while: cutting out the cow's stomach, putting it in this big wheelbarrow, then letting it soak overnight. I also had a job as a heel-puller – in other words, getting the hoofs off the cows. Tripe's one thing, but I don't know who the fuck would ever eat a fucking hoof. I also had a stint killing pigs. They say that the only thing wasted on a pig is the squeal, and it's true. Every single part of those things gets turned into some kind of product, one way or another. My job was to get tongs with sponges on the end of them, dip them in water, put them on the pig's head, press a button on the handle, and make sure the pig zonked out. Again, it didn't always work first time, but no one gave a shit. The guys would fuck around with the pigs sometimes, commit all sorts of atrocities. In was like Auschwitz in that place on a bad day, the evil that went on. Sometimes the pigs would get dropped into a vat of boiling water before they'd even been knocked out. Or they'd still be awake when they were put through a furnace that burned all the hair off their backs. I regret a lot of that stuff now. Killing a pig for a good old fry-up is one thing. But there's no excuse for being cruel, even if you're a bored teenage kid.

You get a different perspective on meat after you've worked in a slaughterhouse for a while. I remember going camping once after Digbeth, and I was cooking these steaks on a barbecue. Some cows from the next field came over to me, sniffing around, like they knew something was up. I started to feel really weird about the steaks. 'I'm sure it's no relation,' I said to them, but they still didn't fuck off. They ruined the fucking meal in the end. It doesn't feel right, eating beef when you're in the company of a cow.

I loved my job at Digbeth, though. The guys I worked with were fucking crazy and always up for the craíc. And once your kills were done you were free to go home. So, if you started early, you could be out by nine or ten o'clock in the morning. I remember we used to get paid on Thursdays and go straight to the pub. Which was always an excuse to practise my favourite practical joke – dropping cows' eyeballs into people's drinks. I'd sneak them out of the slaughterhouse by the dozen for the very purpose. The best thing was to find a young sensitive-looking chick, and when she went to the bog, put an eyeball on top of her can of Coke. They would go crazy when they saw that shit. One time, the landlord threw me out for making someone vomit all over his swirly carpet. So I got another eyeball, stood outside the doorway, and popped it open with a knife. That made another two or three people come out in sympathy, which for some reason I thought was fucking brilliant.

Another great thing about Digbeth was the all-night club across the street called the Midnight City. They played soul music in there, so after staggering out of the pub at closing time I could dance until five in the morning, speeding my balls off on Dexedrine. Then I'd go straight back to the slaughterhouse and kill more cows. I'd keep that up all through the weekend until Sunday night, when I went back to 14 Lodge Road.

It was magic.

I lasted about eighteen months at the slaughterhouse. Having been a puke remover and a cow killer and a tripe hanger and a hoof puller and pig stunner, my final job was fat collector. An animal has what's known as caul fat around its stomach – kind of like a beer belly – and my job was to cut it out, stretch it and hang it up on these poles overnight to dry it out, so you could bag it when you came in the next morning. Most of it was used in girls' make-up. But before you hung it up to dry, you had to clean it. They had this big tank of boiling-hot water, and the trick was to clean the fat using the steam, then wash it off, put it on a rack, and hang it over the poles.

But the guys in the slaughterhouse would fuck around with each other, like they always did. They'd cut the strings on your butcher's apron as you were leaning over the tank, so you'd get this spray of blood and shit and fuck-knows-what-else all down your clothes. I got sick of them doing that to me, and I got a bee up my arse about one guy in particular. So, I'm leaning over the tank and this guy sneaks up behind me and cuts my apron strings. Without thinking, I just turn around and whack him over the head with one of the fat poles. I just lost my cool, man. It was quite a heavy scene. I whacked him a few times, and there was blood spurting out of his face. They had to send him to hospital in the end.

That was the end of the slaughterhouse for me.

'Fuck off and don't come back,' said the boss.

That's why I became John the Burglar. I just couldn't face another factory job. The thought of Harry and his gold watch and the two-quid-a-week wage was too much to handle.

But I soon learned my lesson when they sent me to Winson Green. An hour is a long time in that fucking place, never mind three months. The first thing I did was ask someone what the screws had meant about my long flowing hair and the showers. Then I spent the rest of the week begging for a pair of scissors so I could look less like a girl. Every morning during wash-time I'd have my hand over my balls and my back pressed to the wall, I was so fucking scared. If I dropped the soap, it stayed on the fucking floor.

I wasn't going to be doing any bending over.

But I was worried about more than a rogering. People got killed in that place if they pissed off the wrong guy. There were fights every day, and I was shit at fighting. So I did exactly what I'd done at Birchfield Road with the bullies: I found the biggest, baddest fuckers in the exercise yard and I made 'em laugh by doing crazy things.

That was my protection.

The inside of the prison was just how I'd imagined it would be, with clanging doors and rattling keys, and different levels for different categories of prisoners, each with its own balcony overlooking the central area. I was locked up in the 'YP Wing', which stood for Young Offenders, and on the level above us were adult prisoners who were on remand waiting for trial or sentencing. Murderers, rapists, bank robbers – every kind of undesirable you could imagine was up there. The stuff they could smuggle in was amazing. They had beer, cigarettes, all kinds of shit – although any type of tobacco was very highly prized. Smoking helped kill the boredom, which was your worst enemy on the inside. Even soggy old cigarette butts were worth a fucking fortune in there.

Getting tattoos done was another way to make the time pass more quickly. One of the guys showed me how to do it without a proper needle or any Indian ink. He drew a picture of The Saint on my arm with a ballpoint pen – I'd been a fan of the show since it started in 1962 – and then he used a sewing pin he'd nicked from the workroom and some melted grate polish to poke in the tattoo over the top.

I started tattooing myself all over the place after I came out of Winson Green. I even put a smiley face on each of my knees to cheer myself up when I was sitting on the bog in the morning. Another thing I learned inside was how to split matches. They were a scarce commodity, so the guys had worked out a way to make four out of one by splitting them with a pin. I remember thinking, If they're clever enough to do that, how come these people aren't all fucking millionaires?

My most vivid memory of Winson Green is the time when Bradley came in. He was a notorious child molester, and he'd been given a cell on the level above the YP Wing. They put this big sign outside his door which said, 'RULE 43'. That meant he had to have a twenty-four-hour-a-day guard, to protect him from the other inmates. They'd have strung him up from a light fixture, given half the chance. But the screws hated Bradley as much as the cons did – he was on remand for seventeen offences of sexually abusing kids, including his own – and they did their best to make sure his life was hell on earth. One time I saw this fucking huge guy with a tattoo of a snake on his face beat the shit of Bradley, and the screws just looked the other way, didn't even say anything. The first punch alone must have broken Bradley's nose. There was all this blood and snot and cartilage running down into his mouth and he was fucking howling with pain.

My job in prison was to dole out the food. The inmates would come in with these trays that had little compartments moulded into them, and I'd spoon out the sloppy tripe and peas or whatever disgusting fucking shit they were cooking that day. Whenever Bradley came in, the screw on duty would go to me, 'Osbourne, don't give 'im anything worth a shit.' So I'd give him almost nothing. Bradley would have to be escorted into the canteen by himself to make sure nothing happened to him, but it didn't always work. I remember one time, when he'd been given hardly any food for weeks, he said to the guy who was serving the porridge, 'Can I have some more, please?' The guy with the porridge just looked at him. Then he dipped the big, heavy prison ladle back in the pot, took it out, swung it back, and smashed it into Bradley's face. I'll never forget the sound of that fucking porridge ladle burying itself into his head. *Thwack!* His nose hadn't even healed up from the previous attack, and it just exploded again. Bradley was crying and screaming and staggering around, but the screw just whacked him on the arse with his stick and told him to move along the fucking line. It was heavy-duty.

Bradley refused to come out of his cell again after that.

This became a problem for the screws, because prison regulations meant you had to have a cell search every night and slop out and polish the floor every morning. So when the prison chief noticed that Bradley wasn't coming out to eat, all these fucking whistles and bells started going off. I was in the kitchen at the time. This screw comes up to me and one of the other guys and goes, 'You and you, I want you to get that disgusting piece of shit out of his cell and into the bath. Then I want you to scrub him.'

I don't know how long they'd let Bradley fester in his cell before sounding the alarm, but it must have been a few days, judging by the state of it. The slop bucket he was supposed to use as a bog was knocked over and there was piss and shit everywhere. Bradley himself was covered in it, too. So we dragged him out and into this bath of cold water. Then we used the brooms for the yard to scrub him down. His whole face was swollen and black, his nose was a fucking mess, and he was shivering and crying. I felt sorry for the guy at the end of the day. People say child molesters get a soft time inside. Believe me, they don't. I'm surprised Bradley didn't just top himself. Maybe he was too chicken. Maybe he just didn't have any spare razor blades.

On one of my last days in Winson Green I was walking around the exercise yard and I saw a guy I recognised.

'Hey, Tommy!' I shouted.

Tommy looked up, smiled, and walked over to me, flapping his arms for warmth while smoking a fag.

'Ozzy?' he goes. 'Fucking hell, man, it's you!'

Tommy had worked with me at the Digbeth slaughterhouse. He was one of the guys who roped in the cows before I shot them with the bolt gun. He asked me how long I was in for, and I told him I'd been given three months, but because of my work in the kitchen and my help with Bradley they were going to let me out after six weeks.

'Good behaviour,' I said. 'How long are you in for?'

'Four,' he replied, taking another puff on his fag.

'Weeks?'

'Years.'

'Fucking hell, Tommy. What did you do, mug the Queen?'

'Robbed a bunch of caffs.'

'How much dough?'

'Fuck-all, man. But I got a couple of hundred packets of fags and some chocolate bars and whatnot.'

'Four years for some fags and chocolate?'

'Third offence. Judge said I hadn't learned my lesson.'

'Fucking hell, Tommy.'

A whistle blew and one of the screws told us to get moving.

'See you around then, Ozzy.'

'Yeah, see you around, Tommy.'

My old man had done the right thing by not paying my fine. There was no fucking way I ever wanted to go back to prison after Winson Green, and I never did. Jail, yes. Prison, not a chance.

Having said that, I did have a couple of close calls.

I'm not proud of the fact that I did time, but it was a part of my life, y'know? So I don't try to pretend it never happened, like some people do. If it hadn't been for those six weeks inside, fuck knows what I would have ended up doing. Maybe I'd have turned out like my mate Pat, my apple-scrumping partner from Lodge Road. He just kept getting involved with heavier and heavier things. Got mixed up with a really bad crowd. Drugs, I think it was. I didn't know the details, because I never asked. When I got out of the nick I drifted away from Pat, because I didn't want any more to do with all that dodgy stuff. But every now and again I'd meet up with him and we'd have a bit of a drink and whatever. He was a good guy, man. People are always so quick to put people down, but Patrick Murphy was all right.

He just made some bad choices, and then it was too late. Eventually he turned Queen's Evidence, which means you take a reduced sentence for ratting on someone who's more important. Then, when you get out of prison, they give you a new identity. They sent him off to live in Southend or some out-of-the-way place. He was under police protection twenty-four hours a day. But after years of waiting for him to come out of the slammer, his wife broke down and asked for a divorce. Pat goes into his garage, starts up his car, puts a hosepipe over the exhaust, and feeds it through the driver's window. Then he gets inside and waits until the carbon monoxide kills him.

He was only in his early thirties.

When I heard, I phoned his sister, Mary, and asked if he had been loaded when he'd killed himself. She said they hadn't found anything: he'd just done it, stone-cold sober.

It was the middle of winter 1966 when I got out of the nick. Fucking hell, man, it was cold. The screws felt bad for me, so they gave me this old coat to wear, but it stank of mothballs. Then they got the plastic bag with my things in it and tipped it out on to the table. Wallet, keys, fags. I remember thinking, What must it be like to get your stuff back after thirty years, when it's like a time capsule from an alternative universe? After I signed some forms they unlocked the door, pulled back this barbed-wire-covered gate, and I walked out into the street.

I was a free man, and I'd survived prison without being arse raped or beaten to a pulp.

So how come I felt so fucking *sad*?

2

Ozzy Zig Needs Gig

Knock-knock.

I poked my head through the curtains in the living room and saw a big-nosed bloke with long hair and a moustache standing outside on the doorstep. He looked like a cross between Guy Fawkes and Jesus of Nazareth. And was that a pair of . . . ? Fuck me, it was. He was wearing *velvet* trousers.

'JOHN! Get the door!'

My mum could wake up half of Aston cemetery at the volume she shouted. Ever since I'd got out of the nick, she'd been breaking my balls. Every two seconds, it was 'John, do this. John, do that.' But I didn't want to answer the door too fast. I needed a moment to sort my head out, get my nerves under control. This bloke looked like he was serious.

This could be important.

Knock-knock.

'JOHN OSBOURNE! *GET THE BLOODY—!*

'I'm getting it!' I stomped down the hallway, twisted the latch on the front door, and yanked it open. 'Are you . . .

"Ozzy Zig"?' said Guy Fawkes, in a thick Brummie accent.

'Who wants to know?' I said, folding my arms.

'Terry Butler,' he said. 'I saw your ad.'

That was exactly what I'd hoped he was going to say. Truth was, I'd been waiting a long time for this moment. I'd dreamed about it. I'd fantasised about it. I'd had conversations with myself on the shitter about it. One day, I thought, people might write newspaper articles about my ad in the window of Ringway Music, saying it was the turning point in the life of John Michael Osbourne, ex-car horn tuner. 'Tell me, Mr Osbourne,' I'd be asked by Robin Day on the BBC, 'when you were growing up in Aston, did you ever think that a simple advert in a music shop window would lead to you becoming the fifth member of the Beatles, and your sister Iris getting married to Paul McCartney?' And I'd answer, 'Never in a million years, Robin, never in a million years.'

It was a fucking awesome ad. 'OZZY ZIG NEEDS GIG', it said in felt-tip capital letters. Underneath I'd written, 'Experienced front man, owns own PA system', and then I'd put the address (14 Lodge Road) where I could be reached between six and nine on week nights. As long as I wasn't down the pub, trying to scrounge a drink off someone. Or at the Silver Blades ice rink. Or somewhere else.

We didn't have a telephone in those days.

Don't ask me where the 'Zig' in 'Ozzy Zig' came from. It just popped into my head one day. After I got out of the nick, I was always dreaming up new ways to promote myself as a singer. The odds of making it might have been a million to one – even that was optimistic – but I was up for anything that could save me from the fate of Harry and his gold watch. Besides, bands like the Move, Traffic and the Moody Blues were proving that you didn't have to be from Liverpool to be successful. People were talking about 'Brumbeat' being the next 'Merseybeat'. Whatever the fuck that meant.

I ain't gonna pretend I can remember every word of the conversation I had with the strange, velvet-trousered bloke on my doorstep that night, but it I'm pretty sure it went something like:

'So you got a gig for me then, Terence?'

'The lads call me Geezer.'

'*Geezer?*'

'Yeah.'

'You taking the piss?'

'No.'

'As in "That smelly old geezer just shit his pants"?'

'That's a very funny joke for a man who goes around calling himself "Ozzy Zig". And what's up with that bum fluff on yer head, man? It looks like you had an accident with a lawnmower. You can't go on stage looking like *that*.'

In fact, I'd shaved my head during one of my mod phases, but by then I was a rocker again, so I was trying to grow it back. I was pretty self-conscious about it, to be honest with you, so I didn't appreciate Geezer pointing it out. I almost came back at him with a joke about his massive conk, but in the end I thought the better of it and just said, 'So have you got a gig for me or not?'

'You heard of Rare Breed?'

'Course I have. You're the ones with the strobe light and the hippy bloke with the bongos or whatever, right?'

'That's us. Only we just lost our singer.'

'Oh yeah?'

'The ad said you've got your own PA system,' said Geezer, getting straight to the point.

'That's right.'

'You sang in any bands before?'

'Course I fucking have.'

'Well, the job's yours then.'

*

And that was how I first met Geezer.

Or at least that's how I remember it going down. I was a stroppy little bastard in those days. You learn to be like that when you're looking for a break. I was also getting very restless: a lot of the things that had never bothered me that much before had really started to piss me off. Like still living with my folks at 14 Lodge Road. Like still not having any dough. Like still not being in a band.

The hippy-dippy shit that was all over the radio after I got out of Winson Green was also winding me up, big time. All these polo-necked wankers from grammar schools were going out and buying songs like 'San Francisco (Be Sure to Wear Some Flowers in Your Hair)'. *Flowers in your hair?* Do me a fucking favour.

They even started playing some of that shit in the pubs around Aston. You'd be sitting there with your pint and your fags and your pickled egg, in this yellow-walled shithole of a boozer, staggering to the pisser and back every five minutes, with everyone knackered, broke and dying from asbestos poisoning or whatever toxic shit they were breathing in every day. Then, all of a sudden, you'd hear all this hippy crap about 'gentle people' going to love-ins at Haight–Ashbury, whatever the fuck Haight–Ashbury was.

Who gave a dog's arse about what people were doing in San Francisco, anyway? The only flowers anyone saw in Aston were the ones they threw in the hole after you when you croaked it at the age of fifty-three 'cos you'd worked yourself to death.

I hated those hippy-dippy songs, man.

Really hated them.

They were playing one when a fight broke out in the pub one time. I remember this bloke getting me in a headlock and trying to punch my teeth out, and all I can hear on the jukebox is this *kumbaya* bullshit being tapped out on a fucking glockenspiel while some knob-end with a voice like his marbles are in a vice warbles on about 'strange vibrations'. Meanwhile, the bloke who's trying to kill me drags me out into the street, and he's jabbing me in the face, and I can feel my eye swelling up and blood spurting out of my nose, and I'm trying to reach around so I punch the fucker back, anything just to get him off me, and there's a circle of blokes around us shouting, 'FINISH IT, FINISH IT.' Then, *CRRRAAAAAASSSSSHHHHHH!*

When I open my eyes I'm lying half-conscious in a pile of broken glass, big lumps of flesh torn out of my arms and legs, my jeans and jumper in shreds, people screaming, blood everywhere. Somehow, during the fight we'd both lost our balance and fallen backwards through a plate-glass shop window. The pain was unbelievable. Then I saw this severed head lying beside me and I almost crapped my pants. Luckily it was from one of the shop mannequins, not a *real* head. Then I heard sirens. Then everything went black.

I spent most of the night in hospital being stitched up. The glass ripped off so much skin that I lost half a tattoo, and the doctors told me the scars on my head would be there for life. That wouldn't be a problem though, as long as I didn't become a baldie. On the bus back home the next day I remember humming the tune to 'San Francisco' and thinking, I should write my own fucking anti-hippy song. I even came up with a title: 'Aston (Be Sure to Wear Some Glass in Your Face)'.

The funny thing is, I was never much of a fighter. Better a live coward than a dead hero, that was my motto. But for some reason I just kept getting caught up in all these scuffles during those early days. I must have looked like I was up for it, I suppose. My last big fight was in another pub, out near Digbeth. I've no idea how it started, but I remember glasses and ashtrays and chairs flying all over the place. I was pissed-up, so when this guy fell backwards into me, I gave him a good old shove in the other direction. But the bloke picked himself up, went bright red in the face, and said to me, 'You didn't want to do that, sunshine.'

'Do what?' I said, all innocent.

'Don't play that fucking game with me.'

'How about this game then?' I said, and tried to chin the cunt. Now that would have been a reasonable thing to do, had it not been for a couple of things: first, I fell over when I took the swing; and second, the bloke was an off-duty copper. Next thing I knew I was lying face-down with a mouthful of pub carpet and all I could hear was this voice above me going, 'You just assaulted a police officer, you little prick. You're nicked.'

As soon as I heard that, I jumped up and legged it. But the copper ran after me and pulled some rugby move that sent me crashing down on to the pavement. A week later I was in court with a fat lip and two black eyes. Luckily, the fine was only a couple of quid, which I could just about afford. But it made me think: Did I really want to go back to prison?

My boxing days were over after that.

When my old man found out I was trying to join a band, he offered to help me buy a PA system. To this day, I've no idea why: he could hardly afford to put food on the table, never mind take out a £250 loan on an amplifier and two speakers. But in those days you couldn't call yourself a singer without your own PA. You might as well have tried to get a gig as a drummer without a kit. Even my old man knew that. So he took me down to George Clay's music shop by the Rum Runner nightclub in Birmingham and we picked out this fifty-watt Vox system. I hope my father knew how grateful I was for him doing that. I mean, he didn't even like the music I spent my whole time listening to.

He'd say to me, 'Let me tell you something about the Beatles, son. They won't last five minutes. They ain't got no *tunes*. You can't sing that bleedin' racket down the pub.'

It killed me that he thought the Beatles had 'no tunes'. 'Taxman'? 'When I'm Sixty-four'? You'd have to be deaf not to appreciate those melodies.

I just couldn't understand what was *wrong* with him. Still, I wasn't going to argue – not after he'd forked out £250.

Sure enough, as soon as people found out I had my own PA, I was Mr Fucking Popular. The first band that invited me to join was called Music Machine, and it was led by a bloke named Mickey Breeze.

'Ambitious' wasn't a word you would have used to describe us. Our big dream was to play in a pub so we could earn some beer money. The trouble was, to play in a pub you needed to be able to play. And we never got around to learning how to do that, because we were always in the pub, talking about how one day we could play in a pub and earn some beer money. Music Machine never played a single gig, as far as I can remember.

Then, after a few months of going nowhere, we finally got something done: we changed our name. From then on, Music Machine was The Approach. Didn't make any difference, though. All we'd ever do is have these endless tune-ups, then I'd sing in this high-pitched voice as the others tried to remember the chords to some hokey cover version. I used to joke that you could tell I'd worked in a slaughterhouse, 'cos I did such a good job at slaughtering songs like '(Sitting on the) Dock of the Bay'. Mind you, at least I was able to keep a tune and reach the high notes without windows breaking and the local tomcats trying to mate with me, which was a start. And what I lacked in technique, I made up for in enthusiasm. I knew from my classroom stunts at Birchfield Road that I could entertain people, but to do that I needed gigs. But The Approach could barely get a rehearsal together, never mind a show.

So that's why I put up the ad in Ringway Music. The shop was in the Bull Ring, a concrete mega-mall they'd just finished building in the middle of Birmingham. It was a fucking eyesore from day one, that place. The only way you could get to it was through these subway tunnels that stank of piss and had muggers and dealers and bums hanging around all the time.

But no one cared: the Bull Ring was a new place to meet your mates, so people went there.

And Ringway Music – which basically sold the same kind of stuff as George Clay's – was the best thing about it. All the cool-looking kids would hang around outside, smoking fags, eating chips, arguing about the records they were listening to at the time. All I needed was to get in with that crowd, I thought, and I'd be fucking set. So I wrote the ad and, sure enough, a few weeks later, Geezer came knocking.

Now, he's not your average bloke, Geezer. For a start, he never uses foul language. He always has his nose in a book about Chinese poetry or ancient Greek warfare or some other heavy-duty shit. Doesn't eat meat, either. The only time I ever saw him touch the stuff was when we were stranded in Belgium one time and almost dying of hunger, and someone gave him a hot dog. He was in hospital the next day. Meat just doesn't agree with him – he's not one for a good old bacon sarnie. When I first met him he was also smoking a lot of dope. You'd be out with him at a club, say, and he'd start talking about wormholes in the vibration of consciousness, or some other fucking loony shit. But he also had a very dry sense of humour. I'd always be clowning around with him, just trying to get him to lose his cool and crack up laughing, which would set me off, then we'd be fucking sniggering away for hours.

Geezer played rhythm guitar in Rare Breed, and he wasn't bad at all. But more important than that, he looked the part, with his Jesus hair and his Guy Fawkes moustache. He could afford all the very latest stitches too, could Geezer. He'd been to grammar school, so he had a real job as a trainee accountant at one of the factories. They paid him fuck-all, but he was still probably earning more dough than me, even though he was a year younger. And he must have blown almost all of it on clothes. Style-wise, nothing was too out-there for Geezer. He'd turn up to rehearsals in lime green bell bottoms and silver platform boots. I'd just look at him and say, 'Why the fuck would you ever want to wear *that*?'

I wasn't exactly a conservative dresser myself, mind you. I'd walk around in an old pyjama top for a shirt with a hot-water tap on a piece of string for a necklace. I tell you, it wasn't easy trying to look like a rock star with no fucking dough. You had to use your imagination. And I never wore shoes – not even in winter. People would ask me where I got my 'fashion inspiration' from and I'd tell them: 'By being a dirty broke bastard and never taking a bath.'

Most people reckoned I'd walked straight out of the funny farm. But they'd look at Geezer and think: I bet he's in a band. He had it all. He's such a clever guy, he probably could have had his own company with his name above the door: Geezer & Geezer Ltd. But the most impressive thing he could do was write lyrics: really fucking intense lyrics about wars and superheroes and black magic and a load of other mind-blowing stuff. The first time he showed me them I just said, 'Geezer, we've gotta start writing our own songs so we can use these words. They're amazing.'

We became pretty tight, me and Geezer. I'll always remember when we were walking around the Bull Ring in the spring or early summer of 1968, and all of a sudden this bloke with long, frizzy blond hair and the tightest trousers you've ever seen pops out of nowhere and slaps Geezer on the back.

'Geezer fucking Butler!'

Geezer turned around and said, 'Rob! How are you, man?'

'Oh, y'know . . . could be worse.'

'Rob, this is Ozzy Zig,' said Geezer. 'Ozzy, this is Robert Plant – he used to sing with the Band of Joy.'

'Oh *yeah*,' I said, recognising the face. 'I went to one of your shows. Fucking awesome voice, man.'

'Thanks,' said Plant, flashing me this big, charming smile.

'So, what you been up to?' asked Geezer.

'Well, since you mention it, I've been offered a job.'

'*Nice*. What's the gig?'

'The Yardbirds.'

'*Whoah!* Congratulations, man. That's huge. But didn't they split up?'

'Yeah, but Jimmy – y'know the guitarist, Jimmy Page – he's still around. So is the bass player. And they've got contractual obligations in Scandinavia, so they want to put something together.'

'That's great,' said Geezer.

'Well, I'm not sure I'm gonna to be taking the gig, to be honest,' said Plant, shrugging. 'I've got some pretty good stuff going on here, y'know? Matter of fact, I've just put a new band together.'

'Oh, er . . . cool,' said Geezer. 'What's the name?'

'Hobbstweedle,' said Plant.

Later, when Plant was gone, I asked Geezer if the bloke was out of his fucking mind. 'Is he seriously going to pass up a gig with Jimmy Page for that Hobbsbollocks thing?' I asked.

Geezer shrugged. 'I think he's just worried it won't work out,' he said. 'But he'll do it, as long as they change the name. They can't go around calling themselves the "New Yardbirds" for long.'

'It's better than fucking Hobbstweedle.'

'Good point.'

Bumping into someone like Robert Plant wasn't unusual when you were with the Geezer. He seemed to know *everyone*. He was part of the cool crowd, so he went to the right parties, took the right drugs, hung out with the right movers and shakers. It was a real eye-opener, and I loved being part of it. Still, there was a big problem hanging over us: our band, Rare Breed, was shit. We made Hobbstweedle look like The fucking Who. When I joined they were set on being 'experimental': they had all these trippy stage props and a strobe light, like they were trying to be the next Pink Floyd. Now, there was nothing wrong with trying to be the next Pink Floyd – later on, I would enjoy dropping a few tabs of mind detergent while listening to 'Interstellar Overdrive' – but we couldn't pull it off. Pink Floyd was music for rich college kids, and we were the exact fucking opposite of that. So Rare Breed wasn't going anywhere, and me and Geezer both knew it. Rehearsals were just one long argument about when the bongo solo should come in. Worst of all, there was this bloke in the band who called himself Brick, and he fancied himself as a bit of a San Francisco hippy type.

'Brick's a dick,' I kept telling Geezer.

'Aw, he's all right.'

'No, Brick's a *dick*.'

'Give it a rest, Ozzy.'

'He's a *dick*, that Brick.'

And so on.

I got on fine with the other members of the band. But with Brick on the scene and me getting increasingly pissed off, Rare Breed was never going to last. Even Geezer started to lose his patience after a while.

The only gig I can remember playing in those very early days – and I think it was with Rare Breed, but it could have been under a different name, with different band members, 'cos line-ups changed so often back then – was the Birmingham Fire Station's Christmas party. The audience consisted of two firemen, a bucket and a ladder. We made enough dough for half a shandy, split six ways.

But that gig made an impression on me, because it was the first time I ever experienced stage fright.

And fucking hell, man, did I get a bad case of the brown trousers.

To say that I suffer from pre-show nerves is like saying that when you get hit by an atom bomb it hurts a bit. I was absolutely fucking petrified when I got up on that stage. Sweaty. Mouth drier than a Mormon wedding. Numb legs. Racing heart. Trembling hands. The fucking works, man. I literally almost pissed myself. I'd never felt anything like it in my life. I remember downing a pint beforehand to try to calm myself down, but it didn't work. I would have had twenty pints if I'd had enough dough. In the end I croaked my way through a couple of numbers until we blew out one of the speakers of the PA. Then we fucked off home. I didn't tell my old man about the speaker. I just swapped it with the one in his radiogram.

I'd buy him a new one when I got a job, I told myself. And it seemed like I would have to get a job, because, judging by the fire station gig, there was no way I was ever going to make it in the music business.

A couple of days later, I decided to pack in singing for good.

I remember saying to Geezer down the pub, 'I've had enough, man, this ain't going nowhere.'

Geezer just frowned and twiddled his thumbs. Then, in a dejected voice, he said: 'They've offered me a promotion at work. I'm going to be number three in the accounting department.'

'Well, that's it then, isn't it?' I said.

'Suppose.'

We finished our drinks, shook hands, and went our separate ways. 'See you around, Geezer,' I said.

'Take it easy, Ozzy Zig.'

Knock-knock.

I poked my head through the curtains in the living room and saw a dodgy-looking bloke with long hair and a moustache standing outside on the doorstep. What the fuck was this, *déjà vu*? But no, despite the hair and the tash, the bloke didn't look anything like Geezer. He looked . . . homeless. And there was another bloke standing next to him. He also had long hair and a king-sized ferret on his upper lip. But he was taller, and he looked a bit like . . . Nah, it couldn't be. Not *him*. Parked behind them on the street was an old blue Commer van with a big rusty hole above the wheel arch and faded lettering on the side that said 'Mythology'.

'JOHN! *Get the door!*'

'*I'm getting it!*'

It had been a few months since I'd left Rare Breed. I was twenty now, and had given up all hope of being a singer or ever getting out of Aston. PA system or no PA system, it wasn't going to happen. I'd convinced myself that there was no point in even trying, because I was just going to fail, like I had at school, at work, and at everything else I'd ever tried. 'You ain't no good as a singer,' I told myself. 'You can't even play an instrument, so what hope d'you have?' It was Self-Pity City at 14 Lodge Road. I'd already talked to my mum about trying to get my old job back at the Lucas plant. She was seeing what she could do. And I'd told the owner of Ringway Music to take down my 'OZZY ZIG NEEDS GIG' sign. Stupid fucking name, anyway – Geezer was right about that. All in all, there was no reason whatsoever why two long-haired blokes should be standing on my doorstep at nine o'clock on a Tuesday night. Could they be mates of Geezer? Did they have something to do with Rare Breed? It didn't make any sense.

Knock-knock.

Knock-knock.

Knock-knock-knock-knock.

I twisted the latch and pulled. An awkward pause. Then the shorter and scruffier bloke asked, 'Are you . . . Ozzy Zig?'

Before I could answer, the bigger guy leaned forwards and squinted at me. Now I knew for certain who he was. And he knew me, too. I froze. He groaned. 'Aw, fucking hell,' he said. 'It's *you*.'

I couldn't believe it. The bloke on my doorstep was Tony Iommi: the good-looking kid from the year above me at Birchfield Road, who'd brought his electric guitar to school one Christmas, driving the teachers crazy with the noise. I hadn't seen him for about five years, but I'd heard about him. He'd become a bit of an Aston legend since leaving school. All the kids knew who he was. If you wanted to be in a band with anyone, it was Tony. Unfortunately, he didn't seem to feel the same way about me.

'C'mon, Bill,' he said to the homeless-looking bloke. 'This is a waste of time. Let's go.'

'Wait a minute,' said Bill. 'Who is this guy?'

'I'll tell you one thing: his name ain't "Ozzy Zig". And he ain't no singer, either. He's Ozzy Osbourne and he's an idiot. C'mon, let's get out of here.'

'Hang on a minute,' I interrupted. 'How did you get this address? How d'you know about Ozzy Zig?'

'"Ozzy Zig Needs Gig,"' said Bill, with a shrug.

'I told 'em to take that fucking sign down months ago.'

'Well, you should go and tell them again, 'cos it was up there today.'

'At Ringway Music?'

'In the window.'

I tried not to look too pleased.

'Tony,' said Bill, 'can't we give this guy a break? He seems all right.'

'Give him a break?' Tony had already lost patience. 'He was the school clown! I'm not being in a band with that fucking moron.'

I couldn't think of anything to say, so I just stood there staring at my feet.

'Beggars can't be choosers, Tony,' hissed Bill. 'That's why we're here, isn't it?'

But Tony just huffed and started to walk back towards the van.

Bill shook his head and shrugged at me, as if to say, 'Sorry, mate. Nothing more I can do.'

That seemed to be that. But then something caught my eye. It was Tony's right hand. There was something wrong with it.

'Fucking hell, Tony,' I said. 'What happened to your fingers, man?'

It turned out I wasn't the only one who'd had a rough time with jobs after being turfed out of school at the age of fifteen. While I was poisoning myself with the degreasing machine and going deaf testing car horns, Tony was working as an apprentice sheet-metal worker. Later, he told me his education mainly involved learning how to use an electric welder.

Now, they're lethal fucking things, electric welders. The biggest risk is being exposed to ultraviolet radiation, which can literally melt the skin off your body before you even know it, or burn holes in your eyeballs. You can also get killed by electric shocks, or end up poisoned by exposure to the toxic rust-proofing shit they put on the panels. Anyway, Tony was doing this welding job during the day and playing in a band called the Rocking Chevrolets on the club circuit at night, waiting for his big break. He was always talented, but hammering out all those numbers by Chuck Berry, Bo Diddley and Eddie Cochran every night made him shit fucking hot. Eventually an agent spotted him and offered him a professional gig over in Germany, so Tony decided to quit his job in the factory. He thought he'd made it.

Then it all went wrong.

On Tony's last day in the workshop, the bloke who was supposed to press and cut the metal before it was welded didn't show up. So Tony had to do it. I still don't know exactly what happened – if Tony didn't know how to use the machine properly, or if it was broken, or whatever – but this fucking massive metal press ended up ripping off the tips of the middle and ring fingers on his right hand. Tony is left handed, so they were his fretboard fingers. It makes me shiver just to think about it, even now. You can't imagine what a bad scene it must have been, with all the blood and the howling and the scrambling around on the floor trying to find the tips of his fingers, and then Tony being told by the doctors in the emergency room that he'd never be able to play again. He saw dozens of specialists over the next few months, and they all told him the same thing: 'Son, your days in a rock 'n' roll band are finished, end of fucking story, find something else to do.' He must have thought it was all over. It would have been like me getting shot in the throat.

Tony suffered from terrible depression for a long time after the accident. I don't know how he even got out of bed in the morning. Then, one day, his old shop foreman brought him a record by Django Reinhardt, the Belgian Gypsy jazz guitarist who played all his solos using just two fingers on his fretting hand because he'd burned the others in a fire.

And Tony thought, Well, if old Django can do it, so can I.

At first he tried playing right-handed, but that didn't work. So he went back to left-handed, trying to play the fretboard with just two fingers, but he didn't like that, either. Finally he figured out what to do. He made a couple of thimbles for his injured fingers out of a melted-down Fairy Liquid bottle, sanded them down until they were roughly the same size as his old fingertips, and then glued these little leather pads on the ends to improve his grip on the strings. He loosened the strings a bit too, so he wouldn't have to put so much pressure on them.

Then he just learned to play the guitar again from scratch,

even though he had no feeling in two fingers. To this day, I've no idea how he does it. Everywhere he goes, he carries around a bag full of homemade thimbles and leather patches, and he always keeps a soldering iron on hand to make adjustments. Every time I see him play, it hits me how much he had to overcome. I have so much awe and respect for Tony Iommi because of that. Also, in a strange way, I suppose the accident helped him, because when he learned to play again he developed a unique style that no one has ever been able to copy. And fucking hell, man, they've tried.

After the accident Tony played in a band called the Rest. But his heart wasn't in it. He thought all the hype about 'Brumbeat' was bollocks and he wanted out, so when he was offered an audition with a band called Mythology up in Carlisle, you couldn't see him for dust. He even convinced the Rest's singer to go up there with him. Once the guys in Mythology had heard the two of them in action, they couldn't sign them up fast enough. Then, a couple of months later, Mythology's drummer quit. So Tony called up his old mate Bill Ward from Aston, who was only too happy to take the job.

I never went to a Mythology gig, but I'm told they brought the house down wherever they went: they had this dirty, swampy, heavy blues sound, and they'd cover songs by bands like Buffalo Springfield, the Jimi Hendrix Experience, and John Mayall & the Bluesbreakers – whose new guitarist at the time was Eric Clapton, who'd just quit the Yardbirds, giving Jimmy Page his big break. It was a classic era for rock 'n' roll, and it was all going gangbusters for Mythology. The band quickly built a massive following in Cumberland, playing sold-out shows all over the place, supporting acts like Gary Walker, of the Walker Brothers. But then they started to run into trouble with the law. That's what happened in those days if you had long hair and moustaches and tight leather trousers. From what I heard, the first time they got done was for using the label from a bottle of

Newcastle Brown Ale in place of a tax disc on their tour van. The next time was a lot more heavy-duty, though, and it finished them off. Their dope dealer – a student from Leeds, I think – got busted. Then the cops drew up a list of the guy's clients, got a search warrant, and raided Mythology's flat at Compton House in Carlisle. It was bad news, man.

All four members of the band were done for possession of marijuana. That might not sound like such a big deal now, but in those days it was fucking horrendous. Not so much because of the punishment – they all pleaded guilty and were fined just fifteen quid each – but because of the stigma. No one would book a band that had been done for drugs, 'cos they thought you were a bad crowd. And no one wanted any trouble with the law, not when they had licences that could be revoked. By the summer of 1968, Mythology's gigs had dried up to the point where they were all flat broke. They could barely even afford food. Tony and Bill had two choices: give up full-time music and get proper jobs in Carlisle like their bandmates were planning to do; or fuck off back to Aston, where they could live at their folks' places while they tried to save their careers. They chose Aston, which is how they ended up on my doorstep.

I've no idea what I said to Tony outside my house that night to make him change his mind and give me a chance. The fact that I had a PA system probably helped. And maybe he realised that it had been five years since school, and that we'd both grown up a lot since then. Well, perhaps I hadn't grown up too much, but at least I knew I never wanted to go back to prison or work in a factory again. I think Tony felt the same way after his drugs bust and his accident at the metalworks. And although his folks made a decent living – they owned a little corner shop on Park Lane – he'd left Birchfield Road with a no-hope future just like mine.

Without music, we were both fucked.

Bill also helped to calm Tony down. He's the nicest bloke you'll ever meet, Bill. A phenomenal drummer – as I would soon find out – but also a solid, down-to-earth guy. You could tell that by the way he dressed: he was the anti-Geezer when it came to fashion. If you didn't know better, you'd think he was living in a cardboard box on the hard shoulder of the M6. In all the time I've known him, he's never changed, either. Years later, I went on Concorde for the first time with Bill. He was late, and I was sitting on board thinking, Where the fuck is he? Eventually he strolled into the cabin wearing an old man's overcoat and carrying two Tesco bags full of cans of cider. I looked him up and down and said, 'Bill, you do know that they provide drinks on Concorde, don't you? You don't have to bring your own Tesco cider?' He replied, 'Oh, I don't want to put them to any trouble.'

That's Bill Ward for you.

After Tony had warmed up a bit, we spent the rest of the night sitting in the back of the van, smoking fags, telling stories about prison and Carlisle and drugs busts and severed fingers and Mr Jones from school and how to slaughter cows with a bolt gun and what blues records we'd been listening to lately. Then we started to plot our next move.

'Before we do anything else, we're going to need a name and a bass player,' said Tony.

'I don't know any bass players,' I said. 'But I know a bloke called Geezer who plays rhythm guitar.'

Tony and Bill looked at me. Then at each other. '*Geezer Butler?*' they said in unison.

'Yeah.'

'That bloke's crazy,' said Bill. 'Last time I saw him he was off his nut in Midnight City.'

'That's because Geezer's already a rock star in his own head,' I said. 'Which is a good thing. And he doesn't eat meat, so it'll save us money on the road. *And* he's a qualified accountant.'

'Ozzy's right.' Tony nodded. 'Geezer's a good bloke.'

'I'll go round his house tomorrow and ask him if he wants to do the honours,' I said. 'He'll need some time to learn to play the bass, but how hard can it be, eh? There's only four fucking strings.'

'And what about a name?' said Tony.

The three of us looked at each other.

'We should all take a couple of days to think about it,' I said. 'I dunno about you two, but I've got a special place where I go to get ideas for important stuff like this. It's never failed me yet.'

Forty-eight hours later I blurted out: 'I've *got* it!'

'Must have been that dodgy bird you poked the other night,' said Geezer. 'Has your whelk turned green yet?'

Tony and Bill sniggered into their plates of egg and chips. We were sitting in a greasy spoon caff in Aston. So far, everyone was getting along famously.

'Very funny, Geezer,' I said, waving an eggy fork at him. 'I mean the name for our band.'

The sniggering died down.

'Go on then,' said Tony.

'Well, I was on the shitter last night, and . . .'

'*That*'s your special place?' spluttered Bill, blobs of mushed-up egg and HP sauce flying out of his mouth.

'Where the fuck did you think it was, Bill?' I said. 'The hanging gardens of fucking Babylon? So, I'm on the shitter, and I've got this right old cliffhanger of a Richard the Third coming down the pipe—'

Geezer groaned.

'—and I'm looking straight ahead at this shelf in front of me. My mum's put a tin of talcum powder on there, right? She loves that stuff. When you go to the bog after she's taken a bath it looks like Santa's fucking grotto in there. Anyway, it's that cheap brand of talc, the one with the black and white polka dots on the side . . .'

'Polka Tulk,' said Tony.

'Exactly,' I said. 'Polka Tulk!' I looked around the table, grinning. 'Fucking brilliant, eh?'

'I don't get it,' said Bill, his mouth still full. 'What's your mum's smelly old armpits got to do with our band?'

'The Polka Tulk Blues Band,' I said. 'That's our name!'

The table went so quiet you could almost hear the steam rising from the four mugs of tea in front of us.

'Anyone got a better idea?' said Tony.

Silence.

'It's settled then,' he said. 'We're the Polka Tulk Blues Band – in honour of Ozzy's mum's smelly old armpits.'

'Oi!' I said. 'Enough of that! I won't have a fucking word said against my mum's smelly old armpits.'

Bill roared with laughter, and more blobs of egg and sauce flew out of his mouth.

'You two are just animals,' said Geezer.

The name wasn't the only decision we had to make. Also put to the vote was whether we needed more band members. In the end we agreed that the kind of songs we'd be playing – dirty, heavy, Deep South blues – tended to work better with a lot of instruments, so ideally we could use a saxophonist and a bottleneck guitarist to give us a fuller sound. Tony knew a sax player called Alan Clark, and a mate of mine from school, Jimmy Phillips, could play bottleneck.

To be honest with you, we also wanted to copy the line-up of Fleetwood Mac, whose second album – *Mr Wonderful* – had just come out and blown us all away. Tony was especially taken with Fleetwood Mac's guitarist, Peter Green. Like Clapton before him, Green had played for a while with John Mayall & the Bluesbreakers, but he was now a fully qualified rock god in his own right. That seemed to be how guitarists made the big time: they joined an established act, then they left to front their own projects. Fortunately for us, Tony had been taken off the market by his injury just when he was about to be snapped up by a big-name act.

Their loss was our gain.

That weekend, we met up for our first rehearsal at a community centre in Six Ways, one of the older and shittier parts of Ashton. There was only one problem: we could barely hear the PA above the noise of the A34 underpass outside. Making the din even worse were the cars and trucks circling the massive concrete roundabout they'd just built on top of the fucking thing. They were pouring so much concrete in Aston in those days that we might as well have bought some fur hats and started calling each other comrade. I mean, for fuck's sake, the place was grey enough as it was without adding more fucking grey everywhere.

To cheer things up a bit, I went out one night with an aerosol can – I'd had a few beers – and did some 'decorating'. One of the things I graffitied on a wall by the roundabout was 'Iron Void'. Fuck knows what was going on in my head.

The rehearsals went all right, considering I'd never sung with a proper band before. Basically, the lads would just jam, and then Tony would give me a nod when he thought I should sing. For lyrics, I just came out with whatever bollocks was in my head at the time.

It wasn't easy for Geezer, either. He didn't have enough dough at the time to buy a bass, so he did the best he could with his Telecaster – you can't put bass strings on a normal guitar, 'cos it would snap the neck. I think Tony was worried about Geezer at first, but it turned out that he was a fucking awesome bass player – a total natural. And he looked more like a rock star than anyone else in the band.

Our first gig was up in Carlisle, thanks to Tony's old Mythology contacts. That meant driving two hundred miles up the M6 in Tony's rusty old shitbox of a van, with the motorway stopping and starting all the time, 'cos they hadn't finished tarmacking it. The van's suspension had died along with the dinosaurs, so whenever we went round a corner everyone had to lean in the opposite direction to stop the wheel arch from scraping on the tyre. We soon learned that it's almost impossible to lean in the opposite direction of a turn, so this horrible smell of burning rubber kept wafting into the cabin, sparks were flying all over the place, and you could hear this violent grinding noise as the wheel gradually etched a big fucking hole in the bodywork. 'It's a good job you know how to use a welder,' I said to Tony. Another problem was the windscreen wipers: they didn't work. Well, they did for a bit, but it was raining so hard that by the time we'd reached Stafford the motor had conked out. So Tony had to pull over to the hard shoulder in the pissing rain while me and Bill fed a piece of string out of the window, tied it to the wiper, then strung it back through the other window. That way we could wipe the windscreen manually, with me tugging on one end of the string, then Bill tugging on the other. All the way to fucking Carlisle.

But the eight-hour drive was worth it.

When we finally arrived in Carlisle, I just couldn't stop staring at the flyer for our first official gig. It said:

C.E.S. PROMOTIONS Proudly Present . . .
'68 Dancing for Teens and Twenties
County Hall Ballroom, Carlisle
Saturday August 24th, 7.30 p.m. to 11.30 p.m. –
The New, Exciting Group from Birmingham, POLKA TULK BLUES BAND (With ex-member of MYTHOLOGY)
plus
CREEQUE
Non-stop dancing (Admission 5/-)

This is it, I said to myself.

It's finally happening.

The gig itself was amazing, apart from almost crapping my pants with stage fright. It was afterwards that the trouble started. We were packing up our stuff – roadies were a luxury we couldn't afford – and this giant of a bloke with bright red hair and some kind of pus-filled rash on his face came up to me. He was holding a pint glass and his troll of a chick was standing next to him. 'Oi, you,' he went. 'D'you *like* my girlfriend?'

'Say again?' I said.

'You 'eard me. D'you *like* my girlfriend? You were looking at her. Fancy giving her one, do you?'

'You must have got me mixed up with someone else,' I said. 'I wasn't looking at anything.'

'You were looking at her. I saw ya. With my own two fucking eyes. Fancy having a go, do you?'

By now, the bloke was so close to me that I could smell the sweat on his T-shirt. He was enormous, and he had a head on him like a fucking anvil. He was even bigger than my old mate, the bully-basher from Birchfield Road. There was no way out. I knew exactly what was going to happen next. I'd either say, 'No, honestly mate, I don't like your girlfriend,' and he'd reply, 'You calling her ugly, are you, you Brummie cunt?' then rip my head off. Or I'd go, 'Funny you should say that, 'cos I was just thinking how much I'd love to give your girlfriend a good old seeing to,' and he'd reply, 'Yeah, I thought so, you Brummie cunt,' then rip my head off.

I was fucked, either way.

Then I had an idea: maybe if I got someone else involved, it would take the pressure off.

'Hey, Bill,' I shouted over to the other side of stage. 'Come over here a second, will yer?'

Bill strolled over, hands in pockets, whistling. 'What's up, Ozzy?'

'D'you want to shag his girlfriend?' I said, pointing at the troll in question.

'*What?*'

'His bird. D'you think she's a bit of a slag, or would you give it a go?'

'Ozzy, are you fucking *insa—*'

That was when the bloke went fucking stage-five apeshit. He roared, threw down his pint – beer and shards of glass went everywhere – then he lunged towards me, but I ducked out of the way. Uh-oh, I thought. This could get nasty. Then he tried to take a swing at Bill, who had a look on his face like he was tied to a railway track and the *Flying Scotsman* was coming down the line. At this point I was sure that one or both of us would be spending the next month in hospital, but I hadn't counted on what Tony would do next. He saw what was going on, ran over to the giant redhead, gave him a shove, and told him to fuck off out of it. Now Tony was smaller than the redhead, a lot smaller, but he was an incredible fighter. The redhead didn't know that, of course, so he went for Tony's throat. They wrestled for a bit, the redhead got some jabs in, but then Tony just cracked him full-on in the face and kept pounding away – *bam-bam-bam-bam-bam-bam!* – until the bloke went down like the *Titanic*.

Crraaaasssssshhhh!

I watched, mouth wide open, as Tony shook the pain out of his fist, wiped the blood off his face, then calmly carried on packing up his equipment. No one said a word.

Later, when we were in the van on the way to our next gig down the road in Workington, I thanked him for saving our arses. He just waved me away, told me not to mention it again.

Bill, on the other hand, didn't speak to me for a week.

Can't say I blame him.

*

When we got back to Aston, Tony said he wasn't happy with Alan and Jimmy. Jimmy fucked around too much in rehearsals, he said, and there wasn't any point in having a saxophone player if we didn't have a full brass section. And no one wanted a full brass section – we'd need a double-decker tour bus, for starters, and we'd never make any dough after splitting the takings on the door with half a dozen trombonists and trumpeters.

So that was it: Alan and Jimmy were out, and the Polka Tulk Blues Band became a fourpiece. But Tony still wasn't happy. 'It's the name,' he said, during a rehearsal break. 'It's crap.'

'What's wrong with it?' I protested.

'Every time I hear it, all I can picture is you, with your trousers round your ankles, taking a fucking dump.'

'Well, you lot think of something then,' I huffed.

'Actually,' announced Bill, 'I've been doing a bit of thinking about this and I've got an idea.'

'Go on,' said Tony.

'You've got to imagine it written on a big poster. Like a billboard or something.'

'I'm imagining it,' said Tony.

Bill took a deep breath. Then he said, 'Earth.'

Tony and Geezer looked at each other and shrugged. I ignored them and pretended to look worried.

'Are you OK, Bill?' I said, narrowing my eyes.

'I'm fine. What do you mean?'

'Are you sure?'

'Of course I'm fucking sure.'

'It's just . . . I thought I heard you throw up just then.'

'*What?*'

'UUUUUURRRRRRRRFFFFFF!'

'Fuck you, Ozzy.'

'*UUUUUURRRRRRRRFFFFFF!*'

'Just give it some fucking thought, will you? It's simple, powerful, no bullshit, just five letters – E-A-R-T-H.'

'Bill, honestly mate, I think you should go and see a doctor. I think you just threw up again. UUUURRRRR—'

'Ozzy, cut it out,' snapped Tony. 'It's better than Polka fucking Tulk.'

'I agree,' said Geezer.

That was that.

Officially, we didn't have a band leader. Unofficially, we all knew it was Tony. He was the oldest, the tallest, the best fighter, the best-looking, the most experienced, and the most obviously talented. He'd really started to look the part, too. He'd gone out and bought this black suede cowboy jacket with tassels on the arms, which the chicks loved. We all knew that Tony belonged right up there with the likes of Clapton and Hendrix. Pound for pound, he could match any of them. He was our ticket to the big time.

Maybe that's why I felt so intimidated by him, even after we became friends. Or maybe it was just because he's such a private and reserved person. You never really know what's going on inside Tony Iommi's head. He's the total opposite of me, in other words: no one's ever in any doubt about what's going on in the pile of old jelly inside my thick skull.

I didn't feel intimidated by Geezer, even though he'd been to a proper school and actually knew stuff. As for Bill, he was the fall-guy. We'd always be playing pranks on him. He'd get drunk and pass out and we'd leave him on a park bench somewhere with a newspaper over him, and we'd think it was the funniest thing that had ever happened in the world. He was such a nice guy, he just seemed to be asking for it.

Me? I was still the clown. The madman. The loudmouth who'd do anything for a dare. The others would always get me to do the stuff they didn't want to do – like asking for directions when we were on the road and trying to find the way to some new venue. One time we were in Bournemouth and there was a guy walking across the road with a roll of carpet under his arm. They're all shouting, 'Go on, Ozzy, ask 'im, ask 'im.' So I wind down the window of the van and go, 'Oi! Mister! Can you tell us the way to the M1?' He turns around and says, 'No. Fuck off, cunt.' Another time we're in London, and I shout out to this bloke, 'Excuse me, chief, but d'you know the way to the Marquee?' He says, 'Chief? *Chief?* Do I look like a fucking Indian?'

Fucking priceless, man. We had such a laugh. And that was the thing with us: we always had a sense of humour. It's what made us work together so well – at first, anyway. If you don't have a sense of humour when you're in a band, you end up like fucking Emerson, Lake and Palmer, making eight-disc LPs so you can all have your own three-hour fucking solos.

And who wants to listen to that bollocks?

If it hadn't been for Tony's parents, I'm not sure we'd have made it through the rest of 1968 without starving to death. We were so broke, we'd steal raw vegetables from allotments in the middle of the night, just for something to eat. One time, me and Bill found ten pence, and it was like we'd won the fucking lottery. We couldn't decide what to buy with it: four bags of chips, or ten fags and a box of matches.

We went for the fags in the end.

Tony's mum and dad were our only safety net. They'd give us sandwiches from the shop, tins of beans, the odd pack of Player's No. 6, even petrol money from the till. And it's not like they were rich: they owned a corner shop in Aston, not Harrods of Knightsbridge. I loved Tony's mum, Sylvie – she was a lovely lady. Tony's old man was great, too. He was one of those guys who would buy old bangers and do them up. That's why we always had a van to get around in.

And we needed one, because we never turned down gigs – ever – not even when the pay was only a few quid for a two-hour set, split four ways, before costs. We needed everything we could get. Even Geezer had given up his day job by then, and Earth was the one shot we had at making sure we never had to go back to the factories. We had to make it work – there was no choice.

We were incredibly single-minded. The craziest thing we did – and this was Tony's idea, I think – was to find out whenever a big-name band was coming into town, load up the van with all our stuff, and then just wait outside the venue on the off-chance they might not show up. The odds weren't worth thinking about, but if it ever happened, we reckoned we'd get a chance to show off in front of a few thousand punters . . . even if they were pissed off and throwing bottles because we weren't the band they'd blown a couple of days' wages to see.

And y'know what? *It worked.*

Once.

The big-name band was Jethro Tull. I can't remember where they were supposed to be playing – it might have been in Birmingham, or somewhere like Stafford – but they didn't show up. And there we were, outside in the blue Commer van, ready to spring into action.

Tony went in to see the venue manager.

'Has the band not showed up yet?' he asked, ten minutes after they were supposed to go on.

'Don't fucking start, sunshine,' came the pissed-off reply. Obviously the manager was having a bad night. 'They're not here, I don't know why, I don't know how, but they're not here, and, yes, we've called their hotel. Five times. Come back tomorrow and we'll give you a refund.'

'I'm not looking for a refund,' said Tony. 'I just wanted to let you know that me and my band were driving by the venue – by chance, y'know? – and, well, if your main act hasn't shown up, we can fill in.'

'*Fill in?*'

'Yeah.'

'For Jethro Tull?'

'Yeah.'

'What's the name of your band, son?'

'Earth.'

'*Urf?*'

'Earth.'

'*Urph?*'

'As in the planet.'

'Oh, right. *Hmm*. I think I might have actually heard of you lot. Crazy singer. Blues covers. Right?'

'Yeah. And a few originals.'

'Where's your equipment?'

'In the van. Outside.'

'Are you a Boy Scout or something?'

'Eh?'

'You seem very well prepared.'

'Oh, er . . . yeah.'

'Well, you're on in fifteen minutes. I'll pay you ten quid. And watch out for those bottles, the mob's upset.'

Once the deal was done, Tony ran out of the venue with this huge grin on his face, giving us the double thumbs up. 'We're on in fifteen minutes!' he shouted. '*Fifteen minutes!*'

The jolt of adrenaline was indescribable. It was so intense, I almost forgot about my stage fright. And the gig was a fucking triumph. The crowd grumbled for the first few minutes, and I had to dodge a couple of lobbed missiles, but we ended up blowing them away.

One of the best things about it was that Ian Anderson – Tull's lead singer, who was famous for playing the flute with this bug-eyed look on his face while standing on one leg, like a court jester – finally turned up when we were halfway through the set. The band's bus had broken down on the M6, or something like that, and they'd had no way to contact the venue to warn them. I think Anderson had hitch-hiked there by himself to apologise. So there I was, screaming into the mic, and when I looked up I saw Anderson standing at the back of the hall, nodding his head, looking like he was really into the music. It was fucking fabulous.

We came off stage buzzing. The venue manager couldn't have been happier. Even Anderson seemed grateful. And after that, all the bookers knew our name – even if they couldn't say it.

Over the next few weeks everything started to take off for us. The gigs got bigger, our playing got tighter, and some local managers began sniffing around. One guy in particular took an interest in us: his name was Jim Simpson and he'd been the trumpet player in a fairly well-known Birmingham band called Locomotive. Jim had given up being a musician to set up a management company called Big Bear, which was John Peel's nickname for him, 'cos he was this stocky, hairy, red-faced bloke, who ambled around Birmingham like a big, tame grizzly. He'd also opened a club on the floor above the Crown pub on Station Street, calling it Henry's Blues House. It was one of our favourite hang-outs. One of the earliest shows I remember seeing there was a jam with Robert Plant and John Bonham, probably just before they went off to Scandinavia. It gave me fucking goosebumps, man.

Then, near the end of 1968, Jim invited us to play at the club with Ten Years After, who were a huge blues act at the time. Alvin Lee, the band's guitarist and singer, would later became a good friend of ours. It was a great night – as much of a turning point for Earth as the Jethro Tull gig had been. A few days later, after a few beers, Jim told me and Bill that he was thinking about managing us. Big Bear was already looking after Locomotive and two other local bands, Bakerloo Blues Line, and Tea and Symphony. It was a huge moment. Having Jim on our side would mean a lot more work and a much more realistic chance of making a living out of music without having to rely on handouts from Tony's parents. We could go to London and play the Marquee Club. We could tour Europe.

The sky was the fucking limit.

The next day, me and Bill couldn't wait to tell Tony. We'd booked the rehearsal room at Six Ways, and the second Tony walked in I said, 'You'll never fucking guess what . . .'

But when I told him about the possible deal, he just said, 'Oh', then looked at the floor. He seemed upset and distracted.

'Are you all right, Tony?' I asked.

'I've got some news,' he said quietly.

My heart just about stopped beating. I turned white. I thought his mum or dad must have died. Something terrible, anyway, for him not to be excited about us getting a manager.

'What is it?'

'Ian Anderson got in touch with me,' he said, still looking at the floor. 'Tull's guitarist just quit. He asked me to replace him – and I said yes. I'm sorry, lads. I can't turn it down. We're going to be playing with the Rolling Stones in Wembley on the tenth of December.'

Stunned silence.

It was all over. We'd been so close, and now we were a million light years away.

'Tony,' I said eventually, swallowing hard. 'That's fucking great, man. It's what you've always wanted.'

'Congratulations, Tony,' said Geezer, putting down his guitar and walking over to slap him on the back.

'Yeah,' said Bill. 'If anyone deserves it, you do. I hope they know how lucky they are.'

'Thanks, lads,' said Tony, sounding like he was trying not to choke up. 'You're going to do great, with or without me. You'll see.'

I can say with my hand on my heart that we weren't bullshitting Tony when we said all that stuff. We'd been through a lot together over the last few months, and all three of us were genuinely pleased for him.

Even though it was the worst fucking news we'd ever heard in our lives.

3

The Witch and the Nazi

We were all devastated.

There was only one Tony Iommi, and we knew it.

It had just *worked* with Tony. Maybe it was because all four of us had grown up within a few streets of each other. Or maybe it was because we were all skint and desperate and knew exactly what our lives would be like without rock 'n' roll. Either way, we understood each other. It was obvious to anyone who saw us play.

After getting home from the rehearsal where Tony broke the news, I remember lying on the bed at 14 Lodge Road with my head in my hands. My dad came into the room and sat down next to me. 'Go and have a drink with your pals, son,' he said, pressing a ten-bob note into my hand. I must have looked pretty fucking upset for him to do that, given all the unpaid bills on the kitchen table that my mum was crying over. 'The world doesn't revolve around Tony,' he said. 'There'll be other guitarists.'

He was a good guy, my old man. But this time he was wrong. There were no other guitarists.

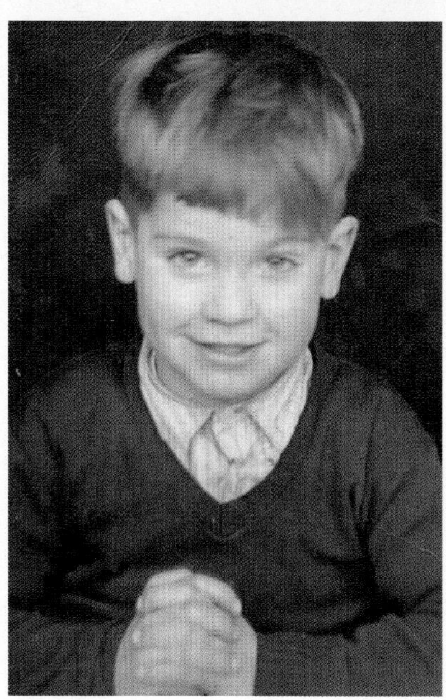

The Boy Prince of Darkness.

My dad promised me long trousers for my sister Jean's wedding. I got these fucking things instead.

With Mum and Dad. They put up with a lot.

Blame this on Jim Simpson. It was his idea to hold the 'Big Fear Follies' – naked.

Bill Ward, Geezer Butler, Tony Iommi and me, at Long Beach Arena. Dunno why we look so miserable – we were all as high as kites.

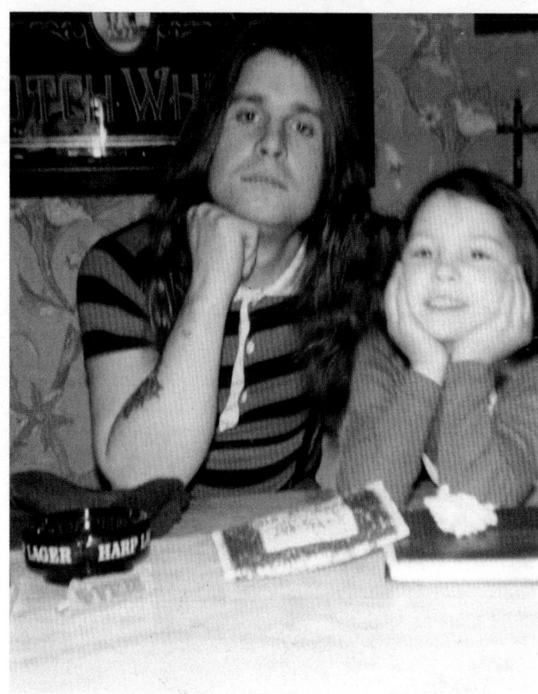

No, I'm not in the pub. I'm in the kitchen of 'Atrocity Cottage', which I'd made to look like a pub. That's my oldest daughter, Jessica.

With Jess again and my son Louis.

Me, the lads from Black Sabbath and, err . . . a rubber chicken. In London. Wearing new clothes 'cos we'd just got a record deal.

Fresh faced. And pissed, probably.

Peace . . .

. . . and love, man.

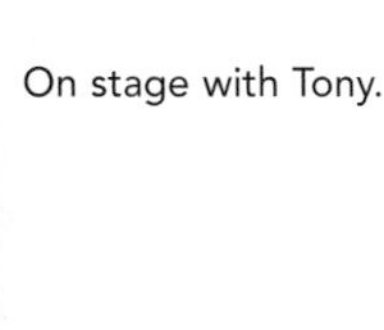

On stage with Tony.

The lads from Aston made good. This was our ten-year anniversary. Unusually, we decided to get completely shitfaced for the occasion. Within a few months I'd be fired.

Going solo. This was the *Diary of a Madman* tour line-up. From left to right: Rudy Sarzo, Randy Rhoads, me and Tommy Aldridge.

Randy Rhoads and Rachel Youngblood, posing next to the tour bus in America. God bless them both.

On stage with Randy. This is how I remember him best.

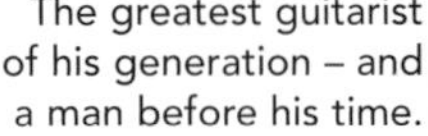

The greatest guitarist of his generation – and a man before his time.

Not like Tony.

So I went down the pub with Bill, and we got completely lollied. Bill was on the cider, as usual: the farm stuff, basically one step removed from poison. He would mix it with blackcurrant juice to take the edge off. They sold it for two bob a pint in those days, which was the only reason why anyone drank it. But Bill kept at it, years after he could afford champagne. He really took cider to heart, did Bill. When you had a few pints of that stuff it wasn't like being drunk, it was like having a head injury.

Tony was the main topic of conversation that night, and I can honestly say that we weren't jealous of what he was doing. We were just heartbroken. As much as we both liked Jethro Tull, we thought Earth could be better – a hundred times better. Before he left, Tony had been coming up with all these heavy-duty riffs of his own – heavier than anything I'd heard anywhere before – and Geezer had started to write far-out lyrics to go with them. As for me and Bill, we'd been improving with every gig. And unlike a lot of the one-hit-wonder Top-Forty bands at the time, *we weren't fake*. We hadn't been put together by some suit-and-tie in a smoky office in London somewhere. We weren't one star, a cool name, and a bunch of session players who changed with every tour.

We were the real fucking deal.

Tony left in December 1968.

It was so cold that winter that I started to have flashbacks to the time when I'd worked as a plumber, bending over manholes while my arse-crack frosted over. Without Tony, me and the lads had fuck-all to do apart from sit around all day, moan, and drink cups of tea. All our gigs had been cancelled, and we'd given up our day jobs long ago, which meant none of us had any dough, so even going down the pub wasn't an option.

No one wanted to think about getting 'real' work, though.

'In 1968, John Osbourne was an up-and-coming rock 'n' roll star,' I would say in this fake movie-announcer voice as I wandered around the house. 'In 1969, he was an up-and-coming binman.'

The one thing we had to look forward to was seeing Tony on the telly. The BBC was going to broadcast the gig in London with the Rolling Stones. It was going to be called 'The Rolling Stones' Rock 'n' Roll Circus'. Nothing like it had ever been done before: the Stones would basically play a private show with a few of their rock star pals at Intertel Studios in Wembley, where the set would be made to look like a circus ring with a big top over it. Jethro Tull would open. Then The Who would play. Mick Jagger had even talked John Lennon into doing a version of 'Yer Blues' with a one-off band called the Dirty Mac – featuring Eric Clapton on guitar, Mitch Mitchell on drums and Keith Richards on bass. I didn't even know Richards could play bass. The press was going nuts about it, because it was going to be the first time Lennon had done a gig since the Beatles' last show in 1966. (Someone told me later that one of those posh BBC producers called up Lennon and asked him what kind of amplifier he wanted to use, and he just replied, 'One that works.' Fucking priceless, man. I wish I could have met that guy.)

In the end, though, the BBC never broadcast the thing. The Stones killed it. I heard that Jagger wasn't too pleased about how the Stones had sounded during the gig. It was twenty-eight years before the footage was finally shown, at the New York Film Festival. If you ever get to see it, Tony's the one in the white hat with the king-sized ferret on his upper lip. He does a great job of playing 'Song for Jeffrey', although there doesn't seem to be much chemistry between him and Ian Anderson.

Maybe that's why he decided to quit after four days.

*

'What d'you mean, you *quit*?' asked Geezer, at an emergency meeting down the pub a few days before Christmas.

'It wasn't my scene,' said Tony, with a shrug.

The drinks were on him.

'How can being in Jethro Tull not be your scene?' said Geezer. 'You played a gig with *John Lennon*, man!'

'I want to be in my own band. I don't want to be someone else's employee.'

'So Ian Anderson's a tosser, then?' I asked, getting to the point.

'No – he's all right,' said Tony. 'He just wasn't . . . We didn't have a laugh, y'know? It wasn't like this.'

Bill, already on his third pint of cider, looked like he was about to burst into tears.

'So are we back together?' said Geezer, trying not to lose his cool by grinning too much.

'If you'll have me.'

'OK. But can we please now find another name?' I said.

'Look, forget about the name,' said Tony. 'We just need to agree that we're all serious. We can't fuck around any more. I've seen how guys like Jethro Tull work. And they *work*, man: four days of rehearsals for one show. We need to start doing that. And we need to start writing our own songs and playing them, even if we get boos. The punters will soon get to know them. It's the only way we're going to make a name for ourselves. And we need to think about an album. Let's go and talk to Jim Simpson in the morning.'

Everyone nodded seriously.

None of us could believe our fucking luck, to be honest with you. Was Tony insane? No one in their right mind would give up the kind of gig he'd just walked away from. Even Robert Plant had eventually gone off to join Jimmy Page in the New Yardbirds, leaving Hobbsbollocks in the dust. And I can't tell you that I'd have done the same thing if I'd been in Tony's position. As much as I was heartbroken when Earth split up, if I'd been the one walking into a band with national recognition, headliner status and a record deal, it would have been, 'Oh, er, see ya!' The bottom line was you had to take your hat off to Tony Iommi. He knew what he wanted, and he obviously believed that he could get it without taking a ride on Ian Anderson's coat tails.

All we had to do was prove he'd made the right decision.

'OK, lads,' said Tony, draining his pint and slamming the glass back down on the table. 'Let's get to work.'

One of the first things Jim Simpson did as our manager was pack us off on a 'European tour'. This meant loading our gear into Tony's van – which by now had been upgraded from a Commer to a Transit – driving it on to a ferry at Harwich, sailing across the North Sea to the Hook of Holland, then hoping the engine would start again when it was time to get off. The temperature in Denmark would be twenty below freezing. From the Hook of Holland, the plan was to drive to Copenhagen, where our first gig had been booked.

I remember taking my entire wardrobe with me on that trip. It consisted of one shirt on a wire hanger, and one pair of underpants in a carrier bag. I was wearing everything else: jeans, second-hand Air Force overcoat, Henry's Blues House T-shirt, lace-up boots.

Day one, the van broke down. It was so cold the accelerator cable froze, so when Tony put his foot down it snapped in half. Which meant we were stranded in the middle of fucking nowhere, halfway to Copenhagen. There was a blizzard outside, but Tony said it was my job – as the band's 'public representative' – to go and find some help. So out I walked into this field, snow blowing into my face, two icicles of snot hanging out of my nose, until finally I saw the lights of a farmhouse up ahead. Then I fell into a trench. After finally pulling myself out of the fucking thing, I waded through the snow until I reached the front door, then knocked loudly.

'Halløj?' said the big, red-faced Eskimo bloke who opened the door.

'Oh, thank fuck,' I said, out of breath and sniffling. 'Our van's knackered. Can you gis a tow?'

'Halløj?'

I didn't know any Danish, so I pointed towards the road, and said, 'Van. El kaputski. Ya?'

The guy just looked at me and started to pick wax out of his ear. Then he said, 'Bobby Charlton, ja?'

'Eh?'

'Bobby Charlton, betydningsfuld skuespiller, ja?'

'Sorry mate, speako Englishki?'

'Det forstår jeg ikke,' he said, with a shrug.

'Eh?'

We stood there and looked at each other for a second.

Then he went, 'Undskyld, farvel,' and shut the door in my face. I gave it a good old kick and set off back through the waist-high snow. I was so cold, my hands were turning blue. When I reached the road I saw a car coming and almost threw myself in front of it. Turned out it was the Danish cops – friendly ones, thank God. They gave me a sip from a flask they kept in the glove box. I don't know what was in that thing, but it warmed me up soon enough. Then they organised a tow-truck to take us to a garage in the next village.

Good guys, those Danish cops.

When they waved us off, they told us to send their regards to Bobby Charlton.

'We'll tell him you said hello,' promised Geezer.

Day two, the van broke down.

This time it was due to a dodgy petrol gauge – the tank ran dry without us knowing it. So off I went to get help again. But this time I had a better idea. We'd conked out next to a little white church, and outside was what I guessed was the vicar's car. I thought he wouldn't mind being a good Samaritan, so I disconnected the hose from the van's engine and used it to siphon fuel from his tank to ours. It worked brilliantly, apart from the fact that I got a mouthful of petrol when it came spurting out of the tube. I had toxic, highly flammable burps for the rest of the day.

Every time it happened I'd screw up my face and have to spit petrol and lumps of vomit out of the window.

'Urgh,' I'd say. 'I fucking hate four star.'

Between gigs we started to jam out some ideas for songs. It was Tony who first suggested we do something that sounded *evil*. There was a cinema called the Orient outside the community centre where we rehearsed in Six Ways, and whenever it showed a horror film the queue would go all the way down the street and around the corner. 'Isn't it strange how people will pay money to frighten themselves?' I remember Tony saying one day. 'Maybe we should stop doing blues and write *scary* music instead.'

Me and Bill thought it was a great idea, so off we went and wrote some lyrics that ended up becoming the song 'Black Sabbath'. It's basically about a bloke who sees a figure in black coming to take him off to the lake of fire.

Then Tony came up with this scary-sounding riff. I moaned out a tune over the top of it, and the end result was fucking awesome – the best thing we'd ever done, by a mile. I've since been told that Tony's riff is based on what's known as the 'Devil's interval', or the 'tritone'. Apparently, churches banned it from being used in religious music during the Middle Ages because it scared the crap out of people. The organist would start to play it and everyone would run away 'cos they thought the Devil was going to pop up from behind the altar.

As for the title of the song, it was Geezer who came up with that. He got it from a Boris Karloff film that had been out for a while. I don't think Geezer had ever seen the film, to be honest with you. I certainly hadn't – it was years before I even knew there *was* a film. It's funny, really, because in spite of our new direction we were still quite a straightforward twelve-bar blues band. If you listened closely, you could also hear a lot of jazz influences in our sound – like Bill's swing-style intro to one of our other early numbers, 'Wicked World'. It's just that we played at eight hundred times the volume of a jazz band.

Today you hear people saying that we invented heavy metal with the song 'Black Sabbath'. But I've always had a bee up my arse about the term 'heavy metal'. To me, it doesn't say anything musically, especially now that you've got seventies heavy metal, eighties heavy metal, nineties heavy metal and new-millennium heavy metal – which are all completely different, even though people talk about them like they're all the same. In fact, the first time I heard the words 'heavy' and 'metal' used together was in the lyrics of 'Born to be Wild'. The press just latched on to it after that. We certainly didn't come up with it ourselves. As far as we were concerned, we were just a blues band that had decided to write some scary music. But then, long after we stopped writing scary music, people would still say, 'Oh, they're a heavy metal band, so all they must sing about is Satan and the end of the world.' That's why I came to loathe the term.

I don't remember where we first played 'Black Sabbath', but I can sure as hell remember the audience's reaction: all the girls ran out of the venue, screaming. 'Isn't the whole point of being in a band to get a shag, not to make chicks run away?' I complained to the others, afterwards.

'They'll get used to it,' Geezer told me.

Another memorable performance of 'Black Sabbath' was in a town hall near Manchester. The manager was there to greet us in a suit and tie when we climbed out of the van. You should have seen the look on his face when he saw us.

'Is that what you're going to wear on stage?' he asked me, staring at my bare feet and pyjama top.

'Oh no,' I said, in this fake-shocked voice. 'I always perform in gold spandex. Have you ever seen an Elvis gig? Well, I look a bit like him – but of course my tits are much smaller.'

'Oh,' he went.

We set up our gear for the tune-up and Tony launched into the opening riff of 'Black Sabbath' – *doh, doh, doooohnnnn* – but before I'd got through the first line of lyrics the manager had run on to the stage, red in the face, and was shouting, 'STOP, STOP, STOP! Are you fucking serious? This isn't Top-Forty pop covers! Who are you people?'

'Earth,' said Tony, shrugging. 'You booked us, remember?'

'I didn't book *this*. I thought you were going to play "Mellow Yellow" and "California Dreamin"'.'

'Who – *us*?' laughed Tony.

'That's what your manager told me!'

'Jim Simpson told you that?'

'Who the hell's Jim Simpson?'

'Ah,' said Tony, finally working out what had happened. He turned to us and said, 'Lads, I think we might not be the only band called Earth.'

He was right: there was another Earth on the C-list gig circuit. But they didn't play satanic music. They played pop and Motown covers. The promotional flyer that Jim Simpson had printed for us had probably only added to the confusion: it made us look like a bunch of hippies, with each of our portraits hand drawn in little clouds around a big sun and 'Earth' spelled out in wobbly psychedelic lettering.

'I told you it was a crap name,' I said. 'Can we please now think of something that doesn't sound like—'

'Look,' interrupted the manger. 'Here's twenty quid for the

trouble of comin' all the way up 'ere. Now fuck off, eh? Oh, and the little hobo is right – you should change yer name. Although I don't know why anyone in their right mind would ever want to listen to that shite.'

'Dear Mum,' I wrote, a few weeks later,

> We're off to do a gig at the Star Club in Hamburg. That's where the Beatles played! Am writing this on a ferry to Dunkirk. Hope you like the picture of the white cliffs (other side). That's what I'm looking at right now. Big news: we're going to change our name to 'Black Sabbath' when we get back to England. Maybe we'll hit the big time now. Love to all,
> John
> PS: Will call Jean from Hamburg.
> PPS: When are you getting a telephone? Tell Dad it's almost the 1970s now!!!

It was 9 August 1969: the day of the Charles Manson murders in Los Angeles. But we weren't looking at the news. In those days it was almost impossible to get an English paper in Europe, and even if you did find one, it would be three or four weeks old. Besides, we were too focused on our next gig to pay much attention to the outside world.

We'd done shows before at the Star Club – which was on the Reeperbahn in Hamburg, where all the dodgy hookers stand around in their skimpy dresses and fishnets – so we knew roughly what to expect. This time, though, we had a 'residency', which meant they would pay us a wage and put us up in this bombed-out shithole of a room above the stage – it had been gutted by fire more than a few times – and in return we'd have to play as many as seven sets a day, in between gigs from visiting bands.

It was a lot of fun, but it was fucking gruelling, man. Every day we'd start at noon and end at two in the morning. You'd do speed, pills, dope, beer – anything you could lay your hands on – just to stay awake. Someone once added up how many shows we did in the Star Club, and it turned out that we'd played more than the Beatles. Mind you, 1969 was seven years after the Beatles' heyday, and the place had gone down the shitter a bit. In fact, we were one of the last British bands to do a residency there: the place closed its doors for good on New Year's Eve of that year.

Then it burned down.

Even so, it was the best training you could ever ask for, playing at the Star Club. A gig's not like a rehearsal: you've got to see it through, even if you're loaded, which we were, most of the time. It's not that I needed any training to be the person I am on stage. I'm a lunatic by nature, and lunatics don't need training – they just *are*. But the Star Club helped us nail all the new songs we'd written, like 'The Wizard', 'N.I.B.' (named after Bill's beard, which we thought looked like the nib of a pen), 'War Pigs', 'Rat Salad' and 'Fairies Wear Boots' (to this day, I have no idea what that song's about, even though people tell me that I wrote the lyrics). The Star Club also helped me get over my stage fright. Once I'd loosened up a bit, I'd just do crazier and crazier things to keep myself amused. And the lads encouraged me. When the crowd was obviously bored, Tony would shout over to me, 'Go and organise a raffle, Ozzy.' That would be my cue to do something fucking mental, to get everyone's attention. One time, I found this can of purple paint backstage, and when I got the call from Tony I dipped my nose in it. Which would have been fine, if the paint hadn't been fucking indelible.

I couldn't get that shit off me for weeks. People would come up to me and go, 'What the *fuck* is wrong with you, man?' Or, more often, they wouldn't come up to me at all, 'cos they thought I was mad.

We all had our moments at the Star Club. One night, Tony is so out of his skull on dope that he decides he's gonna play the flute, but he's lost his sense of distance, so he rests the flute on his chin instead of his lip. So for the entire song he's just standing there, blowing into a microphone, with the flute nowhere near his mouth, and the audience is going, What the *fuck*?

Priceless, man.

The trick to having a really good time at the Star Club was to find some local German chick and then stay at her apartment, so you didn't have to share a bunk bed with one of your farty, ball-scratching bandmates. We didn't care what the chicks looked like – I mean, we weren't exactly much to behold ourselves. And if they bought you beers and gave you fags, that was a bonus. And if they didn't buy you beers and give you fags, you did your best to rob them. In fact, on more than one occasion we used Tony as a honeytrap – 'cos he was the one all the chicks wanted to bang. What would happen is, he'd go upstairs to our room and start fumbling around with some groupie on one of the bunks, and I'd crawl over on my elbows – commando-style – to where she'd left her handbag, and swipe whatever dough I could find. I aint proud of it, but we had to fucking eat somehow.

We used to give these chicks nicknames, which, looking back now, was a bit cruel. More than a bit cruel, in some cases. For example, I shacked up with one girl who everyone called 'The Witch', 'cos she had a conk on her that was even bigger than Geezer's.

We didn't last long, me and The Witch. The morning after she took me back to her place, she got up, made herself a cup of coffee, and said, 'I'm going off to work now. You can stay here, but don't touch anything, OK?' Of course, that's a fatal thing to say to me. So, the second she's out of the door I'm rummaging around in her cupboards, wondering what she doesn't want me to find. And sure enough, at the back of the wardrobe, I come across this perfectly ironed Nazi uniform. It must have been her dad's or something. Anyway, I'm thinking, Fucking-A, man, I've hit the motherlode here. So I put on the uniform, find the drinks cabinet, and before long I'm strutting around the living room, barking out orders to the furniture in this comedy German accent, smoking cigarettes, and getting loaded. I love all that wartime military stuff, me.

After an hour or so of doing that I took off the uniform, put it back in the wardrobe, made sure it was folded up perfectly, and pretended like nothing had happened. But when The Witch came back just before noon, she knew something was up. She went straight over to the wardrobe, threw open the doors, checked the uniform, and went fucking nuts.

Next thing I knew I was on the end of her broom, flying out of the door.

When we got back to England, we had a meeting at Jim Simpson's house to tell him about our change of name to Black Sabbath. He didn't seem too keen, although to be honest with you I think he was distracted by my purple nose. He didn't say anything about it, but I could tell it was on his mind, 'cos he kept staring at me with this worried look on his face. He must have thought I'd picked up some rare disease over in Germany or something. I seem to remember that Alvin Lee from Ten Years After was at that meeting, too. And he was even less keen on the name Black Sabbath than Jim was. 'I don't think you'll get anywhere with *that*, lads,' he told us. The exact order of what happened next is a bit of a blur, to be honest with you. All I know is that Jim had done a deal with a bloke called Tony Hall, who owned a freelance A&R/production company. He agreed to help us make an album as long as he got something back if we turned out to be a success – or something like that. I'm no good with business, me. I'm the last person to ask when it comes to contracts and dough and all that.

Anyway, Tony Hall said he thought we were 'a great little blues band', but that we needed a debut single – even though bands like ours rarely put out singles in those days. He played us this song called 'Evil Woman' by an American group called Crow, and asked if we wanted to cover it. He could tell we weren't that into the idea, so suggested we could make the guitars heavier. We still didn't really want to do it, but Tony offered to pay for some time at Trident Studios in Soho, so we thought, Fuck it, why not?

It was a bit embarrassing in the end. We didn't have a clue what we were doing, so we just set up our equipment, hit the record button, and played our live set. The only vaguely professional thing about us was the fact that one of the roadies had spelled out 'Black Sabbath' with black electrician's tape on the front of Bill's bass drum.

Producing us was a guy called Gus Dudgeon. We were in awe of him because he'd worked with Eric Clapton, the Moody Blues and the Rolling Stones. Looking back, Gus was very good to us, although he also laid down the law a bit, and we weren't used to being told what to do. Still, you couldn't argue with the results – the bloke was a genius. After working on 'Evil Woman' he went on to produce some of Elton John's biggest hits of the seventies and eighties. It was terribly sad when he and his wife Sheila were killed in a car accident in 2002. Gus was one of those guys who made a huge contribution to British music, even though he wasn't a household name. And although we might not have fully appreciated it at the time, we were incredibly lucky to have him help us so early on in our career.

We played a few clubs while we were down in London. At one of those gigs the DJ put on a record before we went on stage, and it just blew me away. Something about the singer's voice sounded familiar. Then it came to me: it was Robert Plant. So I went over to the DJ and said, 'Is that the New Yardbirds' record you're playing?'

'No, it's a new band called Led Zeppelin.'

'*Really?*'

'Yeah, man. I swear.'

We played our gig, but I couldn't get the record out of my mind, so afterwards I went back to the DJ and asked him, 'Are you sure it's not the New Yardbirds? I know that singer, and he ain't in a band called Led Zeppelin. Does it say who the band members are on the sleeve?'

He read out the names: 'Jimmy Page, John Bonham, John Paul Jones, Robert Plant.'

I couldn't believe it: the New Yardbirds must have changed their name to Led Zeppelin . . . and they'd made the best record I'd heard in years. In the van on the way home, I remember saying to Tony, 'Did you hear how *heavy* that Led Zeppelin album sounded?'

Without missing a beat, he replied, 'We'll be heavier.'

By the end of 1969 we were desperate for anything that could take us to the next level. But we were still on the same C-list gig circuit, night after night. Our last gig of the year was on 24 December in Cumberland – we were still getting a lot of work up there – at Wigton Market Hall. As it happened, there was a women's mental hospital right next door to the venue, and every year the doctors would let the patients out for a Christmas dance. We didn't know anything about that, but even if we had, I doubt any of us would have guessed that the funny farm would choose a Black Sabbath gig for its annual outing. But it did. So we're halfway through 'N.I.B.' when all these loony chicks come piling in through the door at the back of the hall, and by the end of the song a riot has broken out. You should have seen it: these chicks were chinning the guys, and then the guys' girlfriends were chinning the mental chicks right back. It was pandemonium. By the time the police showed up there were loads of women lying around on the floor with black eyes and bloody noses and split lips.

Then they started to sing 'Give Peace a Chance'.

Meanwhile, we were just standing there on stage, amps buzzing. I looked at Tony, and Tony looked at me.

'This is fucking *nuts*,' I mouthed to him.

He just shrugged, turned up his amp, and started to play 'We Wish You a Merry Christmas'.

In January 1970, it finally happened.

We got a record deal.

For a few months, Jim Simpson had been shopping us around by inviting all these big-wigs from London to come to our gigs. But no one was interested. Then one night a guy from Philips drove up to Birmingham to see us play at Henry's Blues House and decided to take a bet on us. The name Black Sabbath made a big difference, I think. At the time there was an occult author called Dennis Wheatley whose books were all over the bestseller lists, Hammer Horror films were doing massive business at the cinemas, and the Manson murders were all over the telly, so anything with a 'dark' edge was in big demand. Don't get me wrong, I'm sure we could've done it on the strength of the music alone. But sometimes, when it comes to getting a deal, all these little things have to come together at the right time.

You need a bit of luck, basically.

Another thing that helped was the fact that Philips was setting up a new 'underground' label called Vertigo when we were looking for a deal. We were a perfect fit. But the funny thing was that Vertigo wasn't even up and running in time for our first single, 'Evil Woman', so it was originally released on another Philips label, Fontana, before being reissued on Vertigo a few weeks later.

Not that it made any fucking difference: the song went

down like a concrete turd both times. But we didn't care, because the BBC played it on Radio 1.

Once.

At six o'clock in the morning.

I was so nervous, I got up at five and drank about eight cups of tea. 'They won't play it,' I kept telling myself, 'They won't play it . . .'

But then:

BLAM . . . BLAM . . .
Dow-*doww* . . .
BLAM . . .
Dow-dow-d-d-dow, *dooooow* . . .
D-d-d-d-d-d-d-d-d
DUH-DA!
Do-doo-do
DUH-DA!
Do-doo-*do* . . .

It's impossible to describe what it feels like to hear yourself on Radio 1 for the first time. It was magic, squared. I ran around the house screaming, 'I'm on the radio! *I'm on the fucking radio!*' until my mum stomped downstairs in her nightie and told me to shut up. '*Evil woman*,' I sang to her, at full volume, '*Don't you play your games with me!*' Then I was off, out of the door, singing my head off all the way down Lodge Road.

But if being played on Radio 1 was good, it was nothing compared with the advance we got from Philips: £105 each!

I'd never even had a tenner to call my own before, never mind a hundred quid. It would have taken me a whole year of tuning car horns at the Lucas factory to earn that kind of dough. I thought I was Jack the Lad that week. The first thing I bought was a bottle of Brut aftershave to make myself smell better. Then I got a new pair of shoes, 'cos I'd destroyed my old ones in Denmark. The rest I gave to my mum to pay the bills. But then I kept scrounging it back off her, so I could go down the pub and celebrate.

Then it was back to work.

As far as I can remember, we didn't have any demos to speak of, and there was no official talk about making an album. Jim just told us one day that we'd been booked for a week of gigs in Zurich, and that on our way down there, we should stop off at Regent Sound studios in Soho and record some tracks with a producer called Rodger Bain and his engineer, Tom Allom. So that's what we did. Like before, we just set up our gear and played what amounted to a live set without the audience. Once we'd finished, we spent a couple of hours double-tracking some of the guitar and the vocals, and that was that. Done. We were in the pub in time for last orders. It can't have taken any longer than twelve hours in total.

That's how albums should be made, in my opinion. I don't give a fuck if you're making the next *Bridge Over Troubled Water* – taking five or ten or fifteen years to make an album, like Guns N' Roses did, is just fucking ridiculous, end of story. By that time, your career's died, been resurrected, and then died again.

In our case, mind you, we didn't have the luxury of taking our time. It wasn't an option. So we just went in there and did it. And then the next day we set off for Zurich in the Transit to do a residency at a joint called the Hirschen Club. We hadn't even heard Rodger and Tom's final mix when we left Soho, never mind seen the album cover. That's how the music business was run in those days. As a band, you had less say in what was going on than the guy who cleaned out the shitter in the record company's executive suite. I remember it being a long, long way to Switzerland in the back of a Transit van. To kill time, we smoked dope. Shitloads of it. When we finally got to Zurich, we were so fucking hungry we found one of those posh Swiss caffs and held a competition to see who could eat the most banana splits in the shortest time. I managed to get twenty-five of the fuckers down my throat before the owner chucked us out. My whole face was covered in cream by the end of it. I could have had a couple more of them, too.

Then we had to go and find the Hirschen Club, which turned out to be even sleazier than the Star Club. They had this tiny little stage with the bar just a few feet away, and it was dark and there were hookers hanging around all over the place. The four of us had to share one crappy room upstairs, so getting a chick with her own place was the order of the day.

One night, these two girls in fishnets invited me and Geezer back to their apartment. They were obviously on the game, but I was up for anything that would spare me from another night of sharing a bed with Bill, who spent the whole time complaining about my smelly feet. So when they sweetened the deal by saying they had some dope, I said, 'Fuck it, let's go.' But Geezer wasn't so sure. 'They're *hookers*, Ozzy,' he kept saying. 'You'll catch something nasty. Let's find some other chicks.'

'I ain't gonna bonk either of 'em,' I said. 'I just wanna get out of this fucking place.'

'I'll believe that when I see it,' said Geezer. 'The dark-haired chick isn't so bad-looking. After a few beers and a few puffs of the magic weed, she'll have her way with me.'

'Look,' I said, 'if she makes a move on yer, I'll kick her up the arse and we'll leave, all right?'

'Promise?'

'If she makes *one move* towards your knob, Geezer, I'll pull her off you and we'll fuck off.'

'All right.'

So we go back to their place. It's all dimly lit, and Geezer's on one side of the room with the dark-haired chick, and I'm on the other side with the ugly one, and we're smoking weed and listening to the album by Blind Faith, the 'supergroup' formed by Eric Clapton, Ginger Baker, Steve Winwood and Ric Grech. For a while it's all serene and trippy – the music's playing and everyone's snogging and fumbling around. Then, all of a sudden, this deep Brummie voice rises out of the mist of dope smoke.

'Oi, Ozzy,' says Geezer. 'Time to put the boot in.'

I looked over and this hooker was straddling him as he lay there with his eyes closed and this pained expression on his face. I honestly thought it was the funniest thing I'd ever seen in my life.

I don't even know if he shagged her in the end. I just remember laughing and laughing and laughing until I cried.

Jim Simpson wanted to see us at his house as soon as we got back from Switzerland. 'I've got something you need to see,' he said, in this ominous voice.

So that afternoon we all met up in his living room and sat there, twiddling our thumbs, wondering what the fuck he was going to say. He reached into his briefcase and pulled out the finished record of *Black Sabbath*. We were speechless. The cover was a spooky-looking fifteenth-century watermill (I later found out it was the Mapledurham Watermill on the River Thames in Oxfordshire), with all these dead leaves around it and a sickly looking woman with long dark hair, dressed in black robes, standing in the middle of the frame with a scary look on her face. It was *amazing*. Then, when you opened the gatefold sleeve, there was just black everywhere and an inverted cross with a creepy poem written inside it. We'd had no input with the artwork, so the inverted cross – a symbol of Satanism, we later found out – had nothing to do with us. But the stories that you hear about us being unhappy with it are total bullshit. As far as I can remember, we were immediately blown away by the cover. We just stood there, staring at it, and going, 'Fucking hell, man, this is fucking *unbelievable*.'

Then Jim went over to his record player and put it on. I almost burst into tears, it sounded so great. While we'd been in Switzerland, Rodger and Tom had put these sound effects of a thunderstorm and a tolling bell over the opening riff of the title track, so it sounded like something from a film. The overall effect was fabulous. I still get chills whenever I hear it.

On Friday the thirteenth of February 1970, *Black Sabbath* went on sale.

I felt like I'd just been born.

But the critics fucking hated it.

Still, one of the few good things about being dyslexic is that when I say I don't read reviews, I mean *I don't read reviews*. But that didn't stop the others from poring over what the press had to say about us. Of all the bad reviews of *Black Sabbath*, the worst was probably written by Lester Bangs at *Rolling Stone*. He was the same age as me, but I didn't know that at the time. In fact, I'd never even heard of him before, and once the others told me what he'd written I wished I still hadn't. I remember Geezer reading out words like 'claptrap', 'wooden' and 'dogged'. The last line was something like, 'They're just like Cream, but worse', which I didn't understand, because I thought Cream were one of the best bands in the world.

Bangs died twelve years later, when he was only thirty-three, and I've heard people say he was a genius when it came to words, but as far as we were concerned he was just another pretentious dickhead. And from then we never got on with *Rolling Stone*. But y'know what? Being trashed by *Rolling Stone* was kind of cool, because they were the Establishment. Those music magazines were all staffed by college kids who thought they were clever – which, to be fair, they probably were. Meanwhile, we'd been kicked out of school at fifteen and had worked in factories and slaughtered animals for a living, but then we'd made something of ourselves, even though the whole system was against us. So how upset could we be when clever people said we were no good?

The important thing was *someone* thought we were good, 'cos *Black Sabbath* went straight to number eight in Britain and number twenty-three in America.

And the *Rolling Stone* treatment prepared us for what was to come. I don't think we ever got a good review for anything we did. Which is why I never bother with reviews. Whenever I hear someone getting upset about reviews, I just say to them, 'Look, it's their job to criticise. That's why they're called *critics*.' Mind you, some people just get so wound up they can't control themselves. I remember one time in Glasgow this critic showed up at our hotel, and Tony goes over to him and says, 'I wanna have a word with you, sunshine.' I didn't know it at the time, but the guy had just written a hit-piece on Tony, describing him as 'Jason King with builder's arms' – Jason King being a private-eye type character on TV at the time who had this stupid moustache and dodgy haircut. But when Tony confronted him, he just laughed, which was a really stupid thing to do. Tony just stood there and said, 'Go on, son, finish laughing, 'cos in about thirty seconds you ain't gonna be laughing any more.' Then he started to laugh himself. The critic didn't take him seriously, so he kept on laughing, and for about two seconds they were both just standing there, laughing their heads off. Then Tony swung his fist back and just about put this bloke in hospital. I never read his review of the show, but I'm told it wasn't very flattering.

My old man wasn't too impressed with our first album, either.

I'll always remember the day I took it home and said, 'Look, Dad! I got my voice on a record!'

I can picture him now, fiddling with his reading specs and holding the cover in front of his face. Then he opened the sleeve, went 'Hmm' and said, 'Are you sure they didn't make a mistake, son?'

'What d'you mean?'

'This cross is upside down.'

'It's supposed to be like that.'

'Oh. Well, don't just stand there. Put it on. Let's have a bit of a sing-along, eh?'

So I walked over to the radiogram, lifted the heavy wooden lid, put the record on the turntable – hoping the dodgy speaker that I'd put in there from the PA would work – and cranked up the volume.

With the first clap of thunder, my dad flinched.

I grinned nervously at him.

Then:

Bong!

Bong!

Bong!

My dad coughed.

Bong!

Bong!

Bong!

He coughed again.

Bong!

Bong!

Bong!

'Son, when does—'

BLAM! Dow! Dowwwwwww!!! *Dooooowwwww!!!!!*

My poor old man turned white. I think he'd been expecting something along the lines of 'Knees up Mother Brown'. But I left the record on anyway. Finally, after six minutes and eighteen seconds of Tony and Geezer thrashing away on their guitars, Bill beating the shit out of his drums, and me howling on about a man in black coming to take me away to the lake of fire, my dad rubbed his eyes, shook his head and looked at the floor.

Silence.

'What d'you think, Dad?'

'John,' he said, 'are you absolutely sure you've only been drinking the *occasional* beer?'

I went bright red and said something like 'Oh, er, yeah, Dad, whatever.'

Bless him, he just didn't get it at all.

But it broke my heart, y'know? I'd always felt as though I'd let my father down. Not because of anything he'd ever said to me. But because I was a failure at school, because I couldn't read or write properly, because I'd been sent to prison, and because I'd been fired from all of those factory jobs. But now, finally, with Black Sabbath, I was doing something I was good at, that I enjoyed, that I was prepared to work hard at. I suppose I just really wanted my old man to be proud of me. But it wasn't his fault – it was the way he was. It was his generation.

And I think deep down he *was* proud of me, in his own way.

I can honestly say that we never took the black magic stuff seriously for one second. We just liked how theatrical it was. Even my old man eventually played along with it: he made me this awesome metal cross during one of his tea breaks at the factory. When I turned up to rehearsals with it, all the other guys wanted one, so I got Dad to make three more.

I couldn't believe it when I learned that people actually 'practised the occult'. These freaks with white make-up and black robes would come up to us after our gigs and invite us to black masses at Highgate Cemetery in London. I'd say to them, 'Look, mate, the only evil spirits I'm interested in are called whisky, vodka and gin.' At one point we were invited by a group of Satanists to play at Stonehenge. We told them to fuck off, so they said they'd put a curse on us. What a load of bollocks that was. Britain even had a 'chief witch' in those days, called Alex Sanders. Never met him. Never wanted to. Mind you, we did buy a Ouija board once and have a little seance. We scared the shit out of each other.

That night, at God knows what hour, Bill phoned me up and shouted, 'Ozzy, I think my house is *haunted*!'

'Sell tickets then,' I told him, and put the phone down.

The good thing about all the satanic stuff was that it gave us endless free publicity. People couldn't get enough of it. During its first day of release, *Black Sabbath* sold five thousand copies, and by the end of the year it was on its way to selling a million worldwide.

None of us could believe it.

Not even Jim Simpson could believe it – the poor bloke ended up getting completely overwhelmed. His office was in Birmingham, miles away from the action in London, and he had other bands to look after, no staff, and Henry's Blues House to run. So it didn't take long for us to start getting pissed off with him. For starters, we weren't getting any dough. Jim wasn't robbing us – he's one of the most honest people I've ever met in the music business – but Philips were taking forever to cough up our royalties, and Jim wasn't the kind of bloke who could go down there and bully them into paying. Then there was the issue of America: we wanted to go, immediately. But we had to get it right, which meant going easy on all the satanic stuff, 'cos we didn't want to come across like fans of the Manson Family.

We'd get strung up by our balls if we did.

It didn't take long for all the sharks down in London to realise there was blood in the water, as far as Jim was concerned. So, one by one, they started circling. They looked at us and they saw big fucking neon-lit pound signs. Our first album couldn't have cost more than five hundred quid to make, so the profit margins were astronomical.

The first call we got was from Don Arden. We didn't know much about him apart from his nickname – 'Mr Big'. Then we heard stories about him dangling people out of his fourth-floor Carnaby Street office window, stubbing cigars out on people's foreheads, and demanding all his contracts be paid in cash and delivered by hand in brown paper bags. So we were shitting ourselves when we went down to London to meet him for the first time. When we got off the train at Euston Station, he had his blue Rolls-Royce waiting to pick us up. It was the first time I'd ever been in a Roller. I sat there in the back seat, like the King of England, thinking, Three years ago, you were a puke remover in a slaughterhouse, and before that you were doling out slop to child molesters in Winson Green. Now look where you are.

Don had a reputation as the kind of guy who could make you world famous but would rip you off while he was at it. It's not like he was pulling any complex, high finance, Bernie Madoff-type scams. He just wouldn't fucking pay. Simple as that. It would be like, 'Don, you owe me a million quid, can I have the money please?' And he'd go, 'No, you can't.' End of conversation. And if you ever went to his office to ask for the dough in person, there was a good chance you'd leave in the back of an ambulance.

But the thing with us was, we didn't really need anyone to make us world famous – we were already halfway there. Still, we sat in Don's office and listened to his pitch. He was a short bloke, but with the build and presence of a pissed-off Rottweiler, and he had this incredible shouty voice. He'd pick up the phone to his receptionist and scream so loud the whole planet seemed to shake.

When the meeting was over we all stood up and said how great it was to meet him, blah-blah-blah, even though none of us wanted anything more to do with him. Then, as we filed out of his office, he introduced us to the chick he'd spent half the meeting bawling at over the phone.

'This is Sharon, my daughter,' he growled. 'Sharon, take these lads down to the car, will you?'

I grinned at her, but she gave me a wary look. She probably thought I was a lunatic, standing there in my pyjama shirt, with no shoes and a hot-water tap on a piece of string around my neck.

But then, when Don huffed back to his office and closed the door behind him, I cracked a joke and made her smile. I just about fell on the floor. It was the most wicked, beautiful smile I'd ever seen in my life. And she had the laugh to go with it, too. It made me feel so good, hearing her laugh. I just wanted to make her do it again and again and again.

To this day, I feel bad about what happened with Jim Simpson. I think he got the wrong end of the stick with us. I suppose it's easy to say what he should or shouldn't have done with hindsight, but if he'd admitted to himself that we were too big for him to handle, he could have sold us off to another management company, or contracted out our day-to-day management to a bigger firm. But he wasn't strong enough to do that. And we were so desperate to go to America and get our big break that we didn't have the patience to wait for him to sort himself out.

In the end it was a wide boy called Patrick Meehan who nabbed us. He was only a couple of years older than us, and he'd gone into the management racket with his father, who'd been a stuntman on the TV show *Danger Man* and then worked for Don Arden, first as a driver, then as a general dogsbody, looking after the likes of the Small Faces and the Animals. Patrick had another ex-Don Arden henchman working with him too: Wilf Pine. I liked Wilf a lot. He looked like a cartoon villain: short, built like a slab of concrete, and with this big, tasty, hard-boiled face. I think his hardman routine was all a bit of an act, to be honest with you, but there was never any doubt that he could do some serious damage if he was in the mood. He'd been Don's personal bodyguard for a long time, and when I knew him he'd often go down to Brixton Prison to see the

Kray twins, who'd only just been put away. He was all right, was Wilf. We'd have a laugh. 'You're *crazy*, d'you know that?' he'd say to me.

Patrick was nothing like Don or Wilf, or his own father, for that matter. He was a slick, smooth-talking, good-looking guy, very cool, very sharp, didn't have any problems with the ladies. He'd wear suits all the time, drove a Roller, kept his hair long but not too long. He was also the first guy I ever saw with diamond rings on his fingers. He'd obviously learned a lot from the way Don Arden operated. Patrick threw every trick in the book at us. The chauffeured limo. The champagne dinner. The non-stop compliments and the phoney shock that we weren't all multi-millionaires already. He told us that if we signed with him, we could have *anything* we wanted – cars, houses, chicks, whatever. All we had to do was call him up and ask for it. What he told us were like fairy tales, basically, but we wanted to believe them. And there was at least some truth to what he said . . . The music business is like any other business, y'know? When sales are going well, everything's hunky-fucking-dory. But the second something goes wrong, it's all blood and lawsuits.

I can't remember exactly when or how we left Jim – we never actually fired him, although I suppose that makes no difference – but by September 1970 Big Bear Management was history and we were signed up with the Meehans' company, Worldwide Artists.

It took about three and a half seconds for Jim to sue us. We were served with the writ when we were standing backstage at a venue on Lake Geneva, waiting to go on. It wouldn't be the last time that happened. Jim sued Meehan, too, for 'enticement'. It all took years to go through the courts. To a certain degree, I think Jim got a raw deal. I mean, he had brought Philips out to see us in the first place, which had got us the record deal. And even though he won some dough from the courts, he spent years paying his lawyers. So he didn't really win in the end. It's always the way with lawyers – we found that out for ourselves, later. The funny thing is, I still run into Jim every so often. We're like long-lost friends now. He's done a lot of great things for music in Birmingham, Jim Simpson has. And he's still at it today. I wish him all the very best, I really do.

At the time, though, getting rid of Jim seemed like the greatest thing we'd ever done. It was like we'd just won the lottery: money was falling from the sky. Every day, I'd think of something new to ask for: 'Er, hello, yes, is that Patrick Meehan's office? It's Ozzy Osbourne. I'd like one of them Triumph Herald convertibles. Can you send me a green one? Cheers.' *Click*. Then – *ta-dah!* – the fucking thing would be sitting outside my house the next morning with an envelope tucked behind the windscreen wiper full of paperwork for me to sign and return. Meehan seemed as good as his word: whatever we asked for, we got. And it wasn't all about the big things: we were given allowances, so we could afford beer and fags and platform boots and leather jackets, and we could stay in hotels instead of sleeping in the back of Tony's van.

Meanwhile, we just kept selling more records. One minute we were at the raggedy end of the line when it came to rock bands from Birmingham; the next we'd overtaken just about everybody. What we didn't know was that Meehan was taking nearly everything. Even a lot of the stuff he 'gave' us wasn't actually *ours*. Behind the scenes, he was bleeding us dry. But y'know what, I've thought about this a lot over the years, and I don't think we can complain too much. We'd come out of Aston with nothing to lose and everything to gain, and by our early twenties we were living like kings. We didn't have to carry our own gear, we didn't have to make our own food, we barely had to tie our own shoelaces. And, on top of all that, we could just ask for stuff and it would appear on a silver plate.

I mean, you should have seen Tony's collection of

Lamborghinis. Even Bill got his own chauffeured Rolls-Royce. We were good like that: we split all the dough four ways. The way we saw it, Tony did the riffs, Geezer did the words, I did the melodies, and Bill did his wild drum thing, and each part was as important as the others, so everyone should get the same. I think that's why we lasted as long as we did. For starters, it meant we never argued over who'd done what. Then, if one of us wanted to branch out – like if Bill wanted to sing, or if I wanted to write some lyrics – it was cool. No one was sitting there with a calculator, adding up the royalties they'd win or lose.

Mind you, another reason why we could do what we wanted was because we had total musical control. No record mogul had created Black Sabbath, so no record mogul could tell Black Sabbath what to do. A couple of them tried – and we told them where to stick it.

Not many bands can do that nowadays.

One thing I regret is not giving more dough to my folks. I mean, if it hadn't been for my old man taking out a loan on that PA system, I never would have had a chance. In fact, I'd probably have gone back to burglary. Maybe I'd still be in prison today. But I didn't think about them. I was young, I was loaded most of the time, and my ego was already starting to rule the world. Besides, I might have been rich, but I didn't have much ready cash. All I did was call Patrick Meehan's office and put in my requests, which was different to having your own dough to throw around. In fact, the only time I made any real money was when I realised I could just sell the stuff that the management company gave me, which I did one time with a Rolls-Royce. The others soon learned the same trick too. But how was I supposed to explain that to my folks, when they just saw me swaggering around the place like Jack the Lad? It's not like I gave them *nothing*, but I know now that I never gave them *enough.* You could tell from the atmosphere every time I walked through the door at 14 Lodge Road. I'd ask my mum, 'What's wrong?' and she'd say, 'Oh, nothing.'

'Well, it's obviously something. Just tell me.'

She wouldn't say, but you could smell it in the air: money, money, money. Nothing but money. Not: 'I'm proud of you, son. Well done, you finally made it, you worked hard. Have a cup of tea. I love you.' Just money. It got really ugly after a while. I didn't want to be at home; it was so uncomfortable. I suppose they'd never had any money of their own, and they wanted mine. Which was fair enough. I should have given it to them.

But I didn't.

I met a girl and moved out instead.

4

'You Guys Ain't *Black*!'

I was never the Romeo type, me.

Even after our first album went gold, I never got any good-looking chicks. Black Sabbath was a blokes' band. We'd get fag ends and beer bottles thrown at us, not frilly underwear. We used to joke that the only groupies that came to our gigs were 'two-baggers' – you needed to put a couple of bags over their head before you could shag them; one wasn't enough. And most of the time I was lucky even to get a two-bagger, to be honest with you. The chicks who wanted to shack up with me at the end of the night were usually three- or four-baggers. One night in Newcastle I think I had a five-bagger.

That was a rough night, that was. A lot of gin was involved, if I remember correctly.

But none of that stopped me trying to get my end away.

One of the places where I used to go cruising for a good old bonk was the Rum Runner nightclub on Broad Street in Birmingham, where an old school mate of Tony's worked on the door. It was a famous place, the Rum Runner – years later,

Duran Duran would become the resident band there – so it was magic to have someone on the inside who could get you in without any trouble.

One night, not long after we'd signed the record deal, I went to the Rum Runner with Tony. This was before we'd met Patrick Meehan, so we were still skint. We drove there in Tony's second-hand car, which I think was a Ford Cortina. It was a piece of crap, anyway. Albert greets us at the door as usual, the bouncers unclip the rope to let us through, and the first thing I see is this dark-haired chick behind the counter in the cloakroom.

'Who's *that*?' I asked Albert.

'Thelma Riley,' he told me. 'Lovely gal. Brainy, too. But she's divorced, and she's got a kid, so watch yerself.'

I didn't care.

She was beautiful, and I wanted to talk to her. So I did what I always did when I wanted to talk to a bird: I got fucking lollied. But something strange must have been going on that night, because the old get-as-dribblingly-drunk-as-possible strategy worked: I pulled her on the dance floor while Tony pulled her mate. Then we all drove back to Tony's place in his Cortina, with me and Thelma having a snog and a fumble on the back seat.

Tony dumped Thelma's friend the next day, but me and Thelma kept going. And when I finally couldn't take any more of the bad atmosphere at 14 Lodge Road, we rented a flat together above a launderette in Edgbaston, a posh part of Birmingham.

A year or so later, in 1971, we got married in a registry office.

I thought it was what you did: get some dough, find a chick, get married, settle down, go to the pub.

It was a terrible mistake.

A few months before the wedding, Black Sabbath finally made it to America. Before we went, I remember Patrick Meehan's dad calling us into a meeting at his London office, and telling us that we were going to be 'ambassadors for British music', so we should fucking behave ourselves.

We just nodded and ignored him.

Having said that, I made sure to go easy on the booze until we reached the airport. But what I didn't know is that airports had bars – and I couldn't resist a couple of cheeky ones to calm my nerves. So by the time I got to my seat, I was as pissed as a fart. Then we found out that Traffic were on the same plane. I couldn't get over the fact that I was on the same flight as Steve Winwood. For the first time in my life, I began to feel like a proper rock star.

Even with all the booze I put away on the plane, it seemed to take for ever to get to JFK. I kept looking out of the window, thinking, How the fuck does this thing stay up in the air? Then we flew over Manhattan, where the World Trade Center was being built – half of it was still just scaffolding and steel girders – and landed as the sun was setting. It was a warm night, I remember, and I'd never experienced that warm-night-in-New-York vibe before. It had a distinctive smell, y'know? I thought it was great. Mind you, I was beyond pissed by this point. The flight attendant had to help me out of my seat, and then I fell down the steps.

By the time I got to immigration, the hangover had set it. My headache was so bad that I'd forgotten what I'd written as a joke on the visa-waiver form. Where it asked for your religion, I'd put 'Satanist'. So the bloke takes the form off me and starts reading it. Then he pauses when he gets halfway down.

He looks up at me. 'Satanist, huh?' he says, in this thick Bronx accent, with a bored, tired look on his face.

Suddenly I'm thinking, Oh, *shit*.

But before I can start trying to explain myself, he just stamps the form and shouts, 'NEXT!'

'Welcome to New York' said the sign above his head.

We got our luggage from the carousel and went to queue in the taxi rank outside the arrivals hall. Fuck knows what all the businessmen with their suits and ties and briefcases were thinking, standing next to this long-haired, unwashed, pissed-up Brummie, wearing a tap around his neck and a pair of smelly old jeans with 'Peace & Love' and a CND symbol on one leg, and 'Black Panthers Rule' and a black fist symbol on the other.

As we waited, this massive yellow car drove by. It must have had nineteen or twenty doors on it.

'I knew the cars here were big,' I slurred, 'but not *that* big!'

'It's a *limousine*, you idiot,' said Tony.

Before we left England, we'd already recorded our follow-up to *Black Sabbath*. We had it in the can only five months after the release of the first record – which is unbelievable when you consider the lazy-arsed way albums are made these days. It was originally going to be called *Warpiggers*, which was a term for a black magic wedding or something. Then we changed it to *War Pigs*, and Geezer came up with these heavy-duty lyrics about death and destruction. No wonder we never got any chicks at our gigs. Geezer just wasn't interested in your average 'I love you' pop song. Even when he wrote a boy-meets-girl lyric, it had a twist to it – like 'N.I.B.' off the first album, where the boy turns out to be the Devil. Geezer also liked to put a lot of topical stuff, like Vietnam references, into our songs. He had his ear to the ground, Geezer did.

We went back to Regent Sound in Soho to make the second record, although we'd spent a few weeks beforehand rehearsing in an old barn at Rockfield Studios in South Wales. Studio time cost a fortune back then, so we didn't want to fuck around when the meter was running. And once our work was done at Regent Sound we moved to Island Studios in Notting Hill to do the final mix. That was when Rodger Bain realised we needed a few extra minutes of material. I remember him coming down from the control room one lunch break and saying, 'Look, lads, we need some filler. Can you jam something?' We all wanted to get started on our sandwiches, but Tony launched into this guitar riff while Bill played around with some drum patterns, I hummed a melody, and Geezer sat in the corner, scribbling down some lyrics.

Twenty minutes later, we had a song called 'The Paranoid'. By the end of the day, it had become just 'Paranoid'.

It's always the way with the best songs: they come out of nowhere, when you're not even trying. The thing with 'Paranoid' is that it doesn't fit into any category: it was like a punk song years before punk had been invented. Mind you, none of us thought it was anything special when we recorded it. To us, it just seemed a bit half-arsed compared with 'Hand of Doom' or 'Iron Man' or any of those heavier numbers. But fucking hell, it was catchy; I was humming it all the way home from the studio. 'Thelma,' I said, when I got back to Edgbaston. 'I think we might have written a *single*.'

She just gave me a look that said, *That'll be the day*.

It's funny, y'know: if you'd told us at the time that people would still be listening to any of those songs forty years into the future – and that the album would sell more than four million copies in America alone – we would have just laughed in your face.

But the fact is Tony Iommi turned out to be one of the greatest heavy rock riff-makers of all time. Whenever we went into the studio we'd challenge him to beat his last riff – and he'd come up with something like 'Iron Man' and blow everyone away.

But 'Paranoid' was a different class again. About two seconds after the suits at Vertigo heard that song, the name of the whole album became *Paranoid*. It wasn't that they thought *War Pigs* might upset Americans because of Vietnam – at least not as far as I know. No, they were just freaking out about our little three-minute pop song, because they thought it might get played on the radio, and bands like ours *never* got played on the radio. And it made sense to give the album the same title as the single, to make it easier to promote in the record shops.

The suits were right. 'Paranoid' went straight to number four in the British singles chart and got us on *Top of the Pops* – alongside Cliff Richard, of all people. The only problem was the album cover, which had been done before the name change and now didn't make any sense at all. What did four pink blokes holding shields and waving swords have to do with paranoia? They were pink because that was supposed to be the colour of the war pigs. But without 'War Pigs' written on the front, they just looked like gay fencers.

'They're not gay fencers, Ozzy,' Bill told me. 'They're *paranoid* gay fencers.'

Top of the Pops was probably the biggest thing I'd done in my entire life at that point. Every week when I was growing up in Aston, the entire Osbourne family would get together around the telly to watch that show. Even my mum loved it. So when my folks heard I was going to be on, they were speechless. In those days, fifteen million people tuned in to *Top of the Pops* every week, and Pan's People were still doing those hippy dances between the numbers.

It was fucking awesome, man.

I remember being really impressed by Cliff Richard, 'cos he did his song live, with a full orchestra.

We didn't take the piss out of him or anything – after all, it hadn't been that long since I'd been singing 'Living Doll' in front of my parents. I think the song he did was 'I Ain't Got Time Any More'. I haven't seen the tape for years – maybe it was wiped so the reels could be reused, which was the BBC's policy back then. I'll tell you one thing, though: I wouldn't be in the least bit surprised if Cliff looked older on that 1970 *Top of the Pops* episode than he does now. He ages in reverse, that bloke. Every time I see him, he's lost another couple of years.

When it was our turn to go on, my whole body went numb with fear. The other three didn't have to play a note – they just had to look the part and tap their feet in time to the backing track. But I had to sing live. It was my first time on telly and I was shitting myself like I'd never shit myself before. Pure terror. The inside of my mouth was so dry, it felt like I had a ball of cotton wool in there. But I got through it.

My mum and dad watched us at home on the telly – or so my brothers told me a few days later.

If they were proud, they didn't say so. But I like to think they were.

That song changed everything for us. And I loved playing it. For a week or two we even had screaming girls showing up at our gigs and throwing their knickers at us, which was a nice change, although we were obviously a bit worried about pissing off our regular fans. Straight after *Top of the Pops*, we did a gig in Paris, and at the end of the show this beautiful French chick stayed behind. Then she took me back to her place and fucked the shit out of me. I didn't understand a word she said the entire night.

Which is sometimes the best way with one-night stands.

I thought America was fabulous.

Take pizza, for example. For years, I'd been thinking, I wish someone would invent a new kind of food. In England, it was always egg and chips, sausage and chips, pie and chips . . . anything and chips. After a while it just got boring, y'know? But you couldn't exactly order a shaved Parmesan and rocket salad in Birmingham in the early seventies. If it didn't come out of a deep-fat fryer, no one knew what the fuck it was. But then, in New York, I discovered pizza. It blew my mind wide fucking open. I would buy ten or twenty slices a day. And then, when I realised you could buy a great big pizza all for yourself, I started ordering them wherever we went. I couldn't wait to get back home and tell all my mates: 'There's this incredible new thing. It's American and it's called pizza. It's like bread, but it's better than any bread you've tasted in your life.' I even tried to recreate a New York pizza for Thelma one time. I made some dough, then I got all these cans of beans and pilchards and olives and shit and put them on top – it must have been about fifteen quid's worth of gear – but after ten minutes it just came dribbling out of the oven. It was like somebody had been sick in there. Thelma just looked at it and went, 'I don't think I *like* pizza, John.' She never called me Ozzy, my first wife. Not once in the entire time I knew her.

Another incredible thing I discovered in America was the Harvey Wallbanger – a cocktail made with vodka, Galliano and orange juice. They knocked your fucking head off, those things. I drank so many Wallbangers that I can't even stand the smell of them now.

One whiff and I'll vomit on cue.

And then there were the American chicks, who were nothing like English chicks. I mean, when you pulled a chick in England, you gave her the eye, one thing led to another, you took her out, you bought her this and that, and then about a month later you asked if she fancied a good old game of hide the sausage. In America, the chicks just came right up to you and said, 'Hey, let's fuck.' You didn't even have to make any effort.

We found that out on our first night, when we stayed at a place called Loew's Midtown Motor Inn, which was on Eighth Avenue and 48th Street, a sleazy part of town. I couldn't sleep, 'cos I had jet lag, which was another wild new experience. So I'm lying there, wide awake at three o'clock in the morning, and there's a knock on the door. I get up to answer it, and there's this scrawny-looking chick standing there in a trench coat, which she unbuttons in front of me. And she's completely starkers underneath.

'Can I come in?' she whispers, in this throaty, sexy voice.

What was I supposed to say? 'No thanks, darlin', I'm a bit busy.'

So, of course, I go to town on this chick until the sun comes up. Then she picks up her coat off the floor, gives me a peck on the cheek, and fucks off.

Later, when we're all at breakfast, trying to work out where you put the maple syrup – Geezer was pouring it over his hash browns – I go, 'You'll never guess what happened to me last night.'

'Actually,' said Bill, with a little cough, 'I think I can.'

Turned out we'd all had a knock on our door that night: it was our tour manager's 'Welcome to America' present. Although, judging by the way my chick looked in daylight – she couldn't have been a day under forty – he'd obviously got a bulk deal.

During the two months of our American tour, we covered distances that we couldn't have imagined back in England. We played the Fillmore East in Manhattan. We played the Fillmore West in San Francisco. We even went to Florida, where I swam in an outdoor swimming pool for the first time: it was midnight, I was out of my mind on dope and booze, and it was beautiful. I also saw my first proper turquoise ocean in Florida.

Bill hated flying, so we drove between a lot of the gigs, which became a bit of a ritual for us. Me and Bill's epic road trips ended up being the highlights of all our American tours. We spent so much time together in the back of rented GMC mobile homes, we became as thick as thieves. Bill got his brother-in-law Dave to do the driving eventually, so we could drink more and take more drugs. It's funny, you learn a lot about people when you're on the road like that. Every morning, for example, Bill would have a cup of coffee, a glass of orange juice, a glass of milk, and a beer. Always in the same order.

I asked him why he did it once.

'Well,' he said, 'the coffee's to wake me up, the orange juice is to give me some vitamins to stop me getting sick, the milk's to coat my stomach for the rest of the day, and the beer's to put me back to sleep again.'

'Oh,' I said. 'Makes sense.'

Funny bloke, Bill. I remember one time, we had the GMC loaded full of beer and fags, and Dave was driving. We were going from New York to somewhere a long way further down the East Coast, so we'd got up early, even though we'd had a big night. Dave kept complaining that he'd eaten a dodgy pizza before going to bed. It tasted like rat's piss, he said. So I'm sitting in the passenger seat at seven or eight o'clock in the morning, bleary-eyed and hung over; Bill's crashed out in the back; and Dave's driving along with this funny look on his face. I wind down the window and light up a fag, then look over and see Dave turning green.

'You all right, Dave?' I said, blowing smoke into the cabin.

'Yeah, I'm—'

Then he lost it.

Bleeeeeugh!

He threw up all over the dashboard, and these half-digested lumps of cheese and dough and tomato sauce started to dribble into the air vents and on to my box of cigarettes. Just the sight and the smell were enough to make me come out in sympathy.

'Oh no,' I said. 'Dave, I think I'm gonna—'

Bleeeeeugh!

So now there were two stomachfuls of vomit all over the inside of this van. The smell was fucking abominable, but Bill didn't notice a thing – he was still passed out in the back.

We pulled over at the next truck stop and I ran out and asked the chick in the shop if she had any air freshener. There was no way I was even going to *try* to clean up the puke, but we needed to do something about the smell. It seemed like even the drivers of the cars overtaking us on the freeway were holding their noses. But the chick in the shop didn't understand a fucking word I was saying. Finally, she goes, 'Oh, you mean *this*?' And she gives me a can of spearmint air spray. Then she says to me, 'Personally, I don't recommend it.'

Fuck it, I thought, and I bought it anyway. Then I ran back to the GMC, slammed the door, and while Dave pulled out of the parking spot I started spraying the stuff all over the place.

Then, all of a sudden, there's this grunt and a rustling noise from behind us. I look over my shoulder and see Bill sitting bolt upright, looking very unwell. He could take the smell of our puke, but the spearmint air spray had tipped him over the edge.

'Christ!' he goes. 'What the fuck is that sm—'

Bleeeeeugh!

Our first gig in America was at a caff in New York called Ungano's, at 210 West 70th Street. Then after that we did a show at the Fillmore East with Rod Stewart and the Faces. We were pissed off with the Faces, actually, because they didn't give us any time for a sound check. And Rod kept well out of our way. Looking back now, I don't suppose he was too happy about having Black Sabbath supporting him. We were the unwashed hooligans and he was the blue-eyed boy. He was all right though, Rod; always very polite. And I thought he was a phenomenal singer.

Two months felt like an eternity to be so far away from home, and we missed England like crazy – especially when we started talking about how much we couldn't wait to go down the pub and tell everyone about America, which was like going to Mars in those days. Very few Brits ever made it over, because the air fares were so expensive.

Practical jokes ended up being the best way to take our

minds off home. One of the things we found hilarious was the American accent. Every time a hotel receptionist called me 'Mr Ozz-Burn', we'd all crack up laughing. Then we came up with this prank to play in hotel restaurants. During the meal, one of us would sneak off to the front desk and get them to page a 'Mr Harry Bollocks'. So the others would be sitting there eating their hamburgers and this bellhop would rush into the room, ringing his little bell, and shout, 'Is there a Mr Hairy Bollocks here? I'm looking for Hairy Bollocks.'

Bill would laugh so hard he'd make himself ill.

But the biggest culture shock was at a gig in Philadelphia. It was mostly black guys in the audience, and you could tell they hated our music. We did 'War Pigs' and you could have heard a fucking pin drop. One guy, a big tall fella with a massive Afro, spent the whole gig sitting up on a high window ledge, and every few minutes he'd shout out, 'Hey, you – Black Sabbath!'

I thought, Why the fuck does he keep saying that? What does he want? I didn't realise he thought my *name* was Black Sabbath.

Anyway, about halfway through the gig, at the end of one of the songs, this guy does it again: 'Hey, you – Black Sabbath!'

By this point I'd had enough. So I walked to the edge of the stage, looked up at him, and said, 'All right mate, you win. What the fuck do you want? Just tell me. What is it, eh?'

And he peered down at me with this puzzled look on his face.

'You guys ain't *black*,' he said.

That was our only bad gig, mind you.

None of us could believe how well the *Black Sabbath* album had gone down in America. It was a monster. Warner Bros, our American record company, were so pleased with it they told us they were going to delay the release of *Paranoid* until January the following year.

We were getting such big crowds wherever we played, we even started to get a few groupies.

Our first really crazy groupie experience was in a Holiday Inn, out in California somewhere. Now, usually, Patrick Meehan booked us into the shittiest of places; it wasn't unusual for all four of us to share a single room in some dodgy motel on the outskirts of town for five bucks a night. So the Holiday Inn was luxurious by our standards: my room had a bath and a shower and a phone and a telly. It even had a waterbed – which were all the rage in those days. I loved those things, actually; it was like falling asleep on a tyre floating in the middle of the ocean.

Anyway, so we're in this Holiday Inn, and I've just finished talking to Thelma on the phone when there's a knock at the door. I open it and there's this beautiful chick standing there in a little dress. 'Ozzy?' she goes. 'The gig was awesome. Can we talk?'

In she comes, pulls off her dress, Bob's your uncle, and then she fucks off before I can even ask her name.

Five minutes later, there's another knock on the door. I'm thinking, She probably left something in the room. So I get up to answer it. But it's a different chick.

'Ozzy?' she goes. 'The gig was awesome. Can we talk?'

Off comes her dress, down go my trousers, and after five minutes of my hairy arse bobbing up and down on top of her while we're floating around on this waterbed, it was 'Nice meeting you', 'Cheerio', and off she went.

These Holiday Inns are fucking magic, I thought. Then there was another knock on the door.

You can guess what happened next.

I banged three chicks that night. *Three*. Without even leaving my hotel room. To be honest with you, I was flagging a bit with the last one. I had to use the special reserve tank.

Eventually I decided to find out where the fuck all these groupies were coming from. So I went to the bar but it was completely empty. Then I asked the guy in the lobby, 'Where *is* everyone?' He went, 'Your British friends? Try the pool.' So

I took the lift up to the pool on the roof, and when the doors opened I couldn't believe my eyes. It was like *Caligula* up there: dozens of the most amazing-looking chicks you could ever imagine, all stark naked, and blowjobs and threesomes going on left, right and centre. I lit up a joint, sat down on a recliner between two lesbian chicks, and began to sing 'God Bless America'.

But it wasn't just groupies who followed us around America. We also got a lot of loonies – the kind of people who took the black magic thing seriously. Before we even left for America, someone had sent us a film of a black magic parade in San Francisco, held in our honour. There was a bloke who looked like Ming the Merciless sitting in a convertible Rolls-Royce while all these half-naked chicks danced around him in the streets. The bloke's name was Anton LaVey and he was the High Priest of the Church of Satan or some bollocks, and the author of a book called *The Satanic Bible*.

We just thought, What the fuck?

I have a theory, y'know, about people who dedicate their lives to that kind of bullshit: they're just in it because of all the sexual debauchery they can get up to.

Which is fair enough, I suppose.

But we didn't want anything to do with it. A lot of people were still freaked out by Sharon Tate's murder, so we didn't want to come off like members of Charles Manson's 'Family'. I mean, only a few months earlier we'd been playing at Henry's Blues House in front of a few dozen people, and now we were playing the Forum in LA in front of twenty thousand fans. We loved being big in the US, and we didn't want to do anything to fuck it up.

Mind you, we did bump into some members of the Manson Family at the Whiskey A Go Go on Sunset Boulevard in Los Angeles one night. They were very weird people – somewhere-else people, if you know what I mean. Not on the same wavelength as the rest of the world. They gave me the willies, big time. The funny thing is, though, before he turned psycho, Manson had been a big part of the LA music scene. If he hadn't gone to jail, we probably would have ended up hanging out with him. It blew my mind when I learned that he'd been pals with Dennis Wilson from the Beach Boys. The Beach Boys had even covered one of Manson's songs, 'Never Learn Not to Love'. But from what I heard, Dennis ended up getting so spooked by Manson and his friends that he fled his own house. He just woke up and fucked off one day. Then Manson had a bullet delivered to Wilson's new place. The bloke must have been shitting bricks.

There was a lot of mad stuff like that going on in those days.

LA was a crazy place in 1970. The flower power thing was still a huge deal. When you drove around, you'd see all these people with long hair and bare feet, just sitting around on street corners, smoking weed and strumming guitars. The locals probably thought *we* were crazy, too, I suppose. I remember walking into an offy on Sunset Boulevard one time and asking for twenty fags. The woman behind the counter said, 'What do you want twenty fags for? Get out of here, you fucking pervert!'

She must have thought I was a sex fiend. Of course, at the time I didn't have a clue that 'fag' doesn't mean cigarette in America.

As much as we tried to avoid them, the Satanists never stopped being a pain in the arse. About a year after the first tour, we were playing a gig in Memphis and this bloke wearing a black cloak ran on stage. Under normal circumstances, if a fan climbed on stage, I'd put my arm around him and we'd have a good old head bang for a bit. But this bloke looked like one of the satanic loonies, so I told him to fuck off out of it and pushed him away, towards Tony. Before I knew it, one of our roadies was running on stage with a metal bar raised above his head, and he twatted the guy in the face. I couldn't believe what I was seeing. 'What the fuck are you doing, man?' I shouted. 'You can't do that!'

The roadie turned around and said, 'Yes I fucking can. *Look*.'

The satanic bloke was lying on the stage with his cloak wide open. In his right hand was a dagger.

I almost fell backwards into one of the speaker cabinets, I was so freaked out. If it hadn't been for our roadie, Tony might have been a goner.

By the time we headed back to our motel that night, everyone was shaken up. But the fuckers had found out where we were staying, and in the car park of the motel were more guys in black robes, their hoods up, chanting. We were too knackered to deal with it, so we just ignored them and made our way to our rooms, which faced on to the street. A few seconds later, one of the roadies started jabbering and screaming – it turned out that someone had drawn an inverted cross in blood on his door.

I can't say we were *scared*. But after the incident with the guy on the stage, we weren't in the mood to take any more bullshit. So we called the police. Of course, they found the whole thing extremely funny.

They just wouldn't fuck off, those Satanists. I'd walk out of my hotel room in the morning, and they'd be right outside my door, sitting in a circle on the carpet, all dressed in black hooded capes, surrounded by candles. Eventually I couldn't take it any more. So, one morning, instead of brushing past them as I usually did, I went up to them, sat down, took a deep breath, blew out their candles, and sang 'Happy Birthday'.

They weren't too fucking happy about that, believe me.

We were on the road non-stop for two years after our first American tour. Between 1970 and 1972, we must have crossed the Atlantic six times. We spent so much time in the air, we ended up being on first-name terms with the PanAm flight attendants. And even though we were exhausted and ill half the time from the jet lag, the booze and the drugs, it was a fucking blast. We did everything, saw everything, met everyone.

We even went to an Elvis gig.

It was at the Forum in LA. We were so far up in the gods, it seemed to take longer to get to our seats than it did for the King to do his set. He looked like an ant from where we were sitting, and I couldn't get over the fact that his band played for ages before he came on. Then he did only a few numbers before he buggered off again. We were sitting there thinking, Is that it? Then this voice came booming out over the Tannoy: 'Ladies and gentlemen, Elvis has left the building.'

'Lazy fat bastard,' I said, before remembering where I was.

It was an education, that gig. It was the first time I'd seen merchandising sold so professionally at a venue. You could buy Elvis drinks coasters, Elvis bog-seat warmers, Elvis mug and spoon sets, Elvis dolls, Elvis watches, Elvis jumpsuits. *Anything* you could think of, they'd put the name 'Elvis' on it and wanted to flog it to you with an Elvis Coke and an Elvis hot dog. And the fans seemed only too happy to buy it.

He must have been the richest bloke on the planet.

It didn't take us long to start getting into drugs big time. You couldn't really get cocaine in Birmingham back then, so I didn't try it until a gig in Denver with a band called Mountain in early 1971. Mountain's guitarist and lead singer was a guy called Leslie West, and it was him who introduced me to the old waffle dust – we called it that 'cos it made you stay up all night, talking bollocks – although he insists to this day that I'd been taking it long before then. He's got a bit of a bee up his arse about it, in fact. But I just say to him, 'Listen, Leslie, when you come from Aston and you fall in love with cocaine, you *remember* when you started. It's like having your first fuck!'

We were at a hotel after the show, and Leslie was cutting up a line. 'D'you want a bit?' he asked me.

At first I said, 'Whoa, fucking hell, man, no *way*.'

But he kept saying, 'Go on, just a bit, it's all right.'

He didn't exactly have to try very hard to persuade me.

Then it was, sniff-sniff-*ahh*.

I was in love, immediately. It's the same with just about every drug I've ever taken: the first time I try it, that's how I want to feel for the rest of my life. But it never works out that way. You can chase it all you want, but, believe me, you'll never get that first-time high again.

The world went a bit fuzzy after that.

Every day I'd be smoking dope, boozing, having a few toots of coke, fucking around with speed or barbiturates or cough syrup, doing acid, you name it. I didn't know what day it was most of the time. But at some point we made it back to Island Studios in Notting Hill to record our third album, *Master of Reality*, again with Rodger Bain.

I can't remember much about it, apart from the fact that Tony detuned his guitar to make it easier to play, Geezer wrote 'Sweet Leaf' about all the dope we'd been smoking, and 'Children of the Grave' was the most kick-ass song we'd ever recorded. As usual, the critics hated it, although one of 'em described us as '*Titanic*'s house band on the eve of Armageddon', which sounded about right to me. And the music press obviously didn't put anyone off buying it, because *Master of Reality* was another monster hit, reaching number five in Britain and number eight in America.

But we never had a chance to enjoy our success. And I certainly didn't have much time to enjoy married life. In fact, I was starting to realise that getting married so young might not have been such a clever idea. I would get this crazy restless feeling whenever I was at home, like I was going out of my mind. The only way I could handle it was to get loaded.

Life at home was made more complicated because Thelma's son was living with us. His name was Elliot, and he must have been four or five at the time. I adopted him, actually. He was a good kid, but for some reason we never got on. Y'know, some people just don't hit it off with their children. That was me and Elliot. I spent the whole time when I was home screaming at him or whacking him around the ear 'ole. And it's not like he ever did anything bad to deserve it. I wish I could have been better with him, because he'd had a rough time before I came along: his dad had fucked off before Elliot had ever known him. When he got older, he told me he saw his old man in the pub one time, but he couldn't bring himself to talk to him. Which is terribly sad, really.

But I wasn't much of a substitute. It probably didn't help that my boozing was so over the top, which made me volatile. And, of course, my ego was out of control. To tell you the truth, I must have been a horrendous stepdad.

And if I loved Thelma, I certainly didn't treat her like I did. If I've got any regrets about my life, that's one of them. For years, I acted like a married bachelor, sneaking around, banging chicks, getting so wasted down the pub that I'd fall asleep in the car on the street outside. I put that woman through hell. I should never have married her. She didn't deserve it: she wasn't a bad person, and she wasn't a bad wife. But I was a fucking nightmare.

Nine months to the day after me and Thelma got married, she got pregnant. At that point, we still hadn't seen much dough from all the record sales and the touring, but we knew how well the band was doing, so we assumed that Patrick Meehan would soon be sending us a royalty cheque big enough to buy Buckingham Palace. In the meantime, the usual agreement stood: anything I wanted, I just picked up the phone. So Thelma suggested that we should go house hunting. We couldn't live in a little flat with a screaming baby, she said, so why not move to a proper place? We could afford it, after all.

I was all for it.

'Let's live in the country,' I said, imagining myself in a tweed suit with green wellies, a Range Rover and a shotgun.

For the next few months, every time I came off the road for a few days, we climbed into our brand-new green Triumph Herald convertible – I'd got it for Thelma, because I couldn't drive – and go looking for houses in the countryside. Eventually we found one we both liked: Bulrush Cottage in Ranton, Staffordshire. They were asking just over twenty grand for the place, which seemed reasonable enough. It had four bedrooms, a sauna, there was room for a little studio and, best of all, it had plenty of land. But we kept on looking, just to make sure. Then, one day, in a tea shop in Evesham, Worcestershire, we decided that we'd seen enough: we'd make an offer on Bulrush. It felt like I'd finally grown up. But just as we were starting to get excited about our new life in the country, Thelma suddenly went 'Shhh!' and said, 'Can you hear that?'

'What?' I said.

'That clicking noise.'

'What clickin . . . ?' Then I heard it, too.

It was more of a tick than a click.

Tick, tick, tick, tick.

I looked down and saw a big puddle under Thelma's chair. Something was dripping from under her dress. Then one of the tea ladies started wailing about the mess on the floor.

'Oh my God,' said Thelma. 'My waters have broken!'

'What d'you mean?' I said. 'You've pissed yerself?'

'No, John – *my waters have broken.*'

'Eh?'

'*I'm having the baby.*'

I jumped up so quickly my chair fell over. Then my whole body went numb with panic. I couldn't think. My heart was like a drum roll. The first thing that came into my head was: *I'm not drunk enough*. The bottle of cognac I'd gone through in the car had already worn off. I'd always thought that Thelma would go off to hospital to have the baby. I didn't think it could just *happen* – in the middle of a fucking tea shop!

'Is anyone in here a doctor?' I shouted, looking desperately around the room. 'We need a doctor. Help! We need a doctor!'

'John,' hissed Thelma. 'You just need to drive me to hospital. We don't need a doctor.'

'*We need a doctor!*'

'No, we don't.'

'Yeah, we do,' I moaned. 'I don't feel well.'

'John,' said Thelma, 'you need to drive me to hospital. *Now*.'

'I don't have a driving licence.'

'Since when has the law stopped you from doing anything?'

'I'm drunk.'

'You've been drunk since 1967! C'mon, John. Hurry.'

So I got up, paid the bill, and led Thelma outside to the Herald. I had no idea how to work the thing. My parents had never owned a car, and I'd always assumed that I'd never be able to afford one, so I hadn't taken the slightest bit of interest in learning how to drive. All I knew was the basics, like how to tune the radio and wind down the windows.

But gears? Choke? Clutch?

Nah.

The car jerked backwards and forwards on its springs like a pissed kangaroo for about twenty minutes before I got it moving. In the wrong direction. Then I finally found first gear.

'John, you're going to have to put your foot down,' said Thelma, between groans.

'My foot's shaking,' I told her. 'I can hardly keep it on the pedal.'

My hands were shaking, too. I was terrified that our baby

was going to end up plopping out of Thelma and on to the dashboard, where it might blow away, because the hood was still down. I could imagine the headline: 'ROCKER'S TOT IN FREAK M-WAY TRAGEDY'.

'Seriously, John. *Arrrgh!* Drive faster. *Arrrgh!* I'm having contractions!'

'The car won't go any faster!'

'You're only going *ten* miles an hour.'

After what seemed like a thousand years, we made it to the Queen Elizabeth Hospital in Edgbaston. Then all I had to do was stop the car. But every time I put my foot on the middle pedal it just started bouncing up and down again and making this horrible noise. It's a miracle I didn't crash into the back of an ambulance, to be honest with you. But somehow I managed to get the wheels to stop moving, and then get Thelma out of her seat – not easy when she was screaming and puffing – and into the maternity ward.

A few hours later, at 11.20 p.m., little Jessica Osbourne was born – so I became a father for the first time. The date was 20 January 1972. It was one of those cold, clear winter nights. Through the hospital window, you could see all these gleaming constellations in every direction.

'What should we give her as a middle name?' said Thelma, holding Jessica up to her chest.

'Starshine,' I said.

5

Killing the Vicar (in Atrocity Cottage)

By the summer of 1972 – six months after Jess was born – we were back in America, this time to record a new album, which we'd decided to call *Snowblind* in honour of our new-found love of cocaine. By now, I was putting so much of the stuff up my nose that I had to smoke a bag of dope every day just to stop my heart from exploding. We were staying at 773 Stradella Road in Bel Air, a rented 1930s mansion complete with its own staff of maids and gardeners. The place was owned by the Du Pont family and it had six bedrooms, seven bathrooms, a private cinema (which we used for writing and rehearsing) and a swimming pool in the back, which was on stilts and looked out over all these woods and mountains. We never left the house. Booze, drugs, food, groupies – *everything* was delivered. On a good day there'd be bowls of white powder and crates of booze in every room, and all these random rock 'n' rollers and chicks in bikinis hanging around the place – in the bedrooms, on the sofas, outside on the recliners – all of them as high as we were.

It would be almost impossible to exaggerate how much coke we did in that house. We'd discovered that when you take coke, every thought you have, every word you say, every suggestion you make seems like the most fabulous thing you've ever heard in your life. At one point we were getting through so much of the stuff, we had to have it delivered twice a day. Don't ask me who was organising it all – the only thing I can remember is this shady-looking bloke on the telephone the whole time. But he wasn't shady in the normal sense of the word: he was clean cut and had one of those Ivy League accents, and he'd wear white shirts and smart trousers, like he was on his way to work in an office.

I once asked him, 'What the fuck do you *do*, man?'

He just laughed and fiddled nervously with his aviator shades. At that stage I didn't care, as long as the coke kept coming.

My favourite thing to do when I was high was to stay up all night watching American telly. In those days there was only one thing on after the normal programming ended at midnight – a sales pitch by a bloke called Cal Worthington, who flogged second-hand cars down in Long Beach or somewhere. His big joke was that he always appeared on air with his dog, Spot – but the dog was never actually a dog. It would be an alligator on a lead, or some crazy shit like that. He also had this catchphrase, 'If I can't make you a better deal, I'll eat a bug!', and did these stunts, like being strapped to the wing of an aeroplane as it did a loop-the-loop. After a few hours of snorting coke and watching that shit, you thought you were going insane. The funny thing is, he's still at it today, old Cal. He must be about a thousand years old.

We fucked around so much at 773 Stradella Road, it's a wonder we got any songs written at all. And it wasn't just the coke. We got through a shitload of beer, too. I'd brought over these 'party cans' of best bitter from my local boozer. Each can held five pints, and you could fit six of them in one suitcase. It was like taking coal to Newcastle, but we didn't care, 'cos we missed a good old English pint. We'd sit there by the pool, in ninety-degree sunshine, coked out of our minds, drinking stale Brummie piss, and looking out over Bel Air.

But then we had to tone things down because Thelma came to visit for few days – without the baby. The good behaviour didn't last long, mind you. The second Thelma left for the airport to go back to England, we went straight back to being animals again. During our songwriting sessions, for example, no one could be arsed to walk upstairs for a slash, so we'd just go outside on to this little balcony and piss over the railing, which was only a couple of feet high. Then, one day, Tony gets this can of blue spray paint and sneaks round to the other side of the railing, and when Bill starts pissing, he sprays his dick with it. You should have heard the scream, man. It was priceless. But then, two seconds later, Bill blacks out, falls headfirst over the railing, and starts to roll down the hillside.

I said to Tony, 'Gis a look at that can, will yer?'

He passed it up to me, and there on the side, in big capital letters, it said: 'WARNING. KEEP AWAY FROM SKIN. MAY CAUSE RASH, BLISTERING, CONVULSIONS, VOMITING, AND/OR FAINTING. IF ANY OF THESE SYMPTOMS OCCUR, SEEK MEDICAL CARE.'

'Ah, he'll be all right,' I said.

And he was, eventually.

Although he did have a blue dick for a while.

In spite of all the arsing around, musically those few weeks in Bel Air were the strongest we'd ever been. For me, *Snowblind* was one of Black Sabbath's best-ever albums – although the record company wouldn't let us keep the title, 'cos in those days cocaine was a big deal, and they didn't want the hassle of a controversy.

We didn't argue.

So, after we'd recorded the new songs at the Record Plant in Hollywood, the name *Snowblind* was dropped, and our fourth album became known as just *Vol. 4*. We still managed to get a cheeky reference to cocaine in the liner notes, though. If you look closely enough, you'll see a dedication to 'the great COKE-Cola company of Los Angeles'.

And it was true – that album owed *a lot* to cocaine.

When I listen to songs like 'Supernaut', I can just about taste the stuff. The whole album's like having someone pour a couple of lines into your ears. Frank Zappa once told me that 'Supernaut' was one of his favourite rock 'n' roll tracks of all time, because you can hear the adrenaline. We were flying, y'know? In 1972, it had been only two years since the biggest compliment you could give us was that we were big in Carlisle. Now we had more money than the Queen – or so we thought – with three hit records in the charts, fans all over the world, and as much booze and drugs and chicks as we could ever want.

We weren't on Cloud Nine. We were on Cloud Ten-and-a-Half.

And we still really cared about the music. We wanted to impress ourselves before we impressed anyone else. If other people happened to like what we were doing, that was just a bonus. That's how we ended up doing songs like 'Changes', which didn't sound like anything we'd ever done before. When a lot of people hear the name Black Sabbath, all they think of is the heavy stuff. But there was a lot more to us than that – especially when we started making an effort to get away from all that black magic shit. With 'Changes', Tony just sat down at the piano and came up with this beautiful riff, I hummed a melody over the top, and Geezer wrote these heartbreaking lyrics about the break-up Bill was going through with his wife at the time. I thought that song was brilliant from the moment we first recorded it.

I had to keep listening to it, over and over again. I'm still like that today: if I put it on my iPod, I'll drive everyone nuts by singing along to it for the rest of the day.

Eventually we started to wonder where the fuck all the coke was coming from. All we knew was that it arrived in the back of unmarked vans, packed inside cardboard boxes. In each box there were about thirty vials – ten across, three deep – and each one had a screw-on top, sealed with wax.

I'm telling you: that coke was the whitest, purest, strongest stuff you could ever imagine.

One sniff, and you were the king of the universe.

But as much as we loved being human vacuum cleaners, we knew it would have been a big deal, getting caught with one of our dodgy shipments. Especially in America. And I didn't much fancy the idea of spending the rest of my life bent over in an LA prison with the cock of some twenty-stone gang member up my arse. The trouble was, of course, being constantly strung-out just made me even more paranoid, and after a while I'd convinced myself that our Ivy League dealer was FBI, or LAPD, or the fucking CIA.

Then, one night, me and the lads went down to Hollywood to see *The French Connection* at the cinema. Big mistake, that was. The plot was based on a true story about two undercover New York cops busting an international heroin-smuggling ring. By the time the credits rolled, I was hyperventilating.

'Where the fuck would someone be getting vials of coke with wax seals on them?' I said to Bill.

He just shrugged.

Then we went to the bog to do another couple of lines.

A few days later, I was lying by the pool, smoking a joint and drinking a beer, trying to get my heart to slow down, when the shady-looking bloke came over and sat down next to me. It was morning, and he had a cup of coffee in one hand and a copy of the *Wall Street Journal* in the other.

I hadn't been to bed.

Now's my chance to feel this bloke out, see how dodgy he is, I thought. So I leaned over and said, 'Did you ever see that movie, *The French Connection*?'

He smiled and shook his head.

'Oh,' I said. 'You should, y'know. It's very interesting.'

'I'm sure it is,' the bloke chuckled. 'But why go and see a movie when I had a part in the real thing?'

As soon as I heard that, I broke out into this horrible prickly sweat. This guy was bad news. I just knew it.

'Listen, man,' I said. 'Who do you work for?'

He put down his newspaper and took a sip of his coffee. 'The United States government,' he said.

I almost jumped off my recliner and made a dive for the hedge. But my head was spinning, and I hadn't felt my legs since the night before. That's it, I thought: we're all fucked now.

'Jesus Christ, man, *relax*,' he said, seeing the look on my face. 'I'm not the FBI. You're not about to get busted. We're all friends here. I work for the Food and Drug Administration.'

'The *what*?'

'The FDA.'

'You mean, all that coke . . . it's coming from—'

'Think of it as a gift from Santa Claus, Ozzy. Because you know what they say about Santa Claus, don't you?

'No?'

'There's a lot of snow where he comes from.'

Then the bloke looked at his watch and said he had a meeting to attend. So he finished his coffee, got up, patted me on the back, and fucked off. I thought no more of it. Then I went back inside the house for a bit more coke and a few hits on the bong.

So there I am on the sofa, with all these sealed vials of coke lined up in front of me – along with a big bowl of pot – and I'm cutting up my first line of the day. But then I start to sweat again – that same horrible, prickly sweat as before. Fuck me, I'm thinking, the paranoia's really bad today. At that moment Bill strolls into the room with a beer in his hand and goes, 'It's like a furnace in here, Ozzy. Why don't you switch on the AC?' Then he pokes his head out of the patio door to get his first sunlight in days.

I thought, What's 'the AC' when it's at home? Then it clicked: air conditioning. I always used to forget that the mod cons in America were so much more advanced than they were in Britain. I'd only recently got used to the novelty of an indoor shitter, never mind automated climate control. So I got up and started looking for the thermostat. Must be on the wall somewhere around here, I said to myself. After a few minutes – *bingo!* – I found it in a little nook by the front door. So I turned down the temperature and went back to my coke and pot.

Magic.

But as soon as I'd got the first line up my nose, I heard something.

Was it . . . ?

Nah.

Shit, it sounded like . . .

Suddenly Bill threw himself through the open patio door, with this wild-eyed look on his face. At the same time, I heard doors slamming at the other end of the house and what sounded like three big blokes falling down the stairs. Then Tony, Geezer and one of the roadies – an American bloke called Frank – came puffing into the room. Everyone was half-dressed apart from Frank, who was still in his underwear.

We all looked at each other.

Then in unison, we shouted: '*Sirens!*'

*

It sounded like the entire fucking LAPD was coming up the driveway. We were being busted! Fuck! Fuck! *Fuck!*

'GET THE COKE! GET THE COKE!' I started to scream.

So Frank dived towards the coffee table, grabbed the vials of coke, but then just ran around in circles, his hair standing on end, a fag still in his mouth, his Y-fronts riding up into his arse crack.

Then I remembered something else.

'GET THE POT! GET THE POT!'

Frank dived back towards the coffee table and grabbed the big bowl of pot, but when he did that he dropped the coke. So he ended up scrabbling around on the floor, trying to balance everything in his arms. Meanwhile, I couldn't even move. Even before the sirens, my heart had been going at triple speed. Now it was beating so fast I thought it was gonna crack open my rib cage.

B-b-b-b-b-b-b-b-b-b-bum!

B-b-b-b-b-b-b-b-b-b-bum!

B-b-b-b-b-b-b-b-b-b-bum!

By the time I pulled myself together, Bill, Geezer and Tony had all bolted. So it was just me and Frank, and enough coke to march the Bolivian army to the moon and back.

'Frank! *Frank!*' I shouted. 'Over 'ere. The bog. Quick!'

Somehow Frank managed to haul himself and all the drugs over to the bog, which was just off the hallway near the front door, and we dived inside and locked the door behind us.

The sirens were fucking deafening now.

Then I heard the brakes of the police cars squealing as they pulled up outside. Then a radio crackling. Then a knock at the door.

BAM! BAM! BAM!

'Open up!' shouted one of the cops. 'C'mon, open up!'

By now, me and Frank were kneeling on the floor. In our

panic, we'd tried to get rid of the pot before the coke – first by washing it down the sink, then by flushing it down the bog. Big mistake. The sink and the bog couldn't take it, and they'd started to overflow with all this brown, lumpy water. So we tried forcing some of the pot down the U-bend, using the end of the bog brush. But it wouldn't go. The pipes were backed up.

And we still had to get rid of all the coke.

'There's nothing else for it,' I said to Frank. 'We're gonna have to snort all the coke.'

'Are you fucking out of your mind?' he said. 'You'll die!'

'Have you ever been to prison, Frank?' I said. 'Well, I have, and I'm telling you right now, I ain't going back.'

So I started to break open the vials and tip the coke on to the floor. Then I got down on all fours, pressed my nose against the tiles, and started to vacuum up as much of the stuff as I could.

BAM! BAM! BAM!

'Open the door! *We know you're in there!*'

Frank was looking at me like I was insane.

'Any second now,' I told him, my face bright red, my legs tingling, my eyeballs throbbing, 'they're gonna break down that door, and we'll be fucked.'

'Oh, man,' said Frank, joining me on all fours. 'I can't believe I'm about to do this.'

We must have snorted about six or seven grams each before I heard the tapping noise outside the door.

'SHHH! *Listen*,' I said.

There it was again: *tap, tap, tap, tap . . .*

It sounded like footsteps . . .

Then I heard the front door open and a woman's voice. She was speaking in Spanish. The maid! The maid was letting in the cops. *Fuck!* I broke open another vial and put my nose to the floor again.

A male voice: 'Good morning, ma'am,' he said. 'I believe

someone at this residence pressed the emergency call button?'

I stopped, mid-sniff.

Emergency call button?

The maid said something in Spanish again, the man replied, then I heard two sets of footsteps in the hallway and the man's voice getting louder. *The cop was inside the house!*

'It's usually located right next to the AC thermostat,' he said. 'Yep, here it is – right on the wall. If you press this button, ma'am, it sounds an alarm down at the Bel Air station and we dispatch some officers to make sure everything is OK. Looks as though someone might have pressed it by accident when they were adjusting the thermostat. Happens more often than you'd think. Let me just reset the system – there we go – and we'll be on our way. Any problems, just give us a call. Here's our number. Or hit the button again. We have someone on call twenty-four hours a day.'

'*Gracias*,' said the maid.

I heard the front door close and the maid walk back towards the kitchen. All of the air came out of my lungs. Holy shit: that had been a close one. Then I looked over at Frank: his face was a mask of white powder and snot, and his left nostril was bleeding.

'You mean . . . ?' he said.

'Yeah.' I nodded. 'Someone needs to teach Bill how to use that fucking thing.'

The constant fear of getting busted wasn't the only downside to coke. It got to the point where practically every word out of my mouth was coked-up bollocks. For fifteen hours straight, I'd tell the lads how much I loved them more than anything else in the world. Even me and Tony – who *never* had conversations – would have nights when we'd be up for hours, hugging each other and saying, 'No, really, I love you, man – I *really* love you.'

Then I'd go to bed, wait for my heart to stop beating at eight times its usual speed, then fall into this fucking horrific withdrawal. The comedowns were so bad that I used to pray. I'd say, 'God, please let me sleep, and I promise I'll never do cocaine again, as long as I live.'

Then I'd wake up with my jaw aching from spouting so much bullshit the previous night.

And I'd do another line.

It was amazing how quickly it took over our lives. It got to the point where we couldn't do anything without it. Then it got to the point where we couldn't do anything with it, either.

When I finally realised the pot wasn't enough to calm me down from all the coke, I started getting into Valium. Then eventually I moved on to heroin, but thank God I didn't like that stuff. Geezer tried it, too. He thought it was fucking brilliant, but he was sensible. He didn't want to get involved. Frank, the roadie, wasn't so lucky – heroin ruined him in the end. I haven't heard from Frank in years now, and I'd be amazed if he survived, to be honest with you. I hope he did, I really do, but when heroin gets hold of you, it's usually The End.

During the making of *Vol. 4*, we all had moments when we were so fucked up that we just couldn't function. With Bill, it was when he was recording 'Under the Sun'. By the time he got the drums right on that song, we'd renamed it 'Everywhere Under the Fucking Sun'. Then the poor bloke came down with hepatitis and almost died. Meanwhile, Geezer ended up in hospital with kidney problems. Even Tony burned out. Just after we'd finished the album, we did a gig at the Hollywood Bowl. Tony had been doing coke literally for days – we all had, but Tony had gone over the edge. I mean, that stuff just twists your whole idea of reality. You start seeing things that aren't there. And Tony was *gone*. Near the end of the gig he walked off stage and collapsed.

'Severe exhaustion,' the doctor said.

That was one way of putting it.

At the same time, the coke was fucking up my voice, good and proper. When you're taking heavy-duty amounts of cocaine, this white gunk starts to trickle down the back of your throat, and you find yourself doing that phlegm-clearing thing all the time – like a sniff, but deeper and gunkier. And that puts a lot of stress on that little titty thing that hangs down at the back of your throat – the epiglottis, or the 'clack', as I've always called it. Anyway, I was taking so much coke that I was clearing away the phlegm every couple of minutes, until eventually I tore my clack in half. I was lying in bed at the time in the Sunset Marquis hotel, and I just felt it flop down inside the back of my throat. It was horrific. Then the fucking thing swelled up to the size of a golf ball. I thought: Right, this is it – I'm gonna die now.

So I went to see a doctor on Sunset Boulevard.

He asked, 'What's the problem, Mr Osbourne?'

'I've sucked my clack,' I croaked.

'You've *what*?'

'My clack.'

I pointed at my throat.

'Let's have a look,' he said, getting out his lollipop stick and his little torch. 'Open wide. Say "*ahh*" for me now.'

So I opened my mouth and closed my eyes.

'Holy mother of Christ!' he said. 'How in God's name did you do that?'

'Dunno.'

'Mr Osbourne, your epiglottis is the size of a small light bulb, and it's glowing almost as brightly. I don't even need to use my torch.'

'Can you fix it?'

'I think so,' he said, writing out a prescription. 'But whatever it is you've been doing, s*top doing it*.'

That wasn't the end of our medical problems, though. When

it was time to go back to England, we were all terrified of taking home an STD from one of the groupies and giving it to our other half. Catching some exotic disease was always a big worry when we were in America. I remember one time during a particularly wild night at a hotel somewhere, Tony came running out of his room, going, 'Aargh! My knob! My knob!' I asked him what was wrong, and he told me that he'd been messing around with this groupie when he looked down and saw all this yellow pus coming out of her. He thought he was about to die.

'Did the pus smell funny?' I asked him.

'Yeah,' he said, white in the face. 'I almost puked.'

'Ah.'

'What d'you mean, "ah"?'

'Was it the blonde chick?' I asked. 'The one with the tattoo?'

'Yeah. And?'

'Well, that probably explains it then.'

'Ozzy,' said Tony, getting visibly angry. 'Stop fucking around, this is serious. What are you talking about?'

'Look, I ain't a doctor,' I said. 'But I don't think the yellow stuff was pus.'

'Well what *was* it then?'

'Probably the banana I stuck up there earlier.'

I don't think Tony knew whether to be relieved or even more worried after that.

Of course, one failsafe way to make sure you never gave anything dodgy to your missus was to get a shot of penicillin. I'd learned that after getting the clap one time. But in those days we didn't know any dodgy doctors, which meant the only way to get a 'safety shot' was to check yourself into the emergency room of the nearest hospital.

So that's what we did after making *Vol. 4*.

By then we'd left Bel Air and were on the road in small-town America somewhere, doing a few shows before our flight back home. I'll never forget the scene: me, Tony, Geezer, and pretty much the entire road crew – I don't know what Bill was up to that day – checking ourselves into this hospital one night. And of course no one had the bottle to tell the good-looking chick on the front desk why we were there, so they were all going, 'Go on, Ozzy, you tell her, you don't care, you're fucking crazy, you are.' But even I couldn't bring myself to say, 'Oh, hello there, my name's Ozzy Osbourne, and I've been bonking groupies for a couple of months, and I think my knob might be about to fall off, would you mind terribly giving me a shot of penicillin to make sure my missus doesn't get whatever I've got?'

But it was too late to turn around and walk away.

So when the girl asked me what the problem was, I just turned bright red and blurted, 'I think I broke my ribs.'

'OK,' she said. 'Here's a ticket. See this number? They'll call it out when the doctor's ready to see you.'

Then it was Geezer's turn to go up.

'I've got whatever he's got,' he said, pointing at me.

Eventually the doctors twigged. I don't know who came clean with them, 'cos I certainly didn't. I just remember this bloke in a white suit coming up to me and going, 'Are you with the others?' and me nodding. Then he showed me into this room with Tony, Geezer and about half a dozen other hairy English blokes all bent over with their trousers down, their lily-white arses ready for their penicillin jabs.

'Join the line,' he said.

It was September when we got back to England.

By that time the deal to buy Bulrush Cottage had gone through, and Thelma, Elliot and the baby were already settled in. It always made me smile, going home to Bulrush Cottage – mainly because it was on a little country road called Butt Lane. 'Welcome to Butt Lane,' I used to say to visitors, 'the arsehole of Britain.'

It wasn't just me and Thelma and the baby who got a new place to live around that time. I also sorted out a bigger house for my mum and dad. As always, Patrick Meehan's office took care of the dough side of things, although when the land behind Bulrush Cottage was put up for sale we bought it with our own money – or rather, money we made by flogging the Rolls-Royce that Patrick Meehan had given Tony, which Tony had then given to us. I think that was the first time we'd bought *anything* with our own money. To this day, I don't know why we did it. Maybe it's 'cos Thelma dealt with all the paperwork. I made her do it because the farmer who sold us the land was a cross-dresser, and I didn't want to go anywhere near him. Fucking hell, man, the first time I saw that bloke, I thought I was hallucinating. He had this big bushy beard and he'd drive his tractor down Butt Lane while wearing a frock and curlers in his hair. Other times you'd see him by the side of the road, his frock hitched up, taking a slash. And the funny thing is, no one would bat an eyelid.

Tony and Geezer also bought houses when they got back. Tony got a place in Acton Trussell, on the other side of the M6; and Geezer bought somewhere down in Worcestershire. It took Bill a bit longer to find his rock 'n' roll retreat, so in the meantime he rented a place called Fields Farm, out near Evesham. In less than three years, we'd gone from piss-poor backstreet kids to millionaire country gents. It was unbelievable.

And I *loved* living in the country.

For starters, I suddenly had enough room to get even more toys sent over from Patrick Meehan's office. Like a seven-foot-tall stuffed grizzly bear. And a gypsy caravan with a little fireplace inside. And a myna bird called Fred, who lived in the laundry room. He could do a wicked impression of a washing machine, could Fred. Or at least he could until I put a shotgun in his face and told him to shut the fuck up.

I have to say I really pigged out on the calls to Patrick Meehan's office after we moved into Bulrush Cottage. Everything I'd ever wanted as a kid, I had them deliver. I ended up with a whole shed full of Scalextric cars, jukeboxes, table football games, trampolines, pool tables, shotguns, crossbows, catapults, swords, arcade games, toy soldiers, fruit machines . . . Every single thing you could ever think to ask for, I asked for it. The guns were most fun. The most powerful one I had was this Benelli five-shot semi-automatic. I tried it out on the stuffed bear one time. Its head just *exploded* – you should have fucking seen it, man. Another thing I'd do is get these mannequins and tie them to this tree trunk in the garden and execute them at dawn. I'm telling you, it's really terrifying what booze and drugs will do to your mind if you take them for long enough. I was out of control.

Obviously, the most important thing I needed to sort out after moving to the country was a ready supply of drugs. So I called up one of my American dealers and got him to start sending me cocaine via air mail, on the understanding that I'd pay him the next time I was over there on tour. It worked a treat, although I ended up waiting for the postman all day like a dog. Thelma must have thought I was buying dirty magazines or something.

Then I found a local dope dealer who said he could get me some really strong hash from Afghanistan. He wasn't wrong, either. The first time I smoked that stuff it almost knocked my fucking head off. It came in massive slabs of black resin, which would last even me for weeks. There was nothing I loved more than when someone came over to Bulrush Cottage and said, 'Dope? Nah, I don't smoke that stuff. Never has any effect on me.'

If you said that, you were *mine*.

The first person who claimed to be immune to dope was our local fruit 'n' veg man, Charlie Clapham. He was a right old character, Charlie was, and he became a good friend. One night, after we'd been to the pub, I got out the tin of Afghan hash and said, 'Try this.'

'Nah, never works on me, that stuff.'

'Go on, Charlie, try it, just once. For me.'

So he grabbed the brick out of my hands and before I could say anything he bit off a huge chunk of it. He must have eaten at least half an ounce. Then he burped in my face and said, 'Urgh, that tasted 'orrible.'

Five minutes later, he said, 'See? Nothing,' and went home.

It must have been about one o'clock in the morning when he left, and the poor fucker was meant to be at his market stall by four. But I knew there was no way he'd be doing a normal day's work.

Sure enough, when I saw him a few days later, he grabbed me by the collar and said, 'What the *fuck* was that shit you gave me the other night? By the time I got to the market I was hallucinating. I couldn't get out of the van. I was just lying in the back with the carrots, a coat over my head, screaming. I thought the Martians had landed!'

'I'm sorry to hear that, Charlie,' I told him.

'Can I come over tomorrow night and have some more?' he said.

I rarely slept in my own bed at Bulrush Cottage. I was so loaded every night, I could never make it up the stairs. So I'd sleep in the car, in my caravan, under the piano in the living room, in the studio or outside in a bale of hay. When I slept outside in winter, it wasn't unusual for me to wake up blue in the face with icicles on my nose. In those days, there was no such thing as hypothermia.

Crazy shit would happen all the time at that house. The fact that I was usually pissed up and fucking around with my shotguns didn't help. That's a great combination, that is – booze and shotguns. Very fucking safe. One time I tried to jump over a fence in the back garden while holding one of my guns. I'd forgotten to put the safety on and my finger was resting on the trigger, so as soon as I hit the ground, it went *BAM! BAM! BAM!* and almost blew my leg off.

It's a miracle I ain't an amputee.

I'd shoot anything that moved in those days. I remember when we got rid of Thelma's Triumph Herald and replaced it with a brand-new Mercedes – after yet another call to Patrick Meehan's office. The car was always covered in scratches, and we couldn't work out why. I'd get it resprayed, park it in the garage overnight, but the next morning the paintwork would be covered in all these nicks and gouges again. It was costing me an arm and a leg. Then I realised what was happening: we had a family of stray cats living in the garage, and when it was cold they'd climb up on the Merc's bonnet, because it was nice and warm. So, one day, I came back from a long session at the Hand & Cleaver, got my shotgun, and just fucking obliterated the place. I got two or three of them that first time. Then I kept going back every day, picking them off, one by one.

But y'know, that's one of my regrets – the cruelty to animals. I could have found another way to get rid of those cats, but like I said, I was out of control. It got so bad, people started to call my house Atrocity Cottage, not Bulrush Cottage. It was me who came up with the name – I just blurted it out one night when I was pissed – but from then on it stuck.

People would come to stay with us and they'd never be the same again. Take my old mate Jimmy Phillips, the bloke who'd played bottleneck guitar in Polka Tulk. He got so fucked up on booze and Afghan hash over at Bulrush Cottage one night that he ended up taking a shit in the kitchen sink. Then there was the time when one of my old schoolfriends from Birmingham brought his new wife over for a visit. The day after they arrived, I woke up in the morning with a terrible headache and a big hairy arm around my shoulder. I thought my mate must have been having a go at Thelma while I was asleep, so I jumped out of bed, ready to chin the bastard. But then I realised what had happened: I'd got up in the middle of the night to take a piss and had gone back to the wrong room. Talk about an awkward fucking situation. I was stark naked, too – so I just grabbed my trousers from the floor and dived back into the bed, put them on under the sheets, and then staggered back to my own room, with no one saying a word.

I've never seen them again to this day.

And, as time went on, things got even crazier. At one point – don't ask me why – I started to wear medical uniforms all the time. My assistant, David Tangye, bought them for me. You'd see us staggering up and down these country lanes between the pubs, out of our minds on booze, dope, acid – you name it – wearing these green American-style scrubs, with stethoscopes around our necks.

Every once in a while, the lads from Led Zeppelin would also come over to Bulrush Cottage. Robert Plant didn't live too far away, actually, and I'd go over to his place, too. I remember one night at Plant's house – not long after we'd got back from Bel Air – I taught him how to play seven-card stud. That was a big fucking mistake. As I explained the rules, he said he wanted to place bets – 'just to see how it works, y'know?' – and then he kept raising the stakes. I was just beginning to think what a fucking idiot he must be when he pulled out a royal flush, and I had to give him fifty quid.

He fleeced me, the cheeky bastard.

After a few nights out with Zeppelin, I worked out that their drummer, John Bonham, was as fucking nuts as I was, so we'd spend most of the time trying to out-crazy each other. That was always the way with me, y'know? I'd try to win people over with my craziness, like I had in the playground at Birchfield Road. But, of course, behind the mask there was a sad old clown most of the time. Bonham was the same, I think.

He would just drink himself to fucking bits. One time, we got his assistant, a guy called Matthew, to drive us to a club in Birmingham in my car. But when it was time to go home, Bonham was so pissed, he thought it was *his* car, so he locked all the doors from inside and wouldn't let me in. I ended up standing in the car park shouting, 'John, this is *my* car. Open the door!'

'Fuck off,' he said, through the window, as Matthew revved the engine.

'John, for crying out—'

'I said *fuck off*.'

'BUT THIS IS *MY* CAR!'

Then something finally clicked inside his head. 'Well, you should fucking get in then, shouldn't you?' he said.

Even though I was pissed all the time in the seventies, the one thing I really wanted to do more than just about anything was get my driving licence. And fucking hell, man, I tried. I took my test more times than I can remember while I lived at Bulrush Cottage – and I failed every time. I'd just get intimidated, y'know? After my first couple of attempts, I started to go down to the Hand & Cleaver beforehand to sort out my nerves, but more often than not I'd end up being shitfaced by the time I got in the car with the examiner, and then I'd drive like a cunt. Then I thought the problem might be the car, so I called Patrick Meehan's office and asked for a Range Rover to replace the Merc. When that didn't work, I asked for a Jag. But it was a V12, so every time I put my foot down, I woke up in a hedge.

Eventually I took the test in a Roller.

That didn't work, either.

Finally I went to the doctor and asked for some pills to calm me down, so he wrote me a prescription for a sedative. On the box, it said, 'DO NOT MIX WITH ALCOHOL', which was like showing a red rag to a bull as far as I was concerned. Still, I managed to limit myself to only three or four pints that day. Unfortunately, that just meant I smoked twice as much Afghan hash. The good news was that when I got into the car with the examiner, I didn't feel intimated at all. The bad news was that when I stopped for the first traffic light, I nodded off.

I gave up on the tests after that, but I kept driving anyway. Whenever I gave anyone a ride, they'd ask, 'Do you have a licence yet?' and I'd answer, 'Oh yeah, of course.'

Which was sort of true.

I had a TV licence.

But I didn't want to push my luck too far, so I started trying to come up with other ways of getting around.

Which is why I ended up getting a horse.

Now, I'm generally not cool with horses – they don't have brakes and they've got their own brains. But I was bored of going down to the Hand & Cleaver on my lawnmower, so I went to see a dealer and said, 'Look, can you get me a horse that's a bit on the lazy side?'

A few days later, this chick turned up at the cottage with this pure white gelding – a male with its nuts chopped off – called Turpin. 'He's very laid back,' she told me. 'He won't give you any trouble at all. The only things he doesn't like are very loud hissing noises – like the air brakes on a lorry. But you won't get anything like that around here.'

'Oh no,' I said, laughing. 'It's very quiet out here in Ranton.'

So I called Patrick Meehan's office to get him to send the breeder some dough, and that was that: I was the proud owner of one lazy horse. I kept him at the farm up the road, because they had a little paddock and someone who could feed him and clean out his stable.

Of course, the second I got Turpin I thought I was John Wayne. I started riding him up and down Butt Lane, wearing a cowboy hat and this leather shirt that I'd bought in LA, singing the theme to *Rawhide*. After a few days of that I started to feel pretty comfortable in the saddle, so one lunchtime I decided to take him past the Hand & Cleaver to show the locals, and maybe stop off for a cheeky one at the same time. Off we went down Butt Lane, clippety-clop, clippety-clop. Now, that summer, the Hand & Cleaver had put these picnic tables outside, so I knew I'd have an audience. And I couldn't wait to see everyone's jaws drop when I turned up.

On I went, clippety-clop, clippety-clop.

Two minutes later, I'd arrived.

Sure enough, all these people were sitting outside with their pints and their bags of pork scratchings, and they started oohing and ahhing when they saw this beautiful white horse. Then I pulled on the reins to get Turpin to stop, and started to dismount. But just as I was about to swing my leg over the saddle, a milk delivery lorry came around the bend. At first, I ignored it – that lorry used to drive up Butt Lane every week – but then a thought popped into my head: I hope that thing doesn't have air bra—

TTSSSSSSSHHHHHHHHH went the lorry.

The second those air brakes went off, Turpin's ears went back and he took off like a fucking Grand National winner. First he bolted in the direction of the lorry, with me hanging on to the saddle for dear life, one foot out of the stirrups, my cowboy hat dangling from my neck by the strap. Then he realised he was going in the wrong direction, so he turned around and started galloping back towards the farm. He charged past the Hand & Cleaver at such a fucking speed, the faces of the people outside were just a blur. Meanwhile, I was screaming at the top of my lungs, 'Staaarghp! You *fucker*! Staaarghp!' Which is exactly what he did, as soon as he got back to his paddock – he stopped dead, sending me flying over his head and a fence.

I landed in a cowpat.

Turpin got a new owner after that.

Then, a few days later, I killed the vicar. Or at least I *thought* I did.

It was an accident.

You see, in those days, out in the countryside, vicars would make house calls. They didn't need a reason to come and see you. You'd just hear a knock on your door and there would be a bloke in his frock and his dog collar, wanting to talk about the weather.

So one day, while I was down the pub, the vicar came round to Bulrush Cottage for one of his visits, and Thelma invited him in for a cup of tea. The trouble was, Bulrush Cottage wasn't set up for entertaining vicars – there were beer cans and shotguns and bongs all over the place – and Thelma didn't have a clue what to feed him, either. So she rummaged around in the kitchen until she found this nasty-looking cake in an old tin. With no better option, she gave him a slice, even though it looked and tasted like shit.

What Thelma had forgotten was that the week before, my local dope dealer had given me some dodgy hash. It was stale or something, so it was crap to smoke, but it was still as potent as ever. And rather than letting it go to waste, I'd grated it into a bowl with some cake mix and baked it. The trouble was, the lump of dope was enormous, and I only had half a tin of cake mix in the cupboard, so the cake ended up being about 80 per cent dope and 20 per cent mix. I almost barfed when I tasted it.

'See this tin?' I remember saying to Thelma. 'Don't let *anyone* touch it.'

She mustn't have been listening.

All she knew was that there was a tin with a skull and crossbones marked on it, with some cake inside, and that she had a vicar to feed. So she gave him a slice.

He'd just swallowed his last mouthful when I got back from

the pub. The second I saw him sitting there on the sofa with the little plate in front of him and crumbs everywhere, I knew it was bad news.

'That really was a delicious slice of cake. Thank you very much, Mrs Osbourne,' the vicar was saying. 'Would you mind if I had another?'

'Oh, not at all!' said Thelma.

'Thelma,' I said, 'I don't think we have any more cake.'

'Yes, we do, John, it's in the kitch—'

'WE. DON'T. HAVE. MORE. CAKE.'

'Oh, I don't want to be any trouble,' said the vicar, standing up. Then he started to dab his brow with a handkerchief. Then he turned a funny colour.

I knew exactly what was coming next. You see, eating dope is very different to smoking it – it affects your *whole body*, not just your head. And it takes only the tiniest bit to send you over the edge.

'Oh *my*,' he said. 'I think I'm feeling a little—'

BOOM!

'Fuck! Vicar down!' I shouted, rushing over to see if he was still breathing. Then I turned to look at Thelma. 'What the *fuck* were you thinking?' I said. '*He's gonna die!* I told you not to touch that cake. He's just eaten enough Afghan hash to knock out a bleedin' elephant!'

'How was I supposed to know the cake was dodgy?'

'Because I told you!'

'No, you didn't.'

'It's in a tin with a skull and crossbones on the top!'

'So what are we going to do?' said Thelma, turning white.

'We're going to have to move the body, that's what we're going to have to do,' I said. 'Here, take his legs.'

'Where are we taking him?'

'Back to wherever he lives.'

So we carried the vicar to his car, put him on the back seat, found his address in the glove compartment, and I drove him home. He was out cold. Part of me honestly thought he was a goner, although I'd been drinking most of the day, so I can't say I was thinking completely straight. All I knew is that for a man of the cloth – or anyone else – that much of my hash in one go could be lethal. But I kept telling myself that he'd just wake up with a really bad hangover, and we'd be OK.

When I got to his house I dragged him out of his car and propped him up on the steps to the front door. If I'd have been cleverer, I would have wiped my fingerprints off the car, but I just felt so terrible about what had happened, and I so badly wanted to believe that he'd be fine, I can honestly say it never even entered my head.

Still, I spent the entire night lying awake, waiting for the sirens. Clearly, I'd be the first person to get a knock on the door in the middle of the night if they did any tests on the vicar's body. Who else in his parish would have given him a lethal slice of hash cake? But there were no sirens that night. And none the next day, either.

Then more days passed. Still nothing.

I was out of my fucking mind with guilt. So was Thelma.

But I didn't want to go anywhere near the vicarage – it might look a bit suspicious – so every time I went to the Hand & Cleaver I'd make subtle enquiries. 'Anyone bumped into the vicar lately?' I'd say, all casual. 'He's a nice bloke, that vicar, isn't he? I wonder what his sermon will be about on Sunday.' Eventually someone mentioned that he must be off sick, 'cos he'd missed church and no one had seen him for a while.

That's it, I thought. I killed him. I wondered if I should turn myself in. 'It was an accident, Your Honour,' I imagined myself saying to the judge. 'A terrible, terrible accident.' This went on for at least a week.

Then, one day, I walked into the pub and there he was, at the bar, in his frock, sipping a cranberry juice.

I almost hugged the bloke and gave him a kiss.

'Oh, er, hello there, Vicar,' I said, going light in the head with relief.

'Ah, Mr Osbourne,' he said, shaking my hand. 'You know the funniest thing? I can't remember how I got home from your house the other day. And the next morning I had this terrible, terrible flu.'

'I'm very sorry to hear that, Vicar.'

'Yes, yes, a *very* nasty business, that flu.'

'I'm sure.'

'I've never had flu like it.'

'Well, I'm glad you're feeling bett—'

'I was having hallucinations for three days, you know? The most curious experience. I convinced myself that Martians had landed on the Vicarage lawn and were trying to organise a tombola.'

'That's terrible, Vicar. I hope you're feeling better now.'

'Oh, much better, thank you. Although I must have put on three stone this week, I've been so incredibly hungry.'

'Listen, Vicar,' I said. 'If there's anything I can do for the church, anything at all, just let me know, OK?'

'Oh, how kind of you. Do you play the organ, by any chance?'

'Er, no.'

'But you are in some kind of pop group, aren't you?'

'Yes, I am.'

'Tell me, what do you call yourselves?'

'Black Sabbath.'

'Oh.' The vicar frowned for a while. Then he looked at me and said, 'That's a rather peculiar name, isn't it?'

6

The End is Nigh

We recorded the next Black Sabbath album in a haunted house, out in the middle of absolutely fucking nowhere. I don't know whose brilliant idea that was, but it wasn't mine, that's for sure. The name of the place was Clearwell Castle. It was in the Forest of Dean, on the Welsh border, and it scared the crap out of us from day one. It had a moat, a portcullis, four-poster beds in the rooms, big fireplaces everywhere, animal heads on the walls, and a big old dark musty dungeon, which we used as our rehearsal room. It had been built in 1728 on the site of an old Tudor manor house, and the locals told us that a headless figure would roam the corridors at night, moaning and wailing. We just laughed it off, but as soon as we'd unpacked our bags, we all started to get the willies, big time. At least that took the pressure off us, as far as the next album was concerned. We were more worried about sleeping alone in these spooky old rooms with swords and armour on the walls than coming up with another million-selling LP. We weren't so much the Lords of Darkness as the Lords of Chickenshit when it came to that kind of thing. I remember when we went to see *The Exorcist* that Christmas in Philadelphia: we were so freaked out, we had to go and watch *The Sting* afterwards to take our minds off it. Even then, we all ended up sleeping in the same hotel room, because we were scared out of our minds. It's funny, because years later Linda Blair – who played the satanic kid in that movie – ended up dating my mate Glenn Hughes from Deep Purple. She definitely liked musicians, it turned out. She even went out with Ted Nugent once. But she wouldn't go near me.

Not a fucking chance.

Clearwell Castle certainly wasn't our first choice of venue for making the new album. The plan had initially been to go back to the Bel Air mansion to write the next record, but then we found out we wouldn't be able to do any recording in LA, because Stevie Wonder had installed a giant synthesizer in our favourite room at the Record Plant. So that idea was shelved. Probably a good job, too: we'd almost killed ourselves with cocaine the last time we'd made a record in LA. At Clearwell Castle, meanwhile, the only danger was scaring ourselves to death.

And of course we tried very, *very* hard to do just that.

We hadn't been there a day before the practical jokes started. I was the first culprit: I realised that if you put a cartridge in our eight-track machine and turned down the volume all the way, when it reached the end of a song it would make this loud *CHA-CHUNK-CHICK* noise, which would echo off the stone walls. So I hid the machine under Tony's bed. Just before he turned in for the night – after we'd spent the evening putting the willies up each other with a seance in the dungeon – I sneaked into his room, pressed 'play', and set the volume to zero. Then I ran out and hid in the room next door.

Eventually I heard Tony get into bed.

I waited.

Then, one by one, the lights in the castle went out, until it was pitch black. Apart from the occasional creak from the rafters, and the wind rattling the windows, there was just this eerie silence.

I waited.

And waited.

Then, out of the darkness: *CHA-CHUNK-CHICK.*

All I heard from Tony's room was '*AAAAGGGGGGHHH-HHH!*' and then a thump as he fell out of bed. Then the door burst open and Tony came charging out in his underpants, screaming, 'There's something in my fucking room! There's something in my fucking room!'

I didn't stop laughing for days.

But as much as the castle might have taken our minds off things, it didn't help with the songwriting. The problem was that *Vol. 4* had been a classic – by Black Sabbath's standards, anyway. Which meant we wanted the follow-up to be another classic. But you can't control that. To a certain extent, you've just got to be in the right place at the right time. I mean, I don't think Michael Jackson sat down one day and said to himself, 'Y'know what? Next year I'm gonna write an album called *Thriller*, and every song will be a corker, and then I'll flog a million copies of it every week.' You can't plan that kind of thing.

Then again, we were terrified of becoming one of those bands who started off with a few albums that people thought were amazing, only to follow them up with one turd after another. None of us could really believe how our lives had changed since coming back from the Star Club in 1969. I think we all expected to wake up one day and find that it was all over, that our little scam had been exposed.

Personally, one of my biggest worries was about us moving too far away from what our fans wanted. I mean, I knew we couldn't keep on doing 'Iron Man' for ever – we had to challenge ourselves – but we couldn't put brass bands on every track or start doing abstract jazz bollocks, either. The name of the band was Black Sabbath – and as long as we were called

Black Sabbath, it was gonna be hard to be accepted as anything else.

It's like the guy who plays Batman in the movies. He might be a great actor, but if he goes off and plays a gay waiter in his next role, people will spend the entire movie wondering when he's gonna rip off his tuxedo, put on a rubber suit, and jump out of the window.

So we had to be very careful.

To be honest with you, for a few days at Clearwell Castle, it felt like we didn't know how to move on. For the first time ever, Tony seemed to be having a hard time coming up with new material. Which meant no riffs. And without riffs, we had no songs. It was that Dutch band, Golden Earring, that saved us in the end. We were listening to their latest album, *Moontan*, and something just clicked in Tony's head. A couple of days later, he came down to the dungeon and started playing the riff to 'Sabbath Bloody Sabbath'. Like I said: every time we thought Tony couldn't do it again, he did it again – *and better.* From that moment on, there was no more writer's block.

Which was a huge relief.

But we still couldn't concentrate in that bloody castle. We wound each other up so much none of us got any sleep. You'd just lie there with your eyes wide open, expecting an empty suit of armour to walk into your bedroom at any second and shove a dagger up your arse.

And the fucking seances we kept holding didn't help. I dunno what we were thinking, 'cos they're really dodgy, those things. You've got no idea who's pushing the glass, and then you end up convincing yourself that your great aunt Sally is standing behind you with a sheet over her head. And when you're doing it in a dungeon, it's even worse.

Tony was the one who pulled the most pranks. One day he found an old dressmaker's dummy in a cupboard, put a frock and a wig on it, then threw it out of a third-floor window just as Bill and Geezer were coming back from the pub. They almost shit their pants. Bill legged it so fast back up the driveway, he must have broken the land speed record. Another time – I wasn't around to witness this, but someone told me about it – Tony tied a piece of white thread to an old model sailing ship that was in one of the roadies' bedrooms, and he fed the thread under the door and into another room. Then he waited until the roadie was in there alone and he gave it a little tug. The roadie looked up, and there on this dusty mantelpiece – which was supported by two gargoyles – the ship was 'sailing' all by itself. He ran out of that room and refused ever to go back in.

Bill got the worst of it, though. One night he'd been on the cider and had passed out on the sofa. We got this full-length mirror and lifted it over him, so it was only a few inches from his face. Then we poked him until he woke up. The second he opened his eyes, all he could see was himself staring back. To this day, I've never heard a grown man scream so loud. He must have thought he'd woken up in hell.

Bill started going to bed with a dagger after that.

The jokes got out of hand eventually. People started driving home at night instead of sleeping in their rooms. The funny thing is, the only genuinely dangerous thing that happened during our time at Clearwell Castle was when I got loaded and feel asleep with my boot in the fire. All I can remember is waking up at three o'clock in the morning with a funny feeling at the end of my leg, then jumping up, screaming, and hopping around the room with this flaming boot, looking for something wet to put it in. Everyone else thought it was hilarious.

Geezer just looked at me and said, 'Gis a light, Ozzy.'

But the smile was soon wiped off his face when an ember flew off my boot and set the carpet on fire. All I can say is: thank God for the vat of cider that Bill kept behind his drum kit, which we used to douse the flames. I'm amazed it put the fire out, to be honest with you. I'd tasted Bill's cider, so I half expected it to go up like a Molotov cocktail.

By the time we left Clearwell Castle, we at least had most of the new album written. So we moved on to Morgan Studios, just off Willesden High Road in north London, to finish it off.

Morgan Studios was a very popular place at the time, so whenever you did any work there, you'd run into other bands, and usually you'd end up going over to the little caff they had in there – it had a dartboard and served booze – and having a bit of a laugh. This time, though, when I went over to say hello to the band working next door to us, my heart sank. It was Yes. While we were working on our album in Studio 4, they were making *Tales from Topographic Oceans* in Studio 3. They were hippies, so they'd brought in all of these cut-out cows to make their recording space look 'earthy'. I later found out that the cows even had electrically powered udders. No fucking kidding. They also had bales of hay all over the place, a white picket fence, and a little barn in the corner – like a kid's plaything. I just said to myself, 'And I thought Geezer was weird.'

During the whole time we were at Morgan Studios, the only member of Yes I ever saw in the caff was Rick Wakeman, their superstar keyboard player. He was famous for doing warp-speed Moog solos while dressed in a wizard's cape, and it turned out he was the only regular bloke in Yes. In fact, he was *always* in the caff – usually drinking heavily – and he wasn't into any of that cut-out-cow, hippy bullshit. He'd rather get out of his box and play darts with me.

We used to have a right few laughs, me and Rick – and we've remained friends to this day.

The bloke's a born storyteller. Hanging out with him is like *An Evening with* . . . He once told me that he'd legally changed his name to Michael Schumacher in case the cops ever pulled him over for speeding and asked for his name. Then, when PC Plod told him to fuck off and demanded to see his driving licence, there it would be, in black and white. You've got to admire that kind of dedication to winding up the boys in blue.

He had a collection of about thirty Rollers and Bentleys back then – although I don't know when he ever drove 'em, because whenever I saw him he was shitfaced. He was almost as bad as me. Then, a few years later, he had a bunch of heart attacks in a row and had to give it up.

You could tell that Rick was bored out of his mind with *Tales from Topographic Oceans*. One of the funniest stories I ever heard about him was from the time when Yes went on tour with that album. He got so fed up that halfway through one of the eight-hour twiddly bits, he got his roadie to order a curry and bring it to him on stage. Then he sat there at his keyboards, eating a chicken vindaloo under his cape while smoking a fag.

He didn't last much longer in Yes after that.

Anyway, one day at Morgan Studios, when Rick seemed even more bored than usual, I asked him if he'd like to come over to Studio 4 and hear some of our new tracks. I remember playing the melody of 'Sabbra Cadabra' to him on my ARP 2600 synthesizer. There I was, murdering this riff with one grubby finger, going duh-duh-*duh*, duh-duh-duh-*duh*, with Rick watching me. And when I finally stopped, Rick just went, '*Hmm*, maybe it would sound better like this . . .' leaned over the keyboard, and went diddly-diddly-diddly-diddly-dud-diddly-*duh*. His fingers moved so fast, I swear you couldn't see the fucking things.

I asked him right then if he'd play on the album, and he said he'd love to, as long as we paid him his usual fee.

'How much?' I asked.

'Two pints of Director's best bitter.'

Apart from Rick, though, Yes lived like monks. They didn't eat meat. They looked like they had yoga classes every day. And you'd never see them getting boozed up. The only rock 'n' roll thing they did was smoke dope – and, as it happened, I'd just got another shipment of hash in from Afghanistan, and it was phenomenal. Really heavy-duty shit. Now I considered myself a bit of dope connoisseur in those days, and I was interested to see what Yes thought of this stuff. So one morning I took my brick of hash to the studio, went over to see Yes, and gave them a big lump of it. For some reason, the only one of them who was missing that day was Rick.

'Here, lads,' I said. 'Stick a bit of *this* in your rollies.'

They said they'd try it immediately.

I went back to Studio 4, had a couple of joints myself, did some double-tracking for the vocals, nipped over to the caff for a cheeky five or six at lunchtime, came back, had another joint, then decided to check how Yes were doing.

But when I went into Studio 3, it was empty.

I found the chick from the reception desk and said, 'Have you see Yes anywhere?'

'Oh, they all started to feel very unwell around lunchtime. They had to go home.'

By now, our album had a title – *Sabbath Bloody Sabbath*, after the track that had broken Tony's writer's block – and it was another stonker. Our last truly great album, I think. Even the artwork was spot on: it showed a bloke lying on his bed being attacked by demons in his sleep, with a skull and the number 666 above his head. I fucking loved that cover. And with the music we'd managed to strike just the right balance between our old heaviness and our new, 'experimental' side. On the one hand, you had tracks like 'Spiral Architect', which featured a full orchestra, and 'Fluff', which sounded almost like the Shadows (it was named in honour of Alan 'Fluff' Freeman, the DJ who always played our records on Radio 1). On the other, there was 'A National Acrobat', which was so heavy it was like being hit over the head with a lump of concrete. I even got one of my own songs on the album: 'Who Are You?' I'd written it one night at Bulrush Cottage while I was loaded and fiddling around with a Revox tape machine and my ARP 2600.

We were all happy with *Sabbath Bloody Sabbath*, I think. Even Patrick Meehan and the record company were happy. Which meant only one thing, of course: things could only go downhill from there.

I should have known that bad things were about to happen to Black Sabbath when we flew to America in 1974 and the bloke sitting next to me croaked it halfway across the Atlantic.

One minute I was hearing this choking noise – 'uh, ugh, urrrgh'. The next I was sitting next to a corpse. I didn't know what the fuck to do, so I pressed the button to call for a flight attendant.

'Yes, sir, can I help you?' said the chick, all prim and proper.

'This bloke's a goner, I reckon,' I said, pointing at the lump beside me.

'Sorry, sir?'

'He's kicked the bucket,' I said, holding up the bloke's floppy left arm. 'Look at 'im. Dead as a fucking dodo.'

The stewardess started to panic. 'What happened?' she hissed, trying to cover him with a blanket. 'Did he seem unwell?'

'Well, he was making a bit of a choking noise,' I said. 'I just thought his peanuts had gone down the wrong way. Then he turned white, his eyes rolled back in his head, and Bob's your uncle.'

'Look,' said the stewardess quietly. 'We're going to prop him up here against the window with this pillow. Please don't mention this to the other passengers. We don't want anyone panicking. To compensate for your inconvenience, we can reseat you in first class, if you'd like.'

'What's the difference between business and first?' I asked.

'Champagne.'

'Magic.'

That was the beginning of The End.

What I remember most about the tour to promote *Sabbath Bloody Sabbath* is everyone starting to get pissed off. By now Patrick Meehan had stopped being the magician on the end of the phone line who could get you a Rolls-Royce or a horse or a Scalextric set, and had started to become the annoying flash bastard who never gave you a straight answer when you asked him how much dough you were making.

Meanwhile, Tony was grumbling about doing all the work in the studio, which meant he had no personal life. He had a point. But then again, Tony loved being in the studio – he'd even started to produce the albums himself. Personally, I could never stand all the sitting around, smoking cigarettes, and listening to the same three seconds of guitar solo over and over again. I still can't handle it to this day. It drives me fucking nuts. Once I've done my thing, I have to get out into the fresh air. But as technology improved during the seventies, the temptation was always to add one more track, then another, then another . . . Tony couldn't get enough of all that stuff. He had the patience for it. And no one ever argued with him, because he was the band's unofficial leader.

Geezer was also getting fed up, because he was tired of me asking him for lyrics all the time. I can see how that must have got on his tits after a while, but the guy was a genius. When we were at Morgan Studios, I remember calling him when he was taking a day off at his country house. I said, 'C'mon, Geezer, I need some words for "Spiral Architect".' He grumbled a bit, told me to call him back in an hour, and put the phone down. When I spoke to him again, he said, 'Have you got a pen? Good. Write this down: "Sorcerers of madness/Selling me their time/Child of God sitting in the sun . . ."'

I said, 'Geezer, are you just reading this out of a book or something?'

I couldn't believe it. The bloke had written a masterpiece in the time it took me to read one sentence.

I told him, 'Keep that up and we'll have the whole bloody album done by five o'clock.'

One reason why we weren't getting on so well is that we'd all started to develop these coked-up, rock-star egos.

It was happening to a lot of bands in those days. When we did the CalJam Festival at the Ontario Motor Speedway in 1974, for example, there was all kinds of bollocks going on backstage with the other bands. Things like, 'Well, if he's got a pinball machine, then I want a pinball machine,' or 'If he's got a quadraphonic sound system, then I want a quadraphonic sound system.' People were starting to think they were gods. I mean, the scale of that CalJam thing was unbelievable: about 250,000 fans, with the performances 'simulcast' on FM radio and the ABC TV network. Rock 'n' roll had never been done on that scale before. You should have seen the rig Emerson, Lake and Palmer had. Halfway through their set, Keith Emerson did a solo on a grand piano while it was lifted off the stage and spun around, end-over-end.

CalJam was a good gig for us, actually.

We hadn't played live for a while, so we rehearsed in our hotel room without any amps. The next day we flew in by helicopter, 'cos all the roads were blocked. Then we just ripped through our set, with me wearing these silver moon boots and yellow leggings.

Deep Purple didn't have such a good time, though. Ritchie Blackmore hated TV cameras – he said they got between him and the audience – so after a couple of songs he smashed the neck of his guitar through the lens of one of them, and then set his amp on fire. It was a heavy scene, and the whole band had to fuck off quick in a helicopter, because the fire marshals were after them. ABC must have been well pissed off, too. Those cameras cost an arm and a leg. I remember being on the flight back to England with Ritchie, actually. It was fucking crazy. I had four grams of coke hidden down my sock, and I had to get rid of it before we landed, so I started handing it out to the air hostesses. They were completely whacked out on the stuff after a while. My in-flight meal took a flight of its own at one point. Can you even *imagine* doing that kind of thing nowadays? When I think about it, I shudder.

Another crazy thing that happened around that time was getting to know Frank Zappa in Chicago. We were doing a gig there, and it turned out that he was staying at our hotel. All of us looked up to Zappa – especially Geezer – because he seemed like he was from another planet. At the time he'd just released this quadraphonic album called *Apostrophe (')*, which had a track on it called 'Don't Eat the Yellow Snow'. Fucking classic.

Anyway, so there we were at this hotel, and we ended up hanging out with his band in the bar. Then the next day we got word that Frank wanted us to come to his Independence Day party, which was going to be held that night at a restaurant around the corner.

We could hardly wait.

So come eight o'clock, off we went to meet Frank. When we arrived at the restaurant, there he was, sitting at this massive table, surrounded by his band. We introduced ourselves, then we all started to get pissed. But it was really weird, because the guys in his band kept coming up to me and saying, 'You got any blow? Don't tell Frank I asked you. He's straight. Hates that stuff. But have you got any? Just a toot, to keep me going.'

I didn't want to get involved, so I just went, 'Nah,' even though I had a big bag of the stuff in my pocket.

Later, after we'd finished eating, I was sitting next to Frank when two waiters burst out of the kitchen, wheeling a massive cake in front of them. The whole restaurant went quiet. You should have seen that cake, man. It was made into the shape of a naked chick with two big, icing-covered tits – and her legs were spread wide apart. But the craziest thing about it was that they'd rigged up a little pump, so champagne was squirting out of her vagina. You could have heard a pin drop in that place until the band finally started to sing 'America the Beautiful'. Then everyone had to have a ceremonial drink of the champagne, starting with Frank.

When it was my turn, I took a long gulp, screwed up my face, and said, 'Ugh, tastes like piss.'

Everyone thought that was hilarious.

Then Frank leaned over and whispered in my ear, 'Got any blow? It's not for me – it's for my bodyguard.'

'Are you serious?' I asked him.

'Sure. But don't tell the band. They're straight.'

I saw Frank again a few years later, after he'd done a gig at the Birmingham Odeon. When the show was over, he asked me, 'Is there anywhere we can get something to eat in this town? I'm staying at the Holiday Inn, and the food's terrible.'

I told him, 'At this time of night, there's only the curry house on Bristol Street, but I don't recommend it.'

Frank just shrugged and said, 'Oh, that'll do, I'll have a go.'

So we all went to this dodgy Indian joint – me, Frank, Thelma and some Japanese chick that Frank was hanging out with at the time. I told Frank that the only thing on the menu he shouldn't order, under any circumstances, was the steak. He nodded, looked at the menu for a while, then ordered the steak. When it arrived, I just sat there and watched him try to eat it.

'Like old boots, is it?' I said.

'No, actually,' replied Frank, dabbing his mouth with a napkin. 'More like new ones.'

*

By the mid-seventies, everything had changed with Black Sabbath. In the early days, we used to hang out with each other all the time, and whenever we arrived in a new place for a gig, we'd walk around the town like a little gang, trying out the pubs and clubs, hitting on chicks, getting pissed. But as time went on, we saw less and less of each other. When me and Bill did our road trips, for example, we hardly spent any time with Tony or Geezer. Then even me and Bill started to drift apart. I was the noisy fucker who would always be throwing parties and having chicks in my room and getting up to all sorts of debauchery, and Bill would just want to stay in his bed and sleep.

After all that time on the road, we'd just had enough of each other's company. But when we didn't spend any time together, all our problems grew in our heads, and we stopped communicating.

Then, all of a sudden, everything just blew up. For a start, the publishing rights to a lot of our early work had already been sold to a company called Essex Music 'in perpetuity', which was a posh way of saying for ever.

And there'd been other signs of trouble, like when London & County Bank went bust. I don't know exactly what the deal was – I'm hardly the financial brain of Britain – but I know I had to sell the deeds to the land I'd bought from the cross-dressing farmer in order to save Bulrush Cottage. If me and Thelma hadn't paid for the land with our own money, we'd have been fucked.

The biggest problem was our management. At some point we realised that we'd been stitched up. Although in theory Meehan would send us an allowance for whatever we wanted, whenever we asked for it, we didn't actually have any control. We were supposed to have our own individual bank accounts, but it turned out they didn't exist. So I'd have to go to his office and ask for a thousand quid or whatever. He'd say, 'OK,' and the cheque would turn up in the post. But after a while the cheques started to bounce.

So we fired him. Then all this legal crap started, with lawsuits flying around all over the place. While we were working on the follow-up to *Sabbath Bloody Sabbath* – which we ended up calling *Sabotage*, in reference to Meehan's bullshit – writs were being delivered to us at the mixing desk. That was when we came to the conclusion that lawyers rip you off just as much as managers do. You get charged for every penny they spend while they're working for you, down to the last paperclip. And they're happy to fuck around in court for the rest of their lives, as long as someone's paying the bills. If it takes fifty years to win, that's fine, as far as those guys are concerned.

We had this one lawyer working for us, and I ended up hating him. I just couldn't stand the bloke because he was taking the piss. When we were recording *Sabotage* in Morgan Studios, he came over to see us one day and said, 'Gentlemen, I'm going to buy you all a drink.' I thought, Wow, I can't believe this, the guy's actually getting his wallet out for something. Then, at the end of the meeting, he took out this little notepad and started adding up what we'd all had, so he could bill us later. 'Right. Ozzy, you had two beers, so that's sixty pence,' he went, 'and Tony, you had one beer and—'

I said, 'You're fucking *joking*, right?'

But of course he wasn't. That's what lawyers do. They grease you down and stick their fist up your arse.

You can hear the frustration on *Sabotage*. There's some heavy-duty shit on that album. One incredible track is 'Supertzar'. I remember the day it was recorded: I walked into Morgan Studios and there was an entire forty-member choir in there along with an eighty-six-year-old harpist. They were making a noise like God conducting the soundtrack to the end of the world. I didn't even attempt to put a vocal over the top of it.

One song I'm very proud of on that album is 'The Writ'. I wrote most of lyrics myself, which felt a bit like seeing a shrink. All the anger I felt towards Meehan came pouring out. But y'know what? All that bullshit he pulled on us didn't get him anywhere in the end. You should see him now: he looks like a fat, boozy old fuck. But I don't hate him. Hating people isn't a productive way of living. When all's said and done, I don't wish the bloke any harm. I'm still here, y'know? I still have a career. So what's the point in hating anyone? There's enough hate in the world as it is, without me adding to it. And I got a song out of it, at least.

Aside from 'The Writ', I can't say I'm very proud of much else that happened in that period.

Like pulling a gun on Bill while I was having a bad acid trip at Bulrush Cottage. The gun wasn't loaded. But he didn't know that, and I didn't tell him. He was very cool about it at the time, but we've never talked about it since, which means it was probably quite a big deal.

I had a few bad acid trips around that time, actually. Another night we were at Fields Farm, Bill's old rented house, which a couple of roadies had taken over, and we were getting badly fucked up for some reason. There was a terrible vibe that night, because a kid had just drowned in the lake on the property while pissing around in a canoe, and the cops had torn the place apart, dredging the lake for the body, and searching for drugs. Not exactly the best time to be doing acid, in other words. But that didn't stop us. All I can remember is wandering off into a field and meeting these two horses. Then one of them said to the other, 'Fuck me, that bloke can *talk*,' and I freaked out, big time.

I hit Thelma, too, which is probably the worst thing I ever did in my life. I started to get overpowering with her, and the poor woman must have been frightened to death. What made it even worse was that we'd just had our second kid – little Louis. Thelma really suffered with me, y'know, and I really regret that. If there's one thing I wish for in my life, it's that I could take it all back. But of course you never can never take violence back – of any kind – and I'll take it to the grave with me. My own parents used to fight a lot, so maybe I thought that's just what you do. But there's no excuse. One night, when I was out of my tree on booze and pills, I hit Thelma so hard I gave her a black eye. We were meeting her father the next day, and I thought, Fucking hell, he's gonna beat the crap out of me now. But all he said was, 'So which one of you won, eh?'

The saddest thing is, it wasn't until I became sober that I truly realised how disgusting my behaviour was. But I do now, trust me.

While all that fucked-up stuff was going on, we decided to make another album – this time hauling all our gear and crew to America and booking into Criteria Studios in Miami. The title we'd decided on was *Technical Ecstasy*, although I can't say I was 100 per cent enthusiastic. By now, our albums were getting ridiculously expensive to make. We'd recorded *Black Sabbath* in one day. *Sabotage* took about four thousand years. *Technical Ecstasy* didn't take quite as long, but the cost of doing it in Florida was astronomical.

At the same time as our sales were falling, the record company wasn't as interested as it used to be, we'd just got a million-dollar tax bill from the IRS in America, we couldn't afford to pay our legal bills, and we didn't have a manager. At one point, Bill was the one manning the phones. Worse than all that, though, we'd lost our direction. It wasn't the experimentation with the music. It was more that we didn't seem to know who we were any more. One minute you had an album cover like *Sabbath Bloody Sabbath*, with the bloke being attacked by demons on it, and the next you had two robots having sex while they're going up a fucking escalator, which was the artwork for *Technical Ecstasy*.

I'm not saying the album was all bad – it wasn't. For example, Bill wrote a song called 'It's Alright', which I loved. He sang it, too. He's got a great voice, Bill, and I was more than happy for him to do the honours. But I'd started to lose interest, and I kept thinking about what it would be like to have a solo career. I'd even had a T-shirt made with 'Blizzard of Ozz' written on the front. Meanwhile, in the studio, Tony was always saying, 'We've gotta sound like Foreigner,' or, 'We've gotta sound like Queen.' But I thought it was strange that the bands that we'd once influenced were now influencing us. Then again, I'd lost the plot with the booze and the drugs, and I was saying a lot of bad things, making trouble, being a dickhead.

In fact, my boozing was so bad during the *Technical Ecstasy* sessions in Florida, I checked myself into a loony bin called St George's when I got back home. It's real name was the Stafford County Asylum, but they changed it to make people feel better about being insane. It was a big old Victorian place. Dark and dingy, like the set of a science-fiction movie. The first thing the doctor said to me when I went in there was, 'Do you masturbate, Mr Osbourne?' I told him, 'I'm in here for my head, not my dick.'

I didn't last long in that place. I'm telling you, the docs in those funny farms are more bonkers than the patients.

Then Thelma bought me some chickens.

She probably thought it would help bring me down to earth. And it did, for about five minutes. But then the novelty wore off – especially when I realised that Thelma expected me to feed the fucking things and clean out their shit. So I started trying to find a reason to get rid of them.

Getting hitched in Maui, 1982. There were seven bottles of Hennessy in that cake – later, I passed out in the hotel corridor. Good job the marriage was already consummated.

Fangs for the memories!

I was on so many drugs in 1983, I was on another planet. That must be why Aimee is wearing a space suit.

With my beautiful girls.

Harley Street has some great dentists.

A bad hair day – again. Promo shot for *Bark at the Moon*.

Hitching a ride with Kelly.

Below left: With Sally, my pet donkey. She used to live with us at Outlands Cottage and watch the telly with me.

Below right: With Kelly and Aimee.

Before . . .

. . . After

Getting a load off my mind.

I'd shaved my hair off to get out of doing the gig. Sharon sent me out anyway.

After a grade-one bollocking from the missus.

A postcard from Memphis.

Another quiet night in with Mötley Crüe.

On the *QE2*, bored out of my fucking mind. Sharon was pregnant with Jack so we couldn't fly.

'Thelma,' I said to her, one morning, after I'd finally had enough. 'Where did you get those chickens from? They're broken.'

'What do you mean, they're *broken*?'

'They're not laying any eggs.'

'Well, it would help if you fed them, John. Besides, they're probably stressed out, poor things.'

'Why d'you say that?'

'Come on, John. You put up a sign beside their coop that says, "Oflag 14". I know they can't read, but still.'

'It's just a *joke*.'

'Firing warning shots over their heads every morning probably isn't helping much, either.'

'Everyone needs a bit of encouragement.'

'You're scaring the living daylights out of them. You'll give one of them a heart attack if you keep it up.'

Here's hoping, I thought.

As the weeks and months went by, I kept forgetting to feed the chickens, and they kept forgetting to lay any eggs. All I would hear from Thelma was: 'John, feed the chickens.' Or: 'John, remember to feed the chickens.' Or: 'John, did you feed the chickens?'

It was driving me fucking nuts.

I was trying to have a break – making *Technical Ecstasy* had been knackering, mainly thanks to all the boozing involved – but I couldn't get any peace. If it wasn't Thelma, it was the lawyers. If it wasn't the lawyers, it was the accountants. If it wasn't the accountants, it was the record company. And if it wasn't the record company, it was Tony or Bill or Geezer, worrying about the 'new direction' or complaining about our tax bills.

The only way I could handle it was to get loaded all the time.

Then one day I finally lost it.

I'd been up all night – a lock-in at the Hand & Cleaver,

followed by more boozing at home, then a few toots of coke, then some dope, then some more coke, then a blackout around breakfast time to refresh myself, then some coke to wake me up again. By then it was time for lunch. So I had a bottle of cough syrup, three glasses of wine, some more coke, a joint, half a packet of cigarettes and a Scotch egg. But no matter how much I put away, I couldn't get rid of this horrendous restless feeling. I'd often get that feeling after coming home from America: I'd find myself standing in the kitchen for hours, just opening and closing the fridge door; or sitting in the living room in front of the telly, flipping from one channel to the next, never watching anything.

But this time, something was different.

I was going *insane*.

There was nothing else for it: I was gonna have to go back down the Hand & Cleaver and sort myself out.

I was just about to leave the house when I heard Thelma coming down the stairs. She walked into the kitchen and said, 'I'm going to my mum's to get the kids.' I watched as she picked up a pile of *Good Housekeeping* magazines from the table and started putting them in her bag. Then she stopped and turned to look at me standing there beside the fridge in my Y-fronts and my dressing-gown, fag in mouth, giving my balls a good old scratch.

'Did you feed the chickens?' she said.

'I told you, they're broken.'

'Just feed them, John, for God's sake. Or, y'know what? Let them die – I don't care any more.'

'I'm going down the pub.'

'Wearing the terrycloth bathrobe you got for Christmas?'

'Yeah.'

'Classy, John. Very classy.'

'Have you seen my slippers?'

'Try the dog bed. I'll be back at eight.'

Next thing I knew I was staggering out of the house in a pair of wellies – I couldn't find my slippers – heading in the direction of the pub. As I walked I kept trying to tighten the cord around my dressing-gown. I didn't want to be flashing a loose bollock at any passing farmers; especially not the bearded cross-dressing loony from down the road.

When I got to the gate at the bottom of the driveway I suddenly had a change of heart. 'You know what?' I said to myself. 'I'm going to feed those chickens. Fuck it. If it keeps her happy, I'll do it.' So I turned around and started wobbling back in the direction of the house. But I was thirsty now, so I went over to where the Range Rover was parked, pulled open the door, and reached into the glove box for my emergency bottle of Scotch.

Swig. *Ahhh*. That's better! Burp.

On I went into the garden . . . But then I had another change of heart. Fuck the chickens! I thought. Not one of those little fuckers has ever laid any eggs for me! Fuck them! Fuck them all!

Swig. *Ahhh*. Burp. I lit another fag.

Then I remembered that I still hadn't finished the fag that was already in my mouth, so I flicked it into Thelma's vegetable patch. I changed direction again, this time heading towards the shed.

I threw open the door and stood there, looking up at my Benelli semi-automatic on the gun rack. I picked it up, opened the chamber to see if it was loaded – it was – then I set about stuffing the pockets of my dressing-gown full of cartridges. Next I reached up to the top shelf for the jerry can of petrol that the gardener kept there for my lawnmower – the one I used to ride to the pub every so often for a laugh (Patrick Meehan's office had got it for me, even though I'd asked them for a combine harvester).

So, with the jerry can in one hand, the shotgun in the other, and the Scotch under my arm – still puffing away on my fag – I lurched into the garden and towards the chicken coop. The sun was setting now, and the sky had gone all red and orange. In my head, the only thing I could hear was Thelma saying, 'John, feed the chickens. John, have you fed the chickens?'

Then our accountant going, 'Lads, this is serious. This is a *million-dollar* tax bill from the IRS.'

And Geezer saying, 'We're calling the album *Technical Ecstasy*. We need a new direction. We can't do that black magic shit for ever.'

It wouldn't stop.

Over and over.

'John, feed the chickens.'

'Lads, this is serious.'

'We're calling the album *Technical Ecstasy*.'

'John, did you feed the chickens?'

'A *million-dollar* tax bill.'

'John, feed the chickens!'

'We need a new direction.'

'This is serious.'

'We can't do that black magic shit for ever.'

AAAAAAAAARRRRRRRRRGGGGGGGGHHHHHHH!

When I reached the coop I put down the jerry can and the gun, knelt down by the 'Oflag 14' sign and took a look inside. The chickens clucked and nodded their little beaks.

'Anyone laid any eggs?' I asked – like I didn't already know the answer to that fucking question. 'Didn't think so,' I said, standing up. 'Too bad.'

Then I picked up the gun.

Safety off.

Aim.

Cluck-cluck.

Bang-bang!

Aim.

Squawk!

Bang-bang!

Aim.

Squaaawwwwwwwwwwkkkkkkkkkk!!!!!

BANG!

The sound of the gun was fucking deafening, and it echoed across the fields for what seemed like miles in all directions. And with every shot there was a white flash that lit up the coop and the garden around it, followed by a strong whiff of gunpowder. I was feeling much better now.

Much, much better.

Swig. *Ahhh*. Burp.

The chickens – the ones who hadn't already gone off to meet their maker – were going nuts.

I waited a moment for the smoke to clear.

Aim.

Cluck-cluck.

Bang-bang!

Aim.

Squawk!

Bang-bang!

Aim.

Squaaawwwwwwwwwwkkkkkkkkkk!!!!!

BANG!

By the time I was done there was blood and feathers and bits of beak all over the fucking place. It looked as though someone had thrown a bucket of chicken guts at me and then emptied a pillow over my head. My dressing-gown was ruined. But I felt fucking fabulous – like someone had just lifted a three-ton anvil off my back. I put down the shotgun, picked up the jerry can, and started emptying it over what was left of the chickens. I lit up another fag, took a long drag, stood well back, then flicked it into the coop.

Whooooooooosssshhhhh!

Flames everywhere.

Then I took the leftover cartridges out of my pocket and started throwing them into the fire.

Bang!

Bang!

Bang-bang-bang!

'Heh-heh-heh,' I went.

Then something moved behind me.

I almost fell over the gun and shot myself in the nuts with fright. I turned around to see a chicken legging it away from me. That little fucker! I heard myself letting out this weird, psycho noise – 'Eeeeaaaargggghhhh!' – then, without even thinking, I set off after it. I didn't know what the fuck was wrong with me, or why I was doing what I was doing. All I knew was that I was possessed with this insane, uncontrollable rage at all chickenkind. *Kill the chicken! Kill the chicken! Kill the chicken!*

But let me tell you something: it's not fucking easy, catching a chicken, especially when it's getting dark and you haven't slept for twenty-four hours and you're fucked up on a shitload of booze and coke and you're wearing a dressing-gown and wellies.

So I clomped back over to the shed, found a sword, and came out with it raised above my head, Samurai-style. 'Die, you chicken bastard, die!' I shouted, as the chicken made a last-ditch run for the fence at the end of the garden, its little beak nodding so fast it looked like its head could fly off at any second. I'd almost caught up with it when the front door of my neighbour's house burst open. Then this little old lady – Mrs Armstrong, I think her name was – came running out with a garden hoe in her hands. She was used to all kinds of crazy shit going on at Bulrush Cottage, but this time, I don't even think she could believe it. With the coop burning and the rounds from my gun exploding every few minutes, it was like a scene from an old World War Two movie.

Bang!

Bang!

Bang-bang-bang!

At first I didn't even notice her. I was too busy chasing the chicken, which ended up bolting under the fence and legging it up Mrs Armstrong's driveway, out of her gate, and down Butt Lane in the direction of the pub. Then I looked up and our eyes met. I must have been quite a sight, standing there in my dressing gown with a crazed look on my face, splattered with blood, and holding up a sword, my garden on fire behind me.

'Ah, good evening, Mr Osbourne,' she said. 'I see you're back from America.'

There was a long silence. More cartridges exploded behind me. I didn't know what to say, so I just nodded.

'*Unwinding*, are we?' she asked.

I wasn't the only one going out of my mind with the stress of the band imploding.

I remember one time, Geezer phoned me up and said, 'Look, Ozzy, I'm sick of touring just to pay the lawyers. Before we go on the road again, I wanna know what we're gonna get.'

And I said to him, 'Y'know what, Geezer, you're right. Let's call a meeting.'

So we had a meeting, and I was the first one to speak up.

'Look, lads,' I said, 'I think it's crazy that we're doing gigs to pay the lawyers. What d'you think, Geezer?'

Geezer just shrugged and said, 'Dunno.'

That was it.

I'd had enough. There didn't seem to be any point any more. None of us was getting on. We were spending more time in meetings with lawyers than we were writing songs; we were all exhausted from touring the world pretty much non-stop for six years; and we were out of our minds on booze and drugs. The final straw was a meeting with Colin Newman, our accountant, where he told us that if we didn't settle our tax bills soon, we'd be going to prison. In those days, the tax rate for people like us was something like 80 per cent in the UK and 70 per cent in America, so you can imagine the amount of dough we owed. And after the taxes, we still had our expenses to pay. We were broke, basically. Wiped out. Geezer might not have had the bollocks to say anything in front of the others, but he was right: there was no point in being in a rock 'n' roll band just to worry about money and writs all the time.

So one day I just walked out of a rehearsal and didn't come back.

Then I got a call from Norman, my sister Jean's husband.

Now, he's a lovely guy, Norman – in many ways the older brother I never had. But whenever he called, it usually meant something heavy was going down with the family.

This time was no different.

'It's your dad,' said Norman. 'You should go and see him.'

'What d'you mean?'

'He's not well, John. He might not make it through the night.'

I immediately felt sick and numb. Losing a parent had always been my worst fear, ever since I was a little kid, when I would go up to my dad's bed and shake him awake because I thought he wasn't breathing. Now the fear was coming true. I knew my dad had been ill, but I hadn't thought he was at death's door.

When I pulled myself together, I got in the car and went to see him.

My whole family was already there by his bedside, including my mum, who was just absolutely devastated.

Dad was riddled with cancer, it turned out. It was out of

control, because he'd refused to go and see a doctor until they had to carry him away in an ambulance. He'd stopped working only a few months before. He was sixty-four, and they'd offered him an early retirement deal. 'I'm gonna have some time to do the garden now,' he'd told me. So he did the garden. But as soon as he'd done the garden, that was it. Game over.

I was terrified of seeing him, to be honest with you, because I knew what to expect. My dad's younger brother had died the year before from liver cancer. I'd visited him on the ward and it had shocked the crap out of me, so much so that I'd burst into tears. He bore no resemblance to the guy I'd known. He didn't even look human.

When I got to the hospital this time, my dad had just come out of surgery, and he was up and running. He looked all right, and he managed a smile. They had him on the happy juice, I imagine. Although, as one of my aunties used to say, 'God always gives you one good day before you die.' We talked a little, but not much. The funny thing is, when I was growing up, my dad never used to say anything like, 'You wanna watch those cigarettes,' or, 'Stop going to the pub all the time,' but that day he told me, 'Do something about your drinking, John. It's too bloody much. And stop taking sleeping pills.'

'I've left Black Sabbath,' I told him.

'They're finished then,' he said. Then he fell asleep.

The next day, he took a dive. One of the worst things about it was seeing my mum so distraught. In hospitals back then, the sicker you got, the further they moved you from the other patients. By the end of the day, my dad had been shoved into this broom cupboard in the corner, with mops and buckets and tubs of bleach all over the place. They'd put bandages around his hands like he was a boxer, and they'd tied him to the bars of this giant cot, because he'd kept pulling out his IV tube. It really fucked me up, seeing him like that, the man I adored, the man who'd taught me that even if you don't have a good education, you can still have good manners. At least he was loaded on all kinds of drugs, so he wasn't in too much pain. When he saw me, he smiled, stuck his thumbs up through his bandages and went, 'Speeeeed!' – it was the only drug he knew the name of. Mind you, then he said, 'Take these fucking pipes out of me, John, they hurt.'

He died at 11.20 p.m. on 20 January 1978: in the same hospital, on the same date, at the same time as Jess had been born six years earlier. That coincidence still floors me to this day. The cause of death was given as 'carcinoma of the oesophagus', although he also had cancer of the intestines and cancer of the bowel. He hadn't eaten or gone to the bog by himself for thirteen weeks. Jean was with him when he passed away. The doctors told her they wanted to find out why their Frankenstein experiment on him the previous day in surgery hadn't worked, but she wouldn't let them do an autopsy.

I was in the car, on my way to Bill's house, listening to 'Baker Street' by Gerry Rafferty, at the moment he passed away. As soon I pulled up in Bill's driveway, he was standing there, with a grim look on his face. 'Someone's on the phone for you, Ozzy,' he said.

It was Norman, giving me the news. To this day, whenever 'Baker Street' comes on the radio, I hear Norman's voice and feel that intense sadness.

His funeral was a week later, and he was cremated. I really hate the way traditional English funerals are organised: you're just starting to get over the shock of the death, then you have to go through it all over again. The Jews have a far better idea: when someone dies, you bury them as soon as possible. At least that way you get it all out of your system quickly.

The only way I could handle my father's funeral was to get out of my skull. I got up that morning and poured myself a neat whisky; then I kept going all day. By the time they brought the coffin to the house where my mum and dad had been living, I was halfway to another planet. The coffin was sealed, but for some stupid fucking pissed reason I decided I wanted to see Dad again, one last time, so I got one of the pallbearers to unscrew the lid. A bad idea, that was. In the end, we all took it in turns to look at him. But he'd been dead a week, so as soon as I peered into the coffin, I regretted it. The undertaker had put all this greasepaint on him, so he looked like a fucking clown. That wasn't the way I wanted to remember my father – but as I'm writing this now, that's the picture I see in my head. I'd rather have remembered him being tied to that hospital cot, smiling and sticking his thumbs up, and going, 'Speeeeed!'

Then we all got in the hearse with the coffin. My sisters and my mother started howling like wild animals, which freaked the fuck out of me. I'd never experienced anything like it before. They teach you how to handle life in England, but they don't teach you a thing about death. There's no book telling you what to do when your mum or dad dies.

It's like, *You're on your own now, sunshine.*

If there's one thing that sums up my father, it's the indoor bathroom he built at 14 Lodge Road, so we wouldn't have to use a tin bathtub in front of the fire any more. He hired a professional contractor to do most of the work, but only a few weeks after it was finished all this damp started coming in through the wall. So my dad went off to the hardware shop, bought what he needed, and replastered the wall himself. But the damp came back. So my dad plastered it again. Then it came back again and again and again. By this time he was on a mission. And you couldn't stop my dad when he was on a mission. He came up with all kinds of crazy concoctions to put on that wall and stop the damp. It went on for ever, his anti-damp crusade. Then, finally, after a few years, he got this heavy-duty industrial tar from the GEC factory, smeared it all over the wall, plastered over the tar, then went out and bought some yellow and white tiles, and laid them on top.

'*That* should fucking do it,' I remember him saying.

I'd forgotten all about it until years later, when I went back to the house to do a documentary with the BBC. By that time, there was a Pakistani family living there, and every wall in the house had been painted white. It was eerie, seeing the place like that. But then I walked into the bathroom – and on the wall were my dad's tiles, still up there, like the day they were laid. I just thought, He fucking did it in the end, my old man.

You couldn't wipe the smile off my face for the rest of the day.

I miss my dad a lot, even now. I just wish we could have sat down and had a good old man-to-man conversation about all the stuff I never knew to ask him when I was a kid, or was too pissed and busy being a rock star to ask him when I was in my twenties.

But I suppose that's always the way, isn't it?

The day I left Black Sabbath, we were at Rockfield Studios in South Wales, trying to record a new album. We'd just had another soul-destroying meeting about money and lawyers, and I couldn't take it any more. So I just walked out of the studio and fucked off back to Bulrush Cottage in Thelma's Mercedes. I was shitfaced, obviously. And then, like a pissed dickhead, I started to slag off the band in the press, which wasn't fair. But y'know, when a band splits up, it's like a marriage ending – for a while, all you want to do is hurt each other. The bloke they found to replace me after I walked out was another Brummie, called Dave Walker, a guy I'd admired for a long time, actually – he'd been with Savoy Brown and then Fleetwood Mac for a while.

But for whatever reason things didn't work out with Dave, so when I came back a few weeks later, everything was back to normal – on the surface, at least. No one really talked about what happened. I just turned up in the studio one day – I think

Bill had been trying to act as peacemaker on the phone – and that was the end of it. But it was obvious things had changed, especially between me and Tony. I don't think anyone's heart was in what we were doing any more. Still, as soon as I came back, we picked up where we'd left off with the album, which we decided to call *Never Say Die*.

By now, we were starting to get our finances sorted out, thanks to Colin Newman, who advised us to make the album as tax exiles in another country, to avoid having to give 80 per cent of all our dough to the Labour government. We chose Canada, even though it was January and would be so cold that we wouldn't be able to walk outside without our eyeballs freezing over. So we booked ourselves into Sounds Interchange Studios and flew off to Toronto.

But even three thousand miles away from England the old problems soon came up again.

For example, I spent just about every night getting seriously fucked-up at a place called the Gas Works, opposite the apartment block where I was staying. One night I went over there, came back, passed out, and woke up an hour later with this incredible heartburn. I remember opening my eyes and thinking, What the *fuck*? It was pitch black, but I noticed this red glow in front of me. I had no idea what it was. Meanwhile, the heartburn was getting worse and worse. Then suddenly I realised what had happened: I'd fallen asleep with a cigarette in my hand. *I was on fire!* So I jumped out of bed, tore off my clothes, bundled them up with the smouldering sheets, ran to the bathroom, dumped the whole lot in the bath, turned on the cold water, and waited for the smoke to clear. By the time I was done, the room was a fucking bomb site, I was stark bollock naked, my sheets were ruined and I was freezing to death.

I was thinking, What the fuck do I do now? Then I had an idea: I ripped down the curtains and used them as sheets instead. It worked great, until the boot-faced maid came in the next morning.

She went mental.

'WHAT HAVE YOU DONE TO MY APARTMENT?' she screamed at me. 'GET OUT! GET OUT! YOU ANIMAL!'

Things weren't going much better in the studio. When I mentioned in passing that I wanted to do a side project of my own, Tony snapped, 'If you've got any songs, Ozzy, you should give them to us first.' But then whenever I came up with an idea, nobody would give me the time of day. I'd say, 'What do you think of this, then?' and they'd go, 'Nah. That's crap.'

Then, one day, Thelma called the studio and said she'd just had a miscarriage, so we all packed up our stuff and went back to England. But going home didn't improve things between us, to the point where me and Tony weren't speaking to each other at all. We didn't argue. The opposite, really: just a complete lack of communication. And during the last sessions for the album in England, I'd given up. Tony, Bill and Geezer decided they wanted to do a song called 'Breakout', with a jazz band going *da-dah-da-dah, DAH*, and I just went, Fuck this, I'm off. That's why Bill sang the vocals on 'Swinging the Chain'. The bottom line was that 'Breakout' was stretching it too far for me. With tracks like that on the album, I thought, we might as well have been called Slack Haddock, not Black Sabbath. The only impressive thing about that jazz band as far as I was concerned was how much they could drink. It was incredible. If you didn't get the takes done by midday, you were fucked, 'cos they were all too pissed.

Never Say Die bombed like none of our albums had ever done before in America, but it did OK in Britain, where it went to number twelve in the album charts, and got us a slot on *Top of the Pops*. Which was good fun, actually, 'cos we got to meet Bob Marley. I'll always remember the moment he came out of his dressing room – it was next to ours – and you literally couldn't see his head through the cloud of dope smoke. He was smoking the biggest, fattest joint I'd ever seen – and believe me, I'd seen a few. I kept thinking, He's gonna have to lip-synch, he's gonna have to lip-synch, *no one* can do a live show when they're that high. But no – he did it live. Flawlessly, too.

There were other good things happening for Black Sabbath around that time, too. For example, after sorting out our finances, we'd decided to hire Don Arden as our manager, mainly because we'd been impressed by what he'd done for the Electric Light Orchestra. And for me, the best thing about being managed by Don Arden was getting to see his daughter Sharon on a regular basis. Almost immediately, I began falling in love with her from a distance. It was that wicked laugh that got me. And the fact that she was so beautiful and glamorous – she wore fur coats, and had diamonds dripping from everywhere. I'd never seen anything like it. And she was as loud and crazy as I was. By then, Sharon was helping to run the business with Don, and whenever she came over to see the band, we'd end up having a laugh. She was great company, was Sharon – the best. But nothing happened between us for a long time.

But I knew it was all over with Black Sabbath, and it was clear they'd had enough of my insane behaviour. One of my last memories of being with the band was missing a gig at the Municipal Auditorium in Nashville during our last US tour. I'd been doing so much coke with Bill while driving between shows in his GMC mobile home that I hadn't slept for three days straight. I looked like the walking dead. My eyeballs felt like someone had injected them with caffeine, my skin was all red and prickly, and I could hardly feel my legs. But at five o'clock in the morning on the day of the gig, after we pulled into town, I finally hit the sack at the Hyatt Regency Hotel. It was the best fucking sleep I'd ever had in my life. It was like being six feet under, it was so good. And when I woke up, I felt almost normal again.

But I didn't know that the key I'd used to get into my room was from one of the other Hyatt hotels we'd stayed at earlier in the tour, in another city. So while my bags had been sent to the right room by the tour manager, I'd gone to the wrong room. Which wouldn't normally have been a problem: the key I had in my pocket just wouldn't have worked and I would have gone down to reception and realised the mistake. But when I got to the room, the maid was still in there, plumping the pillows and checking that the minibar was full. So the door was open and I walked straight in. I just showed her the key – which had the right number and the Hyatt logo on it – and she smiled and told me to enjoy my stay. Then she closed the door behind her while I got into the wrong bed in the wrong room and fell asleep.

For twenty-four hours.

In the meantime, the gig came and went. Of course, the hotel sent someone up to my room to look for me, but all they found was my luggage. They had no idea I was zonked out on a different floor, in another wing of the hotel. The lads panicked, my ugly mug was plastered all over the local TV stations, the cops set up a special missing persons unit, the fans began to plan a candlelit vigil, the insurance company was on the phone, venues across America were preparing for the tour to be cancelled, the record company went apeshit, and Thelma thought she'd become a widow.

Then I woke up.

The first thing I did was call down to the front desk and ask them what time it was. 'Six o'clock,' the woman told me. Perfect timing, I thought. The gig was at eight. So I got out of bed and started looking for my suitcase. Then I realised that everything seeemed very quiet.

So I called back down to the front desk.

'Morning or evening?' I asked.

'Sorry?'

'You said it was six o'clock. Morning or evening?'

'Oh, morning.'

'Ah.'

Then I called the tour manager's room.

'Yeah?' he croaked.

'It's me, Ozzy,' I said. 'I think there might be a problem.'

First there was silence.

Then tears – of rage. To this day, I've never had a bollocking like it.

It was Bill who told me I was fired.

The date was 27 April, 1979 – a Friday afternoon.

We were doing some rehearsals in LA, and I was loaded, but then I was loaded all the time. It was obvious that Bill had been sent by the others, because he wasn't exactly the firing type.

I can't remember exactly what he said to me. We haven't talked about it since. But the gist was that Tony thought I was a pissed, coked-up loser and a waste of time for everyone concerned. To be honest with you, it felt like he was finally getting his revenge for me walking out. And it didn't come as a complete surprise: I'd had the feeling in the studio for a while that Tony was trying to wind me up by getting me to sing takes over and over again, even though there was nothing wrong with the first one.

I didn't let it affect my friendship with Bill. I felt bad for the guy, actually, 'cos his mum had just died. Then not long after I was kicked out of Black Sabbath, his father died too. When I'd heard the news, I thought, Fuck the war, I'm still his mate, we're still the same people who lived in a GMC together for months on end in America. So I drove straight up to Birmingham to see him.

He'd taken it really badly and I felt terrible for him. Then his dad's funeral turned into a joke. They were carrying the coffin out of the church when they realised that someone in the funeral party had nicked the vicar's car. The vicar refused to continue with the service until he got it back, but whoever had nicked the fucking thing couldn't get the steering lock off, and ended up crashing into a garden. Imagine that kind of bullshit going down when you're trying to lay your old man to rest. Unbelievable.

But I'd be lying if I said I didn't feel betrayed by what happened with Black Sabbath. We weren't some manufactured boy band whose members were expendable. We were four blokes from the same town who'd grown up together a few streets apart. We were like a family, like brothers. And firing me for being fucked up was hypocritical bullshit. We were *all* fucked up. If you're stoned and I'm stoned, and you're telling me that I'm fired because I'm stoned, how can that fucking be? Because I'm *slightly* more stoned than you are?

But I don't give a fuck any more – and it worked out for the best in the end. It gave me the shove up the arse I needed, and it probably made it a lot more fun for them, making records with a new singer. I don't have anything bad to say about the guy they hired to replace me, Ronnie James Dio, who'd previously been with Rainbow. He's a great singer. Then again, he ain't me, and I ain't him. So I just wish they'd called the band Black Sabbath II.

That's all.

Part Two

Starting Over

7

Des Moines

All of a sudden I was unemployed.

And unemployable.

I remember thinking, Well, I've still got a few dollars in my pocket, so I'll have one last big fling in LA – then I'll go back to England. I honestly thought I'd have to sell Bulrush Cottage and go and work on a building site or something. I just resigned myself to the fact that it was over. None of it had ever seemed real, anyway. The first thing I did was check myself into a place called Le Parc Hotel in West Hollywood, paid for by Don Arden's company, Jet Records. I was amazed Don had forked out for it, to be honest with you. The second he realises I ain't going back to Black Sabbath, I said to myself, they're gonna kick me out of this place – so I might as well enjoy it while I still can. You didn't get a room at Le Parc – you got a little apartment-type thing with its own kitchen where you could make your own food. I never left. I just sat on the bed and watched old war films with the curtains closed. I didn't see daylight for months. My dealer would come over and give me some blow or some pot, I'd get booze delivered from Gil Turner's up on Sunset Strip, and every once in a while I'd get some chicks over to fuck. Although I dunno why anyone was prepared to fuck me, not in those days. I was eating so much pizza and drinking so much beer, I had bigger tits than Jabba the Hutt's fat older brother.

I hadn't seen Thelma or the kids for ages. I'd call them up from the phone in my room, but it felt like they were slipping away from me, which made me feel even more depressed. I'd spent more time with Black Sabbath than I ever had with my family. We'd come back from months on the road, take a three-week break, then go straight off to some farm or castle where we'd fuck around until we came up with some new songs. We did that for a decade, until all our personal lives were ruined: Bill's marriage failed, Tony's marriage failed, Geezer's marriage failed. But I didn't want to accept it, because it would mean losing my home and my kids, and I'd already lost my dad and my band.

I just wanted to shut everything out, make everything go away.

So I hid in Le Parc and drank.

And drank.

And drank.

Then, one day, this bloke called Mark Nauseef knocked on my door. He was a drummer, also managed by Don Arden, and he'd played with everyone from the Velvet Underground to Thin Lizzy. He told me that Sharon from Jet Records was coming over to pick something up from him – he was staying in one of the other apartments – but that he had to leave town for a gig. Then he handed me an envelope.

'Would you do me a favour and give this to her?' he asked. 'I told Sharon just to call for you at reception.'

'No worries,' I said.

As soon as I closed the door, I got a knife and opened it.

Inside was five hundred dollars in cash. Fuck knows what it was for and I didn't care. I just called up my dealer and bought five hundred dollars' worth of coke. A few hours later, Sharon came over and asked if I had something to give her. 'No, I don't think so,' I said, all innocent.

'Are you sure, Ozzy?'

'Pretty sure.'

But it didn't take Einstein to work out what had happened. There was a massive bag of coke on the table next to a ripped-up envelope with 'Sharon' written on it in felt-tip pen.

Sharon gave me a monumental bollocking when she saw it, shouting and cursing and telling me I was a fucking disaster.

I guess I won't be shagging her any time soon, then, I thought.

But she came back the next day, to find me lying in a puddle of my own piss, smoking a joint.

'Look,' she said. 'If you want to get your shit together, we want to manage you.'

'Why would anyone want to manage *me*?' I asked her.

I couldn't believe it, I really couldn't. But it was a good job that *someone* wanted me, 'cos I was down to my last few dollars. My royalties from Black Sabbath were non-existent, I didn't have a savings account, and I had no new income coming in. At first, Don wanted me to start a band called Son of Sabbath, which I thought was a horrendous idea. Then he wanted me to team up with Gary Moore. I wasn't too keen on that, either, even though me and Sharon had gone to San Francisco with Gary and his bird one time, and we'd had a lot of fun. (I really thought I was in with Sharon on that trip, to be honest with you, but nothing happened: she just went back to her hotel at the end of the night, and left me dribbling into my beer.)

The worst idea that Don Arden had was for me and Sabbath to do gigs together, one after the other, like a double bill. I asked Sharon, 'Is he having a laugh?'

But then Sharon started to take more control, and we decided that I should make a proper solo album.

I wanted to call it *Blizzard of Ozz*.

And little by little, things started to come together.

I'd never met anyone who could sort things out like Sharon could. Whatever she said she would do, she'd get it done. Or at least she'd come back to you and say, 'Look, I tried my best, but I couldn't make it happen.' As a manager, you always knew exactly where you stood with her. Meanwhile, Sharon's father would just shout and bully like some mob captain, so I tried to stay out of his way as much as I could. Of course, before I could make an album and go on tour, I needed a band. But I'd never held auditions before, and I didn't have a clue how or where to start. So Sharon helped me out, taking me to see all these young, up-and-coming LA guitarists. But I wasn't really in any state for it. I'd just find a sofa in the corner of the room and pass out. Then a friend of mine, Dana Strum – who'd auditioned to be my bass player – said to me, 'Look, Ozzy, there's one guy you really have to see. He plays with a band called Quiet Riot, and he's red hot.'

So one night this tiny American bloke came over to Le Parc to introduce himself. The first thing that came into my mind was: he's either a chick or gay. He had long, wet-looking hair, and this weirdly deep voice, and he was so thin he was almost not there. He reminded me a little of David Bowie's guitarist, Mick Ronson.

'How old are you?' I asked, as soon as he walked through the door.

'Twenty-two.'

'What's your name?'

'Randy Rhoads.'

'Do you want a beer?'

'I'll take a Coke, if you have one.'

'I'll get you a beer. Are you a bloke, by the way?'

Randy just laughed.

'Seriously,' I said.

'Er, yeah. Last time I checked.'

Randy must have thought I was a fucking lunatic.

Afterwards, we drove over to a studio somewhere so I could hear him play. I remember him plugging his Gibson Les Paul into a little practice amp and saying to me, 'D'you mind if I warm up?'

'Knock yourself out,' I said.

Then he started doing these finger exercises. I had to say to him, 'Stop. Randy, just stop right there.'

'What's wrong?' he said, looking up at me with this worried expression on his face.

'You're hired.'

You should have heard him play, man.

I almost cried, he was so good.

Soon we were flying back to England for rehearsals. I quickly found out that although Randy looked like Mr Cool, he was an incredibly sweet, down-to-earth guy. A real gentleman, too – not at all what you'd expect of a flash American rock 'n' roll guitar hero.

I couldn't understand why he even wanted to get involved with a bloated alcoholic wreck like me.

At first, we stayed at Bulrush Cottage with Thelma and the kids. The first thing we wrote was 'Goodbye to Romance'. Working with Randy was like night and day compared with Black Sabbath. I was just walking around the house one day, singing this melody that had been in my head for months, and Randy asked, 'Is that your song, or a Beatles song?' I said, 'Oh no, it's nothing, just this thing I've got stuck in my head.' But he made me sit down with him until we'd worked it out.

He was incredibly patient – I wasn't surprised at all when I found out that his mum was a music teacher. It was the first time I'd ever felt like I was an equal partner when it came to songwriting.

Another vivid memory of working with Randy was when we wrote 'Suicide Solution'. We were at a party for a band called Wild Horses at John Henry's, a rehearsal studio in London. Everyone else was fucked up on one thing or another, but Randy was sitting in a corner experimenting with riffs on his Flying V, and all of a sudden he just went Dah, Dah, D'La-Dah, DAH, D'La-*Dah*. I shouted over, 'Whoa, Randy! What was that?' He just shrugged. I told him to play what he'd just played, then I started to sing this lyric I'd had in my head for a while: 'Wine is fine, but whiskey's quicker/ Suicide is slow with liquor'. And that was it, most of the song was written, right there. The night ended with everyone on stage, jamming.

Phil Lynott from Thin Lizzy was there. That might have been the last time I saw him before he died, actually. He was a tragic case, was Phil. I mean, I thought he missed his mark so badly. Great fucking performer, great voice, great style, but the old heroin got him in the end.

Thank God I never got into that shit.

Randy loved Britain.

Every weekend, he'd get in the van and drive somewhere, just to have a look around. He went to Wales, Scotland, the Lake District, you name it. He also collected toy trains, so wherever he went, he'd buy one. He was a quiet bloke, very dedicated, didn't like showing off, but he could be a laugh, too. One time we were in this bar and there was a guy in the corner playing classical music on the piano, so Randy goes up to him and says, 'D'you mind if I join you?' The guy looks at Randy, looks around the bar, sees me, and goes, 'Er, sure.' So then Randy gets out his Gibson, hooks up his little practice amp, and starts playing along to this Beethoven piece or whatever it was. But as he goes along, he starts throwing in all these rock 'n' roll moves, and by the end of it he's on his knees, doing this wild solo with his tongue hanging out. It was fucking hilarious. The whole bar was in stitches.

The funny thing is, I don't think Randy really ever liked Black Sabbath much. He was a *proper* musician. I mean, a lot of rock 'n' roll guitarists are good, but they have just one trick, one gimmick, so even if you don't know the song, you go, 'Oh, that's so-and-so.' But Randy could play anything. His influences ranged from Leslie West to jazz greats like Charlie Christian and classical guys like John Williams. He didn't understand why people were into 'Iron Man', 'cos he thought it was so simple a kid could play it.

We had arguments about that, actually. I'd say, 'Look, if it works, who cares if it's simple? I mean, you can't get much easier than the riff to "You Really Got Me" – but it's awesome. When I first bought that single, I played it until the needle on my dad's radiogram broke.'

Randy would just shrug and say, 'I guess.'

One thing Sharon's brother managed to get done when we were in England was find us a bass player – Bob Daisley, an Aussie bloke who'd been signed to Jet with a band called Widowmaker, which was how David knew him. I liked Bob immediately. He was a proper rock 'n' roller – he wore denim jackets with cut-out sleeves and had his hair all blown out – and we'd go down the pub and do a bit of coke once in a while.

Another good thing about Bob was that he wasn't just a bass player. He could chip in with songwriting, too.

And we had a laugh together – at first, anyway.

Getting a drummer wasn't so easy.

We seemed to audition half of Britain before we finally came across Lee Kerslake, who'd played with Uriah Heep. He was all right, Lee – one of those big old pub blokes. Solid drummer, too. But the guy I'd really wanted – Tommy Aldridge, from the Pat Travers Band – wasn't available.

Another early member of our line-up was a keyboard player

from Ipswich called Lindsay Bridgewater. He was a very educated boy, was Lindsay, and he'd never met the likes of us before. I told him, 'Lindsay, you look like a fucking school teacher. I want you to backcomb your hair, put on a white cape, get yourself some black lipstick and some black eyeliner. And while you're playing, I want you to *growl* at the audience.'

The poor bloke didn't last long.

I'd be talking out of my arse if I said I didn't feel like I was in competition with Black Sabbath when we made *Blizzard of Ozz*. I wished them well, I suppose, but part of me was shitting myself that they were going to be more successful without me. And their first album with Dio was pretty good. I didn't rush out and buy it, but I heard some tracks on the radio. It went to number nine in Britain and number twenty-eight in America. But by the time we'd got *Blizzard* in the can at Ridge Farm Studios in Surrey, I knew we had a cracking album of our own. We had a couple of cracking albums, actually, because we had a lot of material left over when we were done.

And it was magic to be in control – like I'd finally pulled something off. Then again, even if you think something's brilliant, you never know if the general public's going to pick up on it. But as soon as the radio stations got hold of 'Crazy Train', it was a done deal. The thing just exploded.

When the album came out in Britain in September 1980, it went to number seven in the album charts. When it came out in America six months later, it peaked at number twenty-one, but it eventually sold four million copies, making it one of *Billboard*'s Top 100 bestselling albums of the decade.

Reviews?

Didn't read 'em.

A few nights before the tour started, I got Sharon in the sack for the first time. It had taken fucking long enough. We'd been at Shepperton Studios in Surrey, rehearsing for our first gig –

which was going to be in Blackpool under the fake name of The Law – and we were all staying at the same hotel across the road. So I just followed Sharon back to her room. I think I might even have used my extra-special pick-up line: 'Can I come back and watch your telly?' The usual reply to this was, 'Fuck off, I ain't got one.'

But this time it worked.

I was shitfaced, obviously. So was Sharon – she *must* have been. All I remember is her deciding to take a bath, and me ripping off my clothes and jumping in with her. Then one thing led to another, as things tend to do when you jump in a bath with a chick.

I fell for Sharon so badly, man.

The thing is, before I met her, I'd never come across a girl who was *like* me. I mean, when me and Sharon went out, people used to think we were brother and sister, we were so similar. Wherever we went, we were always the drunkest and the loudest.

We got up to some crazy shit in those early days.

One night in Germany, we went to a big dinner with the head of CBS Europe, who were releasing *Blizzard of Ozz* over there. He was a big, bearded, cigar-chomping bloke, and very straight. I was out of my fucking clock, of course. So we're all sitting there at this huge table, and halfway through the meal I get the idea to climb on the table and start doing a striptease. Everyone thinks it's funny for a while. But I end up stark bollock naked, take a piss in the CBS guy's carafe of wine, kneel down in front of him, and kiss him on the lips.

They didn't think *that* was very funny.

We didn't get a record played in Germany for years afterwards. I remember being on the plane, flying out of Berlin, with Sharon ripping up the contracts and saying, 'Well, that's another country gone.'

'It was worth it for the striptease though, wasn't it?' I asked.

'That wasn't a striptease you were doing, Ozzy. It was a

fucking Nazi goose-step. Up and down the table. That poor German bloke looked mortified. Then you put your balls in his fucking wine.'

'I thought I pissed in his wine?'

'That was *before* you pissed in his wine.'

Then we went to Paris, and I was still wasted from Berlin. I was *crazy* drunk, because people kept giving us all these free bottles of booze. By then, everyone had heard about what went on in Germany, so these very nervous record company people took us out for a drink at a nightclub. Everyone was talking about business, so to relieve the boredom I turned to the bloke next to me and said, 'Hey, will you do me a favour?'

'Sure,' he said.

'Punch me in the face.'

'What?'

'Punch me in the face.'

'I can't do that.'

'Look, I asked you to do me a favour, and you said you would. You *promised*. So punch me in the fucking face.'

'No!'

'Just punch me.'

'Mr Osbourne, I'm sorry, but I can't do that.'

'Come on! YOU FUCKING PROMIS—'

BLAM!

The last thing I saw was Sharon's fist approaching my face from across the table. Then I was flat out on the floor, my nose bleeding, feeling like half my teeth were gonna fall out.

I opened my eyes and saw Sharon looking down at me. 'Are you happy now?' she asked me.

I spat out some blood and snot. 'Very happy, cheers.'

Later that night, I was lying in bed in the hotel room, having the worst comedown from cocaine you could ever imagine. I was shivering and sweating and having all these paranoid fantasies. So I rolled over and tried to give Sharon a cuddle, but she just moaned and pushed me away.

'Sharon,' I whimpered, 'I think I'm dying.'

Silence.

So I tried again: 'Sharon, I think I'm *dying*!'

Again, silence.

One more time: 'Sharon, I think I'm—'

'Die quietly then. I need to sleep. I've got a meeting in the morning.'

We'd wind each other up all the time, me and Sharon.

One night, we went for a drink together in a hotel. We took a seat in the corner, then I went up to the bar to get the beers in. But I got distracted by a guy in a wheelchair – a Hell's Angel. We ended up having a bit of a laugh, me and this bloke, and I ended up completely forgetting I was supposed to be taking the drinks back to Sharon. Then I heard this voice from the corner of the room.

'Ozzy! OZZY!'

Oh shit, I thought, I'm gonna get a right old bollocking now. So, on my way over, I came up with this ridiculous story. 'Sorry, darling,' I said, 'but you'll never guess what happened to that guy. He was telling me all about it, and I just couldn't tear myself away.'

'Let me guess: he fell off his motorbike.'

'Oh no,' I said. 'It's much worse than that. He's suffering from blowback.'

'He's suffering from *what*?'

'Blowback.'

'What the fuck is blowback?'

'Don't you know?'

The word had just popped into my head, so now I was desperately trying to think of what it could be.

'No, Ozzy, I don't know what blowback is.'

'That's crazy.'

'WELL, WHAT THE FUCK IS IT, THEN?'

'It's this thing you can get from a chick when they give you a handjob. What happens is, they're wanking you off, and then just as you're about to blow your wad, they put their thumb over the end of your knob, and sometimes – if you're really unlucky, like that poor bloke over there – the sperm flies straight back down your tubes and, well, y'know . . .'

'For the millionth time, Ozzy, no, I don't know.'

'Well, it, er . . . knocks out your spinal column.'

'Oh my God!' said Sharon, looking really shocked. 'That's awful. Go and buy that poor man another drink.'

I couldn't believe that she'd bought it.

I never gave it another thought until a couple of weeks later, when I was sitting outside a Jet Records board meeting. All I could hear was Sharon saying the word 'blowback' over and over again, and all the blokes in the room going, 'What? *Blowback?* What the fuck are you talking about?'

Then Sharon came storming out, bright red in the face, and screamed, 'You fucking BASTARD, Ozzy!'

Smack.

Sharon was managing me virtually single-handed when we did the *Blizzard of Ozz* tour. It was the first time in my career that I'd ever seen anyone plan things so carefully. Before we even started, she said, 'We can go two ways, Ozzy. We can open for a bigger act, like Van Halen, or we can headline smaller venues. I think we should headline smaller venues, because that way you'll always have sold-out shows, and when people see sold-out signs, they want to go. Also, you'll be seen as a top-billing act from day one.'

It turned out to be a brilliant move.

Everywhere we went, the venues were full, and there were more people queuing up outside.

Mind you, we worked our arses off for it.

This was my chance, and I knew I was only going to get

Back together for Live Aid in 1985 – Bill, me, Geezer and Tony.

On stage at Live Aid with Tony.

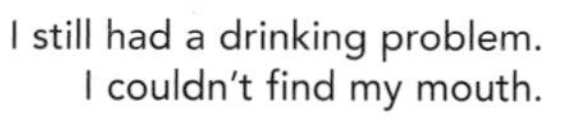

I still had a drinking problem.
I couldn't find my mouth.

A rare picture of the full Osbourne clan.

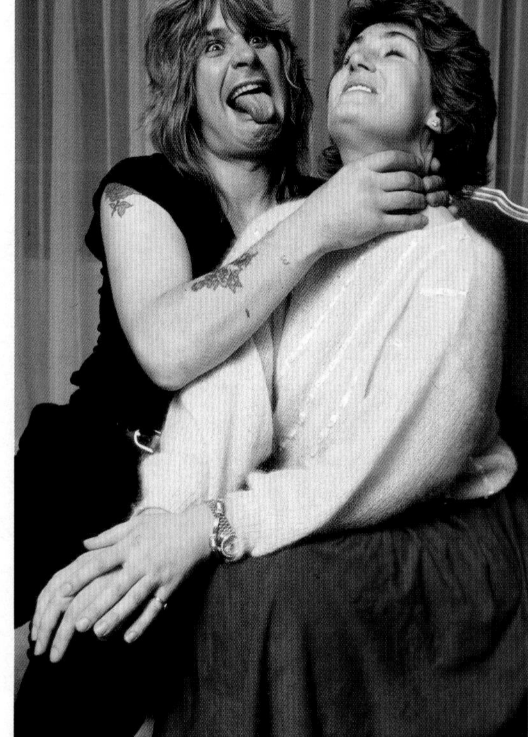

This time, it was just a joke.

Me and Jack. At that age, his favourite thing to do was sit on my shoulders during encores.

Relaxing at home with Jack and Kelly – and the best friend I've ever had, Baldrick the bulldog.

'How many songs do I have left to sing?' At Ozzfest in 1996.

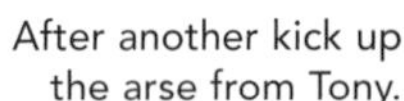

After another kick up the arse from Tony.

Wish I still looked like this.

'I seem to have lost my watch. Can anyone see it up there?'

My sons were taught good manners from an early age. Me, Louis and Jack on my fiftieth birthday in 1998.

My beautiful daughters – Kelly, Jessica and Aimee.

Warming up . . .

. . . and chilling out.

A promo shot for *The Osbournes* in 2002. We had no idea what we were letting ourselves in for.

On *The Tonight Show* with Jay Leno and Sharon, just after the madness began.

one. Me and Sharon both knew it, actually, so we went out and did every radio station, every television station, every interview we could get. Nothing was too small. Every record or ticket we sold counted.

I learned that when Sharon's on a mission, when she wants to get something done, she'll fucking throw herself at it, lock, stock and barrel, and she'll not stop fighting until well after the bell's rung. When she's got a bee up her arse, you can't stop her. Whereas, with me, if it hadn't been for her pushing all the time, I doubt I would have had the same success. In fact, I *know* I wouldn't.

Sharon didn't take anything for granted. It was in her blood and how she was raised. She used to tell me that her family either had the horn of plenty, the cornucopia, or nothing. One day they had the Rolls-Royce and a colour TV in every room; the next they were hiding the car and the tellies were being repossessed. It was a real boom-and-bust household.

I *trusted* Sharon, like I'd never trusted anyone before on the business side of things. And that's essential for me, because I don't understand contracts. I choose not to understand them, I suppose, because I can't stand all the bullshit and backstabbing.

But Sharon wasn't only good with money. She knew how to manage my image, too. She had me out of my grubby old Black Sabbath get-up in a second. 'When Randy's mum came over from LA, she thought you were a roadie,' she told me. Then she got a hairdresser over to bleach my hair. It was the eighties – you had to be flamboyant like that. People laugh at it, but when you go to a gig nowadays, you don't know who's in the band and who's in the audience, because they all look the fucking same. At least when somebody got on stage with a big glossy hairdo, they looked *special*.

Mind you, my stage rags got so outrageous at one point, people used to think I was a drag queen. I'd wear spandex trousers and these long coats studded with rhinestones.

Looking back now, I'm not embarrassed by those clothes, but I am embarrassed by how bloated I was. I was a fat, boozy, pizza-eating fuck. You should have seen my *face*, it was fucking massive. It wasn't surprising, either, given how much Guinness I was putting away on a daily basis. I'm telling you, man, one pint of Guinness is like eating three dinners.

Another person I learned to trust on that tour was Tony Dennis. He was this little Geordie bloke who kept turning up to the gigs every night, without fail. It was the middle of winter, but all he'd wear over his T-shirt was this little jeans jacket. He must have frozen his nuts off when he was queuing up to get in. He came to so many shows I ended up letting him in for free, even though I couldn't understand a fucking word he said. It was all, 'Why-eye, y'nah, Tuhni I-uhmi, haweh man, lyke.' For all I knew, he could have been calling me a cunt.

Anyway, we were in Canterbury, and it was minus five or something, and I asked him, 'How do you get around, Tony?'

'I just hitch-hike, man.'

'And where d'you sleep?'

'Train stations. Telephone boxes. Ahl awa the place, y'nah?'

'I tell you what,' I said. 'If you want to take care of the bags for us, we'll get you a room.'

And he's been with me ever since, has Tony. He's like a family member. He's a great guy, a really wonderful human being. I'm so reliant on him, and he's so efficient, it's amazing. Nothing's ever too much trouble for him, and I trust him completely. I could leave a big pile of dough on the table, come back two years later, and it would be exactly where I'd left it. He was there for my children, too, in the dark years. They still call him Uncle Tony. And all because of that one night in Canterbury when I asked him how he got around.

After our first night in the hotel opposite Shepperton Studios, me and Sharon were bonking all over the place. We couldn't stop. And we didn't carry on behind closed doors, either. The people around us knew exactly what was happening. Some nights Sharon would go out of one door and Thelma would come in the other. I was knackered all the time, having two women on the go. I don't know how those French blokes do it. When I was with Sharon, for example, I'd end up calling her 'Tharon', which earned me more than a few black eyes.

Looking back now, of course, I should have just left Thelma. But I didn't want to because of the kids. I knew that if we got a divorce, it would be terrible for them, because the kids always suffer the most in a break-up. And the thought of losing my family was unbearable to me. It was just too painful, I couldn't take it.

On the other hand I'd never known what it was like to fall in love before I met Sharon – even though we didn't exactly have a normal romance. I mean, Sharon was piggy in the middle when I was still married to Thelma, and in the beginning she was drinking nearly as much as I was. When we weren't shagging, we were fighting. And when we weren't fighting, we were drinking. But we were inseparable, couldn't stay away from each other. On the road we'd always share a room together, and if Sharon ever had to go away on business, I'd spend hours and hours talking to her on the phone, telling her how much I loved her, how much I couldn't wait to see her again. I'd never done that with *anyone* before. In fact, I can honestly say that I didn't have a clue what love was about until I met Sharon. I'd been confusing it with infatuation. Then I realised that when you're in love, it's not just about the messing around in the sack, it's about how empty you feel when they're gone. And I couldn't stand it when Sharon was gone.

But as badly as I'd fallen for Sharon, I knew things couldn't go on the way they were. For a while, I'd thought I could have the best of both worlds – my family, and the woman I loved – but something had to give. So that Christmas, with the British leg of the tour over, I told Thelma everything, because for some stupid drunk reason I thought that would make things better. Not the most fucking brilliant idea I ever had.

Thelma went up like a bottle of pop, kicked me out, and told me she needed time to think.

Then Don Arden put in his size-ten boot. He called Thelma to a meeting down in London and told her he was putting his son David back in charge of me, to get me away from Sharon. But the truth was, he was also shitting himself that Sharon was going to leave Jet Records and go it alone, which could end up costing him a fortune, especially if she took me with her – which is exactly what she did in the end. But Don should have known that if Sharon has her mind set on something, she'll do it, no matter what. And if someone tries to stop her, she'll just try twice as hard.

David didn't last five minutes.

Before we took the *Blizzard of Ozz* tour to America in April 1981, we went back to Ridge Farm and recorded *Diary of a Madman*. To this day, I don't know how we got that album done so quickly. It took us just under three weeks, I think.

We were all living in this crappy little flat while we were doing the sessions, and I'll always remember the morning when I woke up and heard this amazing acoustic riff coming out of Randy's room. I burst through his door, still in my underpants, and he was sitting there with a very uptight-looking classical instructor, having a lesson.

'What was that you just played?' I said, while the instructor stared at me like I was the Loch Ness Monster.

'Ozzy, I'm busy!'

'I know, but what was that you just played?'

'Mozart.'

'Right. We're nicking it.'

'We can't nick Mozart.'

'I'm sure he won't mind.'

It ended up being the intro to 'Diary of a Madman' – although by the time Randy had finished messing around with it, there was hardly any Mozart left.

The rest of the album was a blur. We were so rushed for time that we ended up mixing it on the road. My producer, Max Norman, would send tapes to my hotel room, and I'd call him on payphones and tell him to add a bit more bass here or a bit more midrange there.

It was around then that Bob and Lee started to bitch and moan about everything, which drove me fucking nuts. I'd look over and they'd be huddled in the corner, whispering like schoolgirls. From the very beginning, Bob had always wanted to call the band a name, instead of it just being Ozzy Osbourne. I didn't understand that. Why would I want to leave one band just to join another, with everyone going, 'Shall we do this gig or that gig? Hmm, let's think about that'? I mean, if Bob and Lee had come into Jet's offices and said, 'We want to be in an equal-share band with Ozzy,' I would have said, 'Nah, thanks, I've had enough of that. I want to be my own boss. See ya.' But Bob could be pushy, and if it wasn't for Sharon he probably would have bullied me into doing exactly what he wanted. You see, I have this problem where I just tend to roll over and go along with things. Sometimes I think it's because I don't play an instrument, which makes me feel like I don't deserve to be in the room, y'know?

Anyway, at some point I remember Sharon coming up to us, very excited, and saying, 'Great news, guys. The tickets for the Palladium in New York just went on sale, and they sold out in an hour!' We were all cheering and whooping and doing high fives. Then Sharon went off to take a phone call. When she came back she had an even bigger smile on her face and said, 'You'll never guess what: the Palladium want us to do *two* shows in one night.'

I couldn't believe it: everything was really taking off? But Bob and Lee went very quiet then disappeared for one of their little chin-wags. When they came back, they said, 'Well, if we're doing two shows, we want double our travel expenses and double our pay.' That was a bit much for me. None of us had seen any real dough at that point, and the Ardens had put up the cash for everything – the studio time, the hotels, the food, the equipment, the staff, you fucking name it. Where did they think the money was coming from – the sky? The fact was, every last penny had to be paid back to Don, but Bob and Lee didn't have to worry about that because they were basically session players.

I wanted them gone after that. I said to Sharon, 'If we carry on like this, every five minutes there's going to be another row, and I've had enough of that bullshit.'

So that was the end of Bob and Lee, although I worked with Bob a few times over the years, until he started suing me every other day of the week.

It's sad, y'know, what money does to people. Always money. But I honestly believe that if Bob and Lee had stayed on, I wouldn't be where I am today. The bad vibes would have made it impossible to get anything done. Luckily, Sharon had been working on replacements for them for a while – they'd been getting on her tits for a long time – and she managed to sign up Tommy Aldridge, the drummer I'd wanted from the start, and a bass player called Rudy Sarzo, who'd worked with Randy in Quiet Riot. And that was that.

When the second album was finally done, we packed up our stuff, got on a plane, and went to LA for a week of rehearsals and record company meetings before the tour began in Maryland.

Don't ask me who bought the doves.

All I know is that Sharon showed them to me when we were in the limo on the way over to the Century City headquarters of CBS Records, a few days after we'd flown into LA.

'Aren't they beautiful?' she said. 'Listen. They're *cooing*. Aw.'

Our meeting with CBS was a big deal.

Although *Blizzard of Ozz* had been a hit in England, we badly needed success in America, 'cos we were broke. Everything depended on it. Since going out on the road, we'd been living hand-to-mouth, sleeping in flea-infested hotel rooms, one of us handcuffed to a briefcase full of all the cash we had left in the world. Which was fuck-all, pretty much. We hadn't even been paid the advance for *Diary of a Madman*, 'cos Sharon couldn't prise it out of her father's sweaty hands. Meanwhile, Thelma was talking about a divorce, which meant I could lose everything all over again.

'What d'you want doves for, anyway?' I asked Sharon, swigging from the bottle of Cointreau I'd brought with me.

Sharon gave me one of her looks.

'Don't you remember, Ozzy? Our conversation? Last night? They're for the meeting. When we get in there, you're going to throw the doves in the air so they fly around the room.'

'What for?'

'Because that's what we agreed. And then you're going to say "rock 'n' roll" and give them the peace sign.' I couldn't remember any of it. It was only eleven o'clock in the morning, but I was already on Planet Booze. I hadn't stopped since the night before. Or the night before that.

I'd even forgotten why we were going to see CBS. But then Sharon reminded me: 'They need a kick up the arse because they bought *Blizzard of Ozz* from my father for a *pathetically* small sum of money, so they're probably expecting it to bomb, which is exactly what Black Sabbath's last two albums did in America. You're nothing in this country as a solo artist, Ozzy. Forget about the sold-out shows in Britain. You're starting from scratch here. When you go into this meeting, you've got to make an impression, show them who you are.'

'With doves?' I said.

'Exactly.'

I put down the bottle and took the birds from Sharon.

'Why don't I bite their heads off?' I said, holding them up in front of my face. 'That'll make an impression.'

Sharon just laughed, shook her head, and looked out of the window at the blue sky and the palm trees.

'I'm serious,' I said.

'Ozzy, you're *not* going to bite their heads off.'

'Yeah, I am.'

'No, you're not, silly.'

'Yeah, I fucking am. I've been feeling a bit peckish all morning.'

Sharon laughed again. I loved that sound more than I loved anything else in the world.

The meeting was bullshit. A bunch of fake smiles and limp handshakes. Then someone told me how excited they were that Adam Ant was coming to America. *Adam Ant?* I almost chinned the cunt when he said that. It was obvious none of them gave a shit. Even the PR chick kept looking at her watch. But the meeting went on and on while all these suits with gold watches spouted meaningless corporate marketing bollocks, until eventually I got pissed off waiting for Sharon to give me the cue to throw the doves in the air. In the end I just got up, walked aross the room, sat down on the arm of the PR chick's chair, and pulled one of them out of my pocket.

'Oh, cute,' she said, giving me another fake smile. Then she looked at her watch again.

That's *it*, I thought.

I opened my mouth wide.

Across the room, I saw Sharon flinch.

Then I went *chomp, spit.*

The dove's head landed on the PR chick's lap in a splatter of blood. To be honest with you, I was so pissed, it just tasted of Cointreau. Well, Cointreau and feathers. And a bit of beak. Then I threw the carcass on to the table and watched it twitch.

The bird had shit itself when I bit into its neck, and the stuff had gone everywhere. The PR chick's dress was flecked with this nasty brown-and-white goo, and my jacket, a horrible yellow eighties thing with a Rupert the Bear-style pattern on it, was pretty much ruined. To this day, I have no fucking idea what was going on in my head. I mean, the poor dove. But I'll tell you one thing: it made an impression, all right.

For a split second, all you could hear was everyone taking a breath at the same time and the photographer in the corner going *click-click-click*.

Then pandemonium.

The PR chick started screaming, 'Ew, ew, ew!', while a bloke in a suit ran over to the bin in the corner and puked. Then alarms started going off, as someone yelled into the intercom for security.

'GET THIS ANIMAL OUT OF HERE! NOW!'

At that moment I took the other dove out of my pocket.

'Hello, birdie,' I said to it, giving it a kiss on the head. 'My name's Ozzy Osbourne. And I'm here to promote my new album, *Blizzard of Ozz*.'

Then I opened my mouth and everyone in the room went 'NOOOOOO!' People were covering their eyes with their arms and screaming at me to stop it and get the fuck out. But instead of biting its head off, I let it go, and it flapped happily around the room.

'Peace,' I said, as two massive security guards burst into the room, grabbed me by the arms, and dragged me out backwards.

The panic in that place was insane, man.

Meanwhile, Sharon was pissing herself laughing. Tears were streaming down her cheeks. I think it was just her reaction to the shock of it, more than anything else. She'd also been pretty pissed off with CBS for not showing enough enthusiasm about the album, so in a way she was probably glad I'd just given them the fright of their lives, even if it was the most horrific thing she'd ever seen. 'You are banned from the CBS building, you freakshow,' said the chief security bloke, after he'd pushed me out of the front door of the building into the hundred-degree LA heat. 'If I see you here again, I'll have you arrested, d'you understand?'

Sharon followed me outside, then she grabbed me by the collar, and kissed me.

'That poor fucking *creature*,' she said. 'We'll be lucky if CBS doesn't pull the plug on the whole record after that performance. They might even sue us. You bad, bad, *bad* boy.'

'So why aren't you giving me a bollocking, then?' I asked her, confused.

'Because the press are going to fucking *love* it.'

That night, we went back to Don Arden's house, where we were staying with Rudy and Tommy, our new rhythm section. Don's house was a big Spanish-style deal at the top of Benedict Canyon, above Beverly Hills, with red tiles on the roof and a huge iron gate to keep the little people away. Apparently Howard Hughes had built the place for one of his girlfriends. Don had bought it after making a ton of dough from ELO, and now he lived up there like a king, with Cary Grant as his neighbour. When were in town, Don would put us up in the one of the 'bungalows' on the grounds. He used another one of the bungalows as the LA headquarters of Jet Records.

I was so shitfaced by the time our limo pulled up in the driveway, I barely knew what planet I was on. Then I went off with Rudy to one of the rooms at the back of the house where Don had a TV, a drinks cabinet and a 'wet bar'. I'd moved on from Cointreau to beer by that point, which meant I needed to take a slash every five seconds. But I couldn't be arsed to walk all the way to the bog, so I just pissed in the sink. Which wasn't a problem until Don walked past the door in his dressing-gown, on his way to bed.

All I heard was this voice from behind me, loud enough to register on the Richter scale. 'OZZY, ARE YOU PISSING IN MY FUCKING SINK?'

Oh, *shit*.

I squeezed my dick to stop the piss.

He's gonna kill me, I thought. He's gonna fucking *kill* me.

Then I had an idea: if I whip around really quick while zipping up my fly, everything will be fine. So that's what I started to do. But I was so loaded, my hand slipped off my dick as I turned, and this jet of piss came spraying out – straight at Don.

He jumped backwards and it missed him by a fraction of an inch.

To this day, I've never seen a human being so angry. I swear, I thought he was gonna rip my head off and take a shit down my windpipe. The bloke was livid: red in the face, shaking, spit flying out of his mouth. The whole deal. It was terrifying. When he was done calling me every name under the sun – and a few more – he said, 'GET OUT. GET OUT OF MY HOUSE, YOU FUCKING ANIMAL. GET OUT! GET OUT NOW!'

Then he stomped off to find Sharon. A couple of minutes later, from the other end of the house, I heard, 'AND YOU'RE EVEN WORSE, BECAUSE YOU'RE FUCKING HIM!'

All in all, I have great memories of that first American tour.

And it wasn't just because *Blizzard of Ozz* had sold a million copies by the time we'd finished. It was because I had such fabulous people around me. I don't know what I ever did to deserve Randy Rhoads. He was the only *musician* who'd ever been in my band. He could read music. He could write music. He was so dedicated that he would find a classical guitar instructor in every town we went to and get a lesson. He'd give his own lessons, too. Whenever we were on the West Coast, he'd find time to go to his mother's school and tutor the kids. He worshipped his mum, Randy did. I remember when we were recording *Blizzard of Ozz* at Ridge Farm, he asked if he could write a song and name it 'Dee' in her honour. I told him to go for it.

And I was having the greatest nights of my life with Sharon. We'd do stuff together that I'd never done before, like clubbing in New York. It couldn't have been more different to when I went to New York with Black Sabbath – in those days, I wouldn't even leave my room, 'cos I was always scared shitless. Coming from England, I thought the place was full of gangsters and villains. But Sharon took me out. We used to go to this bar called PJ's, do coke, meet all these random people and have crazy adventures. We even hung out with Andy Warhol a few times – he was friends with a chick called Susan Blonde, who worked for CBS. He never said a word. He'd just sit there and take pictures of you with this freaky look on his face. Strange, strange bloke, that Andy Warhol.

I hung out a lot with Lemmy from Motörhead on that tour, too. He's a very close friend of the family now. I love that guy. Wherever there's a beer tent in the world, there's Lemmy. But I've never seen that man fall down drunk, y'know? Even after twenty or thirty pints. I don't know how he does it. I wouldn't be surprised if he outlived me *and* Keith Richards.

Motörhead opened a few shows for us on that tour. They had this old hippy bus – it was the cheapest thing they could find – and all Lemmy would carry around with him was this suitcase full of books. That's all he had in the world, apart from the clothes on his back. He loves reading, Lemmy. He'll spend days at a time doing it. He came up to stay with us at the Howard Hughes house one time, and he wouldn't leave the library.

Don Arden found him in there and threw a fit. He stormed

to the lounge and shouted, 'Sharon! Who the *fuck* is that caveman in my library? Get him out! Get him out of my house!'

'Relax, Dad. It's just Lemmy.'

'I don't care who he is. Get him out of here!'

'He's in a band, Dad. They're supporting Ozzy.'

'Well, for Christ's sake at least get him a deckchair and put him out by the pool. He looks like the undead.'

Then Lemmy came strolling into the room. Don was right: he looked horrendous. We'd been out on the piss the night before, and his eyes were so red, they looked like puddles of blood.

But as soon as he saw me, he stopped dead in his tracks.

'Fuck me, Ozzy,' he said. 'If I look half as bad as you do, I'm going back to bed, right now.'

When I finally got back to Bulrush Cottage at the end of 1981, I made a big effort to sort things out with Thelma. We even booked a holiday to Barbados with the kids.

Trouble is, if you're a chronic alcoholic, Barbados isn't the place to go. As soon as we got to the resort, I realised you could drink at the beach twenty-four hours a day. Which I saw as a challenge. We got there at five o'clock and I was legless by six. Thelma was used to seeing me pissed, but I was on another level altogether in Barbados.

All I remember is that at some point we bought tickets for a day trip around the bay on this olde worlde pirate ship. They had music and dancing and a walk-the-plank competition and all that kids' stuff. Meanwhile, the big attraction for the adults was a barrel of rum punch they had at the ship's bar. I just about jumped into that thing.

Every two minutes, it was *glug-glug-glug*.

After a few hours of that, I stripped down to my underpants, danced around the deck, then dived off the ship into these shark-infested waters. Unfortunately, I was too pissed to swim, so this big fucking Barbadian guy had to jump in after me and save my life. The last thing I remember is being hauled back on board and then falling asleep in the middle of the dance floor, still dripping wet. When the ship got back to the harbour, I was still there, dribbling and snoring. Apparently the captain came over and asked the kids, 'Is that your dad?' They went, 'Yeah,' then burst into tears.

Not exactly Father of the Year.

When we got on the plane to go home, Thelma turned to me and said, 'This is the end, John. I want a divorce.'

I thought, Ah, she's just pissed off because of the pirate ship incident. She'll come to her senses.

But she never did.

When the plane landed at Heathrow, someone from Jet Records had organised a helicopter to pick me up and take me to a meeting about the *Diary of a Madman* tour. I said goodbye to the kids, kissed them on the heads, then Thelma looked at me for a long time.

'It's over, John,' she said. 'This time, it's really over.'

I still didn't believe her. I'd behaved so badly over the years, I thought she'd put up with anything. So I climbed into the helicopter and off I went to this country hotel, where Sharon was waiting with all these set designers and lighting technicians.

They led me into a conference room with a scale model of the *Diary of a Madman* stage in the middle of it.

It looked incredible.

'The beauty of this stage,' one of the technical guys told me, 'is that it's easy to carry, and easy to put together.'

'It's brilliant,' I said. 'Really brilliant. Now all we need is a midget.'

The idea had come to me in Barbados. Every night on the tour, halfway through 'Goodbye to Romance', we'd stage the execution of a midget. I'd shout, 'Hang the bastard!' or something like that, and this little guy would be hoisted up with a fake noose around his neck.

It would be magic.

So, before we went out on the road, we held midget auditions.

Now, most people don't realise that little people who are in the entertainment business are all in competition for the same jobs, so they're forever backstabbing each other. When you hold auditions, they'll come walking in and say, 'Oh, you don't want to work with that last guy. I did *Snow White and the Seven* with him a couple of years ago, and he's a pain in the arse.' It always cracked me up when a midget talked about being in *Snow White and the Seven*. They'd say it with a completely straight face, too, like they thought it was some hip and cool underground thing to do.

After a few days of searching, we finally found just the right bloke for the job. His name was John Allen, and, funnily enough, he was an alcoholic. He'd get shitfaced after the gigs and start chasing groupies. He was paranoid, too. He carried this little penknife in a holster. One day I asked him what it was for and he said, 'Just in case the noose slips.' I said, 'You're three feet tall and you'll be dangling twenty feet off the ground, so what are you gonna do, cut the rope? You'll end up like a fucking pancake!'

He was a funny guy, that John Allen. He had a completely normal-sized head, so he'd be sitting opposite you on a bar stool, and you'd forget that his feet couldn't touch the ground. But when he got loaded he'd lose his balance, so one moment he'd be there, and the next you'd hear this thump and he'd be on the floor. We used to play jokes on him all the fucking time. When we were on the tour bus, we'd wait until he passed out, then we'd put him on the highest bunk bed, so when he woke up he'd roll over and go, 'Aarrgh!' *Splat*.

He was as bad as me when it came to drinking. One time,

he was so out of his shitter at Los Angeles airport that he missed his flight, so we had to send one of the roadies to pick him up. The roadie just grabbed him by the back of his trousers and threw him into the luggage compartment under the tour bus.

Then this woman came running over and shouted, 'Hey, I saw what you did to that poor little man! You can't treat him like that!'

The roadie just looked at her and said, 'Fuck off. He's *our* midget.'

Then this little head poked out from between the suitcases and went, 'Yeah, fuck off, I'm *his* midget.'

When the tour started at the end of 1981, I was a wreck. I was in love with Sharon, but at the same time I was cut to pieces by losing my family. Then the fights between me and Sharon started to get even crazier than before. I'd get drunk and try to hit her, and she'd throw things at me. Wine bottles, gold discs, TVs – you name it, it would all come flying across the room. I ain't proud to admit that a few of my punches reached their target. I gave her a black eye once and I thought her dad was gonna rip me into pieces. But he just said, 'Watch yourself.' It's shameful, what I did when I was loaded. The fact that I ever raised my hand against a woman disgusts me. It was a fucking atrocious, unforgivable way to behave, and there's no excuse for it, ever. And like I said before, it's something I'll take to the grave with me. I don't know why Sharon stuck around, to be honest with you.

Sometimes she'd wake up in the morning and I'd be gone, 'cos I'd hitch-hiked back to Bulrush Cottage. But every time I got home, Thelma would tell me to fuck off. That went on for weeks. It was fucking me up, fucking up the kids, fucking up Thelma.

And I can only imagine what it was doing to Sharon.

It took me a long, long time to get over the break-up with

Thelma. It tore me apart. I've said to my kids, 'I don't want you to think I jumped away from you and clicked my heels and said, "*bon voyage*". It wasn't like that at all. It just about destroyed me.'

But eventually my little trips to Bulrush Cottage ended. The last time I went there it was pissing it down with rain and already getting dark. As soon as I walked through the gate, this heavy-set bloke popped out of nowhere and said, 'Oi, where d'you think you're going, eh?'

'This is my house,' I told him.

The bloke shook his head. 'No it ain't. This is your ex-wife's house. And you're not allowed within fifty yards of it. Court order. If you take one step further, you're spending the night in jail.'

He must have been a bailiff or something.

From the garden, I could hear Thelma laughing inside the house. She was with her divorce lawyer, I think.

'Can I at least get some clothes?' I asked.

'Wait here.'

Five minutes later, some of my old stage clothes came flying out of the door and landed on the grass. By the time I'd picked them up and stuffed them into a carrier bag they were soaked through. Then the door opened again, and out came my seven-foot-tall stuffed grizzly bear, his head in shreds after the time I opened fire on him with the Benelli. That bear was pretty much the only thing I got out of that divorce, along with the knackered old Merc that the cats had scratched up. Thelma got the house, every last penny I had in the bank, and a weekly allowance. I also wanted to pay for the kids to go to private schools. It was the least I could do.

I felt terribly sorry for myself that night.

Trying to carry a seven-foot bear back to London didn't exactly make things easier. It wouldn't fit in the cab with me, so I had to order a second cab, just for the bear. Then I had to leave it propped up against a bus stop on the street outside Sharon's house on Wimbledon Common while I carried my bags into the hallway. But instead of going back out to get the bear, me and Sharon decided that it would be funnier to put one of her frilly kitchen aprons on it, and then get her friends to come outside and see it. But while we were trying to organise all that, someone nicked the fucking thing. I was heartbroken. I loved that bear.

As for the kids, once the damage is done with a divorce, you can't ever make it right, although we've since become close again. And divorce was a much bigger deal back then.

In LA today, if your marriage breaks up, your wife will marry me, and I'll marry your ex-wife, and we'll all have fucking dinner and holidays in Mexico together. That ain't cool with me. I don't understand how people can do that. I haven't seen Thelma for decades.

And, to be honest with you, I think it's for the best.

By the time we took the *Diary of a Madman* tour to America, we were experts at midget-hanging. But there were some other problems with the show – like the medieval chain-mail suit I used to wear during a few of the numbers. As soon as I worked up a sweat, it was like being wrapped in razor blades. By the end of the night, I was carved up like a slice of roast beef. We also had a lot of trouble with our stage props. For example, we had these kabuki curtains that dropped down from above the stage in two parts, instead of parting in the middle like normal theatrical curtains do. The curtains would go down halfway through the show, and then when they were pulled up again, this mechanical arm with a giant God-like hand on the end of it would come out from under the drum riser and soar above the audience, with me crouching down in the palm. When the arm was fully extended, flames would shoot out of one of the fingers, and I'd stomp on this pedal by my foot, which would activate a catapult behind me, and about fifty pounds of raw meat would be flung into the audience.

Then I'd stand up and shout, 'ROCK 'N' ROLL!'

It was fucking awesome.

But, of course, what can go wrong will go wrong – and pretty much *everything* went wrong on the second night of the US tour. It was New Year's Eve, and we were at the Los Angeles Memorial Coliseum and Sports Arena, playing to a crowd of tens of thousands. First the smoke machine went on the blink. It was coughing out so much dry ice that no one could see what the fuck they were doing. Then, for some reason, one of the kabuki curtains wouldn't come down, so we couldn't get the giant God-like hand ready for its entrance. I remember standing there in my chain-mail suit, watching as Sharon literally swung from this curtain, trying to get it to fall. 'Drop, you bastard, *drop*!' she was screaming.

Eventually, after a couple of roadies joined in, they got the thing unstuck. But then the mechanical arm for the hand got caught up in the carpet on the floor of the stage and started to pull it from under the giant speaker cabinets behind the band, making them wobble like crazy. 'TIMBER!' one of the roadies shouted. For what might have been the longest thirty seconds of all our lives, Sharon, my assistant Tony and a bunch of roadies were wrestling with this carpet, trying to untangle it from the mechanical arm, to stop the whole fucking set collapsing.

Finally the carpet was pulled free, someone gave me a shove from behind, the kabuki curtains went up again, and before I knew it I was crouching down in the hand as it rose into the air, with this ocean of screaming kids below me. By that time I was convinced that something else was going to go wrong. So when the arm was fully extended, I covered my eyes and prepared to get my nuts blown off by the pyro, but the flames shot out of the finger without a problem. I was so relieved I almost wept. Then it was time for the final gimmick, so I stomped on the pedal beside my foot to activate the catapult. But what I didn't know was that some dipshit from the stage crew had set the catapult the previous night rather than just before the show, so the elastic had gone all limp. When I pressed the button, it just went *phut*, and instead of this massive payload of pigs' bollocks and cows' entrails flying into the audience, it smacked me at 20 mph in the back of the head. The last thing I remember is screaming 'Aaaarrgh!' and feeling all this blood and offal dribbling down the back of my neck.

The crowd thought it was all part of the show and went fucking wild.

It became one of our trademarks, throwing butchers' offcuts into the audience. As well as the catapult, we used to get the midget to come on stage with buckets of offal and throw them into the audience before he was hung. It was our version of the custard-pie fights I used to love seeing on telly when I was a kid. But then the audience got involved, and the fans started to bring their own meat, and throw it at us. When we finished a gig, it looked like the Trail of fucking Tears. You'd never get that kind of shit past health and safety today.

And it was amazing how quickly it got out of control.

One time this cop came up to me after a show and said, 'Have you any idea what you're doing to the youth of America?'

Then he showed me this Polaroid photograph of a kid in the queue outside the gig with an ox's head on his shoulders.

'Holy crap,' I said. 'Where did he get that from?'

'He killed it on his way to the gig.'

'Well, I hope he was hungry.'

It was insane what the kids would bring. It started with just cuts of meat, but then it moved on to entire animals. We had dead cats, birds, lizards, all kinds of stuff. One time, someone threw this huge bullfrog on to the stage, and it landed on its back. The fucking thing was so big, I thought it was someone's baby. I got a terrible fright. I started screaming, 'WHAT'S THAT? WHAT'S THAT? WHAT'S THAT?' Then it rolled over and hopped away.

With every gig, it just got crazier and crazier. Eventually people started to throw things on stage with nails and razor blades embedded in them – joke shop stuff, mainly, like rubber snakes and plastic spiders. Some of the crew started to get freaked out about it, especially after a *real* snake ended up on stage one night. It was well and truly pissed off about being on stage with Ozzy Osbourne, that snake was. One of the roadies caught it with one of those big nets on a stick you use to clean swimming pools.

Tony – who had a small walk-on part in the show – was the jumpiest when it came to the creepy-crawlies. Basically, all he had to do was put on this suit of armour and bring me a drink on stage during a break while the scenery was changed. But it took the poor bloke about half an hour to get the suit on and off, and he spent the whole time shitting himself about something being thrown at him. So one night, just to wind him up, I threw a rubber snake in his direction, and when he jumped backwards, one of the roadies dropped a piece of string down his back. Tony went mental. He had that suit of armour off in about three seconds, until he was standing there with nothing on but these grey tights. He was so freaked out I swear his voice went up by three octaves.

It brought the house down.

I'm telling you: something crazy happened on every night of that tour.

And then on 20 January 1982 we played the Veterans Auditorium in Des Moines, Iowa. I'll never forget the name of that place, that's for sure. Or how to pronounce it: 'DEE-Moyn'.

The gig was going great. The God-like hand was working without any hitches. We'd already hung the midget.

Then, from out of the audience came this bat.

Obviously a toy, I thought.

So I held it up to the lights and bared my teeth while Randy played one of his solos. The crowd went mental.

Then I did what I always did when we got a rubber toy on stage.

CHOMP.

Immediately though, something felt wrong. *Very* wrong.

For a start, my mouth was instantly full of this warm, gloopy liquid, with the worst aftertaste you could ever imagine. I could feel it staining my teeth and running down my chin.

Then the head in my mouth twitched.

Oh, *fuck me* I thought. I didn't just go and eat a fucking bat, did I?

So I spat out the head, looked over into the wings, and saw Sharon with her eyes bulging, waving her hands, screaming, 'NOOOOOOOOOOOOOOOOO!!!!!!!!!!!!! IT'S REAL, OZZY, IT'S REAL!'

Next thing I knew I was in a wheelchair, being rushed into an emergency room. Meanwhile, a doctor was saying to Sharon, 'Yes, Miss Arden, the bat was alive. It was probably stunned from being at a rock concert, but it was definitely alive. There's a good chance Mr Osbourne now has rabies. Symptoms? Oh, y'know, malaise, headache, fever, violent twitches, uncontrollable excitement, depression, a pathological fear of liquids . . .'

'Not much chance of that,' muttered Sharon.

'Mania is usually one of the final symptoms. Then the patient gets very lethargic, falls into a coma, and stops breathing.'

'Oh my God.'

'That's why eating a bat is generally a bad idea, from a medical standpoint.'

'Isn't there a vaccine?'

'It's usually best administered beforehand, but, yes, we can give him a shot. A few shots, actually.'

Then the doctor went to get a syringe the size of a grenade launcher.

'OK, Mr Osbourne,' he said. 'You'll need to take off your pants and bend over.'

I did as he said.

'This might sting a bit.'

That was the last thing I heard.

Every night for the rest of the tour I had to find a doctor and get more rabies shots: one in each arse cheek, one in each thigh, one in each arm. Every one hurt like a bastard. I had more holes in me than a lump of fucking Swiss cheese. But it was better than getting rabies, I suppose. Not that anyone would have noticed the difference if I'd gone insane. Meanwhile, the press were going nuts. The next morning, I was the 'And finally . . . ' item on just about every news show on the planet. Everyone thought I'd bitten the head of a bat *on purpose*, instead of it being a simple misunderstanding. For a while, I was worried we might be closed down, and a couple of venues did go ahead and ban us. The fans didn't help, either. After they heard about the bat, they started bringing even crazier stuff to the gigs. Going on stage was like being at a butchers' convention.

And, of course, the animal rights people were going nuts. The American Society for the Prevention of Cruelty to Animals sent people to 'monitor' our gigs. The crew would fuck with them all the time. They'd say, 'Oh, Ozzy's going to throw eighteen puppies into the audience tonight, and he won't sing a note until they've all been slaughtered.'

The ASPCA believed every word of it.

They even pulled over our tour bus in Boston. I remember all these do-gooders jumping on and seeing Sharon's Yorkshire terrier – Mr Pook – and having a fit. One of the guys shouted, 'OK, this bus isn't going any further. I want that dog taken into protective custody. Now!'

What did they think was going to happen? That we were going to start mowing down Yorkshire terriers with a machine-gun halfway through 'You Lookin' at Me Lookin' at You'?

A few nights later, we were playing Madison Square Garden in New York. The whole place stank of shit. It turned out that they'd had a circus in there the week before, and the animals were still locked in their cages underneath the bleachers at the back. One of the venue managers came over and invited the crew to see them. But as soon as he saw me, he went, 'I didn't mean *you*.'

'Why not?' I said.

'You can't be trusted around animals.'

I couldn't believe what I was hearing.

'What the *fuck* do you think I'm going to do?' I asked him. 'Bite the head off an elephant?'

If you'd asked anyone on the *Diary of a Madman* crew which member of the band might not make it through the tour – me, Randy, Rudy or Tommy – they'd have put all their money on me.

Like the song said, the way I was boozing was a kind of suicide. It was only gonna be a matter of time.

Sharon was convinced something bad would happen. So whenever I'd been drinking in the hotel, she'd steal all my clothes, so there was no way I could leave and get into any trouble – unless I was prepared to walk down to the lobby stark bollock naked.

It worked, most of the time.

But then we got to San Antonio, Texas. As usual, I got shit-faced in the hotel. And, as usual, Sharon nicked my clothes. But she made the mistake of leaving one of her evening gowns in the room. It was this dark green frilly thing, and with a bit of ripping and tearing at the seams I got it on. Then I found some running shoes, and I was off.

So there I was in Sharon's evening dress, on the loose, slinging this bottle of Courvoisier around the streets of San Antonio, looking for trouble. I think we might have had a photo shoot going on that day, but I can't remember for sure. I do know that I was blasted. Then I got this sudden urge to take a piss, as you do when you're blasted. Actually, it was more than an urge: my bladder felt like a hot cannon ball. I had to go, right there, right then. But I was in the middle of this strange town in Texas, and I didn't have a clue where the public bogs were. So I looked around, found a quiet corner, and started taking a slash against this crumbly old wall.

Ahhhh. That's *better*.

Then I heard this voice behind me.

'You *disgust* me.'

'What?' I turned around to see this old timer in a cowboy hat, staring at me like I'd just molested his gran.

'You're a *disgrace*, d'ya know that?'

'My girlfriend nicked my clothes,' I explained. 'What else was I supposed to fucking wear?'

'It ain't the dress, you limey faggot piece o' dirt. That wall you're relieving yourself on is the Alamo!'

'The Aalawot?'

Before he could answer, two fat Texan coppers came puffing around the corner, radios crackling.

'That's the one,' said the old bloke. 'Him . . . in the *dress*.'

BAM!

I was face down in the dirt, being handcuffed.

It took a moment for it all to click. I'd definitely heard of the Alamo – I'd seen the John Wayne movie a few times. So I knew it was this big-deal place where lots of Americans had been killed while they were fighting the Mexicans. But I hadn't made the connection between the old wall I was pissing on and the ruins of a sacred national monument.

'You're a Brit, ain'tcha?' one of the cops said to me.

'So?'

'Well, how would you feel if I urinated on Buckingham Palace, huh?'

I gave it some thought. Then I said to him, 'I've no idea. I don't fucking live there, do I?'

That went down a treat, that did.

Ten minutes later, I was sharing a jail cell with a twenty-stone Mexican bloke who'd just murdered his wife with a brick, or some crazy shit. He must have thought he was hallucinating when he saw me show up in a green frock. I was thinking, Christ, he's going to think I'm the ghost of his missus, and then he's going to try to give her one last dick up the arse.

But all he did was grunt and stare.

I was in the cage for about three hours. Some of the cops and their friends came over to look at me. Maybe some of them had bought *Blizzard of Ozz*, I don't know. But they gave me a pretty easy ride. They did me for public intoxication, instead of the more heavy-duty desecration of a venerated object, which would have meant a year in the slammer. And they let me out in time for the gig. Although the chief came down personally to tell me that, as soon as the show was over, I had to leave town and never show my ugly mug again.

That one piss cost me a fortune in lost San Antonio gigs over the years. And rightly so; I suppose: pissing on the Alamo wasn't the cleverest thing I'd ever done. It wasn't so much like pissing on Buckingham Palace as pissing on one of the monuments at a Normandy beach. Unforgivable. A few years later, I apologised in person to the Mayor, promised never to do it again, and donated ten grand to the Daughters of the Republic of Texas. He let me play in the town again after that, although it took more than a decade for it to happen.

When I finally went back, I remember this scrawny Mexican kid coming up to me after the show.

'Ozzy, is it true you got busted for pissing on the Alamo?' he asked me.

'Yeah,' I told him. 'It's true.'

'Shit, man,' he said. 'We piss on it every night on our way home.'

8

While I was Sleeping

We were in the tour bus, on our way from Tennessee to Florida, when Randy broke the news.

'I don't think I want to be a rock 'n' roller any more,' he said.

I waited for him to crack a smile. But he didn't.

We were sitting at a little picnic table in the kitchen area of the bus, which was like a five-star hotel on wheels. It had TVs hanging from the ceiling, shag-pile carpets, air-conditioning, limo-style windows, a flash gold and white paint job, and – of course – a fully stocked bar.

I'd been drinking gin all night. After that bad scene at the Alamo, I'd gone easy on the Courvoisier for a while.

Randy was smoking fags and sipping from a can of Coke. He hardly touched the booze. He only liked that horrible aniseed shit. What's it called? *Anisette*. Like a thick, milky liqueur thing. Didn't do drugs, either. Mind you, he made up for it with the fags. He could have won a gold medal in the Lung Cancer Olympics, could Randy Rhoads.

'Are you joking with me?' I said, trying not to choke on my drink.

'No, Ozzy, I'm serious.'

I couldn't believe what I was hearing.

It was long after midnight – maybe three or four in the morning – and me and Randy were the only ones still awake. Sharon was in the bedroom at the back. Rudy and Tommy were sprawled out on the bunks, along with some of the crew members who travelled with us, like Rachel Youngblood, an older black lady who did all our wardrobe, hair and make-up.

I was amazed they could sleep, 'cos the bus was rattling and shaking and groaning like it was gonna fall to pieces. It was a seven-hundred-mile journey from Knoxville to Orlando, and the driver was going like the clappers. I remember looking out of the window at all the headlamps of the cars and trucks flying past in the other direction and thinking, Any minute now, the wheels are gonna come off this thing. I had no idea that the driver had a nose full of coke. I only found that out later from the coroner's report.

Mind you, I had no idea about anything, me. I was out of my skull with all the booze and the coke and the fuck-knows-what-else I was shoving down my throat, twenty-four hours a day.

But I knew I didn't want Randy to leave.

'How could you quit *now*?' I said to him. 'We've only just broken through, man. Sharon says *Diary of a Madman* might sell even more copies than *Blizzard*. It's going fucking gangbusters all over the world. Tomorrow night we're playing with *Foreigner*!'

Randy just shrugged and said, 'I want to go to university. Get a degree.'

'Are you mad?' I said. 'Keep this up for a couple of years and you can buy your own fucking university.'

At least that made him smile.

'Look,' I went on. 'You're just knackered. Why don't you get some rest, give yourself a bit of a break, y'know?'

'I could say the same thing to you, Ozzy.'

'What d'you mean?'

'That's your fourth bottle of gin in twenty-four hours.'

'Keeps me happy.'

'Ozzy, why do you drink so much? What's the point?'

The right answer to that question was: because I'm an alcoholic; because I have an addictive personality; because whatever I do, I do it addictively. But I didn't know any of that back then.

All I ever knew was that I wanted another drink.

So I just gave Randy a blank look.

'You'll kill yourself, y'know?' said Randy. 'One of these days.'

'Goodnight Randy,' I said, draining my glass. 'I'm off to bed.'

When I opened my eyes a few hours later, it was getting light. Sharon was lying next to me in her dressing-gown. My head felt like a pile of toxic shit.

I couldn't understand why I'd woken up so early. The gin should have knocked me out until at least mid-afternoon.

Then I heard the noise.

It sounded like an engine at full revs. I thought we must have been overtaking a truck.

BBBBBBRRRRRRRRRRRRRRMMMM . . .

Whatever it was that was making the din seemed to move away from the bus, but then all of a sudden it came back, even louder than before

BBBBBBRRRRRRRRRRRRRRRRMMMMMMMMMM-MMMMMMBBBBBBRRRRRRRRRRRRRRRRMMMMMM MMM . . .

'Sharon?' I said. 'What the *fuck* is that noi—'

Then my head smashed into the bed frame as all the windows of the bus exploded.

I could smell fuel.

For a second, there was nothing but blackness.

Next thing I know I'm looking out of the porthole-shaped window next to my left arm. I can see black smoke and people with their heads in their hands, screaming. So I jump out of bed – stark bollock naked apart from a pair of greasy old Y-fronts – and force open the bedroom door. There are tiny fragments of glass everywhere, and a fucking massive hole in the roof. Then I notice that the entire bus has been bent into a V-shape.

The first thing that comes into my head is that the driver must have lost control on the freeway. We must have crashed.

Then I'm coughing from the stench of the fuel and the smoke from the fire outside.

And I think: Fire and fuel. Oh, *fuck*.

'EVERYONE GET OFF THE FUCKING BUS!' I start to shout. 'IT'S GONNA BLOW! IT'S GONNA BLOW!'

Panic.

Numb legs.

Sharon screaming.

I was still sozzled from the gin. My head was throbbing. My eyes were all crusty and raw. I looked for an emergency exit, but there wasn't one. So I ran to the open door at the front of the bus instead, pulling Sharon along behind me. Then I looked around for the others, but all the bunks were empty. Where the fuck had everyone else gone? Where the hell was Randy?

I jumped out of the bus and landed on grass.

Grass?

At that point I thought I must have been dreaming.

Where was the road? Where were the cars? I'd expected to see twisted metal, blood, spinning hub-caps. But we were parked in the middle of a field, surrounded by a bunch of over-the-top, coke-dealer-style mansions. I saw a sign that said, 'Flying Baron Estates'. Then, next to one of the houses, a gigantic fireball – like something from the set of a James Bond film. That's where all the smoke was coming from. There was wreckage strewn around it. And what looked like . . .

Oh, Jesus Christ. I almost threw up when I saw that shit.

I had to turn away.

Aside from the smoke, it was a clear day – but it was early, so there was still a kind of muggy haze in the air.

'Where are we? What's happening?' I kept saying, over and over. I'd never felt so totally fucking out-of-it in my life. It was worse than the worst acid trip I'd ever had. Then I noticed what looked like an air strip and a hangar. Next to the hangar, a woman in riding gear was walking next to a horse, like nothing had happened – like this was an everyday fucking occurrence. I was thinking, This is a nightmare, I'm dreaming, this can't be real.

I stood there, in a trance, while our keyboard player, Don Airey, ran back to the bus, grabbed a miniature fire extinguisher from somewhere, jumped off the bus, then pointed it in the direction of the flames.

It spluttered and dribbled uselessly.

Meanwhile, Sharon was trying to do a head count, but people were scattered all over the field. They were just pointing at the flames and wailing and sobbing.

Now I could make out the remains of a garage around the flames. It looked as though there were two cars inside.

Something must have crashed into it.

And whatever it was must also have ripped the hole in our tour bus and taken out half the trees behind it.

Then Sharon went over to Don – 'El-Doom-O', we used to call him, 'cos he was always expecting the worst – and screamed, 'What happened? Tell me, what the *fuck* happened?' But Don was crouched down in a ball and couldn't talk. So Sharon turned to Jake Duncan, our Scottish tour manager. But he couldn't say anything, either. Next thing I knew, Sharon took off her shoe and just started beating Jake around the head with it.

'Where are Randy and Rachel? Where are Randy and Rachel?'

All Jake could do was point towards the flames.

'I don't understand,' Sharon said. 'I don't *understand*.'

I didn't understand, either. Nobody had said, 'Oh, by the way, Ozzy, on the way to Orlando, we're gonna stop off at a bus depot in Leesburg to fix the air conditioning.' Nobody had said, 'Oh, and by the way, Ozzy, the bus depot is part of this dodgy housing estate with an air strip.' Nobody had said, 'Oh, yeah, and your driver – who's been up all night, out of his mind on cocaine – also happens to be pilot with an expired medical certificate who's going to borrow some bloke's plane without his permission and then, while you're fast asleep, take your lead guitarist and your make-up artist on a sight-seeing trip above the tour bus, before dive-bombing into it.'

Nobody had said anything like that at all.

Then the house next to the garage catches fire, and without even thinking I'm running towards it – still half-pissed, still in my Y-fronts – to make sure no one's inside. When I get to the front door, I knock, wait for about two seconds, then barge in.

In the kitchen an old bloke is making coffee. He almost falls off his chair when he sees me.

'Who the hell are you?' he says. 'Get out of my house!'

'There's a fire!' I shout at him. 'Get out! Get out!'

The guy was clearly insane, 'cos he just picked up a broom from the corner and tried to push me away with it. 'Get out of my house, you little bastard! Go on, fuggarf!'

'YOUR FUCKING HOUSE IS ON FUCKING FIRE!'

'GEDDOUT! GEDDOUT, GODAMMIT!'

'YOUR HOUSE IS—'

Then I realised he was stone deaf. He wouldn't have heard if the entire fucking planet had exploded. He certainly couldn't hear a word this long-haired, raving English loony in his underpants was telling him. I couldn't think what to do, so I just ran to the other side of the kitchen, where there was a door which led to the garage. I opened it, and the fucking thing practically blew off its hinges from the force of the fire.

The old bloke didn't tell me to get out of his house again after that.

We only learned the full story much later. The bus driver was called Andrew C. Aycock. Six years earlier, he'd been involved in a fatal helicopter crash in the United Arab Emirates. Then he'd got a job working for the Calhoun Twins, a Country & Western act who owned the company that was doing the transportation for our tour. When we stopped at the bus depot to fix the air conditioning, Aycock decided to try his luck at flying again. So, without asking, he took a plane belonging to a mate of his.

Don and Jake were the first to go up with him. Everything was fine: the take-off and landing went smoothly. Then it was Randy and Rachel's turn. There's a photograph of the two of them standing beside the plane, just before they got on. They're both smiling. I saw it once, but I could never look at it again. I'm told that Rachel agreed to go up only after Aycock promised not to pull any stunts while they were in the air. If he promised her that, he was a fucking liar as well as a coked-up lunatic: everyone on the ground said he buzzed the tour bus two or three times before the wing clipped the roof a few inches from where me and Sharon were sleeping. But the most insane thing – and the one fact I still can't get my head around, nearly thirty years later – is that the bloke was going through a heavy-duty divorce at the time, and his soon-to-be-ex missus was standing right next to the bus when he crashed the plane into it. He'd picked her up at one of the tour venues, apparently, and was giving her a ride home.

A ride home? The woman he was *divorcing*?

At the time, there was a lot of talk that he might have been trying to kill her, but who the fuck knows? Whatever he was trying to do, he came down so low that even if he'd managed to miss the tour bus, he would have hit the trees behind it.

Don watched the whole thing happen.

I feel bad for him, 'cos it must have been a terrible thing to see. When the wing hit the bus, Randy and Rachel were thrown through the windscreen, or so I was told. Then the plane – minus its wing – smashed into the trees behind, fell into the garage, and exploded. The fire was so intense, the cops had to use dental records to identify the bodies.

Even now I don't like talking or thinking about it.

If I'd been awake, I would have been on that fucking plane, no question. Knowing me, I'd have been on the wing, pissed, doing handstands and backflips. But it makes no sense to me that Randy went up.

He *hated* flying.

A few weeks earlier, I'd been drinking with him in a bar in Chicago. We were about to take a ten-day break from the tour, and Randy was asking how long it would take him to drive from New York to Georgia, where we were starting up again. I asked why the fuck he would want to drive all the way from New York to Georgia when there was an invention called the aeroplane. He told me he'd been freaked out by the Air Florida plane that had crashed into a bridge in Washington a few days earlier. Seventy-eight people had died. So Randy wasn't exactly the type of person to go clowning around in a bullshit four-seat piece of shit. He didn't even want to get on a jet run by a big commercial airline.

Some weird fucking unexplained shit went on that morning, because Rachel didn't like planes, either. She had a weak heart, so she would hardly have wanted to do a loop-the-fucking-loop. A lot of people say, 'Oh, they were pissing around, typical fucking rock stars.' I want to set the record straight: Rachel was in her late fifties and had a heart condition; Randy was a very level-headed guy and he was afraid of flying. None of it makes any sense.

By the time the fire engines arrived, the flames had already burned themselves out. Randy was gone. Rachel was gone. I finally put on some clothes and took a beer from what was left of the fridge in the bus. I couldn't handle the situation. Sharon was running around trying to find a telephone. She wanted to call her father. Then the cops arrived. Good ol' boy types. They weren't too sympathetic.

'Ozzy Ozz-Burn, huh?' they said. 'The bat-eating madman.'

We checked into some shithole called the Hilco Inn in Leesburg and tried to hide from the press while the police did their thing. We had to call Randy's mum and Rachel's best friend Grace, which was horrendous.

All of us wanted to get the fuck out of Leesburg, but we had to stay put until all the paperwork was done.

None of us could get our heads around the situation. Everything had been magic one minute, and the next it had taken such an ugly, tragic turn.

'Y'know what? I think this is a sign that I ain't supposed to do this any more,' I said to Sharon.

By then I was having a total physical and mental breakdown. A doctor had to come over and shoot me up with sedatives. Sharon wasn't doing much better. She was in a terrible state, poor Sharon. The one thing that gave us some comfort was a message from AC/DC saying, 'If there's anything we can do, let us know.' That meant a lot to me, and I'll always be grateful to them for it. You learn who your friends are when the shit hits the fan. In fact, AC/DC must have known exactly what we'd been going through, 'cos it had only been a couple of years since their singer Bon Scott had died from alcohol poisoning, also at a tragically young age.

The morning after the crash I called my sister Jean, who told me that my mother had been on a bus when she'd seen a newspaper stand with the headline, 'OZZY OSBOURNE – AIRCRASH DEATH'. My poor old mum had gone crazy. Then later that day, I went back to the dodgy housing estate with Randy's brother-in-law. The bus was still there, twisted into the shape of a boomerang, next to the ruins of the garage. And there, in the corner, untouched in all the ash and rubble, was a perfect little cut-out section of the Gibson T-shirt that Randy had been wearing when he died. Just the logo, nothing else. I couldn't believe it – it was so spooky.

Meanwhile, outside the hotel, all these kids had started to hang around. I noticed that some of them were wearing the *Diary of a Madman* tracksuits we'd had made for the tour, so I said to Sharon, 'We're not selling those things, are we?' When she said 'no', I walked up to this kid and asked, 'Where did you get the tracksuit from?'

He said, 'Oh, I went in and got it off the bus.'

I went fucking crazy. Almost ripped his head off.

Eventually all the paperwork was done – the only drug they found in Randy's body was nicotine – and the cops let us leave. They were glad to see us go, I imagine.

Then we had to do two funerals in one week, and it was fucking heavy-duty on all of us, especially Sharon, who suffered terribly. She couldn't even listen to the *Diary of a Madman* album again for years.

Randy's funeral was held at the First Lutheran Church in Burbank. I was one of the pallbearers. They had big pictures of Randy all around the altar. I remember thinking: It's only been a few days since I was sitting on the bus with him, calling him mad for wanting to go to university. I felt so bad. Randy was one of the greatest guys who'd ever been in my life. And I suppose I felt guilty, too, because if he hadn't been in my band, he wouldn't have died. I don't know how Randy's mother survived the funeral – she must be some kind of woman. Her little baby had died. She was divorced, Delores was, so her kids meant everything to her. And Randy really loved her – he absolutely adored her. For years after, every time me and Sharon used to see Dee, we felt terrible. I mean, what can you say? It's gotta be any parent's worst nightmare when they lose their child like that.

After the service there was a motorcade from Burbank to San Bernardino, about an hour away. Randy was laid to rest at a place called Mountain View Cemetery, where his grandparents were buried. I made a vow there and then to honour his death every year by sending flowers. Unlike most of my vows, I kept it. But I've never been back to his graveside. I'd like to go there again one day, before I finally join him on the other side.

Rachel's funeral couldn't have been more different. It was at a black gospel church somewhere in South LA. She was very big on her church, Rachel was. And during the service they're all singing gospel and diving on the floor and shouting, 'Jesus Loves You, Rachel!' I'm thinking, What the fuck's all this about? It's a joyous experience, an African-American funeral. There's no moping around.

The following week I did the David Letterman show. It was surreal, man. As soon as I'd sat down and the band stopped playing, Dave said to me, 'Let's just get right to it, Ozzy. From what I hear, you bit the head off a . . .'

I couldn't believe he was going there.

'Oh, don't,' I said. But it was too late.

Dave was very cool with me overall – he was very nice, very sympathetic – but I was in no mood for the bat story. Shock is a very weird thing, and the funerals had been bad.

At the end of the interview, Dave said to me, 'I know that recently there's been a personal and professional tragedy in your life. Quite honestly, I'm surprised that you went ahead with your commitment to be here, and I appreciate that, and I know you want to take a minute to explain.'

'All I can say is that I lost two of the greatest people in my life,' I said, trying not to choke up. 'But it ain't gonna stop me because I'm about rock 'n' roll, and rock 'n' roll is for the people, and I love people, and that's what I'm about. I'm going to continue because Randy would have liked me to, and so would Rachel, and I'm not going to stop, 'cos you can't kill rock 'n' roll.'

If it sounds a bit over-the-top, it's 'cos I was as pissed as a fart. It was the only way I could function.

In private, I wasn't so sure that you couldn't kill rock 'n' roll. 'It's not meant to be,' I kept telling Sharon. 'Let's call it a day.'

But she wasn't having any of it. 'No, we are not calling it a day. This is what you're meant to do, Ozzy. Nothing's gonna stop us.' If Sharon hadn't given me that speech a few times, I'd never have gone on a stage again.

I don't know who started making the calls to find a new guitarist. Sharon was a mess, totally distraught, so maybe her father's office organised it from LA. But eventually the search became a welcome distraction, a way to take our minds off things. I remember at one point I phoned Michael Schenker, the German guy who had played with UFO. He was like, I'll do you this favour, but I want a private jet, and I want this, and I want that. I said to him, 'Why are you stipulating your demands at this point? Just get me though the next show and we'll talk about it.' But he just kept saying, Oh, I'll need this and I'll need that. So in the end I said, 'Y'know what? Go fuck yourself.'

He's nuts anyway, Schenker, so I don't hold it against him.

Our first stand-in was Bernie Tormé, a tall, blond Irish guy who had played with Ian Gillan's band. Bernie was in an impossible situation, trying to take Randy's place, but he couldn't have been more helpful. Having been thrown in at the deep end, he did an incredible job for a few nights, before leaving to record with his own band. Next we hired Brad Gillis, from Night Ranger, and he got us through to the end of the tour.

I honestly don't know how we did any of those gigs after Randy died. We were all in a state of shock. But I suppose being on the road was better than sitting around at home, thinking about the two incredible people we'd lost, and how we'd never get them back.

A few weeks after Randy died, I asked Sharon to marry me. 'If there's one good thing that could come out of all the shit we've been through on this tour,' I told her, 'it would be making you my wife.'

She said yes. So I put a ring on her finger, and we set a date.

Then the booze wore off and I changed my mind.

After everything that had gone down with Thelma, I was terrified of going through it all again. But then I got over the fear. I was in love with Sharon, and I knew I didn't want anyone else. So, a few weeks later, I proposed again.

'Will you marry me?' I asked her.

'Fuck off.'

'Please?'

'No.'

'*Please?*'

'All right then, yes.'

It went on like that for months. We had more engagements than most people have wedding guests. After the first one, it was usually Sharon who called them off. One time, when we were driving to a meeting in LA, she threw her ring out of the car window 'cos I hadn't come home the night before. So I went out and bought her another one. Then I got pissed and lost it, but I didn't realise until after I'd got down on one knee.

So that one was a non-starter.

But a couple of days later, I bought her another ring and we got engaged yet again. But then I was walking home after a twenty-four-hour bender, and I passed a graveyard. There was one freshly dug grave with a bunch of flowers on top. Beautiful flowers, actually. So I nicked them and gave them to Sharon when I got home. She almost burst into tears, she found it so touching.

Then she made this little sobbing noise and went, 'Oh, Ozzy, and you even wrote me a note, how sweet!'

Suddenly I was thinking: *What* note? I can't remember writing any note.

But it was too late. Sharon was already opening up the envelope and pulling out the card.

'In loving memory of our dearest Harry,' it said.

That was another ring out of the fucking window.

And I got a black eye, for good measure.

I proposed to her seventeen times in the end. You could track me home by the trail of rings. They weren't fucking cheap, either. But they got a lot cheaper as time went on, that's for sure.

Then, as soon as I'd signed the decree-whatever-the-fuck-it's-called to make my divorce with Thelma official, Sharon chose 4 July as our wedding day – so I'd never forget the anniversary.

'At least it's not the first of May,' I said to her.

'Why?'

'That's the date Thelma chose so I'd never forget the anniversary.'

With things getting serious with Sharon, she started to get heavy with me about all the cocaine I was doing. She was fine with the booze, but the coke – no way. The fact that our psycho bus driver had been high on coke when he killed Randy and Rachel made it even worse.

Every time I took the stuff, I'd get a bollocking – to the point where I had to start hiding it from her.

But that caused even more problems.

One time, we were staying in one of the bungalows at the Howard Hughes house, and I'd just bought this eight-ball – an eighth of an ounce of coke – from my dealer.

'This stuff's gonna knock your head off,' the bloke had told me.

As soon as I got back to the bungalow I went over to the bookshelves and hid the plastic bag inside this hardback novel. 'Third shelf up, six books to the left,' I kept repeating, so I'd remember. I was planning to save it for a special occasion, but that night I was having a bit of a bad comedown, so I decided to have a little toot. I made sure that Sharon was asleep, tiptoed out of the bedroom, went over to the bookshelves, counted three up and six across, then opened up the novel. No coke. *Fuck*.

Maybe it was six shelves up and three books from the left?

Still no coke.

So I sneaked out of the bungalow and knocked on the window of the room where Tommy was staying. 'Pssst!' I whispered. 'Hey, Tommy! Are you awake, man? I can't find the fucking coke.'

The second I said that, there was this clattering noise behind me.

Sharon had flung open the window of our bungalow.

'IS THIS WHAT YOU'RE LOOKING FOR, YOU FUCKING DRUG ADDICT?' she shouted, emptying the bag of coke on to a sheet of paper.

'Sharon,' I said. 'Be cool. Don't do anything cra—'

But then she goes *puff*, and blows all the coke into the garden.

Before I even have time to react, Sharon's Great Dane comes lolloping out from his kennel, and starts licking up the coke from the grass like it's the best thing he's ever tasted in his life. I'm thinking, This ain't gonna be good news. Then the dog's tail goes straight out – *BOING!* – and he takes this enormous shit. I've never seen such a big shit in my life, and it goes all over the water fountain in the courtyard. Then the dog takes off. He's a fucking huge dog, this Great Dane, so when he runs he does some damage, knocking over plant pots, denting cars, trampling over flower beds, but he keeps it up for three days and three nights straight, his tongue hanging out, his tail still standing on end.

By the time the coke wore off, I swear the dog had lost four pounds. He'd developed a bit of a taste for the old waffle dust, too.

He was always trying to sniff it out after that.

We got married in Hawaii on the way to a gig in Japan. It was a small ceremony on the island of Maui. Don Arden showed up, but only because he wanted Sharon to sign some paperwork. My mum and my sister Jean came, too. Tommy was my best man. The funny thing about getting married in America was that we needed to get a blood test before they'd give us a licence. I wouldn't have been surprised if the bloke from the lab had called back and said, 'Mr Osbourne, we appear to have found some blood in your alcohol.'

There was a lot of drinking at that wedding, not to mention seven bottles of Hennessy in the wedding cake. If you'd been breathalysed after eating a slice of that stuff, you'd have gone to jail. And I was smoking some killer weed, too.

'Maui-wowy', the local dealer called it.

The stag night was a joke. I got so fucked up in the hotel, I missed it. There's a photograph of me crashed out in the room as everyone's getting ready to leave. Fucking classic. The wedding night was even worse. I didn't even make it back to the room to spend the night with my new wife. At five in the morning, the hotel manager had to call her room and say, 'Will you please come and get your husband. He's asleep in the corridor and blocking the maids.'

*

It wasn't long after I almost pissed in my new father-in-law's face that he stopped calling me Ozzy. He took to calling me 'Vegetable' instead. As in, 'Fuck off, Vegetable,' or, 'Die, Vegetable,' or, 'Get out of my fucking house, right now, Vegetable.' I could understand why the bloke was upset – no one likes to get piss splashed in their direction – but I thought that was a bit much.

Mind you, it was nothing compared with how he'd talk to Sharon. I can't even imagine what it would be like to have your own father say such fucking horrific things to you, but Sharon could take it. She was unbelievably tough like that. And I suppose she was just used to it. Most of the time it was *me* who got upset. I'd sit there and ask myself, How can a human being even come up with that shit? Never mind say it to their own flesh and blood. It was just the vilest stuff, from the depths of the lowest places.

Then, the next thing you knew, they were friends again.

That's how Sharon was raised – and why she's so extreme. But I needed someone like her in my life, because she could stand up to me. In fact, standing up to me was *nothing* compared with standing up to her father.

In the end, what happened between Sharon and her old man was tragic. At the time, I was too out of it on booze and drugs to know exactly what went down, and it's not my place to say much about it now. All I know is that Sharon found out that Don was having an affair with a girl younger than she was; that we left Jet Records, which made Don go apeshit; and that we had to pay him $1.5 million to buy out our contract and stop him bankrupting us with lawsuits. There had always been bad blood between the two of them, but it got out of control. Eventually, they stopped talking to each other altogether, and the silence continued for almost twenty years.

If any good came out of that situation, it was that we borrowed as much dough as we could to buy out *all* of my contracts, so that we weren't controlled by anyone. I remember Sharon going in for a meeting with Essex Music and saying, 'OK, how much do you want to fuck off? This is going to get ugly, because we're not playing along any more. Just give us the number, and we'll pay it.'

A week later, I had my own publishing company.

Meanwhile, Don might have thought I was a vegetable, but from the moment Sharon bought out my contract, he never stopped trying to get it back – usually by attempting to fuck up our marriage. He could be a really devious guy when he wanted to be, could my father-in-law. One time, for example, I was staying with Sharon at the Beverly Hills Hotel, and we'd rented this very conspicuous white Rolls-Royce Corniche to ride around town in. But then I got shitfaced, we had this crazy row about something, and Sharon fucked off, saying she was going back to England. Literally two minutes after she walked out of the door, the phone rang. It was Don. 'I need to talk to you, Veg . . . er, Ozzy,' he said. 'It's urgent.'

Looking back, he must have had someone outside the hotel, looking out for Sharon driving the Roller by herself. Otherwise, how would he have known that I was alone? The last thing I wanted to do was talk to him, but I couldn't say no. The guy was terrifying. If you believed the rumours, he kept a loaded gun in his desk.

So Don came over and started telling me the most vile things you could ever imagine about my wife. It was the most disgusting stuff I'd ever heard. It was inhuman, what he said. And he was talking about his *own daughter*.

Eventually, he paused for breath, then asked me, 'Did you know all that, Ozzy? Did you know what your wife's really like?'

Obviously, he wanted me to go crazy, leave Sharon, return to Jet Records, and start over.

But I wasn't gonna give him the pleasure.

He had no right to come to my room and make up all this

horrendous bullshit about my wife. I didn't believe a single fucking word of it. Anyway, whatever Sharon had done, it couldn't have been any worse than what I'd done. And it certainly wasn't anywhere near as bad as what Don himself was doing. But I thought that the best way to piss him off would be just to act like it was no big deal.

'Yeah, Don,' I said. 'I know all that about Sharon.'

'You do?'

'Yeah.'

'And?'

'And what, Don? I love her.'

'If you want to get the marriage annulled, we can always arrange that for you, y'know?'

'No thanks, Don.'

I could never believe what that guy was willing to do to his own family. Years later, for example, we found out that when he'd been managing me – and before then, even – he'd used Sharon as a shield. All of his companies, credit cards, bank accounts and loans were in her name. Basically Don didn't exist on paper, so if he didn't pay his bills, he couldn't be sued. And that included his tax bills, which he just fucking ignored – in England *and* America. Which left Sharon on the hook for everything without her ever knowing it. Then one day, out of the blue, she got a letter from the IRS saying she owed them, big time. By the time they'd added up all the unpaid taxes, interest and penalties, it came to seven figures. Don had taken her to the fucking cleaners.

'I don't know what your father's made of,' I said to her, 'because I could never do that to my children.'

It drove Sharon halfway round the bend, that tax bill.

In the end, I said, 'Look, whatever you've got to pay, just pay it, because I don't want to live another day with this fucking thing hanging over us. You can't avoid tax, so just get it done, and we'll cut back on our expenses and work around it.' That kind of thing happens a lot in the music business. When Sammy Davis Jr died, I heard that he left his wife with a seven-million-dollar tax bill, which took her a fucking eternity to pay off.

And there ain't nothing you can do about it. You've just got to put on a brave face and dig deep.

But it was worth going through all that bullshit with Don to get my freedom. All of a sudden I could do whatever I wanted, no matter what he said. Like when I was in New York one time and I met up with my lawyer, Fred Asis, a great guy, ex-military. He told me that he had a meeting later with another one of his clients, a band called Was (Not Was), who were going crazy because their lead singer hadn't shown up at the studio for a session.

'I'll stand in for him, if you want,' I said, half joking.

But Fred took it seriously. 'OK, I'll ask them,' he said.

Next thing I know I'm in this studio in New York, doing a rap on this song called 'Shake Your Head'. I had a right old laugh – especially when I heard the final version, which had all these hot young backing-singer chicks on it. I still love that song today. It's funny, y'know, because I'd always admired the Beatles for starting out as a bubblegum pop group and then getting heavier and heavier as their albums went on, and here was me going in the opposite direction.

But it wasn't until years later that I heard the full story. I was at the Sunset Marquis Hotel in West Hollywood, and Don Was was there. By that time he'd become one of the biggest producers in the music business, and Was (Not Was) were huge. I remember him rushing over to me and gasping, 'Ozzy, I've gotta tell you something about that song we did, "Shake Your Head". This is gonna blow your mind.'

'Go on,' I said.

'Well, remember how we had all those backing singers on there?'

'Yeah.'

'One of them ended up going off on her own and making a few albums. You might have heard of her.'

'What's her name?'

'Madonna.'

I couldn't believe it: I'd made a record with Madonna. I told Don to re-release it, but for whatever reason he couldn't get clearance. So we ended up re-recording it, with Kim Basinger taking Madonna's place.

I did quite a few duets back in the eighties. One with Lita Ford – 'Close My Eyes Forever' – ended up being a Top-Ten single in America. I even did a version of 'Born to be Wild' with Miss Piggy, but I was disappointed when I found out she wouldn't be in the studio at the same time as me (maybe she'd found out about my job at the Digbeth slaughterhouse). I was just having some fun, y'know? It wasn't about money. Although, after we bought out Don Arden and the publishers and had paid off our tax bills, the dough finally started to roll in. I remember opening an envelope from Colin Newman one morning, dreading another final demand. Instead, there was a royalty cheque for $750,000.

It was the most money I'd ever had in my life.

After the divorce with Thelma went through, a part of me wanted to say to her, 'Fuck you. Look at me – I'm fine.'

So I bought a house called Outlands Cottage in Staffordshire, not far from where she lived. It was a thatched house, and pretty much the first thing I did after moving in was to set the fucking roof on fire. Don't ask me how I did it. All I remember is a fireman turning up in his truck, whistling through his teeth, and going to me, 'Some house-warming party, eh?' And then after he put the fire out, we got shitfaced together. Mind you, he might as well have let the place burn down, 'cos the smell of charred thatch is fucking horrendous, and it never went away after that.

Sharon hated Outlands Cottage from the get-go. She'd fuck off to London and wouldn't want to come home. I suppose I'd half expected or wanted Thelma to call me up in tears and beg me to come back to her. She never did. Although she did call me once to say, 'So, I see you got married again, YOU FUCKING ARSEHOLE,' before slamming the phone down.

Eventually, I began to realise that as much as I loved being close to Jess and Louis, it was bad news, living around the corner from my ex-wife. At one point I even tried to buy back Bulrush Cottage. Then I made the mistake of taking Sharon with me when I went to see the kids. It was fine until we dropped them off and went for a drink at a hotel. Then I got all pissed and sentimental. I told Sharon I never wanted to go back to America, that I missed my kids, that I missed living next to the Hand & Cleaver, that I wanted to retire. Then, when I refused to get in the car to go home – it was actually our accountant Colin Newman's BMW, which we'd borrowed for the day – she went over the edge. She climbed into the driver's seat, put it in gear, and floored the accelerator. It was fucking terrifying. I remember jumping out of the way and then legging it on to the lawn in front of the hotel. But Sharon just crashed the car through this flower bed and kept coming at me, with the wheels churning up all the grass and sending lumps of turf flying all over the place.

And it wasn't just me she nearly killed.

I had this guy called Pete Mertens working for me at the time. He was an old schoolfriend – very skinny, very funny, used to wear these outrageous checked jackets all the time. Anyway, when Sharon drove through the flower bed, Pete had to throw himself into a rose bush to get out of the way. All I remember is him standing up, brushing off his jacket, and going, 'Fuck *this* – this ain't worth two hundred quid a week. I'm off.' (Later, he changed his mind and came back. Working for us might have been dangerous, but at least it was interesting, I suppose.)

In the end, the hotel manager came out and someone called the police. By then, I was hiding in a hedge. So Sharon got out of the car, came over to the hedge, and threw all her rings and jewellery into it. Then she turned around, stomped away, and called for a taxi.

I was there the next day, smelly and hung over, sifting through the soil for a fifty-grand Tiffany's rock.

There were some other wild times at Outlands Cottage, before I finally realised that Sharon was right, and that we should move. One night I met this very strait-laced bloke down the pub – an accountant, I think he was – but he came back to the cottage for a joint afterwards, and then passed out on the sofa. So while he was asleep I pulled off his clothes and threw them on the fire. The poor bloke woke up at six in the morning, stark bollock naked. Then I sent him home to his wife in one of my chain-mail suits. It still makes me laugh to this day, the thought of him clanking off towards his car, wondering how the fuck he's gonna explain himself.

Another one of my favourite tricks at Outlands Cottage was to shave off people's eyebrows while they were asleep. Believe me, there's nothing funnier than a bloke with no eyebrows. People don't realise that your eyebrows provide most of your facial expressions, so when they're gone, it's hard to show concern or surprise or any of those other basic human emotions. But it takes people a while to realise what's wrong. At first, they just look in the mirror and think, Christ, I look like *shit* today. One guy I did it to ended up going to see his *doctor*, 'cos he couldn't work out what the fuck was up.

I went through a period of giving the eyebrow treatment to everyone: agents, managers, roadies, assistants, friends, friends-of-friends. Whenever someone turned up to a management meeting with a face that didn't look quite right, you knew they'd spent the weekend at my house.

Pete Mertens often ended up being an unwilling accomplice

in my drunken practical jokes. For example, one Christmas, I began to wonder what it would be like to get a dog pissed. So me and Pete got a piece of raw meat and put it at the bottom of a bowl of sherry, then we called over Sharon's Yorkshire terrier – Bubbles, this one was called – and waited to see what would happen. Sure enough, Bubbles lapped up the bowl of sherry to get to the meat. Then about five minutes later he went cross-eyed and started to stumble around all over the place while howling along to the music we were playing. We'd done it: Bubbles was absolutely shitfaced. It was brilliant – until poor old Bubbles passed out in the middle of the living room. I was terrified that I'd killed him, so I pulled the fairy lights off the tree and wrapped them around his body, so I could tell Sharon he'd electrocuted himself by accident. But he was all right, thank God – although he had a nasty hangover the next morning, and he kept giving me these dirty looks, as if to say, 'I know what you did, you bastard.'

Bubbles wasn't the only animal who lived with us at Outlands Cottage. We also had a donkey called Sally – who used to sit in the living room with me and watch *Match of the Day* – and a Great Dane and a German shepherd. The thing I remember most about those dogs is the time I came home from the butchers' with some pigs trotters. I put them in a jar on the kitchen table, thinking I could use them in a good old fry up, but when Sharon walked into the room, she gagged and went, 'Ozzy, what the *fuck* is that smell? *And what are those disgusting-looking things on the table*?' When I told her, she literally retched. 'Oh, for Christ's sake, Ozzy,' she said, 'I can't eat that, feed them to the dogs.' So I gave the trotters to the dogs, and they both started to look very unwell immediately. Then one puked while the other one hosed down the walls with shit.

Poor old Pete Mertons got to the point where he just couldn't take it any more. He was living with us at the time, and the craziness was never-ending. The last straw for him was when I downed one too many sleeping pills after an all-night drinking session and had to be taken to hospital to get my stomach pumped. When the doc asked my name, I just went, 'Pete Mertens,' then never thought any more of it. But when Pete went for a check-up a couple of months later, his doctor took him into his office, closed the door, and said to him, 'Now then Mr Mertens, we can't be having that behaviour, can we?' Pete didn't know what the fuck the doc was on about, and the doc just thought Pete was trying to pretend like it never happened. I think the doc might even have sent him off for some counselling. And then eventually Pete found his file, with 'sleeping pill overdose' written at the top, and he went fucking mental with me.

Good bloke, Pete Mertens. Good bloke.

We moved so many times after we left Outlands Cottage that I can't even remember half of the places. It was around this time that I learned my wife loves nothing more than buying and doing up houses. And because it takes so long to do them up, we always end up renting somewhere else while we're waiting for the work to be done. Then, about three seconds after we've moved in, Sharon gets bored, so we sell up and buy another house – and we have to rent again while we're doing that one up. It's gone on like that for decades. Sometimes it feels like all we do with our money is renovate the Western fucking hemisphere. I got Sharon to count up all the houses once, and it turned out that in the twenty-seven years we'd been married, we'd lived in twenty-eight different places.

As I said, Sharon didn't mind my drinking at first. She thought I was funny when I was drunk – probably 'cos she was usually drunk, too. But before long she changed her mind, and started to see the booze as being almost as bad as the coke. She said I'd gone from being a funny drunk to being an angry drunk. But one of the many problems with being an alcoholic is that when people tell you how bad you are when you're drunk, you're usually drunk. So you just keep getting drunk.

The funny thing is, I don't even like the taste of booze. Not unless it's drowned in fruit juice or some other sugary bullshit. It was always the *feeling* I was after. I mean, every now and again I enjoyed a good pint. But I never went to the pub to drink, I went to get fucking blasted.

I tried for a long time to drink like normal people do. When I was still married to Thelma, for example, I went to this wine-tasting at the Birmingham NEC. It was a food market or something around Christmas time. I thought, Fuck me, a wine tasting, that sounds like something a civilised, grown-up person might do. The next morning, Thelma said to me, 'What did you buy?' I said, 'Oh, nothing.' And she said, 'Really? You must have bought *something*.' I said, 'Oh well, yeah – I guess I bought a couple of cases.'

Turned out I'd bought 144 cases.

I was so shitfaced, I'd thought I was buying 144 *bottles*. Then a delivery truck the size of the *Exxon Valdez* pulled up outside Bulrush Cottage and started unloading enough crates of wine to fill every room to the ceiling. It took months for me and the roadies to polish it all off. When we finally emptied the last bottle, we all went down the Hand & Cleaver to celebrate.

Mind you, it's all bullshit with wine, isn't it? It's just fucking vinegar with a fizz, no matter what the tasters say. I should know, I owned a wine bar once: Osbourne's, we called it. What a crock of shit that place was. I remember saying to one of the merchants, 'Look, tell me, what's a *good* wine?' And she says to me, 'Well, Mr Osbourne, if you like Blue Nun at two quid a bottle, then that's a good wine. And if you like Chateau du Wankeur at ninety-nine quid a bottle, then that's a good wine.' I didn't listen. In those days, it was my ego that ordered the wine. The most expensive bottle on the whole list, just to be big-headed. Then I'd wake up the next morning with a two-hundred-quid hangover. But eventually I came to realise something about two-hundred-quid hangovers: they're exactly the fucking same as two-quid hangovers.

It wasn't until Sharon found out that she was pregnant that she really started to try and change the way I was living.

We were on tour in Germany at the time. 'I think something's going on,' she said. 'I've been feeling so sick lately.' So I staggered out to buy one of those pregnancy dip-stick things – and it turned the colour it goes when your missus is expecting. I couldn't believe it, because only a few months before Sharon had gone through a miscarriage after being attacked by one of her mother's dogs. I got a right old bollocking for that, because I was standing right behind her when it happened. I heard the low growl of that Dobermann and just froze on the spot, completely stiff, instead of running over and biting its head off, or whatever the fuck I was supposed to do. I'm a chickenshit when it comes to stuff like that. And I had no idea she was pregnant. It was only when we went to the hospital afterwards that the docs told us.

So it was a big deal when the test was positive in Germany.

'Let's do one more test, just to make sure,' I said.

It went the same colour as the first one.

'I tell you what,' I said, holding the little strip of paper to the light. 'Let's do one more, just to make really sure.'

We must have done five tests in the end. When we were finally convinced it was true, I remember Sharon saying to me, 'Right, Ozzy, I'm going to tell you this once, so you'd better listen. If you ever, *ever* bring any cocaine into this house, I'm going to call the police and have you sent to prison. Do you understand me?'

I had absolutely no doubt whatsoever that she meant it.

'I understand,' I said.

'And what about the shotguns, Ozzy?'

'I'll get rid of them.'

They were sold the next day. I knew I'd never forgive myself if anything happened to Aimee. So that was it: goodbye to the Benelli semi-automatic that I'd used to kill the chickens at Bulrush Cottage, along with all my other guns.

I carried on boozing, though. Even more so, without any coke in the house. I couldn't stop. But Sharon had lost all patience with that too, by then. The second I walked through the door, she'd be on my case.

You wouldn't believe the things I'd do – the time and effort I would dedicate to sneaking a drink behind her back. I'd 'pop to the supermarket' next door, then walk straight through to the back of the grocery section, through the door to the store-room, climb out of the window at the back, jump over a wall, crawl through a hedge, and go to the pub on the other side. And then, after necking six pints in a row, I'd do the same in reverse.

The most unbelievable thing about my behaviour is that I was convinced it was entirely fucking normal.

Then I started trying to sneak booze into the house. One time, I got this big four-gallon bottle of vodka – the kind of bottle they put on display at a bar – but I couldn't work out where to hide it. I ran around the house for ages, looking for the perfect place. Then it came to me: *the oven*! Sharon had never cooked a meal in her life, I said to myself, so she'd never look in there. And I was right: I got away with it for weeks. I'd say to Sharon, 'I've just had an idea for a song. I think I'll pop downstairs to the studio and get it down on tape.' Then I'd pour myself a mug of vodka in the kitchen, neck it as fast as I could, and pretend like nothing had happened.

Then, one day, she twigged.

'Sharon,' I said, 'I've just had an idea for a song. I think I'll just—'

'I found your song idea in the oven this morning,' she said. 'Then I poured your song idea down the sink.'

It was only a week or so after the oven incident, on 2 September 1983, that Aimee was born at the Wellington Hospital in St John's Wood, London. She was a guiding light for us, she really was. It had been just over a year since Randy and Rachel had died, and we were only just starting to get over it. With Aimee, we had a brand new reason to feel good about life. She was such an innocent little thing, when you looked at her, you just couldn't help breaking into a huge smile.

But no sooner had Aimee been born that it was time to go on the road again, this time to promote the *Bark at the Moon* album, which I'd just finished making with my new guitarist, Jake E. Lee. Sharon could have stayed at home, but that wasn't her style, so we put a little cot in the back of the tour bus for Aimee and carried on. It was great for her: Aimee saw more of the world before her first birthday than most people do in a lifetime. I just wish I'd been sober for more of it. I was there physically, but not mentally. So I missed things you can never do over again: the first crawl, the first step, the first word.

If I think about it for too long, it breaks my heart.

In many ways I wasn't really a father to Aimee. I was more like another kid for Sharon to look after.

9

Betty, Where's the Bar?

'Someone's gonna die before this is over,' I said to Doc McGhee, on the second night of the *Bark at the Moon* tour. Doc was the American manager of Mötley Crüe, our support band, and a good mate of mine.

'Someone?' he said. 'I don't think *someone*'s gonna die, Ozzy. I think we're *all* gonna die.'

The problem, basically, was Mötley Crüe – which back then still had the original line-up of Nikki Sixx on bass, Tommy Lee on drums, Mick Mars on guitar and Vince Neil on vocals. They were fucking crazy. Which obviously I took as a challenge. Just as I had with John Bonham, I felt like I had to out-crazy them, otherwise I wasn't doing my job properly. But they took *that* as a challenge. So it was just wall-to-wall action, every minute of every day. The gigs were the easy part. The problem was surviving the bits in between.

The funniest thing about Mötley Crüe was that they dressed like chicks but lived like animals. It was an education, even for me. Wherever they went, they carried around this massive flight case full of every type of booze imaginable. The moment a gig was over, the lid would be thrown open, and the hounds of hell would be set loose.

Every night, bottles would be thrown, knives would be pulled, chair legs would be smashed, noses would be broken, property would be destroyed. It was like bedlam and pandemonium rolled into one, then multiplied by chaos.

People tell me stories about that tour and I have no idea if they're true or not. They ask, 'Ozzy, did you really once snort a line of ants off a Popsicle stick?' and I ain't got a fucking clue. It's certainly possible. Every night stuff went up my nose that had no business being there. I was out of it the whole time. Even Tony Dennis got carried away. We ended up calling him 'Captain Krell' – Krell was our new name for cocaine – because he tried doing a line once, although I don't think he ever did it again. Our wardrobe chick even made him a little suit with 'CK' written in Superman letters on the chest.

We all thought it was hilarious.

One of the craziest nights of all was in Memphis.

As usual, it started as soon as we finished the gig. I remember walking down the corridor backstage to the dressing-room area and hearing Tommy Lee say, 'Hey dude, Ozzy. Check this out!'

I stopped and looked around to see where his voice was coming from.

'In here, man,' said Tommy. 'In *here*.'

I pushed open a door and saw him on the other side. He was sitting on a chair with his back to me. Nikki, Mick, Vince and a bunch of roadies were all standing around, smoking fags, laughing, talking about the show, drinking beer. And there, in front of Tommy, on her knees, was this naked chick. She was giving him the mother of all blowjobs.

Tommy waved at me to come closer. 'Hey, dude, Ozzy. Check it out!'

So I peered over his shoulder. And there it was: his dick. Like a baby's arm in a boxing glove. The fucking thing was so big, the chick could only get about a third of it in her mouth, and even then I was surprised there wasn't a lump sticking out of the back of her neck. I'd never seen anything like it in my life.

'Hey, Tommy,' I said. 'Can you get me one of those?'

'Dude, sit down,' he said. 'Take your pants off, man. She'll do you after she's done me.'

I started to back away. 'I ain't gonna get mine out with that thing filling up the room!' I said. 'It would be like parking a tugboat next to the *Titanic*. Have you got a licence for that, Tommy? It looks dangerous.'

'Oh, dude, you don't know what you're miss— Oh, oh, oh, ah, urgh, urgh, *ahhhhhh* . . .'

I had to look away.

Then Tommy jumped up, zipped up his fly, and said, 'Let's get some eats, dude, I'm starving.'

We ended up in this place called Benihana – one of those Japanese steakhouse joints where they make the food on this big hot plate in front of you. While we waited for the food we drank beer and chasers. Then we got a jumbo-sized bottle of sake for the table. The last thing I remember is getting a massive bowl of wonton soup, finishing it, then filling the bowl to the brim with sake and downing it in one messy gulp.

'*Ahh!*' I said. 'That's *better*.'

Everyone just looked at me.

Then Tommy stood up and said, '*Fuuuuuck*, let's get outta here, man. Any second now, Ozzy's gonna blow.'

Then black.

Complete black.

Like someone yanking the cord from the back of a TV.

From what the others told me later, I got up from the table, said I was going to the bog, and never came back. To this day, I have no memory whatsoever of what I did for the next five hours.

But I'll never forget waking up.

The first thing I heard was the noise:

NEEEEEEEEOOOOWWWWOOOM, NEEEEEEEEO-OOOWWWWOOOM, ZZZZMMMMMMMMMMM . . .

Then I opened my eyes. It was still dark, very dark, but there were thousands of little pinpricks of light everywhere. I thought to myself, What the fuck's going on? Am I dead or what?

And still this noise:

NEEEEEEEEOOOOWWWWOOOM, NEEEEEEEEO-OOOWWWWOOOM, ZZZZMMMMMMMMMMM . . .

Then I could smell rubber and petrol.

Then I heard an air horn, right next to my ear.

BLLLLAAAAAAAAAAAHHHHHHHHHHHMM!!!!!!!!!

I rolled over, screaming.

Then blinding lights – maybe twenty or thirty of them, as tall as an office block – coming towards me. Before I could pick myself up and run, I heard this terrible roaring noise, and a gust of wind blew sand and grit in my face.

I'd woken up on the central reservation of a twelve-lane freeway.

How or why I was there, I had no idea. All I knew was that I had to get off the freeway before I died – and that I had to take a piss, because my bladder was about to explode. So I waited for a gap in the headlamps, then legged it across all these lanes, still too pissed to go in a straight line. Finally I made it to the other side, having just missed a motorbike in the slow lane. I jumped the fence, ran across another road, and began to search for somewhere to take a slash.And that's when I saw it: a white car parked in a lay-by.

Perfect, I thought, this'll give me a bit of cover.

So I whip out my dick, but no sooner have I started to give the tyre of this car a good old watering than all these coloured bulbs in the back window light up, and I hear this horribly familiar noise.

BLOOP-BLOOP-WHOOOO. BAARRRP!

I couldn't fucking believe it. Of all the places in Memphis where I could've taken a piss, I'd managed to choose the wheel of an unmarked cop car, parked in a lay-by, waiting to bust people for speeding.

Next thing I knew this woman police officer was winding down her window. She leaned out and said, 'When you've finished shaking that thing, I'm taking your ass to jail!'

Ten minutes later, I was in the nick.

Luckily, they only kept me in there for a couple of hours. Then I called Doc McGhee and got him to pick me up in the tour bus.

The first thing I heard when I climbed back on board was 'Hey, dude, Ozzy. Check this out, man!' And we were off again, into oblivion.

Someone went to jail for one thing or another every night of that tour. And because Mick and Nikki looked so alike – they both had this long, dark, girly hair – they'd sometimes get locked up for something the other one had done.

One night they're sharing a room and Nikki gets up, stark naked, to go and buy a Coke from the vending machine in the corridor, next to the lift. Just as he's pressing the button for the Coke, the lift doors open and he hears this gasping noise. Then he glances over and sees three middle-aged women standing there with these looks of horror of their faces. 'Hi,' he says, before turning around and walking casually back to his room. A few minutes later there's a knock at the door. So Nikki says to Mick, 'That's probably one of the groupies. Why don't you go and answer it.' So Mick goes off to answer the door and he's greeted by the hotel manager, a cop and one of the chicks from the lift. The chick shouts, 'That's him!' and they drag Mick off to jail, even though he had no idea what he was supposed to have done.

The thing is, though, we were all so out of our minds all the time, it was quite normal not to know what we'd done.

Apart from waking up in the middle of a freeway, the worst moment for me was after we played Madison Square Garden in New York. For the after-show party, we went to this club in an old church. We were all hanging out in this private room, having a few drinks and a bit of coke, when some bloke came up to me and said, 'Hey, Ozzy, would you like to have your photograph taken with Brian Wilson?'

'Who the fuck's Brian Wilson?'

'Y'know, *Brian Wilson*. From the Beach Boys.'

'Oh, him. Sure. Yeah. Whatever.'

Everyone had been talking about Brian Wilson a lot, because the week before, his brother Dennis – the one who'd been mates with Charles Manson in the 1960s – had drowned in LA. Dennis was only thirty-nine, so it was terribly sad. Anyway, I was told to go and meet Brian Wilson on the stairwell, so out I went, loaded up on booze and coke, and waited for him. Ten minutes passed. Then twenty minutes. Then thirty minutes. Finally, after another five minutes, Brian appeared. By then, I was thoroughly pissed off, thinking, What a dick. But at the same time I knew about Dennis, so I decided to give him a break. The first thing I said was: 'Sorry to hear about your brother, Brian.'

He didn't say anything. He just gave me this funny look, then walked off. That was it for me.

'First you show up late,' I said, raising my voice, 'and now you're just gonna fuck off without saying a single fucking word? I tell you what, Brian, why don't we forget about the photograph so you can shove your head back up your arse, where it fucking belongs, eh?'

Next morning, I'm lying in the hotel room, my head pounding. The phone starts ringing and Sharon answers it. 'Yes, no, yes, OK. Oh, he did, did he? Hmm. Right. Don't worry, I'll deal with it.' *Click*. She hands me the phone and says, 'You're calling Brian Wilson.'

'Who the fuck's Brian Wilson?'

I get smacked on the head with the receiver.

Smack.

'Ow! That fucking hurt!'

'Brian Wilson is the Living Musical Legend you insulted last night,' says Shsron. 'And now you're going to call him and apologise.'

The memories start to come back.

'Hang on a minute,' I say. 'Brian Wilson was the one who insulted *me*!'

'Oh yeah?' says Sharon.

'Yeah!'

'Ozzy, when Brian Wilson reached over to shake your hand, the first thing you said was: "Hello, Brian, you fucking arsehole, I'm glad to hear your brother's dead."'

I sit bolt upright.

'I didn't say that.'

'No, the fucking cocaine you keep shoving up your nose said that.'

'But I would *remember*.'

'Everyone else seems to remember perfectly well. They also remember you told him to shove his head up his arse, because that's where it belongs. Here, this is Brian's number. Apologise.'

So I called him and apologised. Twice.

Since then, I've bumped into him a few times over the years. We're cool now, me and Brian. Although we never did get around to taking that photograph.

If any of us had a near-death experience on the *Bark at the Moon* tour, it was me. Amazingly, though, it didn't have anything to do with booze or drugs – not directly, anyway. It happened when we took a forty-eight-hour break after a gig in New Orleans to shoot the video for 'So Tired' in London. It was an insane distance to travel in that amount of time, but in those days MTV was just starting to become a big part of the music business, and if you could get them to play one of your videos on heavy rotation, it just about guaranteed that your album would go platinum. So we always put a lot of money and effort into them.

The plan was to fly from New Orleans to New York, take Concorde to London, shoot the video, take Concorde back to New York, then connect to the next venue. It was a gruelling schedule, not helped by the fact that I was chronically pissed. The only thing that kept me from passing out was all the cocaine I was snorting.

When we finally got to the studio in London, the first thing the director said to me was, 'OK, Ozzy, just sit in front of this mirror. When I give the word, it's gonna explode from behind.'

'All right,' I said, wondering what kind of high-tech special effects they were going to use.

But there were no special effects. There was just an old mirror and a bloke standing behind it with a hammer in his hand. I don't know who the fuck they were using as a props guy, but obviously no one had told him about theatrical mirrors, which are designed to break without killing anyone. So, halfway through the song, the bloke swings his hammer, the mirror explodes, and I get a faceful of glass. It was a good job I was so loaded: I didn't feel a thing. I just spat out all the blood and glass and went, 'Yeah, cheers.'

Then I got up and had another can of Guinness.

I didn't think any more of it until I was halfway across the Atlantic on Concorde. I remember pressing the button for another drink and the stewardess coming over and almost dropping her tray with fright. 'Oh my God!' she squealed. 'Are you OK?' It turned out the pressure from being up at nearly sixty thousand feet had caused all the tiny bits of glass lodged in my skin to rise to the surface, until my face had literally exploded. It had just popped, like a squashed tomato.

When Sharon turned around to look, she almost passed out.

An ambulance was waiting for me at JFK when we landed. It wasn't the first time I'd been wheeled off Concorde. I used to get so pissed on those flights, Sharon would have to carry me through immigration on a luggage trolley with my passport Sellotaped to my forehead. And then when they asked her if she had anything to declare, she'd just point at me and go, 'Him'.

In the hospital in New York they put me under and tried to pull out as much of the broken glass as they could with tweezers. Then they gave me some drugs to reduce the swelling. I remember coming to in this white room, with white walls, and people all around me covered in white sheets and thinking, Fuck, I'm in the morgue. Then I heard a hissing noise next to my bed.

Pssst, pssst.

I looked down and there was this kid holding up a pen and a copy of *Bark at the Moon*.

'Will you sign this for me?' he asked.

'Fuck off,' I told him. 'I'm dead.'

By the time the tour ended, we were all still alive, but my prediction that someone would die still came true. It happened when Vince Neil went back to his house at Redondo Beach in LA and got fucked up with the drummer from Hanoi Rocks. At some point they ran out of booze and decided to drive to the local bottle shop in Vince's car, which was one of those low-slung, ridiculously fast, bright red De Tomaso Panteras. Vince was so loaded he drove head-on into a car coming in the opposite direction. The bloke from Hanoi Rocks was dead by the time they got him to hospital.

I didn't see much of Mötley Crüe after the tour, although I

kept in touch with Tommy, on and off. I remember going to his house years later with my son Jack, who must have been about thirteen.

'Wow, dude, come in,' said Tommy, when I rang the doorbell. 'I can't believe it. Ozzy Osbourne's in my house.'

There were some other guests there, too, and after we'd all been given the tour of his place, Tommy said, 'Hey, dudes, check this out.' He tapped a code into a keypad in the wall, a hidden door slid open, and on the other side there was this padded sex chamber with some kind of heavy-duty harness thing swinging from the ceiling. The idea was that you'd take a chick in there, strap her to this contraption, then fuck the living shit out of her.

'What's wrong with a bed?' I asked Tommy. Then I turned around and realised that Jack had walked into the room with the rest of us. He was standing there, his eyes bulging. I felt so embarrassed, I didn't know where to fucking look.

I didn't take him to Tommy's again after that.

By the time the *Bark at the Moon* tour ended, me and Sharon's fights had reached another level of craziness. Part of it was just the pressure of being famous. I mean, don't get me wrong, I ain't complaining: my first three solo albums eventually sold more than ten million copies in America alone, which was beyond anything I could have hoped for. But when you're flogging that many records, you can't do anything normal any more, 'cos you get too much hassle from the public. I remember one night when me and Sharon were staying in a Holiday Inn. It was maybe three or four in the morning, and we were both in bed. There was a knock on the door, so I got up to answer it, and these guys in overalls just brushed past me and walked into the room.

When Sharon saw them she said, 'Who the fuck are you? What are you doing in our room?'

They went, 'Oh, we're just interested in seeing how you live.'

Sharon threw something at them and they brushed past me again on their way out.

All they wanted to do was come in and stare. That was it.

We stopped staying in cheap hotels after that.

I mean, I'm usually happy to meet fans, but not when I'm asleep with my wife at four in the morning.

Or when I'm eating. It drives me nuts when people come up to me when I'm in a restaurant with Sharon. It's a big taboo with me, that is. The worst is when they say, 'Hey, you look like you're somebody famous! Can I have your autograph?'

'I tell you what,' I want to say to them, 'why don't you go away and find out who you think I am, come back again, and *then* I'll give you my autograph.'

But fame wasn't the biggest problem for me and Sharon. That was my drinking, which was so bad I couldn't be trusted with *anything*. When we were in Germany doing a gig, for example, I went on a tour of the Dachau concentration camp and was asked to leave because I was being drunk and disorderly. I must be the only person in history who's ever been thrown out of that fucking place.

Another thing I did when I was drunk was get more tattoos, which drove Sharon mental. Eventually she said, 'Ozzy, if you get one more tattoo, I'm gonna string you up by your bollocks.'

That night, I went out and got 'thanks' tattooed on my right palm. It seemed like a brilliant idea at the time. I mean, how many times do you say 'thanks' to people during your lifetime? Tens of thousands, probably. Now all I had to do was raise my right hand. But Sharon didn't appreciate the innovation. When she noticed it the next morning – I'd been trying to keep my hand under the kitchen table, but then she asked me to pass the salt – she drove me straight to a plastic surgeon to get the tattoo removed. But he told me he'd have to cut off half of my hand to get rid of the thing, so it stayed.

When we left the hospital, Sharon thanked the doctor for his time.

I just raised my right palm.

Another time we were in Albuquerque in the middle of winter, freezing cold, ice and snow everywhere. I was pissed and coked out of my fucking mind and decided to take a ride on this aerial tramway thing, which goes ten thousand feet up the Sandia Mountains to a restaurant and observation deck at the top. But there was something wrong with the cable car, and it swung to a halt halfway up the mountain.

'What do you do if you get stuck up here?' I asked the bloke at the controls, after we'd been dangling there for ages.

'Oh, there's an escape hatch in the roof,' he said, pointing to this hatch above our heads.

'But how do you climb up there?' I asked.

'There's a ladder right behind you. All you have to do is pull it out. It's very simple.'

'Is the hatch locked?'

'No.'

Big mistake, telling me that. As soon as I knew there was a ladder and an unlocked hatch I had to try it out. So I pulled out the ladder and started to climb up to the ceiling.

The guy went mental.

'What the hell are you doing? You can't do that! Stop! *Stop!*'

That just egged me on even more. I opened the hatch, felt this blast of icy wind, and pulled myself up on to the roof, by which time the guy and everyone else in the cable car was screaming and begging me to come back down. Then, just as I was getting my balance, the car started to move again. I almost slipped and went *splat* onto the rocks thousands of feet below, but I kept my balance by putting out my arms like I was surfing. Then I started to sing 'Good Vibrations'. I stayed up there until we were almost at the top.

The funny thing is I hate heights. I get vertigo going up a doorstep. So when I saw the cable car from the ground the next day – stone-cold sober, for once – I almost threw up. It makes me shiver even now, just thinking about it.

Doing crazy stuff like that always led to another argument with Sharon. On one occasion I lost it so badly with her, I picked up a vodka bottle and threw it in her direction. But the second it left my hand, I realised what I'd done: it was going straight for her head. Oh, *fuck*, I thought, I've just killed my wife. But it missed by an inch, thank God. The neck went straight through the plaster in the wall above her head and just stuck there, like a piece of modern art.

Sharon would always find ways to retaliate, mind you. Like when she'd take a hammer to my gold records. And then I'd retaliate to her retaliation by saying I didn't want to go on stage that night. One time, I shaved my head to try to get out of doing a show. I was hung over, knackered and pissed off, so I just thought, Fuck it, fuck them all.

But that shit didn't work with Sharon.

She just took one look at me and said, 'Right, we're getting you a wig.' Then she dragged me and a couple of the roadies to this joke shop which had a Lady Godiva wig in the window that had been there for five hundred years, with dead flies and dust and dandruff and God knows what else embedded in it. I put it on and everyone pissed themselves laughing.

But it turned out to be quite cool in the end, that wig, because I rigged it with blood capsules. Halfway through the show I'd pretend to pull out my hair and all this blood would come running down my face. It looked brilliant. But after the bat-biting incident, everyone thought it was real. At one gig, this chick in the front row almost fainted. She was screaming and pointing and crying and shouting, 'It's true what they say! He *is* crazy!'

*

'Darling,' said Sharon, a few months after the *Bark at the Moon* tour, when she found out that she was pregnant with Kelly. 'I've heard about this great place in Palm Springs where you can take a break before the next tour. It's a hotel, and they have classes every day where they teach you how to drink like a gentleman.'

'Really?' I said.

In my head, I was going, That's it! I've been doing it wrong. That must be why I've been getting these terrible hangovers. I need to learn how to drink like James Bond!

'What's the name of this place?' I said.

'The Betty Ford Center. Have you heard of it?'

'Nope.'

'Well, it just opened, and it's run by the wife of a former president. I think you'll have a good time there.'

'Sounds magic,' I said. 'Sign me up.'

'Actually, I've already booked you in for the week after the baby's due,' Sharon replied.

In the end, Kelly arrived on 28 October 1984. It was an eventful birth, to say the least. For some insane reason, Sharon had decided that she didn't want an epidural. But then as soon as the contractions started, she went, 'I've changed my mind! Get me the anaesthetist!' Now, for Sharon to say that meant that she was in fucking agony – 'cos my wife can take a bit of pain, certainly a lot more than I can. But the nurse wasn't having any of it. She goes, 'Mrs Osbourne, you do realise that there are people in third world countries who give birth without an epidural all the time, don't you?' Big mistake, that was. Sharon sat up in bed and screamed, 'LISTEN, YOU FUCKHEAD, THIS ISN'T A FUCKING THIRD WORLD COUNTRY, SO GET ME A FUCKING ANAESTHETIST!'

An hour later, Kelly came out into the world, screaming – and she hasn't stopped since, bless her. She's a real chip off the old block, is Kelly. I think that's why I've always felt so protective of her. It certainly wasn't easy, leaving my beautiful little girl with Sharon and the nurses only a few hours after she was born, but at the same time I knew I had to get my drinking under control. With any luck, I thought, I'll come home from Palm Springs a new man. So the next morning I got on the plane, drank three bottles of champagne in first class, landed at LAX twelve hours later, threw up, had a few toots of cocaine, then passed out in the back of a limo as it drove me to the Betty Ford Center. I hope this place is relaxing, I thought, 'cos I'm *knackered*.

I'd never even heard the word 'rehab' before. And I certainly didn't know that Betty Ford – the wife of President Gerald Ford – had been an alcoholic herself. While I was on tour I never spent much time watching telly or looking at newspapers, so I had no idea what a big deal the clinic was, or that the press had been calling it 'Camp Betty'. In my head, I imagined this beautiful oasis of a hotel out in the middle of the Californian desert, with a shimmering swimming pool outside, a golf course, lots of hot chicks in bikinis everywhere, and all these Hugh Hefner types in velvet smoking jackets and bow ties, leaning against an outdoor bar, while a middle-aged woman with a voice like Barbara Woodhouse said, 'OK, gentlemen, after me: take the olive, stir it around the martini, pick up the glass with your fingers arranged like so. *That's right*, good, good. Now, take a sip, count to three, and do it again. Slowly, *slowly*.'

This is going to be my dream holiday of a lifetime, I said to myself.

But when I got there, the place looked more like a hospital than a hotel. Mind you, the grounds were stunning: freshly sprinkled lawns, tall palm trees and man-made lakes everywhere, and these huge, brown, alien-looking mountains looming in the background.

I walk in the door and Betty herself is waiting for me. She's a tiny little thing. Polo-neck sweater, big hairdo. Not much of a sense of humour, by the look of it.

'Hello, Mr Osbourne,' she goes. 'I'm Mrs Ford. I spoke with your wife Sharon a few days ago.'

'Look, Betty, d'you mind if I check in a bit later?' I say. 'I'm gasping. Terrible flight. Where's the bar?'

'I'm sorry?'

'The bar. It must be around here somewhere.'

'You do know where you are, don't you, Mr Osbourne?'

'Er, yeah?'

'So you'll know that we don't . . . have a bar.'

'How do you teach people to drink properly, then?'

'Mr Osbourne, I think your wife might have misled you slightly. We don't teach you *how* to drink here.'

'You don't?'

'We teach you *not* to drink.'

'Oh. Maybe I should stay somewhere else, then.'

'I'm afraid that's not an option, Mr Osbourne. Your wife was . . . How can I put this? She was very *insistent*.'

I can't even begin to describe the disappointment. It was almost as bad as the boredom. After one hour in that place, I felt like I'd been there a thousand years. The thing I hated most about the weeks that followed was talking about my drinking in front of all these strangers during the group sessions. Although I learned some pretty cool things. One bloke was a dentist from LA. His wife found out about his drinking and she was on his case twenty-four hours a day. So he emptied the tank of windscreen-washer fluid in his BMW, refilled it with gin and tonic, disconnected the plastic tube from the nozzles on the bonnet, and re-routed it so it came out of one of the air vents under the dashboard. Whenever he wanted a drink, all he had to do was get in his car, put the tube in his mouth, pull on the indicator stalk, and he'd get a squirt of G&T down his throat. It worked brilliantly, apparently, until one day there was a really bad traffic jam and he turned up at work so out of his shitter that he accidentally drilled a hole in the head of one of his patients.

I'm telling you, the ingenuity of alcoholics is something else. If only it could be put to some kind of good use. I mean, if you said to an alcoholic, 'Look, the only way for you to get another drink is to cure cancer,' the disease would be history in five seconds.

As well as the group sessions, I had to see a therapist on my own. It was hard, being sober and having to discuss all the things I'd just found out were wrong with me. Like being dyslexic and having attention deficit disorder. (They didn't add the word 'hyperactivity' to it until a few years later.) It explained a lot, I suppose. The shrink said that my dyslexia had given me a terrible insecurity complex, so I couldn't take rejection or failure or pressure of any sort, which was why I was self-medicating with booze. She also said that because I was poorly educated, and *knew* I was poorly educated, I always thought people were taking me for a ride, so I didn't trust anyone. She was right, but it didn't help that I usually *was* being taken for a ride – until Sharon came along. Mind you, I had moments of coked-up paranoia when I didn't trust my wife, either.

The shrink also told me that I have an addictive personality, which means that I do *everything* addictively. And, on top of that, I have an obsessive-compulsive disorder, which makes it all ten times worse. I'm like a walking dictionary of psychiatric disorders, I am. It blew my mind. And it took me a long time to accept any of it.

My stay in Camp Betty was the longest I'd been without drink or drugs in my adult life, and the comedown was horrendous. Everyone else was going through the same thing, but I can't say that made me feel any better. At first, they put me in a room with a guy who owned a bowling alley, but he snored like an asthmatic horse, so I moved and ended up with a depressive mortician. I said to him, 'Look, if you suffer from depression, why the fuck do you work in a mortuary?'

'Dunno,' he said. 'It's just what I do.'

The mortician snored even louder than the bowling alley guy – he was like a moose with a tracheotomy. The whole room shook. So I ended up spending every night on the sofa in the lobby, shivering and sweating.

Eventually, Sharon came to get me. I'd been in there six weeks. I looked better – I'd lost a bit of weight – but I'd got the whole rehab thing wrong. I thought it was supposed to *cure* me. But there ain't no cure for what I've got. All rehab can do is tell you what's wrong with you and then suggest ways for you to get better. Later, when I realised it wasn't a solution by itself, I used to go there just to take the heat off myself a bit when things got out of hand. Rehab *can* work, but you've got to want it. If you really want to quit, you can't say, 'Well, I want to quit today, but I might have a drink next week at my friend's wedding.' You've got to commit, then live each day as it comes. Every morning, you've got to wake up and say, 'OK, today's gonna be one more day without a drink,' or a cigarette, or a pill, or a joint, or whatever it is that's been killing you.

That's as much as you can hope for when you're an addict.

The first gig I did after Betty Ford was in Rio de Janeiro.

I was legless before I even got on the plane.

By the time we reached Rio, I'd got through a whole bottle of Courvoisier, and was passed out in the aisle. Sharon tried her best to move me – but I was like a dead fucking body. In the end she got so pissed off with me that she grabbed the stainless steel fork from her meal tray and began stabbing me with it. I soon fucking moved after that. But at least I now knew what I was – a full-blown, practising alcoholic. I couldn't pretend any more that I was just having fun, or that boozing was something everyone did when they got a bit of dough. I had a disease, and it was killing me. I used to think, Even an animal won't go near something again if it makes it sick, so why do I keep going back to this?

The gig was Rock in Rio, a ten-day festival featuring Queen, Rod Stewart, AC/DC and Yes. One and a half million people bought tickets. But I was disappointed by the place. I'd expected to see the Girl from Ipanema on every corner, but I never saw a single one. There were just all these dirt-poor kids running around like rats. People were either outrageously rich or living on the streets – there didn't seem to be anything in between.

I'll always remember meeting Ronnie Biggs, the Great Train Robber, on that trip. In those days he was living in exile in Brazil, and he seemed to be making the best of it – he claimed he shagged two and a half thousand chicks while he was there. But it was still a kind of prison for him, because he was so homesick. He came over to the hotel wearing a T-shirt that said, 'Rio – a Wonderful Place to Escape to', but he just kept asking, 'So, what's it like in England, Ozzy? Do they still have this shop, or that shop, or this beer, or that beer?'

I felt sorry for the guy. No one in their right mind would give him a job, so he'd get all these English tourists over to his house, charge them fifty quid each, get them to buy him some beers and a bag of dope, then tell them the Great Train Robbery story. He called it 'The Ronnie Biggs Experience'. I suppose it was better than being in prison. He was all right, Ronnie, y'know. He wasn't a bad guy, and everyone knew that he wasn't even on the train when the driver was assaulted, yet he was sent down for thirty years. You can rape a kid and kill a granny and get less than thirty years nowadays. People say, 'He got away with it in the end, didn't he?' But I don't think he did. I mean, the bloke was so unhappy. I wasn't surprised when he finally came back to Britain, even though it meant getting arrested at Heathrow and thrown straight in the slammer.

Home's home, in the end, even if it's behind bars. At least he got his freedom at the finish, although it was only 'cos the guy was on his deathbed. Ronnie always said his last wish was 'to walk into a Margate pub as an Englishman and buy a pint'. But from what I've heard, he's going to have to wait until the next life for that pleasure.

The summer after Rock in Rio, I agreed to do Live Aid with Black Sabbath. Sharon was already pregnant again, and we didn't want to fly to Philadelphia, so we decided to take the QE2 to New York instead, then drive the rest of the way.

After the first hour at sea, we regretted it. In those days we were used to getting to New York in three hours on Concorde. The QE2 took five fucking days, which felt more like five billion years. I mean, what the fuck are you supposed to *do* on a ship, apart from puke your guts out 'cos you're feeling sea sick? By the end of day one, I was hoping we might hit an iceberg, just to liven things up a bit. And the boredom only got worse from there. In the end I went to see the ship's doctor and begged him for sedatives to put me out for the rest of the way. I woke up forty-eight hours later, just as we were pulling into port. Sharon was so pissed off – she'd had to entertain herself while I was out cold – it's a miracle she didn't throw me overboard. 'Remember me? You *arsehole*,' was the first thing she said when I opened my eyes.

To be honest with you, I was stressed out about doing Live Aid. I hadn't talked to Tony for years, so it wasn't exactly the most comfortable of situations. Then the organisers put us between Billy Ocean and the Four fucking Tops . . . at ten o'clock in the morning. I don't know what they were thinking. People kept telling us that they needed more black acts in the show, so maybe they thought *we* were black – like when we played Philadelphia on our first American tour.

It didn't get off to a good start.

When I was in the lobby of the hotel, checking in before the gig, this bloke comes up to me and says, 'Hey, Ozzy, can I have a photograph?' and I go, 'Sure, yeah.' Then the bloke goes, 'Sorry, I have to do this,' and hands me a lawsuit. It was from my father-in-law. He'd *served* me – before a fucking charity gig.

When everyone backstage heard about the writ – don't ask me what it was about, or what happened to it, 'cos I left it all to Sharon – one of the roadies came up to me and said, 'He's quite a character, your father-in-law, isn't he?'

'What d'you mean?' I asked him.

'He said the cover of *Born Again* reminded him of his grandchildren.'

If you haven't seen that cover – *Born Again* was Black Sabbath's third album after I left – it's of an aborted demon baby with fangs and claws. What an unbelievable thing to say!

On the one hand, doing Live Aid was brilliant: it was for a great cause, and no one can play those old Black Sabbath songs like me, Tony, Geezer and Bill. But on the other hand, it was all a bit embarrassing. For a start, I was still grossly overweight – on the video, I'm the size of a planet. Also, in the six years since I'd left the band, I'd become a celebrity in America, whereas Black Sabbath had been going in the other direction. So I got preferential treatment, even though I hadn't asked for it. It was just stupid little things, like I got a Live Aid jacket and they didn't. But it still felt awkward. And I didn't handle it with much grace, because my coked-up rock star ego was out of control. Deep down, a part of me wanted to say to them, 'You fired me and now I don't need you, so fuck you.' Looking back now, all I can think is, Why was I like that? Why did I have to be such a dickhead?

But the gig went smoothly enough. We just checked in to the hotel, met up at the sound check, ran through the set list, got up there, did the songs and fucked off home.

As for Don Arden's lawsuit, it probably shouldn't have come as much of a surprise. Jet Records had taken a big hit when we left. And a lot of other things were going wrong for him too.

For example, it was around that time Sharon's brother David ended up in court in England for allegedly kidnapping, blackmailing and beating up an accountant called Harshad Patel. It was a very bad scene. David was sentenced to two years in Wandsworth for whatever part he had in it, but he only served a few months. By the end of it, he'd been moved to Ford Open Prison.

Then they went after Don, who was still living in the Howard Hughes house at the top of Benedict Canyon. In the end, Don realised he was going to be extradited, so he went back of his own accord to stand trial. Then he hired the best lawyers in London and got off, scot-free.

A few months after Live Aid, on 8 November 1985, Jack was born. I was too pissed to remember much of it – I spent most of the time in the pub opposite the hospital – but I remember Sharon wanting to have him circumcised. I didn't put up a fight. I mean, the funny thing is, even though my mother was a Catholic, she had *me* circumcised. None of my brothers had it done – just me. I remember asking my mum what the fuck she was thinking, and she just went, 'Oh, it was fashionable.' I couldn't believe what I was hearing. 'It was *fashionable* to cut my dick off!' I remember shouting at her.

But I have to admit, it is cleaner that way. And because Jack was part-Jewish – because of Don Arden, whose real name was Harry Levy – it seemed like the right thing to do.

The most amazing thing about Jack being born is that he was our third kid in three years. We hadn't planned it that way. It just happened. Every time I came off the road, me and Sharon would get in the sack together – as you do – one thing would lead to another, then nine months later Sharon would be giving birth to another little Osbourne.

It was crazy, really, because I ended up touring the world as the Prince of Darkness with three little kids in tow, which wasn't exactly good for the image. For a few years I spent most of my time between gigs in a panic trying to find Jack's comfort blanket, which was this little yellow teddy bear thing called Baby. Jack would go fucking insane if he didn't have Baby to cuddle and chew on. But we were travelling so much, Baby would always end up getting left behind. I became obsessed with that fucking bear. I'd come off stage after singing 'Diary of a Madman', and the first thing I'd say was, 'Where's Baby? Has anyone seen Baby? *Make sure we don't lose Baby*.'

On more than one occasion we had to send our private jet halfway across America just to get Baby back from the hotel were we'd stayed the previous night. We'd drop twenty grand on jet fuel, just to rescue Baby. And don't think we didn't fucking try to just buy Jack a replacement. He was too smart for that – he wouldn't have any of it. You'd find a comfort blanket that was absolutely identical in every way to Baby, but Jack would take one look at it, throw it back at you, and bawl his eyes out until he got his real Baby back. And of course as time went on, Baby ended up having major surgery after being eaten by Sharon's dog a few times, so in the end there was no mistaking him.

As much as I was drunk and absent a lot of the time, I loved being a dad. It's just so much fun watching these little people you've brought into the world as they develop and grow up. Sharon loved being a mum, too. But enough was enough after a while. After Jack was born, I remember her saying to me, 'Ozzy, I can't have you anywhere near me next time you finish a tour. I feel like I've been pregnant for ever, I can't do it any more.'

So I went and got the snip. What a strange experience that was.

'You know this can't be reversed, don't you, Mr Osbourne?' said the doc.

'Yeah.'

'So you're sure about this?'

'Oh, yeah.'

'Absolutely sure?'

'Doc, believe me, I'm sure.'

'OK then, sign this form.'

After the operation, my balls swelled up to the size of watermelons. They ached terribly, too. 'Hey, Doc,' I said. 'Can you give me something that will leave the swelling but take away the pain?'

All in all, I don't recommend it, as far as elective surgery goes. When you pop your load after you've had the snip, nothing but dust comes out. It's like a dry sneeze. Really weird, man.

Then, nine months later, Sharon got broody again. So I had to go back to the doc and ask him to unsnip me.

'Oh, for fuck's sake,' he said. 'I *told* you that couldn't be done. But we can always try, I suppose.'

It didn't work. As the doc said, it's very hard to reverse a snip. Maybe if I'd gone back to get my pipes cleaned out, it would have been OK. Who knows? But we gave up on having any more kids after that. Still, five kids in one lifetime ain't bad – and I love them all so much.

They're the best things that ever happened to me, no question about it.

Another problem with getting the snip was that it made me think I suddenly had the freedom to do whatever I wanted to – or at least whatever I *thought* I wanted to, when I was pissed out of my skull. But my wife was brought up in a rock 'n' roll environment, and she can sniff out a lie from six thousand miles away. And I'm the world's worst liar, anyway.

So she knew exactly what I was up to. Of course, she hated it, but she put up with it. At first.

It wasn't like I was having affairs. I just wanted to think I was Robert Redford for an hour. But I was never any good at that game. Most of the time, when I was with a chick, she'd be calling an ambulance or carrying me back to my hotel room in a cab while I puked my guts out. I'd start the night like James Bond, and end it like a pile of shit on the floor. And the guilt that followed was always fucking lethal. I hated it. I felt like such an arsehole. And I'm a terrible hypochondriac, so I'd always be shitting myself that I'd caught some rare and deadly virus. I can catch a disease off the telly, me. I'll be taking some pill to help me get to sleep, then I'll see an ad for it on TV, and the voiceover will say, 'Side-effects may include vomiting, bleeding and, on rare occasions, death' and I'll convince myself I'm halfway to the morgue. It got to the point where I had doctors coming over to look at my dick twice a week, just to be on the safe side.

Then AIDS came along.

I wasn't worried at first. Like most people, I thought it was a gay thing. And no matter how drunk or high I got, I never felt the urge to jump in the sack with some hairy-arsed bloke.

But it didn't take long for everyone to realise that you don't have to be gay to get AIDS. Then, one night, I bonked this chick in the Sunset Marquis Hotel in West Hollywood. As soon as I was done, I just *knew* something wasn't right. So, at two in the morning, I called the front desk and asked if they had a doctor on duty. They did – those fancy hotels always have their own in-house quacks – so he came up to my room, checked out my tackle and told me I should go and have a test.

'What d'you mean, a test?' I asked him.

'An HIV test,' he said.

That was it, as far as I was concerned. I was a goner.

For a few days I drove myself halfway insane with worry. I was impossible to be around. Then I blurted everything out to Sharon. You can imagine how that went down. Think of that 100-megaton bomb the Russians once set off in the Arctic.

That was Sharon when I told her that I had to get an HIV test 'cos I'd bonked some dodgy chick from a hotel bar. Angry doesn't even begin to describe it. It was such a bad scene, I began to think that being dead might actually be better than being alive for another bollocking.

Anyway, I got the test. And then a week later, I went with Sharon to get the results.

I'll never forget the doctor walking into that little room, sitting down, getting out his file, and going, 'Well, Mr Osbourne, the good news is that you don't have herpes, the clap or syphilis.'

The second he said that, I knew something was up.

'What's the bad news?' I asked him.

'Well, I'm afraid there's no easy way to tell you this,' he said, as my whole body went numb with fear. 'But you're HIV positive.'

I literally fell to my knees, put my hands over my head, and screamed, 'WHAT THE FUCK DO YOU MEAN I'M HIV POSITIVE? THAT'S A FUCKING DEATH SENTENCE, YOU ARSEHOLE!'

You've got to remember, in those days HIV wasn't treatable like it is now. If you got HIV, it meant you'd get AIDS – and then you'd die. The End. And if I was HIV positive, then it probably meant that Sharon was HIV positive, too. Which meant I'd killed the mother of my kids.

I couldn't even look at Sharon, I felt so fucking terrible. She must have *hated* me at that moment. But she didn't say anything. I suppose the shock of it must have been as bad for her as it was for me.

Then the phone on the doctor's desk rang. I was still on my knees and screaming at this point, but I soon shut up when I realised it was the lab, calling about my results. I listened as the doctor ummed and ahhed for a while. Then he put down the receiver and went, 'Actually, Mr Osbourne, let me clarify: your test was borderline, not positive. That means we need to run it again. Sorry for the confusion.'

Confusion? If I hadn't been such a mess, I would have got up and chinned the bastard.

But I was in no state for anything.

'How long will that take?' I croaked, trying not to throw up.

'Another week.'

'I won't *last* a week,' I said. 'Seriously, doc, I'll have topped myself by then. Is there *any* way of getting it faster?'

'It'll be expensive.'

'I don't care.'

'OK then. I'll get it for you overnight. In the meantime, Mrs Osbourne, I suggest you get a test, too.'

Sharon nodded, her face white.

The next day we went back for my results. I'd been a fucking wreck all night, but Sharon wasn't exactly in the mood to give me any sympathy. The only thing she was in the mood for was divorce. I honestly thought my marriage was over.

'So, Mr Osbourne,' began the doc. 'We ran another test on you, and I'm delighted to say that you don't seem to have HIV – although we should do the test one more time, to be sure.'

I put my head in my hands, released all the air from my lungs, and thanked God like I'd never thanked Him before. Meanwhile, I heard Sharon let out a sob of relief and blow her nose.

'The confusion seems to have arisen from the state of your immune system,' the doc went on. 'Basically, Mr Osbourne, your immune system currently isn't functioning. At all. At first, the lab couldn't understand it. So they did some more blood-work, and then they came across some – well, er, some *lifestyle factors* that probably explain the anomaly.'

'Lifestyle factors?'

'Your blood contains near-fatal quantities of alcohol and cocaine, Mr Osbourne, not to mention a number of other controlled substances. The lab's never seen anything like it.'

'So I really *don't* have HIV?'

'No. But your body thinks it does.'

'Well, that's a relief.'

'Mr Osbourne, you might not be HIV positive, but your life is still in grave danger if you don't take it easier.'

I nodded, but by then I wasn't even listening. I was too busy planning the drink I needed to celebrate. Mind you, I did change my lifestyle in one way – I never cheated on Sharon again.

With the AIDS crisis over, I flew back to England to prepare for the next tour. I'd only been back a week or two when I got a frantic call from Sharon, who was still in California.

'Ozzy, get on the next plane out here.'

She sounded terrible.

'What? *Why?*' I said.

'Just go to the airport, buy a ticket, then call the Beverly Hills Hotel and let me know which flight you're on.'

'Is everything OK?'

'No. One more thing, Ozzy.'

'Yeah?'

'DO. NOT. GET. DRUNK.'

Click.

Fifteen hours later, I was walking through immigration at LAX when about ten thousand flashbulbs went off. I thought there must have been a royal visit going on or something. Then a reporter shoved a TV camera in my face and said, 'What do you think, Ozzy?'

'Oh, er, well, the chicken was a bit soggy,' I said. 'But other than that, it was a pretty decent flight.'

'I mean about the kid. The dead kid. Any comment?'

'*What?*'

'The suicide. Your thoughts?'

'I have no idea what you're talki—'

Before I could say any more, about ten security guards pushed the cameraman out of the way and formed a circle around me. Then they escorted me outside and bundled me into a black limo.

Waiting on the back seat was Howard Weitzman, my lawyer.

'The kid's name is – or rather *was* – John McCollum,' he explained, handing me a copy of the *Los Angeles Times*. 'Nineteen years old. Big fans of yours. According to his parents, he was drinking and listening to *Speak of the Devil* when he shot himself with his father's .22. He was still wearing headphones when they found him. And they're blaming it all on you.'

'Me?'

'The father says his son was just doing what the lyrics of "Suicide Solution" told him to do.'

'But *Speak of the Devil* is a live album of Black Sabbath songs. "Suicide Solution" isn't even on there.'

'Right.'

'And has he actually *read* the lyrics?'

'Look, you and I both know the song's about the perils of too much liquor, but he doesn't see it that way.'

'He thinks I want my fans to kill themselves? How the fuck does he think I plan to sell any more records?'

'That's not all, Ozzy. They're saying that your songs have subliminal messages embedded in them, instructing the young and impressionable to "get a gun", "end it now", "shoot-shoot-shoot", that kind of thing. It's all in the lawsuit. I'll have a copy sent over to your hotel.'

'How much are they suing me for?'

'Everything. Plus damages.'

'You're kidding me.'

'Unfortunately not. We're on our way to a press conference right now. Let me do the talking.'

The press conference was at a tennis club. I was jet-lagged, pissed (I couldn't help myself) and in shock. It got even worse when I was led on to this little podium to face the cameras. I was used to being interviewed by music magazines or whatever, but not by this hardcore national media gang. It was like being back in the classroom with Mr Jones. The reporters were throwing questions at me so hard and so fast, I almost wanted to duck for cover.

One guy said, 'Listen, Mr Osbourne, isn't it true that you sing on one of your songs, "Paranoid", "I tell you to *end* your life"?'

I had to take a moment to run through Geezer's lyrics in my head. Then I said to him, 'No, I sing "*enjoy* life".'

But the other reporters were already shouting their follow-up questions, so no one could hear.

'It's ENJOY life,' I kept repeating. 'ENJOY life.'

No one listened.

'Ozzy,' said another reporter. 'Mr McCollum's attorney says he went to one of your concerts, and that it was like being at Nuremberg, with the crowd chanting your name. Any comment?'

'*Nuremberg?*' I should have said, 'I don't think Hitler spent much of his time at Nuremberg making the peace sign and shouting "rock 'n' roll".' But I didn't. I couldn't get my words out. I just froze.

Then they started asking about 'Suicide Solution'. All I can remember is Howard Weisman shouting above the crowd, 'The song is autobiographical. It's about Mr Osbourne's well-publicised battle with alcoholism, which he believes is a form of suicide, as evidenced by the tragic death of Mr Osbourne's good friend Bon Scott, lead singer of the Australian band AC/DC.'

'But Ozzy,' shouted the reporters, 'isn't it true that . . .'

Finally, it was over and I went back to the hotel, shaking. I flopped down on the bed, flicked on the TV, and there was Don Arden, discussing the case. 'To be perfectly honest, I would be doubtful as to whether Mr Osbourne knew the meaning of the lyrics – if there was *any* meaning – because his command of the English language is minimal,' he said.

I suppose it was his way of showing support.

The press conference was very frightening, and it gave me a taste of what was to come. I became public enemy number one in America. I opened a newspaper one morning in New York and there was a picture of me with a gun pointed at my head. They must have cut and pasted it together 'cos I'd never posed for it, but it freaked me out. Then I started to get death threats wherever I went. The cops would use them to try to get me to cancel gigs. One time in Texas, the local police chief called up our tour manager and said, 'There's been some dynamite stolen from the local quarry, and we've had a letter from an anonymous source saying it's going to be used to blow up Ozzy.'

I was scared for the kids, more than anything. I told the nannies never to stop for anyone on the street. It was 1986, just over five years since John Lennon had signed a copy of *Double Fantasy* for a fan and then been shot by the same bloke. And I was well aware that it was often the fans who could be the most psycho. One guy started to follow me around with this five-million-year-old mammoth tusk. Another bloke sent me a video of his house: he'd painted my name over every single thing, both outside and in. Then he sent me another video of this little girl wearing a pair of wellies and dancing to 'Fairies Wear Boots'.

He was insane, that guy. He built a tomb so that me and him could spend the rest of eternity together. I could think of better fucking things to do with eternity, to be honest with you. It got to the point where the cops had to take him into custody every time I played a gig anywhere near where he lived. And if I did a signing at a record shop in the area, they'd make me wear a bullet-proof jacket, just to be safe.

I got well and truly pissed off with the crazy stuff after a while. I remember one time, me and my assistant Tony were on a flight from Tokyo to LA. There'd been a six-hour delay at the gate, and they'd handed out free drinks coupons, so everyone was pissed. But this one American chick wouldn't leave me alone. She was sitting behind me, and every two seconds she'd tap me on the back of my head and go, 'I *know* you.'

Tony kept saying to her, 'Now, missus, please just go away. We don't want to be bothered,' but she wouldn't listen.

In the end, she got out of her seat, came round, and wanted a photograph. So I let her take one. Then she went, 'I got it! You're Ozzy Bourne!'

I'd had enough. 'FUCK OFF!' I shouted.

A stewardess came over and told me not to be rude to the other passengers.

'Well, keep that woman away from me then!' I told her.

But she kept coming back. And back. And back.

Finally, I thought, Right, I'm gonna do something about this.

In those days, I used to carry around these things called Doom Dots. They're basically chloral hydrate, and they come in little gel caps. All you do is stick a pin in the end and squirt the stuff into someone's drink. When you hear about people being 'slipped a Mickey', that's what they're being given – a Doom Dot. Anyway, I waited for this chick to get up and go for a piss, then reached behind me, and squirted a Doom Dot into her glass of wine.

When she came back, I told Tony, 'Keep looking behind me, and tell me what's happening.'

He said, 'Whey, she's ahl-reet right now, but she's leaning

forward a bit. She's lookin' a bit dazed. Oh, hang on now – she's goin', she's goin', she's—'

I felt a jolt in the back of my seat.

'What happened?' I asked Tony.

'Face down on the tray. Fast asleep.'

'Magic,' I said.

'Aye. It's just a shame she didn't get her soup oot the way first, lyke. Poor lass. She's gonna be covered.'

But the Jesus freaks were the worst. While the 'Suicide Solution' case was going through the courts they followed me around everywhere. They would picket my shows with signs that read, 'The Anti-Christ Is Here'. And they'd always be chanting: 'Put Satan behind you! Put Jesus in front of you!'

One time, I made my own sign – a smiley face with the words 'Have a Nice Day' – and went out and joined them. They didn't even notice. Then, just as the gig was about to start, I put down the sign, said, 'See ya, guys,' and went back to my dressing room.

The most memorable Jesus-freak moment was in Tyler, Texas. By then, the death threats were coming in pretty much every day, so I had this security guy, a Vietnam vet called Chuck, who was with me at all times. Chuck was so hardcore he couldn't even go into a Chinese restaurant. 'If I see anyone who looks like a Gook, I'm gonna take 'em out,' he'd say. He had to turn down a tour with me in Japan 'cos he couldn't handle it. Whenever we stayed in a hotel, he'd spend the night crawling around on his belly through the undergrowth in the garden or doing push-ups in the corridor. Really intense guy.

Anyway, in Tyler, we did the gig, went out on the town, and got back to the hotel at about seven in the morning. I'd agreed to meet a doctor in the lobby at noon that day – my throat had been bothering me – so I went to bed, got a few hours' kip, then Chuck knocked on my door and off we went to see the quack. But the doctor was nowhere to be found, so I said to the chick on the front desk, 'If a bloke in a white coat turns up, just tell him I'm in the coffee shop.'

But I didn't have a clue that the local evangelist guy had been doing this TV campaign about me in the run-up to the gig, telling everyone that I was the Devil, that I was corrupting the youth of America, and that I was going to take everyone with me to hell. So half the town was out to get me, but I had no idea. There I was, sitting in this coffee shop, with Chuck twitching and muttering beside me. Thirty minutes went by. No doctor. Then another thirty minutes. Still no doctor. Then, finally, this guy comes in and says, 'Are you Ozzy Osbourne?'

'Yeah.'

'PUT SATAN BEHIND YOU! PUT JESUS IN FRONT OF YOU! PUT SATAN BEHIND YOU! PUT JESUS IN FRONT OF YOU! PUT SATAN BEHIND YOU! PUT JESUS IN FRONT OF YOU!'

It was the preacher from the telly. And it turned out that the coffee shop was full of his disciples, so as soon as he started to do his nutty Jesus bullshit, all these other people joined in, until I was surrounded by forty or fifty Jesus freaks, all red in the face and spitting out the same words.

Then Chuck went fucking mental. The whole thing must have triggered some sort of 'Nam flashback, 'cos he just flipped. Stage-five psycho. The guy must have taken down about fifteen of the Jesus freaks in the first ten seconds. There were teeth and Bibles and glasses flying everything.

I didn't stick around to see what happened next. I just elbowed the preacher in the nuts and legged it.

The funny thing is, I'm actually quite interested in the Bible, and I've tried to read it several times. But I've only ever got as far as the bit about Moses being 720 years old, and I'm like, 'What were these people smoking back then?' The bottom line is I don't believe in a bloke called God in a white suit who sits on a fluffy cloud any more than I believe in a bloke called the Devil with a three-pronged fork and a couple of horns. But I believe that there's day, there's night, there's good, there's bad, there's black, there's white. If there is a God, it's nature. If there's a Devil, it's nature. I feel the same way when people ask me if songs like 'Hand of Doom' and 'War Pigs' are anti-war. I think war is just part of human nature. And I'm fascinated by human nature – especially the dark side. I always have been. It doesn't make me a Devil worshipper, no more than being interested in Hitler makes me a Nazi. I mean, if I'm a Nazi, how come I married a woman who's half Jewish?

All those Jesus freaks ever had to do was listen to my records, and it would have been obvious. But they just wanted to use me for publicity. And I suppose I didn't care that much, 'cos every time they attacked me, I got my ugly mug on the telly and sold another hundred thousand records. I should probably have sent them a Christmas card.

But in the end, even the American legal system came down on my side.

The 'Suicide Solution' lawsuit was filed in January 1986, and was thrown out in August of that year. At the court hearing, Howard Weitzman told the judge that if they were gonna ban 'Suicide Solution' and hold me responsible for some poor kid shooting himself, then they'd have to ban Shakespeare, 'cos *Romeo and Juliet*'s about suicide, too. He also said that the song lyrics were protected by the right of free speech in America. The judge agreed, but his summing up wasn't exactly friendly. He said that although I was 'totally objectionable and repulsive, trash can be given First Amendment protection, too'.

I had to read that sentence about five times before I realised that the bloke had actually ruled in our favour.

The one thing the McCollums were right about was that

there *was* a subliminal message in 'Suicide Solution'. But it wasn't 'Get the gun, get the gun, shoot-shoot-shoot'. What I actually say is 'Get the flaps out, get the flaps out, bodge-bodge-bodge'. It was a stupid dirty joke we had at the time. If a chick took her kit off, we said she was getting her flaps out – her piss flaps. And 'bodge' was just a word we had for fuck. So I was basically saying, 'Get a chick naked and give her one,' which was a whole fucking lot different to saying, 'Blow your brains out.'

But the media was obsessed with that stuff for a long time. Which was great PR as far as we were concerned. It got to the point where if you put a 'parental advisory' sticker on your album saying it contained explicit lyrics, you sold twice as many copies. Then you *had* to have one of those stickers, otherwise the album wouldn't chart.

After a while, I started to put subliminal messages in as many of my songs as I could. For example, on *No Rest for the Wicked*, if you play 'Bloodbath in Paradise' backwards, you can clearly hear me saying, 'Your mother sells whelks in Hull.'

The saddest thing about that period wasn't that the Jesus freaks kept giving us a hard time. It was that my old bandmates Bob Daisley and Lee Kerslake decided to have a go, too. It started to feel like someone had put a bull's-eye on my forehead, just 'cos I'd made a bit of dough.

They claimed we owed them money for *Blizzard of Ozz* and *Diary of a Madman*, so they sued us. And we fought, because we didn't owe them anything. Bob and Lee were what's known as paid-to-play musicians. They got a weekly rate for recording, a different rate for touring and another rate to stay at home. I even paid for the fucking petrol they used to drive to and from the studio. Yes, they helped write some of the songs on the first two albums, but they got publishing royalties for that – and they still get them to this day. So what more did they want? I'm obviously no great legal brain, but from what I understand they said I wasn't a solo artist and that we were all part of a band. But if I was just the singer and we were all at the same level, how come I auditioned them? And how come I was talking about *Blizzard of Ozz* for years before I met them? And where the fuck are all *their* hit records, before and after the two albums with me?

People ask me why we didn't just settle. But that's what Michael Jackson did, and look what happened to him. If you've got a bit of hard-earned dough in the bank and you say to someone who's suing you, 'OK, how much will it cost to make this go away?' that opens the door for every loony and arsehole in the world to try to get the next load off you. You have to stand up for yourself, 'cos it can be a nasty game, this business – especially when people think you go to bed at night on a big mountain of cash.

In the end Bob and Lee's lawsuit got thrown out of every court in America. What really pisses me off is that Bob and Lee never said to me, 'Ozzy, we've gotta sit down. We wanna have a talk to you.' They just kept blasting off in all fucking directions. The first I knew about it was when I got served. They'd been creeping around behind my back, calling up other people who'd played on my albums and trying to get them involved. I'd done fuck-all wrong, but they made me feel like the criminal of the century, and it really got up my arse after a while.

Sharon protected me from a lot of the details, 'cos she knows how much I worry. In the end she just snapped and re-recorded Bob and Lee's parts on those two albums. When they were re-released, a sticker was put on the covers telling people all about it. I didn't have anything to do with that decision, and I can't say I feel good about it. I told Sharon that I was uncomfortable with it, but I get it, y'know? I understand why she felt she had to do it. Every time we got past one hurdle, another one would come up. It never stopped. The case went on for *twenty-five years* after *Blizzard of Ozz* was recorded. All I wanted to do was get on with being a rock 'n' roller, and instead I ended up being Perry fucking Mason, giving depositions here, there and everywhere.

What really kills me is that I worked with Bob for years, and I was very fond of him and his family. He's a very talented bloke. We were good friends. I certainly didn't turn around and sue him when they put my balls to the fire for 'Suicide Solution', even though he wrote some of the lyrics. But sometimes in life you've gotta move on. Eventually, I had to stop talking to him or seeing him, 'cos I was frightened I might say the wrong thing – and then it would be lawsuit time again. Also, I just hate fucking confrontations. It's one of my biggest failings.

I never want to go through any of that bullshit again. Before I work with anyone now, I tell them to get themselves a lawyer, have their lawyer write up a contract with my lawyer, then read it, think about it, make sure they're happy with it, make double and triple sure they're happy with it, and then *never* say that anyone ripped them off.

Because I don't do that – no matter what Bob Daisley and Lee Kerslake might say.

My last good memory of the eighties, before everything went dark, was being sent to Wormwood Scrubs. Not because I'd broken the law again – amazingly – but because I was asked to play a gig there.

What a crazy experience that was. I might have been in a few police station lock-ups over the years, but I hadn't set foot in a proper slammer since I'd walked out of Winson Green in 1966. The iron bars, the balconies, even the screws all looked the same as they had twenty years before, but it was the smell that really brought it all back to me: like a public shitter, times ten. Bad enough to make your eyes water. I can't for the life of me figure out why anyone would want to work in one of those places. I suppose they're all ex-army, so they're used to it.

Maybe that's what I would have done in the end if the army hadn't told me to fuck off.

I was invited to do the gig because the prison had its own band, called the Scrubs, which had both screws and inmates in it. They'd written a song and donated the royalties to charity. Then they wrote to me and asked if I fancied doing a gig with them. The deal was that they'd play a set, then I'd play my set, then we'd do a jam of 'Jailhouse Rock'.

So we get to the prison and they let me through all the fences and gates and doors, then they show me into this back room where there's a big fat guy making a pot of tea. He's a nice jolly chap, very friendly, and offers me a cuppa.

I ask him, 'How long are you in here for, then?'

'Oh,' he says, 'I'll never get out of here.'

We keep chatting for a while and I'm drinking this cup of tea, but then curiosity gets the better of me and I say, 'So, how come you're in here for such a long stretch?'

'I murdered eight people.'

That's a bit heavy duty, I think, but we carry on talking. Then curiosity gets the better of me again. 'So, how did you do it?' I ask, taking another sip of my tea. 'I mean, how did you kill all those people?'

'Oh, I poisoned them,' he says.

I just about threw the mug of tea at the wall. And whatever had been in my mouth came out of my nose. It's funny, when you think of a murderer, you always picture some tall, dark, evil-looking monster. But it can be just a nice, normal, jolly fat bloke, with a loose wire somewhere.

The gig itself was surreal.

The smell of dope in the hall where we played almost knocked me off my feet. It was like a Jamaican wedding in there. Another thing that amazed me was that they had a bar right outside, where all the screws went. As for the members of the Scrubs, the bass player was a Vietnamese guy who'd burned thirty-seven people to death a few years earlier by pouring petrol through the letterbox of an underground club in Soho and putting a match to it (the biggest mass killing in British history at the time); the guitarist was a kid who'd murdered a drug dealer by beating him to death with an iron bar; and then there were a couple of screws who sang and played the drums.

I'll never forget the moment when it was our turn to go on stage. Jake E. Lee had just left the band and Zakk Wylde had taken over as lead guitarist. He was young, with ripped muscles and long blond hair, and the second he walked out from the wings, the entire place started to wolf-whistle and scream, 'Bend over, little boy, bend over, little boy!' Then they all started to jump around, stoned out of their minds, while the riot-screws stood guard. It was insane. I'd said to Sharon before we went on, 'At least if we're crap, no one will walk out.' Now I was thinking, No, they'll just kill me.

At one point, I looked down and there in the front row was Jeremy Bamber, the bloke who murdered his entire family with a rifle at a farmhouse in Essex and then tried to make it look like his mentally ill sister had done it. His face had been on the front page of every tabloid in Britain for months. He gave me a big smile, did the old Bambinator.

At the end, when we were playing 'Jailhouse Rock', there was a full-on stage invasion, led by one of the kids who had tried to cut the head off that police officer, Keith Blakelock, during the Broadwater Farm riot. I knew it was him 'cos one of the screws on stage told me. The last thing I saw was this kid taking off a shoe and hitting himself on the head with it.

Fuck this for a game of soldiers, I thought. Nice seeing ya, I'm off now.

And I didn't look back.

*

Getting a star on the Hollywood Walk of Fame in April 2002. Left to right: Jack, Marilyn Manson, me, Robbie Williams and Kelly. Not sure I want to know what Marilyn's thinking about.

With my biggest fan.

Having a blast with Kelly. Our duet of 'Changes' went to number one in 2003.

At Welders House, messing around on my dirt bike.

Before . . .

. . . and after. I broke my neck, my collarbone, eight ribs and punctured my lungs, and was in a coma for eight days.

With Elton, the most generous man I've ever met.

Meeting Liz Taylor. My father once told me she was the most beautiful woman in the world.

My rock 'n' roll hero.

Shaking hands with the Queen. She didn't have to bring me flowers.

And meeting, err . . . me. Filming with impersonator Jon Culshaw. That's him on the left. I think.

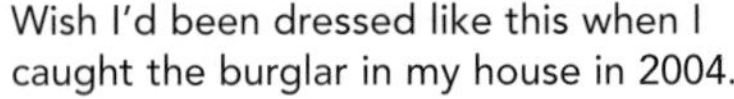

Wish I'd been dressed like this when I caught the burglar in my house in 2004.

With Maggie, one of my seventeen dogs.

Me and Sharon, just after the burglary. We lost £2 million worth of jewellery.

On stage at the Tower of London for the Prince's Trust in 2006.

Black Sabbath being inducted into the Hall of Fame with Tony (centre) and Bill (far right).

Arm in arm with my sisters. From left: Gillian, me, Iris and Jean.

Sharon, trying to keep my hand away from the knife, at my sixtieth in December 2008.

My incredible family.

One morning, not long after that gig, Sharon asked me, 'Did you have a good night last night, Ozzy?'

'What d'you mean?'

'At Kelly's birthday party. Did you have a good time?'

'Yeah, I suppose.'

All I could remember was playing with the kids in the garden, making Jack laugh by tickling his tummy, telling a few funny jokes, and eating one too many slices of Kelly's birthday cake. We'd even hired a clown for the occasion – a bloke called Ally Doolally – who'd put on a little puppet show. The rest was a bit of a blur, 'cos I'd also had one or two drinks.

'You should have seen yourself,' said Sharon.

'What d'you mean?'

'I mean *you should have seen yourself*.'

'I don't understand, Sharon. I was a bit tipsy, yes, but it was a birthday party. Everyone was a bit tipsy.'

'No, honestly, Ozzy, you should have *seen* yourself. Actually, would you like to see yourself? I have a video.'

Oh *crap*, I thought.

Sharon had filmed the whole thing. She put the tape in the machine, and I couldn't believe my eyes. In my mind, I'd been the fun dad that everyone wants to have around. Then I saw the reality. Jack was terrified and in tears. Kelly and Aimee were hiding in the shed, also in tears. All the other parents were leaving and muttering under their breath. The clown had a bloody nose. And there was me, in the middle of it all, fat, pissed, cake all over my face, dripping wet from something or other, raving, screaming drunk.

I was a beast. Absolutely terrifying.

After I'd come out of the Betty Ford Center, I'd started to say to myself, 'Well, I might be an alcoholic, but I have the perfect job for an alcoholic, so maybe it's kind of all right that I'm an alcoholic.'

In a way, it was true. I mean, what other occupation rewards you for being out of your brains all the time? The more loaded I was when I got on stage, the more the audience knew it was gonna be a good night. The trouble was the booze was making me so ill that I couldn't function without taking pills or cocaine on top of it. Then I couldn't sleep – or I had panic attacks, or I went into these paranoid delusions – so I turned to sedatives, which I'd get from doctors on the road. Whenever I overdosed, which I did all the time, I'd just blame it on my dyslexia: 'Sorry, Doc, I thought it said *six* every *one* hour, not *one* every *six* hours.'

I had a different doctor in every town – 'gig doctors' I called them – and played them off against each other. When you're a drug addict, half the thrill is the chase, not the fix. When I discovered Vicodin, for example, I used to keep an old bottle and put a couple of pills in it, then I'd say, 'Oh, Doc, I've got these Vicodins, but I'm running low.' He'd look at the date and the two pills left in the jar, then whack me up another fifty. So I'd get fifty pills before every gig. I was doing twenty-five a day at one point.

Mind you, in America, if you're a celebrity, you don't have to try very hard to get doctors to give you whatever you want. One gig doctor would drive out to see me in his pick-up. In the back he had one of those tool cabinets full of little drawers, and in each drawer he had a different kind of drug. All the heavy shit you could ever want. Eventually Sharon found out what was going on and put her foot down. She grabbed the doc by the scruff of the neck and said, 'Do not give my husband any drugs under any circumstances or you're going to jail.'

Deep down, I knew that all the booze and drugs had turned sour on me; that I'd stopped being funny and zany and had started to become sad. I'd run miles to get a drink. I'd do anything for a drink. I used to keep a fridge full of beer in the kitchen, and I'd get up, first thing in the morning, knock off a

Corona, and by twelve o'clock I was fucking blasted. And when I was doing Vicodin and all that other shit, I was always playing with my fucking nose. You can see how bad I was on Penelope Spheeris's documentary *The Decline of Western Civilization Part II*. Everyone thought it was hysterical, me trying to fry an egg at seven o'clock in the morning after I'd been out on the piss all night, drinking bottle after bottle of vino.

Booze does terrible things to you when you drink as much as I did. For example, I started to shit myself on a regular basis. At first I made a joke out of it, but then it just stopped being funny. One time, I was in a hotel somewhere in England, and I was walking down the corridor to my room, but suddenly I felt this turd rumbling down the pipe. I had to go. Right then. It was either do it on the carpet or do it in my pants, and I'd had enough of doing it in my pants. So I squatted down, dropped my trousers, and took a dump right there in the corridor.

At that exact moment, a bellboy came out of the elevator, looked at me, and shouted, '*What the hell are you doing?*'

I couldn't even begin to think how to explain. So I just held up my room key and said, 'It's all right, I'm staying here.'

'No you're fucking not,' he said.

A lot of alcoholics shit themselves. I mean, think about it: a gallon of Guinness makes enough tarmac to pave ten miles of the M6. And when you come round the following day, your body wants to get rid of everything: it just wants to expel all the toxic crap you forced into it the night before. I tried to stop it by switching from Guinness to Hennessy. But I was fruiting it up with orange juice or Coca-Cola the whole time, which made it just as bad. And I was drinking four bottles of Hennessy a day, plus the cocaine and the pills and the beer. At first, I would barely get hangovers, but as time went on they started to get worse and worse, until I couldn't handle them any more.

So I went back to rehab. I was just so sick and tired of feeling sick and tired. If you drink a liquid that makes you feel better, then that's one thing. But if you drink a liquid that makes you feel worse than you did originally, then what's the point? And I felt like I was *dying*.

I couldn't face Betty Ford again, so I went to the Hazelden Clinic in Center City, Minnesota. It was winter, freezing cold. I spent the whole time shivering, throwing up and feeling sorry for myself.

On the first day, the therapist got a bunch of us together and said, 'When you go back to your rooms tonight, I want you to write down how much you think drink and drugs have cost you since you started doing them. Just add it all up and come back to me.'

So that night I got out a calculator and started to do some sums. I kind of wanted to get a big number, so I grossly exaggerated a lot of things, like how many pints I had each day – I put twenty-five – and how much each of them cost. In the end I came up with this obscene number. Just a huge, ridiculous number. Something like a million quid. Then I tried to get some sleep, but I couldn't.

The next day, I showed my calculations to the bloke, and he said, 'Oh, very interesting.'

I was surprised, 'cos I thought he was gonna say, 'Oh, come off it, Ozzy, give me some real numbers.'

Then he said, 'So is this just from drinking?'

'And drugs,' I said.

'Hmm. And you're sure this is *everything*?' he asked me.

'It's a million quid!' I said. 'How much more could it be?'

'Well, have you ever been fined because of drinking?'

'A few times, yeah.'

'Have you ever missed any gigs or been banned from any venues because of drinking?'

'A few times, yeah.'

'Had to pay lawyers to get you out of trouble because of your drinking?'

'A few times, yeah.'

'Medical fees?'

'Big time.'

'And d'you think you might have lost record sales because your work was affected by drinking?'

'Probably.'

'*Probably?*'

'OK, definitely.'

'Final question: have you ever lost property or other assets in a divorce caused by your drinking?'

'Yeah, I lost everything.'

'Well, Ozzy, I did some research and some calculations of my own last night, and d'you want to know what *I* think your addictions have cost you?'

'Go on then.'

He told me. I almost threw up.

10

Blackout

I woke up groaning.

Fuck me, I thought, as my eyes began to focus: must have been another good one last night. I was lying on a bare concrete floor in a square room. It had bars on the window, a bucket in the corner, and human shit up the walls. For a second I thought I was in a public toilet. But no: the bars on the window were the giveaway.

One of these days, I thought, I really need to stop waking up in jail cells.

I touched my face. Argh! *Shit*, that hurt.

For some reason, all I was wearing one of my smelly old T-shirts – the kind I used to sleep in – and a pair of shiny black tuxedo trousers. At least it's better than waking up in one of Sharon's frocks again, I thought.

I wondered what time it was. Seven in the morning? Nine? Ten? My watch was gone. So was my wallet. The coppers must have bagged my stuff when they booked me. The only thing left in my pockets was a scrunched-up receipt from my local Chinese restaurant, the Dynasty. I pictured the inside of the place – red, like hell – and saw myself sitting in one of the leather booths, arguing with Sharon, and crushing powder and pills in one of those . . . what d'you call them? A pestle and mortar. What the fuck had I been doing last night? Coke? Sleeping pills? Amphetamines? All that and more, knowing me.

I felt disgusting. My whole body ached – especially my face, and my teeth, and my nose.

I needed a bag of ice.

I needed a shower.

I needed a doctor.

'HELLO?' I shouted through the bars. 'ANYBODY THERE?'

No reply.

I tried to think what my drunk, coked-up evil-twin brother could have done to put me behind bars. But my brain was empty. Blank. Just that image of me in the Dynasty, then static. I'd probably been caught pissing in the street again, I thought. But if that was the case, why was I wearing my pyjama T-shirt? Had I been arrested at my *house*? Whatever I'd got up to, it had given me the mother of all headaches. I hoped I hadn't already used up my telephone call, 'cos I needed to tell Sharon that I was in jail, so she could come and get me. Or maybe she'd gone to America. She was always fucking off to America to get out of my way, especially after a big argument. In which case I'd need to call Tony Dennis.

Good old Tony.

He'd sort me out.

It was 3 September 1989.

By then, we'd moved back to England full time. We'd bought a place called Beel House, in Little Chalfont, Buckinghamshire. The house dated back to the seventeenth century, or so Sharon told me. Dirk Bogarde once lived there. It was a *real* house, not the fake, movie-set bullshit you get out in California. But my favourite thing about it was our next-door neighbour, George, who lived in what used to be the gatehouse. George was a chemist, and he made his own wine. Every day I'd knock on his door and say, 'Gis a bottle of your super stuff, George.' It was like rocket fuel, that wine of his. People would come over from America, take one swig, their eyes would widen, and they'd go, 'What the fuck *is* this stuff?' A few glasses of Chateau d'George was enough to put you under for good. The funny thing was George didn't even drink. He was a teetotaller. He'd say, 'Oh, Mr Osbourne, I saw that you set fire to the kitchen last night. That must have been a good one. Remind me, was it the elderberry or the tea leaf?'

But Sharon was on my back, big time, so I couldn't drink George's brews in front of her. And I couldn't hide the bottles in the oven any more, either. So I started to bury the stuff in the garden. Trouble was, I would always hide the booze when I was pissed, so the next night I could never remember where the fuck I'd put it. I'd be out there with a shovel until two o'clock in the morning, digging holes all over the place. Then Sharon would come down for breakfast and look out of the window, and there'd be all these trenches everywhere. 'Fuck me, Sharon,' I'd say to her, 'them moles have been busy, haven't they?'

In the end, I had floodlights installed to help me find the booze. Cost me an arm and a leg.

Then Sharon twigged, and that was the end of that.

'I should have known better than to think you would develop a sudden interest in horticulture,' she said.

It was probably good that I got caught, 'cos my body could hardly take the hard stuff any more. I was forty, and my system had started to give up. I knew something was badly wrong when I went to the pub one time and woke up *five days* later. People would come up to me and say, 'Hello, Ozzy,' and I'd ask, 'Do I know you?' And they'd go, 'I spent three months living at your house over the summer. Don't you remember?'

I'd been warned about blackouts when I went to the Betty Ford Center that time after Kelly was born. The doc told me that my tolerance would eventually hit zero, and then my body and brain would shut down. But I thought it was just bullshit to frighten me. 'You know what my real drinking problem is?' I said to him. '*I can't find a fucking bar in this place.*'

But then the blackouts started, just like he said they would. They didn't stop me drinking, though. They just made me worry, which made me drink even more. After what had happened with Vince Neil and the car crash, my biggest fear was waking up in a courtroom one day with someone pointing at me and saying, 'That's him! He's the one who ran my husband down!' Or, 'That's him! The one who killed my baby!'

'But I had a blackout, Your Honour' would be my last words before they locked me up and threw away the key.

'HELLO?' I shouted again. 'ANYBODY THERE?'

I was getting nervous now – which meant all the booze and the coke from the night before must have been wearing off. As soon as I get out of this shithole, I told myself, I'm gonna have a nice drink to calm myself down.

Silence.

I waited.

And waited.

And waited.

Where the fuck was everybody?

I was sweating and shivering now. And I really needed to take a shit.

Finally this copper showed up: big bloke, my age – maybe older – with a right old pissed-off look on his face.

'Excuse me,' I said to him. 'Will someone please tell me what I'm doing in this place?'

He just stood there, looking at me like I was a cockroach in his dinner. 'You really want to know?' he said.

'Yeah.'

He came up to the bars, took an even better look at me, and said, 'Normally I don't believe people when they have a convenient loss of memory while they're breaking the law. But in your case, after seeing the state of you last night, I might make an exception.'

'Eh?'

'*You should have seen yourself*.'

'Look, are you gonna tell me why I'm in here or not?'

'I'll tell you what,' said the copper. 'Why don't I just go and get your file? Then I can read you the charges.'

Read me the charges?

I almost crapped my pants when he said that.

What the fuck had I done? Killed someone? I began to think about the documentary I'd watched a few weeks before on American telly, about a murderer in New York. He was on trial, this bloke, and he knew he was going to get for ever in jail, so he got some peanut butter and smeared it up his arse crack, then, just before the jury went out to consider its verdict, he put his hand down his trousers, scraped it up, and started to eat it out of his hand.

And he got off for being insane.

Trouble was, I didn't have any peanut butter. So if I wanted to look like I was eating my own shit, *I'd have to eat my own shit.*

Y'know, even after Sharon played me the video of Kelly's birthday party – the one where I made all the kids cry – I never really thought of myself as a *frightening* drunk. I couldn't see why I was doing any harm. I thought I was just going out, having a few beers, going home, shitting myself, then wetting the bed. Everyone did that, didn't they? It was just a bit of a laugh, par for the course, what you did. But in rehab they said,

'Look, what you've got to do is reverse the role. How would you feel if you went home and it was Sharon who was lying on the floor in a puddle of her own shit and piss, and she was out of her mind, and the kitchen was on fire, and she couldn't look after the kids? How long would you stay with her? How would you feel about your marriage?'

When they put it like that, I could see their point.

But it's taken me until now to realise how scary and wrong it all was. I was just an excessive fucking pig. I would drink a bottle of cognac, pass out, wake up, then drink another. I'm not exaggerating when I say I was drinking four bottles of Hennessy a day.

Even now, I have a lot of trouble understanding why Sharon stayed – or why she married me in the first place, come to think of it.

I mean, she was actually afraid of me half the time.

And the truth was *I* was afraid of me, too. Afraid of what I'd do to myself or, even worse, to someone else.

A lot of the time, Sharon would just leave the country when I went on a bender. 'See ya, I'm off to America,' she'd say. It was around then that she'd started to manage other acts, because I was so fucking volatile, she didn't want to be totally dependent on me. But that made me worry that she was gonna run off with some young fucking hot shot. I mean, I wouldn't have blamed her – I wasn't exactly much fun to be around. Being with me was like falling into an abyss.

One night, when Sharon was away, I paid George the chemist fifty quid for this extra-super-strong bottle of wine, and got well and truly shitfaced with my old keyboard player, John Sinclair. It so happened that I'd been to see a doctor that day, so I had this scoopful of pills: sleeping pills, pain meds, temazepam, you name it. Doctors would give me jars and jars of that shit, all the time. So while I was getting pissed, I was also popping these things, one after the other, until eventually I blacked out.

When I woke up the next morning, I was in bed with

Johnny, and we were all tangled up with each other. But when I reached down to check my dick, to make sure nothing had happened, I realised I couldn't feel anything. I was numb. Totally numb.

So I was lying there, and I started to scream, 'Fuck! Fuck! I can't feel my legs!'

Then I hear this grunt next to me.

'That's because they're *my* legs,' said Johnny.

I had to take three showers after that. It makes me shudder just to think about it. In fact, I felt like such a fucking mess, I said, 'Right, that's it. No more booze, no more pills, no more nothing. This is ridiculous. Sharon's gonna leave me at this rate.'

I went cold turkey.

Which, as any drug addict will tell you, is the stupidest thing you can ever do. When Sharon came home, Jack ran up to her and shouted, 'Mum! Mum! Dad's stopped drinking! He's stopped drinking!' Then I crawled off to bed, feeling horrendous, but couldn't sleep from the comedown. So I scoffed my face full of Excedrin PM, because I thought Excedrin PM didn't count as a drug.

Then I really *did* go numb.

I couldn't feel a thing.

By the time I opened my eyes again, all I could see was Sharon leaning over me and going, 'What's my name? What's my name?' I couldn't answer because I felt like I was underwater. Then she was going, 'How many fingers am I holding up? How many fingers, Ozzy?' But I couldn't count. All I wanted to do was sleep. For the first time in years, all my pain had gone. Suddenly I knew what the phrase 'out-of-body experience' meant. It was the richest, warmest, most comforting feeling I'd ever had.

I didn't want it to end.

It was beautiful, so beautiful.

Then Sharon and Tony were dragging me on to the back

seat of the car, and we were driving round and round, trying to find a doctor. Finally, I was on a bed with all these drips coming out of me, and in a muffled voice I could hear the doc saying to Sharon, 'Your husband has gone into an alcoholic seizure. It's very, very serious. We've put him on anti-seizure medication, but we're going to have to keep monitoring him overnight. He might not come out of it.'

Then, little by little, the feeling returned.

Toes first. Then legs. Then chest. I felt like I was being lifted up from deep, deep under the sea. Then, all of a sudden, my ears popped and I could hear an EKG machine behind me.

Bleep. Bleep. Bleep. Bleep.

'How many fingers?' Sharon was saying. 'How many fingers, Ozzy?'

Bleep. Bleep. Bleep. Bleep.

'Ozzy, what's my name? What's my name?'

Bleep. Bleep. Bleep. Bleep.

'Your name's Sharon. I'm so sorry, Sharon. I'm so fucking sorry for everything. I love you.'

Clomp, clomp, clomp, clomp.

The copper walks up to the bars of my cell holding a sheet of paper in his hand. I'm looking at him, sweating, breathing fast and shallow, fists balled, wanting to fucking die.

He's looking back at me.

Then he clears his throat and starts to read:

> John Michael Osbourne, you are hereby charged with the attempted murder by strangulation of your wife, Sharon Osbourne, during a domestic disturbance that took place in the early hours of Sunday, 3 September 1989, at Beel House, Little Chalfont, in the county of Buckinghamshire.

It was like someone had hit me over the head with a shovel. I staggered backwards, fell against the shit-smeared wall, then slumped on to the floor, head in my hands. I wanted to throw up, pass out and scream, all at the same time. *Attempted murder? Sharon?* This was my worst nightmare. I'm gonna wake up in a minute, I thought. This can't be happening. 'I love my wife!' I wanted to tell the copper. 'I love my wife, she's my best friend in the world, she saved my life. *Why the fuck would I want to kill my wife?*'

But I didn't say anything.

I couldn't speak.

I couldn't do anything.

'I hope you're proud of yourself,' said the copper.

'Is she all right?' I asked him, when I finally got my voice back.

'Her husband just tried to kill her. How d'you *think* she is?'

'But why would I do that? I don't understand.'

'Well, it says here that after returning home from a Chinese restaurant – you'd gone there after celebrating your daughter Aimee's sixth birthday, during which time you became heavily intoxicated on Russian vodka – you walked into the bedroom naked and said, I quote, "We've had a little talk and it's clear that you have to die."'

'I said *what*?'

'Apparently, you'd spent the entire night complaining about being overworked, because you'd just come back from the Moscow Festival of Peace – fitting that, ain't it? – and then you had to go to California. Sounds more like a holiday than work to me.'

'It can't be true,' I said. 'I'd *never* try to kill her.'

But of course it *could* be true. Sharon had been saying for years that she never knew which version of me was going to walk through the front door: Bad Ozzy or Good Ozzy. Usually it was Bad Ozzy. Especially when I'd just come off the road, and I had that horrendous restless feeling. Only this time I'd decided to kill more than my chickens.

'Another thing,' said the copper. 'Your wife told us that if she'd had access to a gun at the time of the assault, she would have used it. Although I see she had a pretty good go at scratching your eyes out. She's quite a fighter, your missus, isn't she?'

I didn't know what to say. So I just tried to make light of it, and said, 'Well, at least it'll give the press something to write about.'

The copper didn't like that.

'Given the severity of the charges,' he said, 'I don't think this is very fucking *funny*, do you? You're up for attempted murder, you piss-head. Your wife could very well be dead if others in the house hadn't heard her screaming. They're gonna put you away for a *long* time, mark my words.'

'Sharon knows I love her,' I said, trying not to think of Winson Green and Bradley the child molester.

'We'll see about that, won't we?'

It would be fair to say that the coppers in Amersham jail didn't take much of a shine to me. My little dance, my little ego, it didn't do me any favours in there. I wasn't the bat-biting, Alamo-pissing, 'Crazy Train'-singing rock 'n' roll hero. All that celebrity shit counts for nothing with the Thames Valley Police.

Especially when they've locked you up for attempted murder.

They kept me in the cell for about thirty-six hours in the end. The only thing I had for company was the shit up the walls. Apparently Don Arden tried to call me when I was in there. So did Tony Iommi. But they didn't get through – and I wouldn't have spoken to them, anyway. A few reporters called, too. The coppers told me they wanted to know if it was true that Sharon was having an affair, or if it was true that I was going back to Jet Records to re-form Black Sabbath. Fuck knows where they'd heard all that bullshit from.

All I wanted was to keep my family.

Then I had to go to Beaconsfield Magistrates' Court. They let me out of the cell to clean myself up a bit first, but whoever had pebble-dashed the walls of the cell had done the same thing to the shower, so I didn't want to get in. Then Tony Dennis came over with a tuxedo jacket, a black shirt and a pair of earrings. I put it all on and tried to feel smart and respectable, but I was going into severe withdrawal. I looked terrible. I felt terrible. I smelled terrible. When the time came to leave, the cops walked me through the jail and out of the back door – away from all the press – and bundled me into the back of a jam sandwich. Tony followed close behind in the Range Rover.

The courtroom was a zoo. It was the 'Suicide Solution' press conference all over again. Only this time it was *really* serious. I was shitting blue cobblers, as my old man used to say. Don Arden had sent one of his heavies to sit at the back and listen. My accountant Colin Newman was there. The funny thing is I can't remember if Sharon was there – which probably meant she wasn't. Thankfully, all the lawyer-talk and gavel-bashing didn't go on for very long. 'John Michael Osbourne,' said the judge, at the end, 'I'm granting you bail on three conditions: that you immediately enter a certified rehabilitation programme of your choosing; that you do not attempt to make contact with your wife; and that you do not attempt to go back to Beel House. Understand?'

'Yes, Your Honour. Thank you, Your Honour.'

'Ozzy!' went the press. 'Is it true that Sharon wants a divorce? Is it true about the affair? Ozzy! *Ozzy!*'

Tony had already booked me into a rehab place: Huntercombe Manor, about twenty minutes away. On the way we passed a newsagent's. 'DEATH THREAT OZZY SENT TO BOOZE CLINIC,' said the sandwich board outside. It feels strange, y'know, when you see the most private moments of your life put on display like that. Very strange.

Huntercombe Manor was all right. I mean, it wasn't exactly Palm Springs, but it wasn't a dump, either. The rate was steep enough: about five hundred quid a night in today's dough.

After I checked in, I just sat there alone in my room, smoking fags, drinking Coke, feeling very sorry for myself. I wanted to hit the bottle so badly, man – so badly, it physically hurt.

I must have been in that joint for a couple of months in the end.

The other people in there were the usual chronic boozers and junkies. There was a gay bloke who'd been involved in the Profumo Affair; there was an aristocrat, Lord Henry; and there was a young Asian woman whose name I can't remember. Rehab wasn't as advanced in England in those days as it is now. There was still a lot of shame attached to it.

Eventually, Sharon came to visit. I told her how sorry I was, how much I loved her, how much I loved the kids, how much I wanted to keep our family together. But I knew it was useless.

'Ozzy,' she said, in this low, quiet voice, 'I've got some important news that I think you'll want to hear.'

That's it, I thought. It's over. She's found someone else. She wants a divorce. 'Sharon,' I said, 'it's OK. I underst—'

'I'm going to drop the charges.'

I couldn't believe what I'd just heard.

'What? *Why?*'

'I don't believe you're capable of attempted murder, Ozzy. It's not in you. You're a sweet, gentle man. But when you get drunk, Ozzy Osbourne disappears and someone else takes over. I want that other person to go away, Ozzy. I don't want to see him again. *Ever.*'

'I'm gonna stop,' I said. 'I promise, I'm gonna stop.'

Meanwhile, the press was going nuts. They had photographers hiding in the bushes, hanging from the treetops. The story wasn't over, as far as they were concerned. And even though Sharon dropped the charges, the Crown Prosecution

Service said it was determined to put me away on the lesser charge of assault. I still wasn't allowed to go back to Beel House, either. But then – on Hallowe'en – they dropped the case.

It was finally over.

The press didn't fucking care, though. One of the newspapers sent a reporter to my mum's house in Walsall, and then printed some exaggerated bullshit about what a terrible parent she was, and what a shitty upbringing she'd given me. It was horrendous. Then my mum got into a slagging match with them, which just kept the story going. It got to the point where my kids had to stop going to school, because they were being hounded at the gate. So I called up my mum and said, 'Look, I know it ain't true what they said, but you can't win a slagging match with the tabloids. And if you keep making a fuss, they're going to keep making my kids' lives hell. Why don't I go on the BBC this week and put the record straight. Then we can put it all behind us, eh?'

My mum agreed, so I went on the Tommy Vance show on Radio 1 and said my bit – that my parents had been great, that the press were telling lies, the whole lot.

Settled. Over. Done. No more.

The next thing I know, my mum's demanding a retraction from one of the papers, and the whole thing blows up again. So it drags on for another three months, the kids have to keep staying away from school.

Finally, she called me and said, 'You'll be glad to know I got that retraction.'

'Are you happy now?' I said, still pissed off with her.

'Yes, very happy. They're just working on the settlement.'

'Settlement?'

'I asked them for fifty thousand, and they've just come back with forty-five thousand.'

'So it was all about *money*? I would have given you the fucking money, Mum. I was trying to protect my kids!'

Looking back now, I can't blame my mum for acting the way she did. She'd grown up poor, so fifty grand was a massive amount of dough. But I still found it very depressing. Was it just all about money? Was that the meaning of life? I mean, friends said to me at the time, 'It's all right for you, 'cos you've *got* money,' and there's some truth in that. But what killed me was the fact that if one of *my* kids ever said, 'Look, Dad, please stop doing this because it's hurting my family,' I'd stop doing it immediately. And it's not like my mum was skint – I gave her an allowance every week. But for some reason she couldn't understand that the more she bugged the press and complained, the more the press wanted to be on my back. It really hurt my relationship with her, in the end. We were always falling out about one thing or another, and we always made up, but I didn't go and see her much after she got the retraction. It just seemed that we always ended up talking about money, and I've never liked that topic of conversation.

I went on a big mission to clean myself up after rehab. I lost a lot of weight. Then I went to a plastic surgeon to get forty-four of my forty-five chins removed. All he did was cut a hole, stick a vacuum cleaner in there, and suck out all the blubber. It was magic. Mind you, part of the reason I did it was just to get shot up with Demerol, which I thought was the best drug ever.

While I was in there, I had some fat taken off my hips, too. I've got no problem with cosmetic surgery, me. If something bothers you, and you can get it fixed, then fix it, that's what I say. Sharon's had a shitload of it done – she'll draw you a map if you ask her. And she looks great. Mind you, it's like anything in life: you get what you pay for.

I felt a lot better after dropping a few stone. And I managed to stay off the booze for quite a while, even though I hardly ever went to the AA meetings. I've just never felt comfortable in those places. It's my worst zone. I'll get up and sing my heart out in front of two hundred thousand people at a rock festival, but when I've got to talk about the way I feel to people I've never met before, I can't do it. There's nothing to hide behind.

Mind you, in LA, those meetings are like rock star conventions. One time, at this clinic in LA, I was sitting in a room with a bunch of other sorry-looking alcoholics, and I looked over and saw Eric Clapton. It was terrible moment, actually, 'cos at the time I was convinced that Clapton hated me. We'd met at an awards show about ten years earlier, and someone had wanted a photograph of me and him and Grace Jones, so we posed for this picture, but I was off my nut on booze and coke, and ended up making all these crazy faces. I got the impression Clapton was either scared of me or just didn't like me, and for some reason I became convinced he'd personally called up the photographer and had the picture destroyed.

So when I saw him at that meeting, I fucked off as fast as I could out of a back door. Then I saw him there again a few days later, and again I tried to avoid him, but this time Clapton went after me.

'Ozzy!' he shouted, as I was about to cross the street to my car.

'Oh, er, hello, Eric,' I went.

'You living over here now?' he asked.

'Yeah.'

'How are you finding it?'

And it went on from there. We had a really nice chat, actually. And then a fortnight later I was browsing through a magazine and there was the picture of me and Eric Clapton and Grace Jones, with me pulling a stupid face and Eric smiling. I'd been imagining the whole thing.

I still hated those AA meetings, though. Eventually I stopped going completely. Whenever I fell off the wagon, I'd just get someone to come over and do one of those home detox things to get me back on the right track again. I was really into all that stuff for a while. Potions, massages, organic herbal fruit baths – any bollocks you can imagine, I did it. Then, one day, this bloke came over and gave me a bottle of colon-cleansing solution.

'Flush yourself out with this stuff every morning,' he said, 'and you'll feel absolutely amazing, I promise.'

I didn't get around to using it for a long time – I didn't fancy the thought of it, to be honest with you – but then finally, one morning, I said to myself, 'Fuck it, I bought the stuff, I might as well give it a go.' The solution was made from seed husks, and the instructions said you just had to pour yourself a glass of it and down in it one, before it had a chance to expand in your throat. So that's what I did. It tasted fucking horrendous – like wet sawdust, but worse. Then I went out with Sharon to look at houses, which was actually a rarity for me, because as far as I'm concerned there's nothing fucking worse than house-hunting. But on this occasion Sharon really wanted me to see a place that was owned by Roger Whittaker, the easy-listening guy, because it had a recording studio in the basement. I had nothing else going on, so I couldn't say no.

When we get to the house, the estate agent is waiting for us outside. She's a posh chick in her late thirties, green Barbour jacket, pearls, the whole deal. Then she gets out this big chain of keys and lets us in through the front door. But as soon as I step foot inside the hallway, I begin to feel this apocalyptic rumbling in my arse. I'm thinking, Aye-aye, here we go, the colon cleanser's kicking in. So I ask the chick where the nearest bog is, shuffle over there as fast as I can without looking conspicuous, slam the door behind me, sit down, and set free this massive torrent of liquid shit. It goes on for so long, it feels like I'm giving birth to the Mississippi River. When it's finally over, I start looking around for some shit roll. But there isn't any. I stand up and think, Fuck it, I'll just have to go unwiped until we get home. Then I realise the shit's gone all over the back of my legs, so I don't have any choice – I've *got* to wipe myself down with something. But there isn't even a flannel.

So I end up just standing there, trousers down, paralysed, trying to work out what to do.

Then Sharon knocks on the door.

Bam! Bam! Bam!

'Ozzy? Are you OK?'

'I'm, er, fine, thank you, darling,' I say.

'You're taking an awfully long time.'

'Won't be long, darling.'

'Hurry *up*.'

Finally, it comes to me: the curtains. *I'll wipe my arse with the curtains!* So I rip 'em down and do what needs to be done. But then I've got another problem on my hands: what the fuck am I supposed to do with a pair of Roger Whittaker's shitty curtains? I can hardly bring them out of the bog with me and ask the estate agent for directions to the nearest toxic dump. Then I think, Well, maybe I should leave a note. But what would it say? 'Dear Roger, sorry for shitting on your curtains. Love the whistling! Cheers, Ozzy.'

In the end, I just rolled them up and hid them in the bath, behind the shower curtain.

If you're reading this, Roger, I'm terribly, terribly sorry. But how about buying some shit roll in future, eh?

A lot of people think you have to be fucked up to write good material, but I reckon the album I did after coming out of Huntercombe Manor, *No More Tears*, was my best in years. Maybe part of that was because I said to the band before we even started, 'Look, we have to treat every song like it could be a hit single, but without being too hokey or try-hard.'

And it worked, pretty much.

Everything about that album seemed to go right. My new

guitarist, Zakk Wylde, was a genius. My producers were amazing. And Sharon got the artwork spot on. She's very artistic, my wife, which a lot of people don't realise. The cover is a sepia portrait of me with an angel's wing on my shoulder. The idea was to give the album more of a mature vibe. I mean, I couldn't keep doing the blood-out-of-the-mouth thing – it was starting to get hammy. I remember the shoot for the cover in New York very well, actually: normally, it takes about five hundred rolls to get a photograph like that in the can, but for *No More Tears* it was just *click-click-click*, 'OK, we've got it, see ya.'

The only thing I didn't like about *No More Tears* was the video for 'Mama I'm Coming Home'. It was one of those high-tech, million-dollar jobs, but all I wanted was something simple, like the video for Nirvana's 'Smells Like Teen Spirit'. So in the end I did a second video for $50,000 using the Nirvana camera guy, and it was perfect. It had a huge impact on me, 'Smells Like Teen Spirit' – and I was very proud when I found out that Kurt Cobain was a fan of mine. I thought he was awesome. I thought that whole *Nevermind* album was awesome. It was such a tragedy the way it ended.

Mind you, it's amazing I didn't end up the same way as Kurt Cobain. I might have been sober after *No More Tears* – most of the time, anyway – but whatever I'd cut out in booze I was making up for with pills. I was already an expert at scamming doctors, and I'd go to a different one every day of the week, picking up a new prescription for something each time. For a while, it was enough just to fake symptoms, but when Sharon cottoned on and started calling the doctors in advance to warn them about me, I had to give myself real symptoms. So I'd whack myself over the head with a piece of wood and say, 'I fell off my bike, can I have some Vicodin, please?'

The doc would go, 'Are you sure you fell off your bike, Mr Osbourne?'

'Oh, yes.'

'It's just that you have a nail sticking out of your head with a splinter attached to it, Mr Osbourne.'

'Oh, I must have fallen on a piece of wood, then.'

'Right. OK. Take five of these.'

'Cheers.'

But I didn't just go to doctors. I had dealers, too. I remember one time, in Germany I think it was, I visited this guy to buy some sleeping pills – I was more addicted to sleeping pills than just about anything else. He was out of sleeping pills, but he asked if I wanted to try some Rohypnol instead. Now, as it happened, I'd heard all about Rohypnol. The press were going crazy about it at the time, calling it the 'date-rape drug', but, to be honest with you, I thought it was all bullshit. A drug that could completely paralyse you while you remained fully awake? I mean, c'mon, it seemed too good to be true. But I bought a couple of doses of the stuff and decided to try it out, as a kind of science experiment.

I gulped down the pills with a bit of cognac as soon as I got back to my hotel room. Then I waited. 'Well, this is a load of bollocks,' I said to myself. Two minutes later, while I was lying on the edge of the bed, trying to order a movie on the telly with the remote control, it suddenly kicked in. *Fuck me, this stuff is real!* I couldn't move. Totally paralysed. But I was also wide awake. It was the weirdest feeling. The only trouble was that I'd been dangling on the edge of the bed when my muscles had seized up, so I ended up sliding to the floor and banging my head on the coffee table on the way down. It hurt like a motherfucker. Then I was trapped between the bed and the wall, unable to move or talk, for about five hours.

So I can't say I'd recommend it.

My health took a real dive around that time.

I started to notice a tremor in my hand. My speech was slurred. I was always exhausted. I tried to escape from it all by getting loaded, but I'd developed such a tolerance to all the drugs I was taking, I had to overdose to get high. It reached the point where I was getting my stomach pumped every other week. I had a few very close calls. One time, I scammed a bottle of codeine off a doctor in New York and downed the whole fucking lot. I nearly went into respiratory arrest. All I remember is lying in this hotel bed, sweating and feeling like I was suffocating, and the doc telling me over the phone that if you take too much codeine, your brain stops telling your lungs to work. I was very lucky to survive. Although, the way I was feeling, I would have been happy never to wake up again.

The worse I got, the more I worried that Sharon would leave me. And the more I worried, the worse I got. In fact, I couldn't understand why she hadn't already left me. I've heard people say, 'Oh, your wife only wants to spend your money.' But it's only because of her that I'm alive to make any money. And people forget that when we met, *she* was the one with the money, not me. I was halfway to the bankruptcy court.

The bottom line is: Sharon saved my life, Sharon *is* my life, and I love her. And I was terrified that I was going to lose her. But as much as I wanted everything to be normal and right, I was terribly sick, physically and mentally. I couldn't even face being on stage any more.

So I tried to kill myself a few times to get out of gigs. I mean, I wasn't *really* trying to kill myself. If you're determined to commit suicide, you'll blow your brains out or you'll jump off a tall building. You'll do something that you can't take back, in other words. When you 'try to kill yourself' by taking too many pills – like I did – you know you're probably gonna get found by someone. So all you're doing is sending a message. But it's a deadly fucking game to play. Look what happened to my old mate Steve Clark from Def Leppard. All it took was a bit of brandy, a bit of vodka, some painkillers and some anti-depressants, and that was the end of it. Lights out.

For ever.

Then, one day, Sharon said to me, 'Right, Ozzy, we're going to Boston. There's a doctor I want you to see.'

'What's wrong with going to a doctor in England?'

'This one's a specialist.'

'A specialist in *what*?'

'In what's wrong with you. We're leaving tomorrow.'

I presumed she just meant a doctor who knew a lot about drug addiction, so I said, 'OK,' and off we went to Boston.

But this doc was a hardcore guy. The best of the best. He worked out of a teaching hospital – St Elizabeth's Medical Center – and he had more qualifications hanging on his office wall than I had gold records.

'OK, Mr Osbourne,' he said. 'I'd like you to stand in the middle of the room, then walk towards me, slowly.'

'Why?'

'*Just do it*,' hissed Sharon.

'All right then.'

So I walked towards this bloke, and I mustn't have been drinking that day, 'cos I managed to go in a straight line.

More or less.

Then he got me to follow his finger as he moved it up and down, and from side to side. What the fuck does this have to do with being a drug addict? I kept thinking to myself. But that wasn't the end of it. Next thing I knew I was hopping across the room on one leg, doing lifting exercises, and jogging around in circles with my eyes closed.

It felt like a fucking PE class.

'Hmm, OK,' he said. 'Well, I can tell you this much, Mr Osbourne. You don't have multiple sclerosis.'

What the—?

'But I never thought I *did* have multiple sclerosis,' I spluttered.

'And you don't have Parkinson's.'

'But I never thought I *did* have Parkinson's.'

'Nevertheless,' he went on, 'you clearly have some symptoms that could be caused by both of those conditions, and diagnosis can be difficult. All I can say is that, for now, you're one hundred per cent clear.'

'*What?*'

I looked at Sharon.

She looked at the floor. 'Ozzy, I didn't want to tell you,' she said, sounding like she was trying hard not to cry. 'But after your last couple of physicals, the doctors told me they were worried. That's why we're here.'

All this had been going on for six months, apparently. My doctors in LA were pretty much convinced that I either had MS or Parkinson's, which is why we'd had to come all the way to Boston to see this specialist. But even though the doc had given me the all-clear, just the sound of the words 'MS' and 'Parkinson's' set me off into a panic. The worst thing was, if I'd had either of those diseases, it would have made a lot of sense – my tremor was out of fucking control. That's why both me and Sharon wanted to get another opinion. So the doc recommended that we go and see a colleague of his who ran a research centre at Oxford University, and off we went. He did the exact same tests on me as before, and told me the exact same thing: I was clear. 'Aside from your drug addiction and your alcoholism, you're a very healthy man, Mr Osbourne,' he said. 'My considered medical opinion is that you should leave my office and go and live your life.'

So I decided to retire. In 1992 I went on tour to promote *No More Tears*. We called it the *No More Tours* tour. That was it. I was done. The end. I'd been on the road for twenty-five years, pretty much. I was like a mouse on a wheel: album, tour, album, tour, album, tour, album, tour. I mean, I'd buy all these houses, and I'd never fucking live in them. That's the thing about being working class: you feel like you can never turn down work. But after seeing the doc in Boston I thought, Why am I doing this? I don't need to work. I don't need the dough.

Then, when we got back to England, Sharon said, 'Don't go crazy, but I've bought us a new house.'

'Where?'

'It's called Welders House. In a village called Jordans in Buckinghamshire.'

'Is there a pub near by?'

'It's a Quaker village, Ozzy.'

She wasn't fucking kidding, either. Welders is probably further away from a pub than any other house in England. I was seriously pissed off with Sharon for buying that place – I didn't talk to her for about six months because it was in such a dreadful state. 'Dilapidated' doesn't even begin to describe it, and we had to rent a place in Gerrards Cross for a year while it was being done up. Even now, I don't think it's anywhere near as attractive as Beel House. But on the inside it's magnificent. Apparently, it was built by the Victorian Prime Minister Benjamin Disraeli as a wedding present for his daughter. Then it became a convalescent home for army officers during World War Two. By the time Sharon came along, it was owned by one of the special-effects guys who'd worked on *Star Wars*.

I forgave Sharon eventually, because when we finally moved in it was magic. The weather was perfect that summer, and suddenly I had all this land – two hundred and fifty acres – and I could just fuck around all day on my quad bikes, without having to worry about anything. My health improved dramatically. I even stopped worrying about MS and Parkinson's disease. I just thought, Well, if I get it, I get it.

But as soon as I felt better, I got bored. Crazy bored. I started to think about my dad – about how he'd taken early retirement and then ended up in hospital as soon as he'd finished the garden. I started to think about the bills for the renovation, and the cost of the staff at the management company, and how all the money to keep the whole machine up and running was now coming out of my savings. Then I thought, How can I retire at the age of *forty-six*? I mean, it's not like I worked for anyone other than myself.

And what I do for a living isn't a job, anyway. Or if it is, it's the best fucking job in the world, hands down.

So one morning I got up, made myself a cup of tea, and said to Sharon, all casual, 'Can't you get me a gig at one of those American festivals this year?'

'What d'you mean, Ozzy?'

'I'd like to do a gig. Get back in the game.'

'Are you *sure*?'

'I'm bored out of my fucking brains, Sharon.'

'OK, then. If you're serious, I'll make some calls.'

So she called the organisers of Lollapalooza.

And they told her to fuck off.

'Ozzy Osbourne? He's a fucking dinosaur,' they said, in not so many words.

That wound Sharon up no end, as you can imagine. So a few days later, she said, 'Screw it, we'll do our own bloody festival.'

'Hang on a minute, Sharon,' I said. 'What d'you mean, "We'll do our own festival"?'

'We'll book some venues and we'll do it ourselves. Screw Lollapafuckinglooza.'

'Won't that be expensive?'

'I'm not going to lie to you, Ozzy, it could be very expensive. But life's all about taking risks, isn't it?'

'OK, but before you start going around booking stadiums left, right and centre, let's test the ground first, eh? Start off small, like we did with *Blizzard of Ozz*. Then, if it takes off, we'll get bigger.'

'Well, listen to you, Mr Businessman all of a sudden.'

'What are you planning to call this festival?'

'Ozzfest.'

As soon as she said the word, I could think of only one thing: 'Beerfest'. It was fucking perfect.

That's how it started. Our strategy was to take all the undesirables, all the bands that couldn't find an outlet anywhere else, and put them together, give them an audience. It worked better than we ever could have expected, 'cos nothing existed for those bands at the time. It had got to the point in the music business where if you wanted to play a gig, the venues made you buy all the tickets in advance, so you had to give them away for free or sell them on your own, which is bullshit. Black Sabbath never had to deal with that kind of bollocks in the early days. We'd never have left Aston, if that had been the case. Where would we have found the dough?

A year later, in 1996, we were ready.

And we did exactly what we said we'd do. We started out small in just two cities – Phoenix and Los Angeles – as part of my tour to promote the *Ozzmosis* album (the *Retirement Sucks* tour, as it was known). It couldn't have gone better. It was a monster, from day one.

As soon as it was over, Sharon turned to me and said, 'D'you know who would be the perfect band to headline Ozzfest '97?'

'Who?'

'Black Sabbath.'

'*What?* Are you kidding? I think Tony's the only one left. And their last album didn't even chart, did it?'

'No, the *real* Black Sabbath: you, Tony, Geezer and Bill. Back together after eighteen years.'

'Yeah, right.'

'It's time, Ozzy. Hatchets buried. Once and for all.'

I'd spoken to Tony only once or twice since Live Aid. Although we had done a gig together, of sorts, in Orange County at the end of the *No More Tours* tour in 1992. I can't remember if it was me who called him first, or the other way around, but once the word got out about a reunion, we had a few 'big talks' on the phone. During one of them I finally asked him why Black Sabbath had fired me. He told me what I already knew – that I'd been slagging off the band in the press, and that my drinking had become unmanageable – but for the first time I actually got it. I ain't saying it was right, but I got it, y'know? And I could hardly complain, because if Tony hadn't kicked me out, where would I be now?

That summer, we went out on the road.

At first, it wasn't the full original line-up: it was just me, Tony and Geezer, with Mike Bordin from Faith No More standing in on drums for Bill. I honestly don't know why we couldn't get Bill to play those first few shows. But I was told he'd had a lot of health issues, including a bad case of agoraphobia, so maybe the rest of us were trying to protect him from the stress. By the end of the year, though, he was back with us to do two gigs at the Birmingham NEC, which were fucking phenomenal. Even though I've always played Sabbath songs on stage, it's never as good as when the four of us do them. Today, when I listen to the recordings of those shows – we put them out the following year on an album called *Reunion* – I still get chills. We didn't do overdubs or anything. When you put that album on, it sounds *exactly* as it did on those two nights.

Everything went so well that we decided to have a go at making a new album together, which would have been our first since *Never Say Die* in 1978. So off we went to Rockfield Studios in South Wales – where I'd quit the band twenty years before.

At first, it all went smoothly enough. We did a couple of bonus songs for the *Reunion* album – 'Psycho Man' and 'Selling My Soul'. But then the practical jokes started again.

Or so I thought, anyway.

'Ozzy,' said Bill, after we'd finished the first rehearsal, 'can you give me a massage? My hand's hurting.'

Here we go, I thought.

'Seriously, Ozzy. *Argh*, my hand.'

I just rolled my eyes and walked out of the room.

The next thing I knew, this ambulance was coming up the driveway with all its lights flashing. It skidded to a halt in front of the studio, then four paramedics jumped out and ran into the studio. About a minute later they came out again with Bill on a stretcher. I still thought it was a joke. We'd relentlessly been taking the piss out of Bill about his dodgy health, so we thought he was just getting his own back with a wind-up. Part of me was quite impressed: he was putting so much effort into it. Tony thought he was fucking around, too. He was on his way out for a walk when the ambulance arrived, and he just looked at it and said, 'That'll be for Bill.'

Bill had always been the boy who cries wolf, y'know? I remember one time, back in the day, I was at his house and he said, 'Oh, 'ello Ozzy. You'll never guess what? I've just come out of a coma.'

'What d'you mean, a coma? That's one stage removed from being dead. You know that, don't you, Bill?'

'All I know is I went to bed on Friday, and now it's Tuesday, and I only just woke up. That's a coma, isn't it?'

'No, that's taking too many drugs and drinking too much cider and sleeping for three days in a row, you dick.'

But this time it turned out that Bill wasn't fucking around. His sore hand was the first sign of a major heart attack. Both his parents had died of heart disease, so it ran in the family. He was kept in hospital for ages, and even when he was let out he couldn't work for a year. So we had to tour without him again, which was a terrible shame. When he finally felt up to it, we gave it another shot in the studio, but by then it just wasn't happening.

The press blamed my ego for our failure to record a new album. But in all honesty I don't think that was the problem. I'd just changed. We all had. I wasn't the crazy singer who spent most of his time getting blasted down the pub but could be called back to do a quick vocal whenever Tony had come up with a riff. That wasn't how I worked any more. And by then I'd been solo for a lot longer than I'd ever been with Black Sabbath. If I'm honest, being sober probably didn't help the creativity, either – although I was still a chronic drug addict. I latched on to a doctor in Monmouth in no time, and got him to prescribe me some Valium. I was also taking about twenty-five Vicodins a day, thanks to a stash I brought over from America. I needed *something* to calm me down. I mean, the expectations for the album were just so high. And if it wasn't as good as before, what was the point of doing it? There *wasn't* a point, as far as I was concerned.

So it never happened.

I was back in LA, staying at a rented place in Malibu, when the phone rang. It was Norman, my brother-in-law.

Oh shit, I thought. This ain't gonna be good news.

It wasn't.

'John?' said Norman. 'It's your mother. She's not doing very well. You should come home and see her.'

'Now?'

'Yeah. I'm sorry, John. But the docs say it's bad.'

It had been eleven years since the argument about the newspaper retraction, and I hadn't seen much of my mum since – although we had made up over the phone. Of course, I now wish I'd spent more time with her. But my mum didn't exactly make it easy for me, talking about money all the time. I should just have given her more of it, I suppose. But I always thought that whatever I had was temporary.

As soon as I got the call from Norman, I flew back to

England with my assistant Tony. Then we drove up to Manor Hospital in Walsall, where she was being treated.

My mum was eighty-seven, and she'd been ill for a while. She was diabetic, had kidney trouble, and her ticker was on the blink. She knew her time was up. I'd never known her go to church before, but all of a sudden she'd become very religious. She spent half the time I was there reciting prayers. She'd been raised a Catholic, so I suppose she thought she'd better catch up on her homework before going over the great divide. But she didn't seem frightened, and she wasn't suffering – or, if she was, she didn't let me know. The first thing I said to her was: 'Mum, are you in pain? You're not just putting on a brave face, are you?'

'No dear, I'm all right,' she said. 'You've always been such a worrier. Ever since you were a little baby.'

I stayed for a few days. Mum sat up in bed for hours talking to me with her arm hooked up to this whirring and bleeping dialysis machine. She seemed so well, I began to wonder what all the fuss was about. Then, on my last day there, she asked me to pull my chair closer to the bed, because she had something very important to ask me.

I leaned in really close, not knowing what to expect.

'John,' she said, 'is it true?'

'Is what true, Mum?'

'Are you really a *millionaire*?'

'Oh, for fu—' I had to stop myself. After all, my mum was dying. So I just said, 'I don't really want to talk about it.'

'Oh, go on, John, tell me. *Pleeeease*.'

'OK, then. Yeah, I am.'

She smiled and her eyes twinkled like a schoolgirl's. I thought, Well, at least I finally made her happy.

Then she said, 'But tell me, John, are you a multi-multi-multi-*multi*-millionaire?'

'C'mon, Mum,' I said. 'Let's not talk about this.'

'But I want to!'

I sighed and said, 'OK, then. Yeah, I am.'

Her face broke into that huge grin again. Part of me was thinking, Is this really *that* important to her? But at the same time, I knew this moment was the closest we'd been in years.

So I just laughed. Then she laughed, too.

'What's it like?' she asked, with a giggle.

'Could be worse, Mum,' I said. 'Could be worse.'

After that we said our goodbyes and I flew back to California with Tony. As soon as I landed, I had to go and do a gig with Black Sabbath at the Universal Amphitheatre. I can't remember much of it, 'cos I couldn't concentrate. I just kept thinking about my mum, asking me if I was a millionaire. After the gig, I went back to the house in Malibu. When I opened the door, the phone was ringing.

It was Norman.

'John,' he said. 'She's gone.'

I sobbed, man.

I sobbed and sobbed and *sobbed*.

It was 8 April 2001 – just forty-eight hours since we'd been talking in the hospital.

I don't know why, but I took it very hard. One thing I've learned about myself over the years is that I'm no good at dealing with people dying. It's not that I'm afraid of it – I know that everyone's gotta go eventually – but I can't help thinking that there are only one or two ways of being brought into this world, but there are so many fucked-up ways of leaving it. Not that my mum went out in bad way: Norman told me that she just went to sleep that night and never woke up.

I couldn't face the funeral – not after what had gone down at my father's. Besides, I didn't want it to be a press event, which it would have been, with people asking me for a photograph outside the church. I just wanted my mum to go out in peace, without it being about me. I'd given her enough grief over the years, and I didn't want to add to it. So I didn't go.

I still think it was the right decision – if only because my final memory of my mum is such a fond one. I can see her so clearly, lying in the hospital bed, smiling up at me, asking what it's like to be a 'multi-multi-multi-*multi*-millionaire', and me answering, 'It could be worse, Mum. It could be worse.'

11

Dead Again

The first time we allowed TV cameras into our house was in 1997, the year Black Sabbath got back together. We were renting Don Johnson and Melanie Griffith's old place in Beverly Hills. I was off the booze – most of the time, anyway – but I was still scamming as many pills as I could from any doctor who'd write me a prescription. I was smoking my head off, too. Cigars, mainly. I thought it was quite acceptable to fire up a foot-long Cuban while lying in bed at nine o'clock at night. I'd say to Sharon, 'D'you mind?' and she'd look up from her magazine and go, 'Oh no, please, don't mind me.'

I don't think the TV guys could believe what they were seeing most of the time. On the first day, I remember this producer turning to me and saying, 'Is it *always* like this?'

'Like what?'

'A sit-com.'

'What d'you mean, "a sit-com"?'

'It's the timing,' he said. 'You walk in one door, the dog walks out of the other, then your daughter says, "Dad, why does the dog walk like that?" and you say, "Because it's got four legs." And then she goes into a huff and storms off, stage left. You couldn't script this stuff.'

'We're not *trying* to be funny, you know.'

'I know. That's what makes it so funny.'

'Things just happen to my family,' I told him. 'But things happen to *every* family, don't they?'

'Not like this,' he said.

A company called September Films made the documentary – *Ozzy Osbourne Uncut*, they called it – and it was shown on Channel Five in Britain and the Travel Channel in America. People went crazy over it. In the year after it came out, Five repeated it over and over. I don't think anyone could get over the fact that we had to deal with the exact same boring, day-to-day bullshit as any other family. I mean, yes, I'm the crazy rock 'n' roller who bit the head off a bat and pissed on the Alamo, but I also have a son who likes to mess around with the settings on my telly, so when I make myself a nice pot of tea, put my feet up, and try to watch a programme on the History Channel, I can't get the fucking thing to work. That kind of stuff blew people's minds. I think they had this idea in their heads that when I wasn't being arrested for public intoxication, I went to a cave and hung upside down, drinking snakes' blood. But I'm like Coco the Clown, me: at the end of the day, I come home, take off my greasepaint and my big red nose, and become Dad.

The documentary won a Rose d'Or award at the Montreux TV festival in Switzerland, and all of a sudden everyone wanted to make TV stars out of us. Now, I've never much liked being on telly. I just feel so hokey doing it. Plus, I can't read scripts, and I when I see myself on screen, I get a fucking panic attack. But Sharon was all for it, so we did a deal with MTV to do a one-off appearance on *Cribs*, which was a bit like a cooler American version of *Through the Keyhole*. By then, we'd long since stopped renting Don Johnson's old place and I'd forked out just over six million dollars for a house around the corner at 513 Doheny Road. We were living there full-time, going to Welders House only when we were in England for business or on family visits.

Again, people went crazy for it. That *Cribs* episode became a cult classic overnight. So one thing led to another, and MTV ended up offering us a show of our own.

Don't ask me how all the business stuff went down, 'cos that's Sharon's department. As far as I was concerned, I just woke up one morning and we had this thing to do called *The Osbournes*. I was happy for Sharon, 'cos she loved all the chaos in the house. She loved doing TV, too. She'll openly say, 'I'm a TV hoo'er.' She'd be the next fucking test card, if she had her way.

But if I'm honest, I was hoping that it would all be shelved before it ever made it on to the air.

A few days before we agreed to the filming, we had a family meeting, to make sure the kids were OK with it. You often hear people say, 'How could they expose their kids to that kind of fame?' but we had no idea how popular our little MTV show would become. And our kids had been born into show business, anyway: Aimee went on tour with us when she was less than a year old; Kelly was the kind of girl who'd stand up at the front of a jumbo jet and sing 'Little Donkey' to all the passengers; and Jack used to sit on my shoulders when I did encores on stage. It was the life they knew.

So we weren't surprised when Jack and Kelly said they were all for *The Osbournes*.

Aimee felt differently, though. From the very beginning, she didn't want anything to do with it.

We respected her for that. Aimee likes to be anonymous, and we'd never have forced her into doing anything she wasn't comfortable with. In fact, I said to all my kids, 'Look, if you decide you want to get involved with this, it's gonna be like being on a fairground ride – you won't be able to make it stop.'

Jack and Kelly both understood. Or at least they said they understood. To be honest with you, I don't think any of us really understood.

Meanwhile, Aimee's mind was made up. 'Have fun, guys. See ya.'

She's a smart one, Aimee. Don't get me wrong – I'm not saying we were all idiots for signing on the dotted line, 'cos in many ways *The Osbournes* was a great experience – but I'd never have agreed to any of it if I'd known what I was letting myself in for. No fucking way, man. I agreed to do it mainly because I thought there was very little chance it would ever happen. Even if it *does* happen, I remember thinking, it won't get any further than one or two shows. American telly is very brutal. The bitching and backstabbing that go on when the cameras aren't rolling are ridiculous – it's enough to make the rock 'n' roll business look like a fucking joke. And it's like that because very, very few shows ever make it. I was convinced *The Osbournes* would be one of the failures.

Our first big mistake was letting them do all the filming at our real house. Most of the time on telly, everything's recorded in a studio, then they cut to stock footage of a street or a bar or whatever to make you think that's where the scene's being shot. But no one had done a show like *The Osbournes* before, so MTV just made it up as they went along.

First they set up an office in our garage – Fort Apache, I called it, 'cos it was like some military command post. They put all these video monitors in there, and little office cubicles, and this big workboard, where they kept track of everything we had planned for the days ahead. No one slept in Fort Apache, as far as I know. They just staggered the shifts so they had all these technicians and camera operators and producers coming in and out all the time. It was very impressive, the way MTV organised the logistics; those guys could invade a country, they're so good.

And I have to admit, it was a laugh for a week or two. It was fun having all these new people around. And they were good guys – they became like family after a while. But then it was like, *How much longer is this going to go on?* I mean, if you'd have taken me aside after those first few weeks of filming in 2001 and told me that I'd still be doing it three years later, I'd have shot myself in the balls, just to get out of it. But I didn't have a fucking clue.

None of us did.

In the early days, the production team's life was made a lot easier because I had a very specific routine. Every morning, come what may, I'd get up, have a coffee, blend some juice, and go and work out in the gym for an hour. So all they had to do was put static cameras in those places and leave them running. But after a while these cameras started to appear all over the house, until I felt like I couldn't get away from the things.

'Right, that's it,' I said one day. 'I need a bunker – a safety zone – or I'm gonna go out of my mind.'

So they taped off this room where I could go to scratch my balls, or pick a zit, or knock one out, without it ending up on the telly. I mean, you want reality only up to a point.

But then one day I was sitting in the safe room, smoking a joint and having a good old rummage under my ballsack, when I started to get this creepy feeling. At first I thought, The stress of this show's driving me insane, 'cos I'm starting to get an attack of the old paranoia. But I searched the room anyway. And there in the corner, hidden under a pile of magazines, was a little spy-camera. I went apeshit about that. 'What's the point of having a safe room if there's a fucking TV camera in it!' I yelled at them.

'Don't worry, Ozzy, it's not recording anything. It's just so we know where you are.'

'Bollocks,' I said. 'Get rid of it.'

'But how will we know where you are?'

'If the door's closed, that's where I am!'

The show was broadcast for the first time on 5 March 2002 – a Tuesday night. By Wednesday morning, it was like I'd moved to another planet. One minute I was a dinosaur who'd been told to fuck off by Lollapalooza; the next I was strapped to a rocket and being blasted through the stratosphere at warp factor ten. I can honestly say that I never knew the power of telly until *The Osbournes* aired. When you've got a hit TV show in America, that's as big as it gets, fame-wise. Bigger than being a movie star. Bigger than being a politician. And *a lot* bigger than being the ex-lead singer of Black Sabbath.

I can't say that I ever sat down and watched any of the shows all the way through. But from the clips I saw, it was obvious that the production team had done a phenomenal job – especially when it came to editing down the thousands of hours of footage they must have had. Even the title sequence – Pat Boone doing a jazzy version of 'Crazy Train' in that silky voice of his – was genius. I love it when people mess around with musical styles like that – it's so clever. And the funny thing was we'd lived next door to Pat Boone for a while at Beverly Drive. He's a lovely bloke, actually: a born-again Christian, but he never gave us a hard time.

We knew immediately that *The Osbournes* was big. But it took a few days for us to realise just *how* big. That weekend, for example, me and Sharon went down to Beverly Hills for a little walk around this market they have in the park, just like we often did. But literally the second I got out of the car, this girl turned around, screamed, then ran up to me with her mobile phone and went, 'Ozzy! Ozzy! Can I take my picture with you?'

'Oh, sure,' I said.

But then all these other people turned around, then *they* screamed, which made even more people turn around, then *they* screamed. Within about three seconds, it seemed like thousands of people were screaming and wanted a fucking picture.

Having the MTV crew trailing along behind didn't exactly help matters, either.

It was terrifying, man. I mean, I ain't complaining, 'cos *The Osbournes* had given me a completely new audience, but the whole thing felt like Beatlemania on LSD. I couldn't believe it. And I certainly couldn't understand it. I'd never been that famous before – not even close. So I fucked off back to England to get away from it. But the same thing happened there. The moment I got off the plane at Heathrow, there was this wall of flash-bulbs and thousands of people shouting and screaming and going, 'Oi, Ozzy! Over 'ere! Gis a picture!'

Obviously, I was no longer famous for being a singer. I was famous for being that swearing bloke on the telly – which felt very strange, and not always in a good way.

I got a lot of flak for it, too. Some people said that I'd sold out 'cos I was on the telly. But that's a load of bollocks, that is. The thing is, no one like me had done a reality show before. But I've always believed that you've got to move with the times. You've got to try and take things to the next level, or you'll just get stuck in a rut. If you stay the same you might keep a few people happy – like the ones who think that any kind of change is a sell-out – but sooner or later, your career will be fucked. And a lot of people forget that in the beginning, *The Osbournes* was just an MTV experiment. No one expected it to blow up in the way it did. But it didn't change me at all. When I was on the show, I never pretended to be anyone other than who I am. Even now when I'm doing ads on the telly, I'm not pretending to be anyone other than who I am. So how's that selling out?'

Mind you, there are things that happened on *The Osbournes* that I still can't get my head around to this day. Like when Sharon got a call from Greta Van Susteren, one of the anchors at Fox News.

'I was wondering if you and Ozzy wanted to have dinner next week with the President of the United States,' she said.

'Is he in trouble again?' asked Sharon.

Greta laughed. 'Not that I know of, no.'

'Thank God for that.'

'Will you come?'

'Of course we will. It would be an honour.'

When Sharon told me, I couldn't believe it. I always thought I'd be on a 'Wanted' poster on the Oval Office wall, not invited over for tea. 'What does President Bush want to talk about, anyway?' I said. 'Black Sabbath?'

'Don't worry,' said Sharon, 'it won't be just the four of us. It's the annual White House Correspondents' Dinner. Fox News has a table, so there'll be plenty of other people there.'

'George Bush used to be the Governor of Texas, didn't he?' I said.

'Yes?'

'Well, I pissed on that Alamo thing once. He's gonna be cool with that, is he?'

'I'm sure he's forgotten all about it, Ozzy. He used to like a drink or two himself, y'know.'

'He did?'

'Oooh yeah.'

So off we went to Washington. The dinner was at the Hilton, where Ronald Reagan had been shot. It wasn't long after 9/11, so I was feeling really paranoid about the security situation. Then, when we got there, it was pandemonium. They had about five thousand TV cameras outside, and just one little metal detector with a couple of guys manning it. I had to cling on to Greta's jacket just to get through the crowd.

Meanwhile, my assistant Tony – who's only a little fella – skipped over the rope and walked behind the metal detector without anyone even noticing. It was a joke, man. I could have smuggled a ballistic fucking missile into that place, and no one would have said a word.

Then the dinner started, and I started to have this horrendous panic attack. There I was, this half-baked rock star, in a room with all these Great Brains and the Leader of the Free World. What the *fuck* was I doing there? What did all these people want from me? *The Osbournes* had only been on air for about two months, and my brain was already struggling to process it all.

In the end, I just snapped. I couldn't survive one more second in that place without being pissed out of my mind. So I grabbed a bottle of vino from one of the waiters, filled my wine glass, downed it, refilled it, downed it, refilled it, and carried on until the bottle was empty. Then I got another. Meanwhile, Sharon was glaring at me from the other end of the table. I ignored her. Not tonight, darling, I thought.

Then the First Lady walked into the room, with George W. Bush following her. And the first thing he said when he reached the podium was: 'Laura and I are honoured to be here tonight. Thanks for the invitation. What a fantastic audience we have tonight: Washington power-brokers, celebrities, Hollywood stars . . . and Ossie Ozz-Burn!'

By that time I was well and truly blasted, so as soon as I heard my name, I jumped up on the table like a drunken arsehole and screamed, '*Yeeeeeeeehhaaaaaa!!*' It brought the fucking house down. But I was *fucked*, so I didn't know when to stop. I just stayed up there, going, '*Yeeeeeeeehhaaaaaa!!*' until the whole room of eighteen hundred people went silent.

Bush looked at me.

'*Yeeeeeeeehhaaaaaa!!*' I screamed again.

Silence.

'*Yeeeeee*—'

'OK, Ozzy,' snapped Bush. On the tape, you can even hear him say, 'This might have been a mistake.'

I finally climbed down from the table – actually, I think Greta might have pulled me down. Then Bush started to tell this joke about me: 'The thing about Ozzy is he's made a lot of big hit recordings: "Party with the Animals", "Face in Hell", "Bloodbath in Paradise" . . .'

I was about to get back up on the table and tell him that none of those were big hits, but then he delivered the punchline.

'Ozzy,' he said, 'Mom loves your stuff.'

The whole room went crazy.

I don't remember much after that.

Y'know, ever since I went to that dinner, people ask me what I think of Bush. But I can't say I have an opinion, because I don't know enough about all that political stuff. I mean, *somebody* must have voted for him, right? In 2000 *and* 2004. And I think a lot of that crazy terrorist shit had been going on for a long time before he got into power. I don't think they were sitting around in their cave and suddenly said, 'Oh, look, Bush is in the White House. Let's fly some planes into the World Trade Center.'

The thing is, I'm living in America as a guest, so it's not up to me to say anything, y'know? I keep trying to explain that to Jack: 'Don't talk about politics here, because you're not an American. They'll just say to you, "Get the fuck out of our country, if you don't like it."' We've made a good living from America. We should be grateful.

A month later, I met the Queen.

She came up to me and shook my hand after I'd done a song at the Party at the Palace concert, during the Golden Jubilee weekend. Magnificent woman, I've always thought. I have so much respect for her. Then I met her again, not long after, at the Royal Variety Performance. I was standing next to Cliff

Richard. She took one look at the two of us, said, 'Oh, so *this* is what they call variety, is it?' then cracked up laughing.

I honestly thought that Sharon must have slipped some acid into my cornflakes that morning.

Seriously, though, I get on very well with the royals. I'm even an ambassador for the Prince's Trust now, so I've met Charles a few times. Very nice guy. The press keep giving him stick, but if you get rid of the monarchy, what do you replace it with? President Gordon 'Wet Fart' Brown? Personally, I think the royal family do a hell of a lot of good. People think they live in that palace and spend their whole lives just holding up sceptres and watching the telly, but they work their arses off. They have to be on all the time. And the dough they make for Britain adds up to a ridiculous fortune every year.

I'm not so comfortable with politicians. Meeting them always just feels weird and a bit creepy, no matter who it is. For example, I met Tony Blair during *The Osbournes* period at this thing called the Pride of Britain Awards. He was all right, I suppose; very charming. But I couldn't get over the fact that our young soldiers were dying out in the Middle East and he could still find the time to hang around with pop stars.

Then he came over to me and said, 'I was in a rock 'n' roll band once, y'know?'

I said, 'So I believe, Prime Minister.'

'But I could never work out the chords to "Iron Man".'

I wanted to say, 'Fuck me, Tony, that's a staggering piece of information, that is. I mean, you're at war with Afghanistan, people are getting blown up all over the place, so who honestly gives a fuck that you could never work out the chords to "Iron Man"?'

But they're all the same, so there's no point getting wound up about it.

For a while after *The Osbournes* went on air, it seemed like everyone in the world wanted to be around me. Then we had a party at our house, and Elizabeth Taylor showed up. For me, that was the most surreal moment of all, 'cos when I was a kid, my dad had said to me, 'I want you to see the most beautiful woman in the world.' Then he'd let me stay up late to watch *Cat on a Hot Tin Roof.* So that's what Elizabeth Taylor has always been to me – the most beautiful woman in the world. But, of course, I can't even remember what I said to her, 'cos I was fucking wasted again.

Of all the people I got to meet, though, the most special was probably Paul McCartney. I mean, I'd looked up to that man since I was fourteen. But what the fuck are you supposed to talk to him about, eh? It's like trying to strike up a conversation with God. Where d'you start? 'Oh, I see you made the Earth in seven days. What was that like?' We were at Elton John's birthday party: Paul on one side of me, Sting on the other, and Elton opposite. It was like I'd died and gone to rock star heaven. But I'm useless when it comes to making conversation with people I admire. I'm a big believer in just leaving them alone, generally. In that way, I'm very shy. There were some rumours going around in the press for a while that me and Paul were gonna do a duet, but I can honestly say I never heard a word about it from the man himself. And I'm glad I didn't, 'cos I would have shit my pants, big time.

He played at the Brits when me and Sharon were hosting, though. I remember Sharon turning to me halfway through his set and whispering, 'Did you ever think you'd be standing on stage with a Beatle?'

'Never in a million years' was the answer.

It didn't even seem so long since I'd been looking up at his picture on the wall of 14 Lodge Road.

We e-mail each other from time to time now, me and Paul. (Which means I speak and Tony taps what I've said into the computer, 'cos I don't have the patience for all that internet bollocks.) It started when I heard a song called 'Fine Line' on a Lexus commercial. I thought, Fucking hell, that's not a bad tune, I think I'll nick it. So I mentioned it – just in passing – to a guy who used to work with me called John Roden, who also happened to work with Paul.

John said, 'Y'know who wrote that, don't you?'

I told him I didn't have a clue.

'My *other* boss,' he said.

Obviously I left the song well alone after that.

Then, out of the blue, came this letter saying, 'Thanks for not nicking "Fine Line", Ozzy.' You couldn't get the smile off my face for days. And it just went on from there. We don't e-mail very often, but if he's got an album coming out, or if he's getting some flak in the press, I'll drop him a line. The last one I sent was to congratulate him on that *Fireman* album he did. If you haven't heard it, you should, 'cos it's fucking phenomenal.

Not everyone loved *The Osbournes*.

Bill Cosby, for example.

He got a right old bee up his arse about it.

I suppose he got offended 'cos the press kept comparing our show to his: one of the newspapers even said I was 'America's New Favourite Dad'. So he wrote us a letter. It was along the lines of 'I saw you on the telly, and your foul language sets a bad example.'

Fair enough, I thought.

But, y'know, swearing is just part of who we are – we're forever effing and blinding. And the whole point of *The Osbournes* was to be real. But I have to say I always thought that bleeping out the swearing actually improved the show. In Canada, they didn't have any bleeps, and I reckoned it wasn't anywhere near as funny. It's just human nature – isn't it? – to be more attracted to something that's taboo. If someone tells you not to smoke, you wanna smoke. If they say, 'Don't do drugs,' you wanna do drugs. That's why I've always thought that the best way to stop people taking drugs is to legalise the fucking things. It would take people about five seconds to realise that being an addict is a terribly unattractive and pathetic way to be, whereas at the moment it still has that kind of rebel cool vibe to it, y'know?

Anyway, Sharon replied to Bill Cosby.

'Stop me if you've heard this one before, Mr Cosby,' she wrote, 'but people in glass houses shouldn't throw stones, and we all know about your little affair, which has been all over the newspapers, so how about you put your own house in order before having a go at ours?'

She also pointed out that when you switch on the telly in America, there's always a guy being shot or chopped up or scraped off the tarmac, and no one bats an eyelid. But if you say 'fuck', everyone freaks out. It's insane when you think about it.

Killing's fine, but swearing isn't.

To be fair to Bill, we got a very nice reply from him, saying, 'Hands up, you got me, I'm sorry.'

So he was very cool about it in the end.

MTV shit themselves when *The Osbournes* got so big, so quickly, 'cos they hadn't signed a long-term deal with us. So then all the games started – and you know me, I can't stand all that bullshit.

But it didn't stop them trying to drag me into it.

Not long after the ratings went crazy, I remember me and Sharon were in New York to do the *Total Request Live* show at the MTV building in Times Square. As soon as we went off air, this exec in a suit came up to us and said, 'Hey, I've got a surprise for you guys.'

'What kind of surprise?' I said.

'Follow me, and I'll show you.'

So this guy took us up to a boardroom on one of the highest

floors in the building. There was a big conference table in the middle with telephones on it and chairs all around, and these huge windows looking out over the New York skyline.

'Are you ready?' he asked us.

I looked at Sharon, and she looked back at me. Neither of us knew what the fuck was going on. Then the bloke hit the speakerphone button, and this *Charlie's Angels* voice came on the line.

'Have you got the gift?' it said.

'Yep,' said the bloke.

'OK, give them the gift.'

The bloke reached into his jacket pocket, took out this gold-embossed envelope, and handed it to me.

I opened it and saw a cheque for $250,000.

'What *is* this?' I said.

'A gift,' the guy told me. 'From MTV.'

Now, I might not be much of a businessman, but even I knew that cashing a cheque for $250,000 could be seen as some kind of contract. If that thing had landed in my bank account, the negotiations for the next few seasons would have been a whole different ball game. I mean, maybe it *was* just a gift. Maybe they weren't trying to pull any funny stuff. But it still creeped me out. Even Sharon was speechless, for once.

'Thanks very much,' I said. 'Would you mind sending it to my lawyer's office? He deals with all that.'

Talk about swimming with fucking sharks.

By the summer of 2002, it seemed like *The Osbournes* was the biggest thing on the planet. And the stress of it was killing me. After falling off the wagon at the Correspondents' Dinner, I'd been getting pissed every day. And I was still necking as much prescription medication as I could get my hands on – which was *a lot*. At one point I was on forty-two different pills a day: sedatives, sleeping medication, anti-depressants, amphetamines, anti-seizure medication, anti-psychotics. You fucking name it, I was on it. I was taking an unbelievable quantity of drugs. Half the pills were just to cancel out the side-effects of the others.

And none of them seemed to be making me any better. My tremor was so bad that I was shaking like an epileptic. My speech was terrible. I'd even started to develop a stammer, which I'd never had before – although stammers run in my family. If someone asked me a question, I would panic, and by the time the words reached my mouth from my brain, they would be all jumbled. And that just made me even more stressed, 'cos I thought it was the beginning of the end for me. Any day now, I thought to myself, a doctor was gonna take me aside and say to me, 'I'm very sorry, Mr Osbourne, but the tests have come back, and you have MS.' Or Parkinson's disease. Or something equally horrific.

I started to get very self-conscious about it. I remember watching some clips from *The Osbournes* – and even *I* didn't have a clue what I was talking about. I mean, I've never had a problem playing the clown, but when it became a national joke that no one could understand a fucking word I said, it was a bit different. I began to feel like I had when I was at school and I couldn't read out a page from a book, and everyone laughed and called me an idiot. So I just got more pissed and more stoned. But the drink and the drugs made my tremor worse – which was the exact opposite of what I'd expected, because alcoholics get the DTs when they come *off* the booze, not when they're *on* it. And the pills my docs were giving me were supposed to make the shaking go away.

There seemed to be only one rational explanation for all of it.

I was dying.

So every other week I had a new test. It was like a new hobby. But none of the results ever came back positive. Then I began to wonder if I was getting tested for the wrong things. I mean, it was cancer that had killed my father, not Parkinson's disease. So I went to see a cancer specialist.

'Look,' I said to him, 'is there some kind of high-tech scan you can do that'll tell me if I'm gonna get cancer?'

'What kind of cancer?'

'Any kind of cancer.'

'Well,' he said. 'Yes there is . . . sort of.'

'What d'you mean, "sort of"?'

'There is a machine. But it won't be available for another five years, at the very least.'

'Why not?'

'Because they haven't finished inventing it yet.'

'Is there anything else you can do, then?'

'You could always get a colonoscopy. Although, y'know, I really don't see any warning—'

'It doesn't matter,' I said. 'Let's do it.'

So he gave me this kit to get my arse ready for its close-up. It was basically four bottles of liquid, and you had to drink a couple of them in the afternoon, shit through the eye of a needle, rinse yourself out, drink the next two, shit through the needle again, then not eat anything for twenty-four hours. You could have seen daylight through my arse by the end of it, it was so clean. Then I went back to the doc's for the test.

First he got me to lie on this table and put my knees up to my chest. 'Right,' he says, 'I'm going to put you under with some Demerol. Then I'm going to insert this camera up your rectal passage. Don't worry: you won't feel a thing. And I'll record everything on a DVD, so you can watch it yourself at your leisure.'

'OK.'

So he jabs me with a needle, and while I'm waiting to pass out I notice this massive flat-screen TV to the side of me. Then, all of a sudden, I feel something the size of a small house go up my arse. I yelp and close my eyes, and when I open them again, the TV screen is showing a high-definition image of a big red cave.

'Is that the inside of my arsehole?' I ask.

'Why the *hell* aren't you asleep?' says the doc.

'Dunno.'

'Don't you feel groggy?'

'Not really.'

'Not even a little bit?'

'Nope.'

'I'm going to give you some more Demerol then.'

'Whatever it takes, Doc.'

So he gives me another shot of the good stuff. *Ahhh.* Two minutes later, he says, 'How are you feeling?'

'Fine, thanks,' I say, still glued to *Journey to the Centre of my Arse* on the TV screen.

'Jesus *Christ*,' he says. 'You're *still* awake? I'm going to give you some more.'

'Go on then.'

Another couple of minutes go by.

'How about now, Mr Osbourne? Blink if you can hear me?'

'Blink? Why can't I just tell you?'

'That's impossible! You're not human!'

'How can I fall asleep during this?' I say. 'Any minute now you're going to find some long-lost cufflinks up there, or maybe an old watch, or a pair of Sharon's tights.'

'I can't have you awake right now. I'm going to give you one last sh—'

Black.

When it was over, the doc told me he'd found a couple of abnormal growths up my arsehole – polyps, they're called – and he needed to send them away for testing. Nothing much to worry about, he said. And he was right, 'cos when the results came back, everything was fine.

But then I convinced myself that Sharon also needed to get

a colonoscopy – 'cos she never went for regular check-ups. In the end I nagged her so much that she finally agreed to go before flying off to New York with the kids to do some filming. She was still there when the results came back. This time, they weren't good: the lab had found 'cancerous tumours'. But as devastating as that news was, the way we found out was fucking unbelievable. The woman from the doctor's surgery just called Sharon's work number in LA and left a voicemail. It should have been *me* who broke the news to her, in person. Instead she found out when some chick from the office called up with her list of end-of-day messages: 'Oh, by the way, are you sitting down for this? You've got cancer.'

The first thing Sharon did was call me.

'Ozzy, please don't freak out,' she said. 'I'm coming home tonight and going into hospital tomorrow.'

Stunned silence.

'Ozzy, it's gonna be OK. Stop freaking out.'

'I'm not freaking out.'

As soon as she hung up, I was literally on the floor, howling. When I was growing up, no one *ever* recovered from cancer. I mean, the doc would always tell you it was survivable, but everyone knew that was just bullshit to calm you down.

But I had to pull myself together before Sharon's plane landed in LA. So I showered, put on the brand of aftershave that Sharon loved, and got dressed up in a black evening suit with a white silk scarf. I wanted to look as good as possible for my wife.

Then off I went to the airport. When Sharon finally stepped off the plane with the kids and the dogs, we all hugged and cried on the tarmac. As much as I was trying to put a brave face on things, I was a fucking wreck. I'd been bad enough *before* the cancer scare, but this had pushed me into an abyss. My doctors were working overtime, upping my dosage of this, that and the other. My head felt like it was floating three feet above my shoulders.

'I'm going to deal with this,' was the first thing Sharon said to me.

Then we went back home, and the crew from MTV were waiting. They said, 'Look, it's OK if you want us all to go home now. Just let us know. It's your decision.'

But Sharon wouldn't have any of it.

'This is *reality* TV,' she said. 'It doesn't get any more fucking real than this. Keep your cameras rolling.'

I thought it was very courageous of her to say that. But that's my wife for you. Tougher than tough.

Looking back now, I had a full-on nervous breakdown in July 2002, which was made ten times worse by all the shit I was putting down my neck, twenty-four hours a day. It's not enough to say that I love Sharon. I owe my life to Sharon. The thought of losing her was unbearable. But I never gave up. When something heavy like that happens, you get this force field around you, and things that would normally rattle your cage just don't mean anything any more. It's hard to describe – I just went to this other place in my head.

Sharon's operation was on 3 July 2002. When it was done, and the cancer had been removed, the doctor said that she'd make a full recovery. But while they were digging around up there, they took out a couple of lymph nodes for testing. Days later, the lab confirmed that the cancer had spread into her lymph nodes. Which meant the worst wasn't over – not by a long shot. I didn't know it at the time, but Sharon's chances of survival were only about 33 per cent. All I knew was that she'd have to go through months of horrific chemotherapy.

They were the darkest, most miserable, terrible, fucked-up days of my life. And I can't even begin to imagine how bad it must have been for Sharon. Almost immediately, her hair started to fall out, so she had to get hairpieces made. And every time she got zapped by the chemo, she'd come home so badly dehydrated – because of all the vomiting – that she'd have a seizure. What would happen is, the first day she got back from the hospital she'd be wired, the second day she'd be all spaced out, and the third day she'd go into a seizure. And the seizures got worse every time.

One evening I went out for dinner with the kids, and when we got back, Sharon was worse than I'd ever seen her before: instead of just having one seizure, she was having them one after the other. It was fucking terrifying. There was no way we could wait for an ambulance, so I ran into Fort Apache, and shouted at the MTV guys, 'Get us one of your trucks. We need to drive Sharon to the emergency room, *right now*, because if we wait for an ambulance, it's gonna be too late.' Then I then ran back to the bedroom, picked up Sharon from the bed, and carried her down the stairs and out to the driveway.

The guys had a truck waiting by the time we got outside. Two of the crew members sat up front while I climbed into the back with Sharon. We'd strapped her to this gurney, but she was bouncing off the fucking thing like you wouldn't believe. It was wild, like something out of *The Exorcist*. The spasms were so intense it was like she was levitating. Then, when we got to the hospital – it took us three minutes – all these nurses were running around, screaming. It was a terrible scene, the worst vibe you can possibly imagine.

After that, I got a team of nurses to live with us at Doheny Road, 'cos I never wanted Sharon to go through that again. I also got my agent to call Robin Williams to ask him if he would come over and cheer up Sharon. I've always believed that if you can get someone to laugh when they're sick, it's the best way of helping them to get better – and I got the feeling that Robin felt the same way after seeing that movie he did, *Patch Adams*. So he came over one day when I'd gone off to the studio, and apparently Sharon was crying with laughter the whole afternoon. To this day I think that's the greatest gift I've ever given my wife, and I'm for ever in Robin's debt for it. I mean, 'thanks' is nowhere near enough, is it? The guy is just a really wonderful human being. But in spite of Robin's comedy show, Sharon had another seizure that night and she ended up in hospital again.

I got terribly paranoid whenever Sharon was in hospital. One stray germ, I thought, and she could get an infection and die. At first, I ordered the kids to wear face masks and gloves whenever they were around her. But then they'd bring the dogs, which drove me crazy. In fact, Sharon's dog Minnie didn't leave her side for one second during the chemo. I never saw that dog eat. I never saw it piss. By the end of the treatment, the dog was as dehydrated as Sharon was. One time I went to the hospital and they were both lying there, side by side, with matching drips. Minnie was like a guardian angel for Sharon. But she didn't like me one bit. In fact, she didn't like men, full stop. Even when she was on her last legs, that dog would always find the energy to growl at me. The last thing Minnie ever did was give me one of her withering looks, as if to say, '*Urgh.*'

I suffered physically during Sharon's illness, too, but in my case it was self-inflicted. I'd drink a case of beer in the morning, smoke a shitload of dope at lunchtime, try to wake myself up again with speed, then go jogging. At least it dimmed the reality of the situation, but by the end I was a fucked-up shell of a human being. Then, one day, Sharon said to me, 'For God's sake, Ozzy, go and do some gigs. You're driving everyone crazy.'

So that's what I did. I'd already missed a few Ozzfest dates by then, but I rejoined the tour on 22 August in Denver. I was so uptight, I wouldn't let anyone talk about cancer. If I heard the c-word, I freaked out. But a few nights later, when we were in another city – don't ask me where – I was halfway through the set and I just thought, Fuck this, I can't keep denying that this is happening. So I said to the crowd, 'I want to tell you about Sharon's progress. She's doing well, and she's going to beat this cancer. She's going to kick it up the fucking arse!'

The crowd went mental. I swear to God, they lifted me up. It was magical. The power of people, when they focus on something positive, never fails to amaze me. A few days after that I went to see my physiotherapist about some back problems I'd been having. 'There's something I want to tell you,' he said. 'I can see by the look on your face that you're terrified, but I want you to know that ten years ago I had what your wife's got. And I made a full recovery.'

'You survived the chemo?' I said.

'I didn't even have chemo,' he said.

It was the first truly positive thing I'd heard from anyone about Sharon's illness. Or at least the first time I'd *listened* to anything positive. In my mind, cancer equalled death. And I think a lot of other people thought the same way I did. They'd say to me, 'I'm so sorry to hear about Sharon,' without even looking at me, like they *knew* she was dying. But this guy was different, and he changed my attitude right there and then.

And he was right: when the chemo was over, Sharon's cancer seemed to have been completely destroyed.

I remember going to the hospital, and one of the doctors telling me, 'Just so you understand, your wife's going to spend as much time getting over the chemo as she did getting over the cancer.'

I said, 'Let me tell *you* something about my wife. The second you give her the all-clear, she'll be off and running – and you won't be able to stop her.'

'I don't want to argue, Mr Osbourne,' he said, 'but, believe me, she's not going to be able to do very much.'

A week later, she got the all-clear.

And you couldn't see her for dust.

*

When we started to film *The Osbournes*, Sharon hadn't spoken to her father for almost twenty years. It was terribly sad, because I knew that deep down, somewhere, she loved the guy. But after everything he'd done, she'd pretty much given up on him. She'd even told the kids that their grandfather had died during the war – although it didn't take long for them to find out the real story. I remember the day it happened, in fact: we were all in the car together, driving through Beverly Hills, when Sharon suddenly hit the brakes, made an illegal U-turn, and pulled up outside Nate 'n Al's delicatessen.

Before anyone could ask her what the fuck she was doing, she was leaning out of the window and screaming, 'You fucking arsehole! YOU FUCKING ARSEHOLE!'

Then I saw Don standing there on the street. He immediately started to shout back. The last thing I remember is him coming right up to the car window, until he was only inches from Sharon's face, and calling her a 'fucking whore'. Then Sharon put her foot down and sped off, leaving him coughing and spluttering in a cloud of black smoke from the tyres.

Meanwhile, inside the car, there was just this stunned silence. I had no fucking idea how to explain what had just happened to the kids. Then Aimee's little voice piped up from the back seat.

'Mum, why did Tony Curtis call you a whore?'

'BECAUSE TONY CURTIS IS A FUCKING ARSEHOLE,' came the reply.

To this day, I have no idea why Aimee thought Don was Tony Curtis. Maybe that's what Sharon had told her, or maybe she'd seen Tony Curtis on telly – at the time he was a dead-ringer for Don. But it didn't matter, 'cos that's when Sharon told the kids everything.

It wasn't the only time we bumped into Don in LA. On another occasion we'd been to see a movie at the Century City shopping mall, and we were waiting for our car at the valet stand. All of a sudden, I spotted Don behind Sharon.

'Promise me you won't go nuts,' I said.

'*Why?*'

'Just promise me.'

'OK, I promise.'

'Your father's standing right behind you.'

The moment I said it, one of the valet guys turned up with our car. Thank God for that, I thought.

'Get in the car,' barked Sharon.

'You're not gonna do anything crazy, are you?' I said to her.

'No.'

'You're sure about that?'

'GET IN THE FUCKING CAR.'

I got in the passenger side and closed the door. Sharon climbed into the driver's seat. Then she turned into this Satan woman. She floored the accelerator, mounted the kerb, and drove straight at her father. He had to dive into a hedge to get out of the way. She almost killed him – with about fifty people standing around as witnesses. It was terrifying.

After that we didn't see or hear from Don for years. Then, at the end of the nineties, Sharon's mother died. I don't know all the ins-and-outs of it, but Sharon's mum had taken a few funny turns over the years, and the upshot was that the two of them had stopped talking, too. They're a very intense family, the Ardens. They've always gone in for a lot of verbal abuse – which sometimes I think can be even worse than physical abuse. Anyway, a year or so after her mother died, we heard from the family in England that Don was sick and had fallen on hard times. Even though they still weren't talking, Sharon sorted him out with a place to live. Then I got a call from Sharon's brother, David. 'I've got some bad news,' he said. 'Don's got Alzheimer's.'

There was *no way* I could keep that from Sharon.

At first she brushed it off, and said she was supporting him financially anyway. But I said to her, 'Look, I don't know what your real feelings are towards your father, but I strongly advise you, if you've got anything to say to him, even if it's just to call him an arsehole again, do it now. Because with every day that goes by, he's gonna be like a dying flame.'

The thing is, I've never believed in feuds. Don't get me wrong: I've been angry with people. *Very* angry – with people like Patrick Meehan, or that lawyer who tried to bill me for a drink, or Bob Daisley. But I don't hate them. And I don't wish them any harm. I reckon hating someone is just a total fucking waste of time and effort. What do you get out of it in the end? Nothing. I'm not trying to come over like the Archangel Gabriel here. I just think that if you're pissed off with someone, call them an arsehole, get it out of your system, and move on. It's not like we're on this earth very long.

Anyway, Sharon finally decided she wanted to see him again, so he came back into our lives. He even ended up in a couple of episodes of *The Osbournes*. And I was happy about it, y'know – even though he'd called me Vegetable for most of the time I knew him. Then, when Sharon decided she wanted to renew our wedding vows – she was still going through chemo at the time – we made Don part of the ceremony, which we held on New Year's Eve at the Beverly Hills Hotel. We did it Jewish-style – with the little canopy, the broken glass, everything.

A lot of people came up to me that night and asked, 'How come you and Sharon have stayed together all this time?' My answer was the same then as it is now: I've never stopped telling my wife that I love her; I've never stopped taking her out for dinner; I've never stopped surprising her with little gifts. Unfortunately, back then, I'd never stopped drinking and taking drugs, either, so the ceremony ended much the same as our original wedding had: with me slumped in a corridor, pissed out of my brains.

The Don Arden I'd known since the early seventies just disappeared after that. The light was on but no one was home. It was a terrible way to die. I'm telling you, having seen what happened to my father-in-law, I wouldn't wish Alzheimer's on my worst fucking enemy. Even after everything that had gone down between us over the years – even though he'd played a part in Bob Daisley's lawsuit – I felt truly sorry for him during his final years.

In the end, we put him in a care home.

I remember he had this wax build-up in his ears, and whenever we went to see him, I used to put these drops in for him. I don't know why I thought it was my job, I just did it. I suppose it probably had something to do with the immense pity I felt for him. This vicious, powerful, frightening man had become a child.

'Dad,' said Jack one day. 'When you're on the telly, d'you think people are laughing *with* you or *at* you?'

The question had obviously been bothering him for a while.

'Y'know what,' I said to him, 'as long as they're laughing, I don't care.'

'But why, Dad? Why would you want to be a clown?'

'Because I've always been able to laugh at myself, Jack. Humour has kept me alive over all these years.'

And it's true, y'know. I mean, it doesn't take much to rattle my cage, either – although, as I'm getting older, I increasingly think, Fuck it, what's the point, it'll all work out one way or another – but humour has saved my life too many times to count. And it didn't start with *The Osbournes*. Even in Black Sabbath, I was the clown. I was always the one making the others crack up.

But I felt bad for Jack.

It couldn't have been easy for him, especially during those first two years of the show, when I was this shaking, mumbling, fucked-up wreck. I can't even imagine it, to be honest with you. Same goes for Kelly. When we all became these mega-celebrities, it was the first time I really understood why all these young Hollywood starlets get doped up and go into rehab every other day of the week. It's the pressure – it's fucking ridiculous. Non-stop. Day-in, day-out. I mean, the first year we went on air, Kelly sang 'Papa Don't Preach' at the MTV Movie Awards. She had to come down this big flight of stairs with every star in the business sitting there, watching her. But she just took it by the horns. And of course she ended up loving every minute of it, as did the audience.

But she had her problems, like we all do. And it broke my heart when Jack started to get fucked up too. He took Sharon's cancer as hard as I did, to the point where he ended up on OxyContin, which they call 'hillbilly heroin' in LA. I remember we had this huge row about it, and I said, 'What the fuck, Jack? Why are you going around getting pissed all the time? You've never wanted for a thing! *What have you ever wanted for?*'

He just looked at me and said, 'A father.'

I won't forget that moment in a hurry.

It was the first time I'd really had to face the cost of how I'd been living all those years – the cost to my son, who I loved so much, who I was so proud of, but who I'd never been there for. It was a terrible feeling.

All I could say was: 'Jack, I'm so sorry.'

Jack got sober after that. But I didn't.

By August 2003, I was shaking so much that I couldn't walk, I couldn't hold anything, I couldn't communicate. It got to the point where Sharon started to get pissed off with my doctors. The stuff they were giving me seemed to be making me *worse*, not better.

So then I got a new doctor, Allan Ropper, who was based in the same teaching hospital in Boston where I'd been told I didn't have MS in the early nineties. He was treating Michael J. Fox's Parkinson's disease at the time – Sharon had read an article about him in *People* magazine. The first thing Dr Ropper did when we flew out to see him was throw away all the pills I was on. Then he checked me into hospital for five days and ran every test ever invented on me. After that, I had to wait another week for the results,

Finally, me and Sharon went back to his office to find out what the fuck was wrong with me, once and for all.

'I've think I've got to the bottom of this,' he said. 'Basically, Mr Osbourne, you have a very, very rare condition, which is caused by your mother and your father both having the same damaged chromosome in their DNA. And when I say it's very rare, think one-in-a-billion rare. The good news is that it's not MS or Parkinson's disease. The bad news is that we don't really have a name for it. The best description is probably Parkinsonian syndrome.'

'Is that what's been giving me the tremor?'

'Absolutely.'

'And it's hereditary? It has nothing to do with the booze or the drugs?'

'The alcohol and some of the drugs you were taking were definitely making it worse. But they weren't the primary cause.'

'Can you treat it?'

'Yes. But first I have to tell you something, Mr Osbourne. If you keep drinking, and if you keep abusing drugs, you'll have to find another doctor, because I won't have you as a patient. I'm a busy man, I have a *very* long waiting list, and I can't afford to have my time wasted.'

I'd never been spoken to like that by a doctor before. And the way he looked at me, I knew he was serious.

'OK, doc,' I said. 'I'll try my hardest.'

'Good. I'm going to put you on two pills a day. You should see a vast improvement in your health.'

That was the understatement of the century, that was.

My tremors calmed down almost overnight. I could walk again. My stammer improved. I even managed to get back into the studio and record a new version of 'Changes' with Kelly.

I'd been promising to do a song for Kelly ever since I named one of the tracks on *Ozzmosis* after Aimee. She was always saying, 'How come Aimee got a song and I didn't?' In fact, I'd done a song for Jack, too – 'My Little Man' – which is also on *Ozzmosis*. So I owed Kelly – and I wanted to help her out, anyway, 'cos she's my special girl, y'know? I mean, I love all my children the same, but Kelly always seems to end up in the firing line, for some reason.

So we did 'Changes', one of my favourite songs of all time, with the lyrics changed slightly for a father and daughter. It was so good, I thought we might have a Christmas number one on our hands. Then we flew back to England in December to promote it. By then, I was off the booze – on Dr Ropper's orders – but I was still fucking around with all kinds of pills. You don't just stop being a drug addict overnight. I was Russian Rouletting it every day. At the time, I was into chloral hydrate, which is the world's oldest sleeping medication or something. But it was still a big improvement on the ridiculous amount of narcotics I'd been taking only a few months earlier, and I got through an appearance with Kelly on *Top of the Pops* with no problems. Then I drove up to Welders House with my assistant Tony for the weekend.

MTV already had a camera crew up there, because by then a lot of our family routines had become old hat, and they were desperate for some new material. But there wasn't much to shoot. I had this Yamaha Banshee 350cc quad bike – like a bullet on wheels – and I'd gun it around the fields for hours on end. So I spent most of the weekend doing just that. And on Monday morning, 8 December – the day 'Changes' went on sale – I took the bike out again.

By this point, the crew were a bit cheesed off, I think. They didn't even have the cameras rolling. I remember getting off the bike to open a gate, closing it after everyone had gone through, getting back on the bike, racing ahead along this dirt trail, then slamming on the brakes as I went down a steep embankment. But the trouble with that quad bike was that it didn't have one of those twisty throttles like you get on a motorbike. It just had a little lever that you pushed to go faster. And it was very easy to knock the lever by accident, while you were trying to control the bike, especially when it became unstable. That's exactly what happened when I got to the bottom of the embankment: the front wheels hit a pothole, my right hand slipped off the handlebar and slammed into the lever, the engine went fucking crazy, and the whole thing shot out from under me and did a backflip in the air, throwing me on to the grass. For about a millionth of a second, I thought, Oh well, that wasn't so bad.

Then the bike landed on top of me.

Crack.

When I opened my eyes, my lungs were full of blood and my neck was broken – or so my doctors told me later.

OK, *now* I'm dying, I thought.

It was the Nazis' fault, believe it or not. The pothole was a little crater, made by a German bomb that had been dropped during the war. I didn't know it at the time, but the land around Welders is full of them. The German pilots would bottle out before they reached the big cities – where they might get shot down – so they'd dump their bombs over Buckinghamshire, claim they'd carried out their mission, then fuck off home.

I can't remember much of the next two weeks. For the first few hours, I was slipping in and out of consciousness all the time. I have this vague memory of Sam, my security guard, lifting me on to the back of his bike and driving me back across the field. Then all I can remember are glimpses of the inside of an ambulance, followed by lots of doctors peering down at me.

'How did you get him to an ambulance?' one of them said.

'We put him on the back of a bike,' replied a voice I didn't recognise.

'You could have paralysed him! He's got a broken *neck*, for God's sake. He'll be lucky to walk again.'

'Well, how were we *supposed* to get him out of the forest?'

'A helicopter was on its way.'

'*We didn't know that.*'

'Clearly.'

Then everything started to melt away.

Apparently the last thing I did before losing consciousness was to pull on a doctor's sleeve and whisper in his ear, 'Whatever you do, don't fuck up my tattoo.'

Sharon was in LA, so Tony called her and put the chief doc on the line. He told her everything, and they agreed I had to go straight into surgery.

I was very badly injured. As well as breaking my neck, I'd fractured eight of my ribs and punctured my lungs, which was why they were filling up with blood. Meanwhile, when my collarbone broke it cut through a main artery in my arm, so that there was no blood supply. For a while the docs thought they were gonna have to chop it off. Once they were done operating on me, they put me into a 'chemical coma', 'cos it was the only way I was going to be able to handle the pain. If I'd copped it then, it would have been a fitting end for me: I'd spent my whole adult life trying to get into a chemical coma. They kept me under for eight days in the end. Then they started to bring me slowly back to consciousness. It took another six days for me to fully wake up. And during that time I had the most fucking insane dream. It was so vivid, it was more like a hallucination. All I can say is that the NHS must have loaded me up with some top-quality gear, 'cos I can still picture every detail like it was yesterday.

It started off with me in Monmouthshire – where I used to go to rehearse with Black Sabbath and my solo bands. It was raining – pissing it down. Then I was in this corridor at Rockfield Studios, and in front of me was a camouflaged fence, like something they might have had in the trenches during World War Two. To my left was a window. When I looked through it, on the other side was Sharon, having a party. She couldn't see me, but I could see her. I followed her out of this party and watched as she met up with some handsome, wealthy guy, who had his own plane. In the dream I thought, There's my wife, and she's leaving me. It was terribly sad. The guy had a landing strip in his back yard, and at the end of it was a big gun. Then, all of a sudden, he could see me – so I offered him some telescopic night-vision sights, because I wanted him to like me. He told me to fuck off, and I felt rejected all over again. At that point, all the guests from the party came running on to the lawn. The crowd got bigger and bigger until in the end it became this big music festival.

That was when Marilyn Manson showed up.

It was fucking nuts, man.

Next, I was on the rich guy's plane going to New Zealand, and they were serving draught Guinness in the cockpit. I suppose that must have had something to do with my son Louis's wedding in Ireland, which I was missing because I was in hospital. In New Zealand it was New Year's Eve. Jack was there – he'd bleached his hair completely white and he was letting off fire crackers. Then he got arrested.

At that point, Donovan strolled into the dream and started to play 'Mellow Yellow'.

What made all this even freakier was that I kept coming around, so some aspects of the dream were real. For example, I thought I was living in a fish 'n' chip shop, but in fact my bed was right next to the hospital kitchen, so I could smell them cooking. Then I saw my guitarist Zakk Wylde – which in the dream I thought was impossible, because he lived in America – but I later learned that he'd flown over to see me, so he was really there.

I also saw him wearing a frilly dress, dancing with a mop and a bucket.

But that *wasn't* real.

Or at least I hope it wasn't.

'Ozzy, *Ozzy*, can you hear me?'

It was Sharon.

After almost two weeks, they'd finally brought me out of the coma.

I opened my eyes.

Sharon smiled and dabbed at her face with a tissue.

'I've got news for you,' she said, squeezing my hand.

'I had a dream,' I told her, before she could say anything more. 'You left me for a rich guy with an aeroplane.'

'What are you talking about, Ozzy? Don't be silly. No one's leaving anyone. Everyone loves you. You should see the flowers that your fans have left outside. You'll be touched. They're beautiful.' She squeezed my hand again and said, 'Do you want to hear the news?'

'What is it? Are the kids OK?'

'You and Kelly are at number one. You finally fucking did it.'

'With "Changes"?'

'Yes! You even broke a record, Ozzy. It's never taken anyone thirty-three years from having their first song in the charts to getting a number one. Only Lulu has even come close.'

I managed a smile. 'Is that supposed to make me feel better?' I said. Then I laughed.

Not a good idea, with eight broken ribs.

Normally, I hate Christmas. I mean, if you're an alcoholic and you're drinking, Christmas is the best thing in the world. But if you ain't drinking, it's fucking agony. And I hate the fact that you have to buy everyone a gift. Not because I'm tight – it's just that you do it out of obligation, not because you want to.

It's always seemed like total bullshit to me.

But Christmas 2003 was the exception. Me and Kelly might not have got the Christmas number one – we were outsold in the last week by Michael Andrews and Gary Jules, with their cover version of 'Mad World' – but I got to live another day. Which is pretty unbelievable, when you think about it. The only sadness I have from that time is that none of my old Black Sabbath bandmates called to say they liked 'Changes', or to say, 'Well done on getting to number one.' Even if they'd called to say they thought it was a piece of shit, it would have been better than silence. No wonder it was raining so hard in Monmouthshire when I was there in the dream.

But whatever, man. It ain't a big deal.

The hospital where I'd been in the coma, Wexham Park, couldn't have been better. But I pissed them off in the end. I wanted to go home, 'cos I'd had enough, but they told me there was no way I could leave. I mean, at that point I couldn't walk; I had a neck brace on; my arm still hadn't come back to life; and I was in excruciating fucking pain. But my dream had fucked me up. I was convinced that Sharon was flying around the world in a private jet with a hot tub in the back, while being shagged senseless by some billionaire. If I was in hospital, I thought, I had no chance of getting her back. But by the time Sharon had raced over to the hospital with the kids to tell me for the millionth time that everything was OK, that it was all just a dream, it was too late: I'd managed to sign myself out. So Sharon had to get a hospital bed for me at Welders House and a home-help nurse to wipe my arse and shake my dick. For weeks, the only way I could get from room to room was in a wheelchair, and every night I had to be carried upstairs to go to bed.

But eventually I made a full recovery. Or as full as anyone could expect. My short-term memory seemed worse, but maybe that was just age, or the sleeping pills. And my ribcage is still full of screws and bolts and metal rods. When I walk through an airport metal detector these days, a klaxon goes off in the Pentagon.

But I can't complain, y'know? I remember when I first went back to America after the crash, and I had to go to the doc for a check-up. He took all these X-rays of my chest, put them up on the viewing box, and started to whistle through his teeth. 'Nice work,' he said. 'Must have been a bit pricey, though. What did it cost ya? Seven figures? Eight?'

'Nothing, actually,' I said.

He couldn't believe it. 'What d'you mean?'

'NHS,' I said, and shrugged.

'Holy crap,' he went. 'No wonder you guys put up with the weather.'

Once I was out of the wheelchair and the neck brace, it was time to renegotiate our contract with MTV – *again*. But I couldn't face another season of *The Osbournes*.

Enough was enough.

Anyway, by then MTV had killed the show by trying to wring every last ounce of dough out of it. It seemed to be on twenty-four hours a day. And when you overdo a show like that, people get bored. You want the folks at home to be saying, 'Oh, it's nine o'clock. Time for *The Osbournes*.' You want them to be jacked up for it. But when it's on every night, they just say, '*Meh*, it'll be on tomorrow.' They did the exact same thing with *Who Wants to be a Millionaire?* It was brilliant for five minutes, then you couldn't get away from it.

Another problem was that after three years of doing the show, we'd filmed just about everything we could ever film. So, for the last season, we had to come up with all these gimmicks – and we were so famous that we were mobbed whenever we left the house. It started to feel a bit fake, which was the exact opposite of what *The Osbournes* was all about.

So that was the end of it. By 2005 the show was over, Fort Apache was taken down, and the crew moved out. Not long after, Jack and Kelly moved out too. But I like to think we made our mark on TV. And especially on MTV. They love reality shows now, that lot. You have to stay up until three in the morning just to catch a music video these days. And, of course, a lot of people have tried to take credit for *The Osbournes* now that it's over. But I've never been in any doubt about who were the *true* creators of *The Osbournes*.

They're called the Osbournes.

One of the great things about the show was that it allowed Sharon to go off and have a successful career in TV. After she got through her chemotherapy, all I wanted was for Sharon to be happy, and when she got the gig as a judge on *The X Factor*, she loved it. When Sharon wanted to leave after the fourth season, I said to her, 'Look, are you absolutely sure this is what you want to do, because if it is then I'm completely behind you.' And in the end, it worked out very well for her, because now she's having the time of her life doing *America's Got Talent*.

I must say I thought my life would become a bit more normal after *The Osbournes* ended. Fat fucking chance. Welders House almost burned down three times, for a start. Then I nearly murdered a cat burglar in the middle of the night in my own bathroom.

I swear this kind of crazy shit only ever happens to me.

If it hadn't been for my dodgy bladder, I wouldn't even have seen the guy. But I'm up and down during the night like a fiddler's elbow, I am. It's because I drink so much liquid, even when I'm not boozing. The cups of tea I make are the size of soup bowls. And I can get through a dozen of them a day. Whatever I do, it's always to excess.

Anyway, the break-in happened just before dawn on Monday, 22 November 2004. I woke up busting for a piss, and luckily I wasn't loaded on anything more than the usual pills, so I wasn't staggering around, falling into things. I just got out of bed, stark bollock naked, and walked into the bathroom, which leads through to this little vanity area. I switched on the lights and lifted up the toilet seat, and as I did so, I glanced towards Sharon's dressing table.

There he was: a bloke about my height, dressed head-to-toe in black, a ski mask over his face, crouched down, but with nowhere to hide.

It's hard to describe the kind of fright you get when something like that happens. But then the urgency of the situation takes over. As soon as he knew that I'd seen him, the bloke legged it to the window and tried to climb out. For some reason – God knows why, given how much of a chickenshit I am – I ran after him and got him in a headlock before he could get his whole body through the gap. So there he is, this cat burglar, on his back with his eyes twinkling up at me, and I've got my arm around his throat. Suddenly I'm thinking: Right, what now? We seemed to be there for ages, neither of us saying anything, while I decided what to do.

If I pull him back inside, I thought, he might have a crowbar, or a gun. I also thought he might have had a friend outside, waiting to help out in an emergency. And I wasn't exactly up for a fight at four o'clock in the morning. I didn't have my Rambo attire on, put it that way. So then I thought, Why don't I just kill the bastard? I mean, he was in my house, and I hadn't invited him. But did I really want to live with the fact that I'd taken someone's life, when I knew I could have let him go?

In the end, I just threw the fucker out of the window, which was on the second floor. I could hear him crash through the branches of a tree on his way down. Then I watched him hobbling across the field, yelping with every step. With any luck, he broke something.

He got away with two million quid's worth of jewellery, and the cops never caught him. The stuff was insured, but you never get back the full value with those things. I suppose I should have shouted for Sharon to press the alarm button, but I didn't think. And she didn't know anything about it until it was all over.

But it's only stuff, isn't it? And it could have been a lot worse. He could have beaten me over the head with a baseball bat while I was asleep. He could have raped Sharon. I mean, you hear people down the pub saying, 'Oh, I'd fucking *love* that to happen to me, I'd show the bastard,' but believe me, when you're taken by surprise like that, it's a lot different.

I've bought a few guns since then, mind you, so if there's ever another bloke, he won't have it so easy. Then again, I don't know if I'd have the nerve to shoot someone. And you've gotta be fucking careful with guns. It's like my father always said to me, if you ever pull a weapon on somebody – no matter what it is – you've got to be fully prepared to use it, because if you're not, the other guy will see the doubt in your eyes, and he'll take it off you and use it on you instead. Then you're *really* in trouble.

The day after the burglary, the press went crazy, as they always do with stories about me. 'NAKED OZZY'S RAGE AS HE FIGHTS JEWELLERY ROBBER AT HIS HOME' said the *Sun*'s headline. Then some of the other papers sent reporters to Aston to write about how I'd robbed Sarah Clarke's clothes shop, and how it was ironic that I was now complaining about being a victim of burglary. I thought that was a bit of a stretch, to be honest with you. I was just a stupid kid when I broke into Sarah Clarke's; I was hardly the fucking night stalker. And I learned my lesson.

In 1965, the clothes I nicked were worth about twenty-five quid, and I thought that was all the money in the world. I never would have believed that forty years later I'd have two million pounds' worth of stuff for someone to pinch – and enough left over to not really notice when it was gone. It's ridiculous, really. My life should never have happened the way that it did. But, believe me, I'm grateful. Not a day goes by without me thinking about where I came from, and where I ended up, and how no one in their right fucking mind would have put a bet on it turning out that way.

Patient Notes

Hidden Hills, California
2009

'OK, Mr Osbourne, I'm going to ask you a question,' said the doc. 'Have you ever taken any "street drugs"?'

This was the new guy I went to see when I decided to get clean. I'd spent almost forty years blasting the booze and the pills, so it seemed like a good idea to see what kind of damage I'd done.

'Well,' I told him, with a little cough, 'I once smoked some pot.'

'Is that it?'

'Yeah, that's it.'

The doc carried on prodding me and checking his notes. Then he stopped and asked, 'Are you *sure*?'

'Well,' I said, with another little cough, 'I've taken a bit of speed. A long time ago, y'know?'

'So just the pot and a bit of speed?'

'Pretty much, yeah.'

The doc carried on doing his thing. But after a while, he stopped again. 'Are you *absolutely* sure it was just the pot and the speed?'

'Well, I suppose I've had a few toots of the old waffle dust in my time,' I said. I was starting to warm up now.

'So pot, speed and . . . a few lines of cocaine?'

'Pretty much, yeah.'

'And you're sure about that?'

'Uh-huh.'

'I just want to make absolut—'

'Does heroin count?'

'Yes, heroin counts.'

'Oh. And heroin, then. Just once or twice, mind.'

'Are you *sure* it was just once or twice?'

'Oh, yeah. Fucking crap drug, heroin is. Have you tried it?'

'No.'

'Too much throwing up for my liking.'

'The nausea can be intense, yes.'

'It's a waste of booze, that's what it is.'

'OK,' the doctor snapped, 'let's just stop this. Are there any drugs you *haven't* taken, Mr Osbourne?'

Silence.

'Mr Osbourne?'

'Not that I'm aware of, no.'

More silence.

Finally, the doc said, 'And what about alcohol? You mentioned that you drink. How many units per day?'

'Oh, about four? Give or take.'

'Can you be more specific?'

'Bottles of Hennessy. But it depends.'

'On what?'

'On how long I pass out between them.'

'And it's just the Hennessy?'

'Well, beer doesn't count, does it?'

The doc shook his head, let out a big sigh, and started to rub his eyes. He looked like he wanted to go home. Then he asked, 'And do you smoke, Mr Osbourne?'

'Now and again.'

'What a surprise. How many per day, would you say?'

'Oh, thirty-ish?'

'What brand of cigarettes?'

'Cigars. I don't count the cigarettes.'

The doc started to go very white. Then he said, 'For how long has this been your typical daily routine?'

'What year is it?' I asked him.

'2004.'

'Nearly forty years, then.'

'And is there anything else in your medical history I should know about?' asked the doc.

'Well,' I said, 'I got hit by an aeroplane once – sort of, anyway. And I broke my neck on a quad bike. Then I died twice during the coma. I had AIDS for twenty-four hours, too. And I thought I had MS, but it turned out to be a Parkinsonian tremor. I broke my clack that other time. Oh, and I've had the clap a few times. And one or two seizures, like when I took the codeine in New York, or when I date raped myself in Germany. That's it, really – unless you count the abuse of prescription medication.'

The doctor nodded

Then he cleared his throat, loosened his tie, and said, 'I've got one last question for you, Mr Osbourne.'

'Go ahead, Doc.'

'*Why are you still alive?*'

He was right: there's no plausible medical reason why I should still be alive. There's even less of a reason why I should be so healthy. Nowadays there's pretty much fuck-all wrong with me – seriously.

I mean, yes, my short-term memory hasn't been too great since the quad bike accident – I have a memory therapist now, to help me with it – and I still have a mild stammer. But my heart's in great shape, and my liver's like brand new. After a million and one tests, the best the doc could come up with was that I had 'a little bit of cholesterol'. But that's hardly unusual for a sixty-year-old man brought up on lard sandwiches and chips.

I can honestly say I never expected to last into my seventh decade – never mind still be viable. When I was a kid, if you'd put me up against a wall with the others from my street and asked me which one of us was going to make it to the year 2009, which one of us would end up with five kids and five grandkids and houses in Buckinghamshire and California, I'd never have put any money on me. I have to laugh every so often, 'cos I grew up with the entire system against me. I got thrown out of school at the age of fifteen without even being able to read a sentence properly.

But I won in the end.

We all did – me, Tony, Geezer and Bill.

And I'm feeling great now. Better than ever.

I mean, I still have my issues. I get very phobic about meeting new people, although it comes in waves. And I'm very superstitious. If I'm working out in the gym, I'll always do more than thirteen repetitions. *Always*. And I won't, under any circumstances, wear the colour green. It freaks me out, green does. I've no idea why – maybe it's just because I had a green car once that was always breaking down. And I swear that being sober has made me a bit psychic, too. I'll say to Sharon, 'I wonder how so-and-so is' – someone I haven't seen for years – and the next day he'll pop out of the woodwork.

I had something similar when Princess Diana died, y'know. The week before the crash, I had a dream about it. It was so vivid I told Tony Dennis about it. Then, a few days later, she was gone.

'Don't have any fucking dreams about *me*,' Tony said.

People ask me if I'm really, *truly* clean now.

I can't give them the answer they want. All I can say is I'm clean today. That's all I've got. That's all I'll ever have.

But I'm certainly cleaner than I've been for the last forty years. One of the last times I got seriously fucked up was a few years ago now, after a gig in Prague. The beer was so good, man, I couldn't help myself. And I was out with Zakk, my guitarist, who's the most dangerous company in the world if you're an alcoholic. The bloke can knock 'em back like you wouldn't believe. He's a machine. That was a memorable night, that was. After hitting the town big time, we went back to my suite on the ninth floor of this fancy high-rise hotel and got stuck into the minibar. Then, at about one in the morning, this thought came to me.

'D'you know what I've never, *ever* done?' I said to Zakk.

'That must be a short fucking list, man,' he replied.

'Seriously, Zakk,' I said. 'There's one rock 'n' roll thing that I've never got around to doing, in all these years.'

'What?'

'I've never thrown a telly out of a hotel window.'

'Shit, man,' said Zakk. 'We'd better do something about that.'

So we pulled the telly out of the cabinet and hauled it over to the window, which we started to crank open. But they'd designed the window so you could open it only a few inches. Which meant we had to smash off the hinge by bashing it with a paperweight, until the thing finally opened wide enough to slide out this fifty-inch TV.

Then we gave it a good old shove.

Whooooooossssssssssssssssh!

Down it went, past the eighth floor, the seventh floor, the

sixth floor, the fifth floor, the fourth floor . . .

'Is that a bloke down there smoking a fag?' I said to Zakk.

The TV kept falling.

'Don't worry,' said Zakk. 'He's miles away.'

BANG!

You shoulda seen that thing explode, man. Holy crap. It was like a bomb going off. The poor bloke having a smoke almost swallowed his cigarette, even though he was on the other side of the plaza.

When we got bored of staring at the wreckage, I climbed into the cabinet where the TV had been and pretended to read the news. Then the phone rang. It was the hotel manager.

'May I speak to Mr Osbourne?' he said. 'There's been an . . . incident.'

'He's not here,' said Zakk. 'He's on TV.'

In the end, the manager just moved me to another room – the window was in a pretty bad state – and when I checked out they added a 'miscellaneous item' to my bill: $38,000! They justified it by saying the room couldn't be used for a month. Which was bullshit. Zakk was billed another $10,000. And they charged us $1000 for the booze from the minibar.

But it was worth it, in a way.

When I paid that bill, I realised I didn't want to be that person any more. It reached the point where I just thought, What are you gonna do, Ozzy? Are you gonna carry on being that one-foot-in-the-grave, one-foot-out-of-the-grave type of person, until you end up like so many other tragic rock 'n' roll cases? Or are you gonna climb out of the hole for good?

I'd hit rock bottom, in other words. It had taken me four decades to get there, but I'd finally arrived. I disliked everything about myself. I was terrified of living, but I was afraid to die.

Which is no kind of existence, take it from me.

So I cleaned myself up.

First I quit the cigarettes. People ask, 'How the fuck did *you* do *that*?' but I was just so fed up with buying patches, taking them off, smoking a fag, putting them back on, that I thought, *Fuck it*, and went cold turkey. I simply did not want to do it any more.

Then I did the same with the booze. After I'd been sober for a while, I asked Sharon, 'Can I have a drink now?'

All she said to me was, 'You're old enough to make up your own mind.'

'But I've never been any good with choices,' I said. 'I always make the wrong ones.'

'Well, do you *want* a drink, Ozzy?' she said.

For the first time in my life, the honest answer was 'no'. In the old days, whenever I stopped boozing, I always used to think about the good times I was missing. Now, all I think about is how the good times always – and I mean fucking *always* – turned bad.

I couldn't tell you how much a pint of beer costs now, and I don't want to know. Which is amazing, considering how much my life used to revolve around the pub. I just ain't interested any more. The other week, I was in the Beverly Hills Hotel and I ran into Ronnie Wood from the Rolling Stones. He looked like he'd had a few. And I just thought, Fucking hell, he's still going. I also bumped into Keith Richards recently, at an awards show. 'How are you doing, Keith?' I asked him. He replied, 'Oh, not bad for a living legend.' I almost said, '*Living?* Keith, you and me are the walking fucking dead.'

A lot of my old drinking buddies are still going, actually. But they're getting to the age where they just can't handle the damage any more. One of them died not long ago from cirrhosis of the liver. And everyone went to the pub after the funeral. They were all standing there at the bar with their black armbands, drinking rum and black. 'Are you trying to catch up with him or something?' I said to them.

But that's just what people do in England – they go to the

pub to celebrate the life of someone who's just killed themselves by going to the pub too much. It's an alcoholics' culture. When I was younger, I used to think the whole world was drunk. Then I moved to America and realised it's just *England* that's drunk.

I got off the drugs, too, eventually. Apart from the stuff I take for my tremor and my anti-depressants, I'm a narco-free zone. When I go to a doctor now, the first thing I say is, 'Look, I'm an addict, I'm an alcoholic, so please don't listen to a word of my bullshit.' Tony comes with me to all of my appointments, too, as a kind of insurance policy.

The drugs I'm taking now don't have many side-effects – unlike the ones I got from some of those other docs I used to go to. Although the anti-depressants have played havoc with my sex drive. I can get a boner, but no fireworks. So I end up pumping away on top of Sharon like a road drill all night, with nothing happening. I tried Viagra, but by the time it kicked in, Sharon was fast asleep. So it was just me and this tent pole in front of me, with nothing to do but watch the History Channel.

When I asked the doctor about it, he said, 'Oh, you don't still do *that*, do you?'

'It's the only fucking pleasure I have left!' I told him.

Mind you, I've never felt the temptation to run off with a younger chick, like some guys my age do. I mean, what do you fucking talk about with a twenty-year-old? The real estate market? The situation in Afghanistan? It would be like talking to a child.

I must have been clean for at least four or five years now. I don't keep count. I don't know the exact date when I stopped. It's not a fucking race. I just get out of bed every morning and *don't* drink, and *don't* take drugs. I still avoid those AA meetings, though. To me, it feels too much like substituting an addiction to booze with an addiction to the programme. I ain't saying it's unhelpful, 'cos it can be very helpful. But the change had to come from *me*.

Therapy's helped a lot, mind you, even though I didn't understand it at first. I made the same mistake as I had with rehab – thinking it would cure me. But it's just a way of relieving a problem by talking about it. It helps because if you ain't talking about something it stays in your head and eventually you get whacked out on it.

I have a sponsor, too: Billy Morrison, the guitarist from Camp Freddy. I met him through AA. If I ever get the feeling that I should have a joint, 'cos it would help me write a song or whatever, I pick up the phone to Billy. And that defuses the thought. He'll say, 'A joint might feel good for the first two minutes, but by the end of the day you'll be throwing bottles of Scotch down your neck.' It's a good system because it's the secrets and the lies that get you drunk again.

I couldn't be a sponsor, though. I have too much of a problem trusting people, and, like I said, I don't go to the meetings, so I've never worked my way through the twelve steps, like you're supposed to. It's not the God thing that puts me off, because you don't have to believe in God to do the programme. You just have to accept that there's a higher power – it could be the lamp in the corner of the room, for all they care. Some people use nature, the ocean, their dick – whatever comes to mind.

The thing about being clean is, if I fell off the wagon now there's a good chance I'd die. Your tolerance falls off a cliff when you quit. A couple of drinks, and I'd be fucked. So I don't go out much when I'm not on the road. I don't need to: I've got my wife, I've got my friends, I've got my dogs – all seventeen of them – and I've got my land. And you should see our new house up in Hidden Hills. Talk about a rock-star mansion. When I'm lying in bed, all I have to do is press a button and this giant flat-screen TV rises out of the floor and dangles above my head. And the bogs – fucking hell, man, I wish my old man could have lived long enough to try out one of my bogs. I grew up having to piss in a bucket 'cos there was no indoor shitter, and now I have these computerised Japanese super-loo things that have heated seats and wash and blow-dry your arse at the touch of a button. Give it a couple of years and I'll have a bog with a robot arm that pulls out my turds, so I don't have to strain.

It ain't a bad life, put it that way.

And I keep myself busy. For example, I'm going to take my driving test again. I mean, I've been driving for the best part of forty years – but never legally and usually drunk. So I might as well do it properly before I pop my clogs. Mind you, my driving instructor wants me to learn in a car with two steering wheels. Bollocks to that. I said to the guy, 'We're doing it in my Range Rover or we're not doing it at all.' But after the last lesson we had, I wouldn't be surprised if he turns up next week in a crash helmet. He thinks I'm crazy, that bloke. Every time I go around a corner, he flinches like I'm gonna play chicken with an eighteen-wheeler.

I suppose it's understandable, given the crazy things they've said about me over the years. 'He bit the head off a bat.' OK. 'He bit the head off a dove.' Fair enough. But I ain't a puppy-killer, or a Devil-worshipper, or someone who wants his fans to blow their heads off. It haunts me, all that crazy stuff. People embellish the stories, y'know? It's like kids in a schoolyard: one of them says, 'Johnny's cut his finger,' but by the time it's reached the other side of the playground, Johnny's cut his fucking head off.

Nowadays, when I'm at home, I draw pictures while listening to old Beatles albums on my headphones. They're just doodles, really. I ain't good at it. I just do patterns and fuck around and make crazy shapes in bright colours – like sixties Pop Art. It keeps me out of trouble. Oh, and I collect Nazi memorabilia. I've got flags, SS daggers, leather overcoats, everything – but I don't get many chances to put up the swastikas, not with a half Jewish missus. Most of the stuff I buy eventually finds its way to Lemmy, who's even more into it than I am.

You should see his house, man. It's like a museum.

These days, I spend much more time with my family than I ever did when I was drinking. Aimee, Kelly and Jack are doing great. And I see Jess and Louis all the time now, too. They both got Thelma's brains: Jess is a surveyor and Louis got a law degree. Between them, they've given me five grandchildren, which is a crazy thought. And I still talk to my older sister Jean every Sunday. 'Anything to report?' I always ask her. 'Everyone doing OK?'

Things are OK with Black Sabbath, but at the moment there's an issue over who owns the name. My position is that we should all own it equally. We'll see what happens, but I hope it gets resolved, 'cos I have the greatest respect for Tony Iommi. I haven't spoken to Geezer for a while – he's still always got his nose in a book – but I've kept in touch with Bill. He's been clean and sober for twenty-five years now. And if you'd known him a quarter of a century ago, you'd know that's nothing short of a miracle.

As for me, I just want to spend the rest of my days being a rock 'n' roller. I certainly don't want to do any more telly, except for a few ads here and there, as long as they're funny. Y'know, I used to get upset by people not understanding me, but I've made a career out of it now. I even ham it up a bit, 'cos it's what people expect of me.

I suppose the one ambition I have left is to get a number one album in America. But if it doesn't happen, I can't really complain. I've managed to do just about everything else. I mean, I'm so grateful that I'm *me*, that I'm here, that I can still enjoy the life that I have.

If I don't live a day longer, I'll have had more than my fair share. The only thing I ask is that if I end up brain-dead in a hospital somewhere, just pull the plug, please. But I doubt it'll get to that. Knowing me, I'll go out in some stupid way. I'll trip on the doorstep and break my neck. Or I'll choke on a throat lozenge. Or a bird will shit on me and give me some weird virus from another planet. Look what happened with the quad bike: I'd been taking lethal combinations of booze and drugs for decades but it was riding over a pothole in my back garden at two miles an hour that nearly killed me.

Don't get me wrong: I don't worry about that kind of heavy-duty stuff on a daily basis. I've come to believe that everything in life is worked out in advance. So whenever bad shit happens, there ain't nothing you can do about it. You've just gotta ride it out. And eventually death will come, like it comes to everyone.

I've said to Sharon: 'Don't cremate me, whatever you do.' I want to be put in the ground, in a nice garden somewhere, with a tree planted over my head. A crabapple tree, preferably, so the kids can make wine out of me and get pissed out of their heads.

As for what they'll put on my headstone, I ain't under any illusions.

If I close my eyes, I can already see it:

Ozzy Osbourne, born 1948.
Died, whenever.
He bit the head off a bat.

Acknowledgements

My darling wife Sharon, who has always been there for me – I love you.

My wonderful children: Aimee, Kelly, Jack, Jessica (and my son-in-law, Ben) and Louis (and my daughter-in-law, Louise).

My amazing grandchildren: Issy, Harry, Maia, Elijah and Kitty.

Colin and Mette Newman; I couldn't have done it without you.

To my brothers and sisters: Paul, Tony, Iris and Gillian, and not forgetting my big, wonderful sister Jean – who has always been like my other mum and not my big sister – and of course my brothers-in-law, Norman, Russell and Tom and my nephew Terry.

My dear Mum and Dad, who made it all possible.

Gina and Dean Mazlin and their children, Oliver and Amelia.

My great friends Billy and Jen Morrison – who helped me to find my way back.

My lifetime friends in Black Sabbath: Bill Ward, who has always given me support. God bless you always. Tony Iommi and Terence 'Geezer' Butler.

To my extended family, my staff: Michael Guarracino, his wife Denny and son Jesse; John Fenton and his wife Sandee; Kevin Thomson; Silvana Arena; Lynn Seager; Claire Smith; David and Sharon Godman; Jude Alcala; Bob Troy; Saba; Dari; Trino; Steve and Melinda Varga, Lukey and Scarley girl (who said that?).

Very special thanks to my best friend Tony Dennis (way'ye son, cumin' have a pint, his dad's got a boat and his mam's got a bike).

My dear friends, Mrs Delores Rhoads; Pete Mertens, his wife Danielle and daughter Phoebe; Gloria Butler; and my friend and co-producer Kevin Churko.

Antonia Hodgson, who has driven me mad to write this book.

Chris Ayres, my co-author on this book. Thank you for organising my life stories into book form. I couldn't have done it without you.

Zakk and Barbaranne Wylde, my godson Jesse, Haley-Rae and Hendrix Wylde.

My band: Mike Bordin and his family; Merilee, Abby and Violet; Blasko and his wife Carol; Adam Wakeman and his family.

And all my four-legged angels who shit in my house every day.

Picture Credits

Section One

Page 2: (bottom) © Neil Preston/Corbis
Page 4: (top) © WireImage; (bottom) © Michael Putland/Retna
Page 5: (top left) © Chris Walter/Photofeatures/Retna; (top right) © Chris Walter/WireImage; (bottom) © Richard E. Aaron/Redferns/Getty Images
Page 6: (top) © Michael Putland/Retna UK; (bottom) © Richard E. Aaron/Redferns/Getty Images
Page 8: (top) © Chris Talter/WireImage; (bottom) © Jon Sievert/Getty Images

Section Two

Page 9: (bottom) © Preston/Retna UK
Page 10: (bottom) © David McGough/Time & Life Pictures/Getty Images
Page 11: (top and bottom) © London Features International
Page 12: (top) © Tony Mottram
Page 13: (bottom) © Lynn Goldsmith/Corbis
Page 14: (top) © London Features International
Page 15: (top) © Ron Galella/WireImage; (bottom) © Rex Features

Section Three

Page 17: (top) © Ann Clifford/Time & Life Pictures/Getty Image; (bottom left and right) © David McGough/Time & Life Pictures/Getty Images
Page 18: (top) © Terry Smith/Time & Life Pictures/Getty Images; (bottom) © David McGough/Time & Life Pictures/Getty Images
Page 19: (bottom) © George Chin
Page 20: (top) © Joe Giron/Corbis; (bottom) © Christina Radish/Redferns/Getty Images
Page 21: (top) © Mick Hutson/Redferns/Getty Images; (bottom) © Christina Radish/Redferns/Getty Images
Page 23: (top and bottom) © Mark Leialoha
Page 24: (top) © Rex Features; (bottom) © Getty Images

Section Four

Page 25: (top) © Vince Bucci/Stringer/Getty Images; (bottom) © Albert L. Ortega/WireImage
Page 26: (top) © Getty Images; (bottom) © George Chin
Page 27: (top) © George Chin
Page 28: (top left) © Rex Features; (top right and bottom) © Frank Micelotta/Stringer/Getty Images
Page 29: (bottom) © Advertising Archives
Page 30: (top left) © George Chin; (bottom) © Getty Images
Page 31: (top) © Ken McKay/Rex Features
(middle) © Frank Micelotta/Stringer/Getty Images